THE SOVIET UNION

A Systematic Geography

Leslie Symons
Professor of Geography, University College of Swansea

J. C. Dewdney
Reader in Geography, University of Durham

D. J. M. Hooson
Professor of Geography, University of California

R. E. H. Mellor
Professor of Geography, University of Aberdeen

W. W. Newey
Senior Lecturer in Geography, University of Edinburgh

THE SOVIET UNION

A Systematic Geography

BARNES & NOBLE BOOKS

TOTOWA, NEW JERSEY

*The photograph reproduced on the title page is of
a Caucasus mountain settlement.*

Library of Congress Cataloging in Publication Data

The Soviet Union, a systematic geography.

   1. Soviet Union—Description and travel—1970–
I. Symons, Leslie.

<u>DK29.S725</u>   914.7   82–6683
ISBN 0–389–20309–2   AACR2
ISBN 0–389–20310–6 (pbk.)

First published 1983 by Hodder and Stoughton Educational

First published in the USA 1983 by
BARNES & NOBLE BOOKS
81 ADAMS DRIVE
TOTOWA, NEW JERSEY, 07512

Typeset by Macmillan India Ltd., Bangalore

Printed and bound in in Hong Kong

Contents

Preface   vii

Acknowledgements   viii

Transliteration   viii

Maps and diagrams   ix

Photographs   x

Introduction   1

1 The Evolution of the Russian State   6

2 Physiography   21

3 Climate   38

4 Biogeography—the Vegetation, Soils and Animal life   52

5 Water Resources   71

6 Population   88

7 Agriculture   112

8 Minerals, Fuel and Power Resources   133

9 Industry   160

10 Urban and Rural Settlement   184

11 Transport   202

12 The regions   224

Index   249

Preface

The Soviet Union, from its very size and diversity in landscape, peoples, economies and cultures, deserves much more attention than it has hitherto received in geographical studies. This book aims to fill some of the gaps that exist in the material at present easily available to schools and colleges. Though there are a number of excellent textbooks available on the USSR, certain topics have not been covered adequately in them. The present volume provides not only an up-to-date account of the basic aspects of the physical and economic geography of the USSR but also deals in detail with topics such as vegetation and water resources not usually adequately covered in textbooks.

The study of the Soviet Union, through the very diversity that it encompasses, presents some difficulties. This diversity, which defies brevity of description in the case of the physical features, poses even more problems in the variety of the human geography. This is best illustrated by the matter of different nationalities, of which over 90 are recognised in the current classification used by the Soviet authorities, with many additional lesser ethnic groups. Each of these nationality groups has its own language but access to material on the Soviet Union is simplified by the status of Russian, the language of the dominant ethnic group, as a *lingua franca*. Soviet atlases and maps show place names in Russian and it is the Russian forms that are used here, transliterated by the standard system used by British and American geographers, reproduced on page viii. A few of these names may appear unfamiliar to the reader, because of the adherence to the transliteration system, e.g. Baykal rather than Baikal, Tadzhikistan instead of Tajikistan. The system is extended to transliteration of other Russian words, *tayga* rather than *taiga*. As this word should be pronounced ap-proximately *taygá*, not 'taeega', as commonly in English usage, the transliteration gives a better idea of correct Russian pronunciation. For simplification, soft and hard signs have been omitted throughout. Where English forms of names are in general use, e.g. Moscow (*Moskva*), Georgia (*Gruzinskaya Respublika*), these are used, and where alternative names, such as Turkmeniya and Turkmenistan are equally acceptable, the authors' usage has not been standardised by the editor. With these exceptions the spellings will be found to coincide with the Times Atlas as this uses the same transliteration system.

Capital letters are used for regions defined administratively e.g. North-west, North Caucasus economic regions, while north-west Russia, north Caucasus, etc. indicate geographical areas not so defined.

All the contributors to this volume have specialised in the geography of the Soviet Union. John Dewdney, Reader in Geography at the University of Durham (Chapters 2, 6 and 12), has studied, especially, Soviet demography and regional development; David Hooson, Professor of Geography at the University of California at Berkeley (Chapter 3), is the author of regional and methodological studies in particular; R. E. H. Mellor, Professor of Geography at the University of Aberdeen (Chapters 10 and 11), has specialised in the economic and urban geography of the region; and Walter W. Newey, Senior Lecturer in Geography at the University of Edinburgh (Chapters 4, 5 and 8), specialises in biogeography. Leslie Symons (editor and contributor of Chapters 1, 7 and 9) is Professor of Geography in the Centre of Russian and East European Studies and the Department of Geography at the University College of Swansea.

Acknowledgements

Acknowledgements are made to Associated Book Publishers (NZ) Ltd for permission to reproduce material from a series of booklets produced in New Zealand and written by the same authors. This material includes Figs 6.1, 10.4, 11.2, 11.3 and 11.4 of this book. All other maps and diagrams were drawn by Mr G. B. Lewis and Mr T. Fearnside, Department of Geography, University College of Swansea, from material supplied by the authors and based mainly on the following sources: *Atlas SSSR, Atlas razvitiya khozyaystva i kul'tury SSSR, Atlas sel'skogo khozyaystva SSSR, Fiziko-geograficheskiy atlas mira,* and Soviet statistical publications, with supplementary information derived from other sources referred to in the text with *Soviet Geography, Review and Translation* particularly valuable for a wide range of articles and comments from geographers of both the Soviet Union and the West. The photographs on pages 136, 144, 146, 165, 167, 177 and 178 are reproduced by courtesy of the Novosti Press Agency (A.P.N.). Other photographs are by Dr C. G. Alvstam (pages 217 and 240), Dr T. E. Armstrong (page 48), Dr E. M. Bridges (page 73), Dr G. Humphrys (page 126) and Mrs Wendy Playfoot (pages 45 and 64). The cover photograph is by M. S. Hackforth-Jones (Robert Harding Picture Library) and the remaining photographs by the editor. Special thanks are due to the secretaries in the several Universities involved, especially the University College of Swansea, for the typing of the manuscripts, and to Mrs G. Symons and Miss A. H. C. Symons for assisting the editor in reading and checking of typescripts and other material.

Transliteration system

Russian	English rendering	Russian	English rendering
Аа	a	Рр	r
Бб	b	Сс	s
Вв	v	Тт	t
Гг	g	Уу	u (pronounced o͞o)
Дд	d	Фф	f
Ее	ye	Хх	kh
Ёё	yo (short o)	Цц	ts
Жж	zh	Чч	ch
Зз	z	Шш	sh
Ии	i	Щщ	shch
Йй	y	Ъъ	" (hard sign, not pronounced)
Кк	k	Ыы	y
Лл	l	Ьь	' (soft sign)
Мм	m	Ээ	e (eh)
Нн	n	Юю	yu
Оо	o	Яя	ya
Пп	p		

Maps and Diagrams

A	The Soviet state	2
B	Political-administrative structure of the USSR	4
1.1	Tatar invasions of the thirteenth century, Kievan Rus and medieval princedoms	8
1.2	The expansion of the Russian Empire	11
1.3	Heavy industry in 1913	17
2.1	Structure of the USSR	22
2.2	Physiographic regions of the USSR	24
2.3	Relief of the USSR	26
2.4	Geology of the USSR	28
3.1	Accumulated temperatures	40
3.2	Effective moisture	42
3.3	Climatic characteristics of cities studied	47
4.1	Vegetation zones of the USSR	53
4.2	Soil zones of the USSR	56
4.3	Soil erosion	67
5.1	Irrigation schemes, southern European USSR	75
5.2	Irrigation schemes in Central Asia	77
5.3	River diversions in European USSR	83
5.4	Proposed diversion of river water from Siberia to Central Asia	85
6.1	Major ethnic groups of the USSR	89
6.2	Distribution of the Soviet population in 1979	94
6.3	Population density	96
6.4	Age and sex structure of the Soviet population in 1959 and 1970	100
6.5	Population change, 1959–79	102
6.6	Types of population change, 1959–79	107

7.1	Agricultural land	118
7.2	Agricultural regions of the USSR	120
8.1	Coal, oil and natural gas	135
8.2	Oilfields, pipelines and refineries	138
8.3	Gas resources and pipelines	142
8.4	Nuclear power stations	149
8.5	Hydro-electric power stations	152
8.6	Ferrous and non-ferrous metals	155
9.1	Distribution of major iron and steel plants	166
9.2	Major centres of the engineering industry	170
9.3	Major centres of the chemical industry	173
9.4	Major industrial regions	180
10.1	Percentage of urban dwellers in the total population	186
10.2	Dates of foundation of towns	189
10.3	Distribution of the largest contemporary towns in the Soviet oecumene	195
10.4	Rural settlement types	198
11.1	Terrain problems for transport	203
11.2	Waterways, ports and icing of seas and rivers	205
11.3	Dominant flows of railway freight traffic	216
11.4	Railway passenger services and isochrones	218
12.1	Major Economic Regions, 1940–1960	228
12.2	Sovnarkhoz Regions, 1957	230
12.3	Industrial Management Regions, 1963	231
12.4	Major Economic Regions, 1961	232
12.5	Major Economic Regions (current)	233

Photographs

St Basil's Cathedral and the Kremlin, Moscow   9

Tamara's Castle, in the glaciated Terek Valley, one of the main routes through the Caucasus mountains   10

A medieval tower in Baku, Azerbaydzhan   12

Petrodvorets, the summer palace of Peter the Great near Leningrad   13

Dvortsovaya (Palace) Square, Leningrad, from the Winter Palace   14

Lenin's portrait and name dominate a Moscow intersection   19

Erosion scars on the sides of valleys cut into the loess of the southern Russian steppes near Rostov-on-Don   27

Limestone ranges of the Crimea, a vineyard in the foreground   32

Snow covered peaks in the Gissar mountains, Tadzhikistan   33

Lake Baykal, in southern Siberia, is the deepest lake in the world   34

A pass in the Pamir mountains in May   44

A chair lift in the Dombai valley in the Caucasus   45

Collapse of part of an apartment house following subsidence caused by melting of permafrost   48

Seaside crowds at Yalta in the Crimea   50

A riverside clearing in the Siberian tayga   58

A notice at a conservation park (Zapovednik) in the Caucasus mountains   64

Accelerated soil erosion on the slopes of a valley, Tadzhikistan   66

Accelerated erosion in the Caucasus mountains resulting from deforestation and overgrazing   68

Nurek Lake, high in the Pamir Mountains, supplies water to the giant Nurek hydro-electric scheme   73

Water being piped to a Crimean vineyard   76

Water power in Uzbekistan, an old water wheel with a hydro-electric plant in the distance   78

Much of the tayga is swampland, with an excess of water useless for cultivation because of the low temperatures that prevail   86

Armenian children in the uniform of the Pioneers   91

Soviet citizens and tourists watch the guard leaving Red Square after the changing-over ceremony at Lenin's tomb   104

An Uzbek taxi driver eating shashlick (roast mutton)   105

Grain silos on an Ukrainian farm   115

A livestock farm in the Ukraine   122

Cultivation, using contour terraces to control erosion, on a Tadzhik hillside   125

A tea farm near Sochi on the Black Sea coast   126

Mil-2 helicopter crop-spraying   130

Oilfield plant in the Siberian tayga, Tyumen in the Ob river basin   136

Oil rigs in the Caspian Sea   137

The most northerly gas pipelines in the world are in the USSR: the Mesoyakha-Norilsk line in June, with pipes for doubling the line being brought by truck and trailer   144

The Kharanor open-cast coal mine in East Siberia is planned to increase output from 6.5 to 9 million tonnes by 1985   146

The Berezniki (Urals) titanium-magnesium plant   165

PHOTOGRAPHS

A blast furnace of the Karaganda iron and steel works at Temirtau 167

Paper factory timber yards in Siberia—one of the industrial plants using power from the Bratsk hydro-electric scheme 175

Designing clothes in the Salut garment factory, Moscow 177

Quality inspectors checking tomatoes in a cannery in the Kirgiz SSR 178

A boulevard in Tbilisi. People are gathered around a kvass cart, kvass being fermented fruit juice 187

A view of Moscow from the river 190

Soviet and foreign tourists stream into Petrodvorets, the summer palace of Peter the Great near Leningrad 191

Flats in Ordzhonikidze in the north Caucasus region 194

A Tadzhik village with new houses and farm buildings among the old 200

A trolleybus line; Simferopol to Yalta, Crimea 209

A mainline train passing through the Donetsk coalfield 212

A railway station on the Trans-Siberian Railway 217

A public service bus in the mountains, Tadzhikistan 219

The harbour at Yalta 220

Tupolev Tu 134 airliner of Aeroflot on display in the Exhibition of Economic Achievement in Moscow 222

A village on river terraces in a Caucasus mountain valley 237

A Siberian valley with limited cultivation and livestock rearing 240

Summer day at a Simferopol suburban market, Crimea 243

The Registan square in Samarkand, one of the oldest cities in Central Asia 244

Introduction

The Union of Soviet Socialist Republics is, in terms of area, the largest state in the world, covering about one-sixth of the land surface of the earth. For mankind, however, much of this land area is inhospitable and difficult to utilise, and the population (about 267 million in 1981) is largely concentrated in the more favourable parts. It was in one of these more favoured areas, today usually referred to as European Russia, that the Russian state originated and from which explorers, traders, soldiers and settlers moved out into all the other areas and eventually brought them under Russian control.

It is for this reason that the name of Russia is commonly used to apply to the whole of the USSR, but such a use can lead to confusion and is not geographically satisfactory, so 'Russia' will not be used in this widest sense here. At the same time, it is not easy to lay down hard and fast rules about the use of names like 'Russia' and we shall sometimes use it, particularly in its adjectival form, in a rather wider use than if used only for European Russia. This is, indeed, necessary in the case of the pre-communist Russian Empire, while today the largest of the republics that constitute the USSR, or Soviet Union, is called the Russian Soviet Federal Socialist Republic, although it stretches far beyond the traditional limits of European Russia to embrace Siberia and the Soviet Far East (see Fig. A).

Altogether there are 15 Soviet Socialist Republics, including the RSFSR, making up the USSR. The name of each indicates the nationality group for which it is a 'national home' and which makes up the majority of the population, except that in Kazakhstan the population is only about 30 % Kazakh, compared with over 50 % Slav. An SSR is intended to give a measure of self-expression to each of the major national groups within the USSR, while smaller national and linguistic groups are recognised by other divisions, notably the Autonomous Soviet Socialist Republic (ASSR) usually an enclave within the great RSFSR, while other divisions are purely administrative and not connected with nationality or language. Further details are given in the table on page 3, Fig. B (page 4) and in Chapter 12.

During the years when revolutionary groups were preparing the way for the overthrow of the Tsar the term 'soviet' (council) became adopted for a revolutionary group or cell, and seizure of power by the Bolshevik Party was achieved largely through the efforts of the members of the soviets of workers, soldiers and sailors. The word thus became an honoured term in the language of the revolution and its adoption in national and regional administrative divisions symbolised the transfer of power.

Similarly, the term 'socialist' in the titles signifies the organisation of the state for the common good, rather than for the benefit of royal, aristocratic and other powerful groups. The term does not represent all the ideas that it does in western countries and the Russians do not consider it contradictory that the power in the Soviet socialist state is held mainly by the officers of the Communist Party. It is assumed by the leaders that everybody in the Soviet Union wishes to support the Communist Party and so no other political party is allowed to exist and the power of

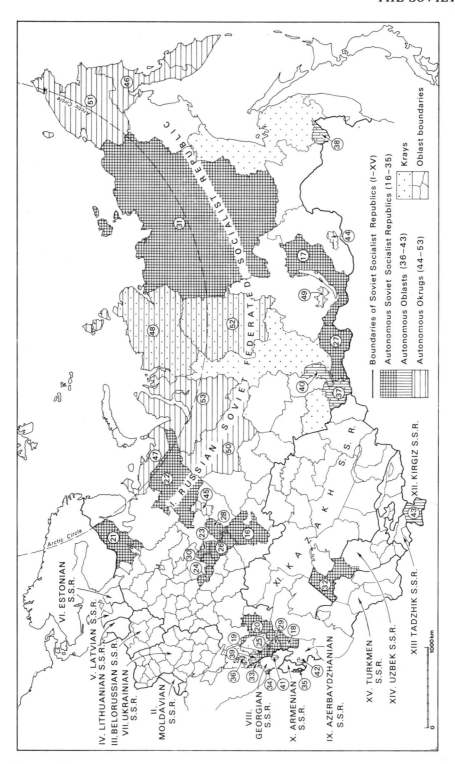

Fig. A Political and administrative divisions of the Soviet state (Numbers key pp. 225–6)

ADMINISTRATIVE DIVISIONS OF THE SOVIET UNION

The Soviet system of local administration involves the following major units:

English name	Russian name	Description
Union of Soviet Socialist Republics (USSR)	Soyuz Sovetskikh Sotsialistiches-kikh Respublik, i.e. SSSR (Cyrillic letters CCCP)	Originated as a union of several nominally separate republics, as indicated by its name.
Russian Soviet Federated Socialist Republic (RSFSR)	Rossiyskaya Sovetskaya Federativ-naya Sotsialisticheskaya Respublika	Comprises European Russia and other areas where Russians are dominant, i.e. Siberia and the Far East.
Soviet Socialist Republic (SSR)	Sovetskaya Sotsialisticheskaya Respublika	The term is applied to the 14 republics (e. g. Kazakhstanskaya SSR) which, together with the RSFSR, constitute the Soviet Union.
Autonomous Soviet Socialist Republic (ASSR)	Avtonomnaya Sovetskaya Sotsialis-ticheskaya Respublika	Are contained within the RSFSR or an SSR and represent the homelands of important minority groups, e.g. Tatarskaya ASSR.
Autonomous Oblast, (AOb) and Autonomous Okrug (AOk)	Avtonomnaya Oblast, Avtonomnyy Okrug	Administrative divisions with a limited degree of local autonomy. The bulk of the population belongs to one of the smaller minority groups, e.g. Khakasskaya AOb, Koryak-skiy AOk. Prior to 1977, Autonomous Okrugs were known as National Okrugs.
Oblast	Oblast	The basic administrative division of the RSFSR and most SSRs; usually named after its 'capital' and consisting of a town and the surrounding area, e.g. Leningradskaya Oblast.
Kray	Kray	A larger administrative division, found only in the RSFSR, e.g. Primorskiy (Maritime) Kray in the Far East.

For smaller divisions see page 227

English name	Russian name	Description
Economic Region	Ekonomicheskiy Rayon	In some cases subdivisions of republics comprising several oblasts; in others they consist of a single republic (e.g. Kazakhstanskiy Ekonomicheskiy Rayon); or may unite several republics, e.g. the Central Asian Economic Region (Sredneaziatskiy Ekonomicheskiy Rayon).

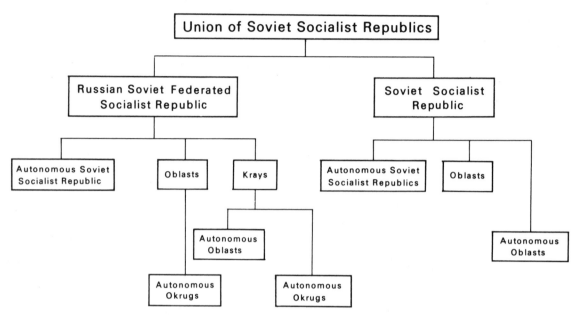

Fig. B Political-administrative structure of the USSR. The term 'Autonomous okrug' was adopted in 1977 for the areas previously known as 'National okrugs'

an elector is limited to recording votes for or against the candidate nominated by the Party.

We are not here concerned with politics, but it is necessary to understand the elementary facts of organisation of the country politically because many aspects of its economic development can only be properly understood with this knowledge. It is widely known that the dictates of the Communist Party are followed closely, with little public discussion or criticism of government policy, but it is less widely appreciated that within the ranks of the Communist Party and the government there is scope for considerable difference of opinion and conflict between alternative policies. No leader of the Soviet Union since Stalin has been permitted by his colleagues to establish himself as a dictator.

The Communist Party speaks, at least in public, with one voice. It exercises its power through the Supreme Soviet, which is the elected body, though it is not a parliament in our sense of the word (implying a body almost continuously in session and devoting its time to arguing over the actions of the executive, or government, and often trying to put some check on them). The Supreme Soviet does not have to be convened more than twice a year, but elects a Presidium which carries on the

work of government between sessions, its measures being subject to the approval of the larger body. The elective structure is maintained in soviets at republic and local levels, and the various committees and administrative bodies of all these organisations provide continuous opportunities for members to carry out useful work when the soviets themselves are not sitting.

The Supreme Soviets of the republics are now, since the adoption of a new Constitution of the USSR in 1977, elected for a period of five years, instead of four as formerly. The reason for the change is that the term of office now coincides with the Five Year Plans, thus emphasising the role of the soviets in economic planning. Local soviets are elected for two and a half years (formerly two years), their work being largely concerned with educational and health matters, cultural affairs and supervision of various bodies. They are assisted in their tasks by voluntary helpers.

Real power, however, resides in the Communist Party. The chief policy-making body is the Politburo, its political committee. The larger Central Committee and the Secretariat, the Party's own civil service, share the powers of government at national level. The Communist Party is, however, also organised right through from national down to local level, and every organisation, be it factory, farm or theatre, has its 'cell' of local party members. Membership is not easy to attain, so is looked on as an indication of success and vigour in one's profession and service to the country. Some western critics tend to assume that the local party 'bosses' are always concerned with the implementation of policy handed down from above and aimed at curbing local initiative, but this seems now hardly a correct interpretation. In the local party offices, as in the soviets, there is scope for local initiative. Also, persons holding important posts in the Central Committee of the party and the Council of Ministers, the executive group of the Presidium, are open to persuasion from the rank and file as well as having their own personal backgrounds of local interests. Thus, N. S. Khrushchev, before becoming First Secretary of the Central Committee and then Chairman of the Council of Ministers (or Prime Minister) held a succession of posts in his native Ukraine and, when in higher office, never failed to take note of Ukrainian interests, and, on a broader front, of the needs of the agricultural industry. His programmes for the widespread planting of maize, the ploughing of the 'virgin and unused lands' of Kazakhstan and western Siberia and his policies of livestock improvement resulted in major changes in the face of the countryside. These were policies in which he himself believed but they were founded on the ideas of officials, important and unimportant, throughout the country. Similarly, there were opponents of these policies at all levels and a continuous ebb and flow of power between the competing groups, with resulting 'stop–go' trends in economic development not entirely unlike those to which we are accustomed in the parliamentary democracies.

BIBLIOGRAPHY

Brown, A. *et al.* (eds) (1982), *Cambridge encyclopedia of Russia and the Soviet Union*, Cambridge University Press, Cambridge.

Campbell, R. (1974), *Soviet-type economies*, Houghton Mifflin, Boston.

Churchward, L. G. (1975), *Contemporary Soviet government*, Routledge and Kegan Paul, London.

Davies, R. W. (ed.), *The Soviet Union*, Allen & Unwin, London.

Dyker, D. A. (1976), *The Soviet economy*, Crosby Lockwood Staples, London.

Frolic, B. M. (1972), Decision making in Soviet cities, *American Political Science Review*, **66**, 38–52.

Lane, D. (1972), *Politics and society in the USSR*, Weidenfeld and Nicolson, London.

Pallot, J. and Shaw, D. (1981), *Planning in the Soviet Union*, Croom Helm, London.

Schöpflin, G. (ed.) (1970), *The Soviet Union and Eastern Europe, a handbook*, Anthony Blond, London.

1 The Evolution of the Russian State

The history of the Soviet Union is the combined history of many different ethnic groups. These groups are described in a later chapter, and for a brief summary here of the historical geography of the Soviet Union and of its predecessor, the Russian Empire, it must suffice to summarise the development and geographical diffusion of the dominant ethnic group, the Slavs, who eventually brought the other groups under their control. The Slav civilisation of central and eastern Europe was itself the result of a long period of evolution. From early Paleolithic times there was a gradual northward movement from the Middle East and the Black Sea coasts into the steppe and forest regions. As the ice retreated groups of hunters penetrated into the northern forest zones and an important Mesolithic settlement has been identified by archaeologists as far north as Kunda in the Estonian SSR.

While hunting, fishing and gathering of food remained the basis of life for most communities, agriculture in the form of forest-fallow cultivation with the rearing of livestock began to appear in the Neolithic period (fifth to second millenium BC). This was particularly so in the southern areas where climatic and soil conditions were most favourable and nearness to the hearths of agriculture in the Middle East and central Asia facilitated the transfer of ideas, seeds, plants and livestock. A pastoral – agricultural economy was well developed in the succeeding Bronze Age over a large part of the present-day territories of the USSR. Metal working was particularly well developed in the Caucasus and Transcaucasian areas, and this was also the region in which iron working developed first, but in the Iron Age such crafts spread northward and also eastward into Siberia and encouraged trade as well as agriculture.

From about the eighth century BC new raiders and colonists were appearing along the Black Sea coast and establishing settlements there and trade developed, particularly under the stimulus provided by the Greeks. Then the area fell under Roman domination, but there were also many incursions by a variety of raiders and the towns fell into decay, and migration northward reinforced the communities that had developed in the steppes and forests. It is to this period that the Soviet archaeologists and historians look for the signs of the first Slavonic groups in central and eastern Europe, notably in the basins of the Vistula and Dnepr and in Volynia, and for the split of the Slavs by about 500 BC into eastern, southern and western groups, with the former becoming much the largest group and providing the basis of the future Russian state.

During the first to ninth centuries AD the east Slav tribes developed agricultural and trading communities along the Dnepr, Desna, Dnestr, Volga and other river valleys. They were subject to raids by marauding tribes including the Goths, Huns, Avars, Khazars and Bulgars from the east and south, while from the north the forest lands were penetrated along the river routes by the Vikings, or Varangians, as the Slavs called them. The Scandinavians became the most consistent raiders and colonists. Trading and intermarrying with the Slavs, they appear to have played an important role in the development of the still separate communities to which the name Rus became attached. By 862 Rurik had established Novgorod as the capital of a small but distinct princedom in the northern forest zone which had become known as Rus. On the southern fringes of the forest-steppe belt, Kiev had evolved as a leading city state and in 882 this fell to Oleg, Rurik's successor. Kievan Rus became the most advanced of the embryos of the Russian state but there were many other communities evolving into small states, many of them coming under the rule of the Kievan princes for a time. In spite of raids by the Pechenegs and others Kievan Rus flourished and the adoption of Christianity late in the tenth century facilitated the forging of links with Constantinople and royal houses throughout Europe.

In Kievan Rus forest-fallow forms of cultivation persisted but there was some transition to permanent fields, and cultivation was aided by a variety of implements—ard irons, plough shares, coulters, sickles and scythes. Archaeological investigations reveal well-made grain pits, with millet as the favoured crop, no doubt because of its drought-resistant qualities appropriate to forest-steppe conditions. Established field systems with wheat and rye (more suitable in northerly latitudes) gradually became common in the central forest areas and even in Novgorod by about the eleventh century. By this time also there was increased reliance on domestic livestock, as opposed to hunting, with pigs probably most numerous, but cattle, sheep and goats also common.

Other raiders came to Kiev, which was particularly exposed to the nomads of the steppes and after the city was sacked by the Polovtsy or Cumans it failed to regain its previous eminence and the areas more protected by the forests from marauders gained in strength, notably Vladimir–Suzdal. Exports from the forest lands included furs, honey and wax, while from the farms came flax, hemp, hides, skins, suets, tallow and grains. Local craftsmen developed manufactures based on these raw materials. Under the growing pressure of population, improved field systems developed, and two-field agriculture, in which one field was left fallow after a crop, merged into three-field systems, in which two out of three fields were productive each year. The light *sokha* plough was generally used in the northern districts, where glaciation had deposited numerous boulders, while the *ralo* was used on heavy soils. This more cumbersome plough needed a team of draught

animals and may have been one of the factors encouraging the growth of the commune and the gradual introduction of slavery and of serfdom by the more powerful members of the community.

By the eighth to ninth centuries towns were becoming an important factor in economic, social and administrative systems. The need to establish strongholds to control areas over which princes claimed suzerainty, to keep out raiders and to store tribute led to the creation of many towns. The security they offered, as well as trade links, would then lead to the growth of craft industries, trading rows and markets. Churches, cathedrals and monasteries also stimulated urban developments.

THE TATAR PERIOD

The thirteenth century saw a reversal of the progress that was being made throughout the Russian lands, as the Tatar nomads began sustained raiding of the steppes and repeated incursions into the forest zone. These people, also known as Mongol, possessed superior military skill and exploited to the full their horsemanship, which gave them total supremacy in open land. They inflicted a series of defeats on Slav forces from 1223 onward and gradually conquered Transcaucasia and southern Russia, culminating in the fall of Kiev in 1240. The principalities which had emerged in the forest zone as independent of Kiev and Vladimir–Suzdal fell under Tatar control, although in due course their princes were permitted to remain leaders if they collected tribute for the Khan who had established the capital of the Golden Horde at Saray on the Volga.

Novgorod remained independent and had trade links with the Baltic and Finnish lands, trading especially in the furs collected in the forests from as far as, and occasionally beyond, the Ural Mountains. However, it had its own campaign to fight against the incursions of the Swedes and Germans who were organised in orders of Knights. In 1242 the victory of Alexander Nevsky in the 'battle on the ice' assured the survival of Novgorod, but it was not entirely free of raids and partial control by the Tatars. During the second half of the thirteenth century, the Tatar yoke fell heavily on the Russian people as trade, agriculture and crafts were affected by the disruption and exaction of tribute. Nevertheless, firm administ-

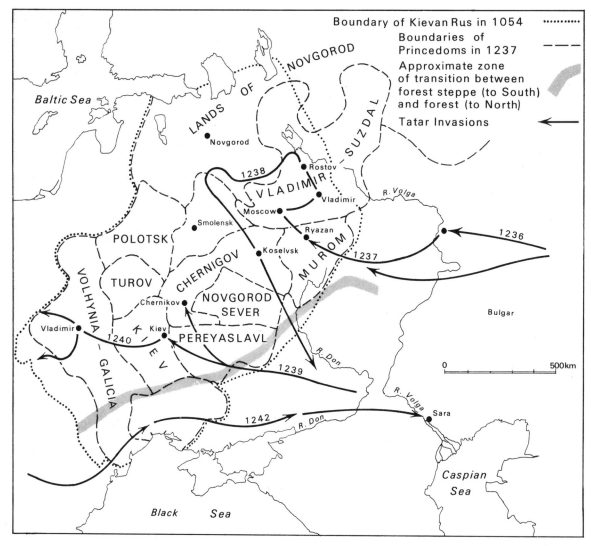

Fig. 1.1 Tatar invasions of the thirteenth century and the boundaries of Kievan Rus in 1054 and the princedoms of 1237. The forests provided some protection from the raiders who easily penetrated the forest steppe from the more southerly treeless steppe

ration by the Tatars gradually re-established the trade routes and eventually disruption within the Tatar state itself facilitated the rise of new forces within Russia.

It was Moscow, first mentioned in the Annals of 1143, that emerged as the nucleus of the new Russian state. It had no doubt benefited from its sheltered position in the forest lands and from a strategic position in relation to communications. Its merchants had access to river routes in all direc-

tions, for here the upper reaches of the Volga make a great loop to the north of the city, and southward the Oka cuts across to join it, and so also gives access to the upper Don and other rivers by easy portages. As in the wooded steppe near Kiev, the soils were relatively easy to cultivate with the available implements, so facilitating the development of agriculture.

Moscow, however, was not free from the attacks of the Tatars and not until 1328, when it acquired the task of collecting the tribute from

St Basil's Cathedral and the Kremlin, Moscow

other principalities for the Tatars, did it begin to assume the role of leadership. In 1326 the seat of the Metropolitan of the Orthodox Church was moved from Kiev to Moscow and when Constantinople fell to the Turks in 1453 its mantle was held to have fallen on Moscow—the 'Third Rome'. Meanwhile, the Tatar leaders had been converted to Islam, which helped to prevent any union between the rivals and stimulated more church support for the Russian princes. In 1380 Dmitry Donskoy defeated the Saray Tatars at Kulikovo on the Don. Two years later Moscow was burnt by Tokhtamysh, but before the end of the century Tokhtamysh's Golden Horde was in turn defeated by a rival eastern prince, Timur the Lame, or Tamerlane. The Golden Horde remained strong enough to besiege Moscow again in 1408, but soon after began to disintegrate and a partial split took place with the formation of the khanates of the Crimea, Kazan, Astrakhan and

Siberia. In 1480 a final, unsuccessful, campaign by the Tatars was followed by the denunciation of the 'Yoke' by Ivan III, 'the Great'. Novgorod, Tver, Vyatka and other local princedoms were gradually absorbed into Muscovy.

Moscow was now firmly set on the road of expansion and during the long reign of Ivan IV 'the Terrible', who was crowned 'Tsar' (derived from Caesar) and grand prince of all Russia, the khanates of Kazan and Astrakhan were subjugated and the whole of the Volga area was brought under Russian rule. During this time, Russia was visited by the Englishman, Richard Chancellor, and the Muscovy Company was formed for trade between England and Russia, leading later to the founding of the port of Arkhangelsk (Archangel) on the White Sea.

Thus, by the middle of the sixteenth century, the forest state of Moscow had emerged to undisputed leadership of the east Slavs, and one of the major

Tamara's Castle, in the glaciated Terek Valley, one of the main routes through the Caucasus mountains, now used by the Georgian Military Highway. Queen Tamara ruled 1184–1213 when Georgia was a powerful and cultured state

themes of Russian history and geography was already beginning to develop—the search for outlets to the sea to enable the benefits of trade to be realised. Sweden, Lithuania and Poland blocked the way to the Baltic Sea while, in the steppes to the south, the Tatars were still strong enough to bar Russian access to the Black Sea. As late as 1571 the Crimean Tatars raided Moscow and fortifications were built along the line of the wooded steppe, where forest shelter was available. In this frontier zone there grew up communities of a semi-military nature, formed by people who sought independence from serfdom and oppression in Poland, Lithuania and Muscovy and took the name of Cossacks, meaning 'free warriors'. They are known mainly for the part they later played in the expansion of the Russian empire, being employed by the Tsars as frontiersmen and soldiers to occupy and control conquered areas.

The conquest of Siberia

The Ural Mountains and the Ural River, which flows from the mountains to the Caspian Sea, have long been regarded as a border between Europe and Asia. Today, this border has no meaning, but in the first half of the sixteenth century it was a frontier zone beyond the limits of Russian civilisation, developed from Slav, Greek, Roman, Scandinavian and Germanic cultures, with the way barred by the Tatar khanate of Kazan. When Kazan was captured in 1552 the Russians could advance into this vast, almost untapped hunting-ground from which could be obtained great quantities of furs, the greatest source of wealth in Russia.

The Stroganov family, possessors of great estates in Russia, acquired new lands in and beyond the Urals and sent a Cossack army to conquer the Siberian Tatars. This they did, though they lost their leader, Yermak, in battle. Tyumen fort was built in 1585 and soon there was a string of strongholds and trading posts along the valleys of the Tobol, Irtysh and Ob, a vast river system flowing from the mountains and steppes through the forest to the tundra and the Arctic Sea. Now began in earnest the battle against nature in the frozen north and the *tayga*—the great coniferous forest that stretches in a belt some 8000 km across northern Russia and Siberia. Incredible hardships were tolerated by the traders, soldiers and administrators who would trek by river valley and forest trail from Moscow or, in the brief summer, would be shipped round from the White Sea to the mouth of the Ob, many of them being shipwrecked and falling among hostile tribes on the way. From Moscow to a base at Tobolsk or Tyumen could be (depending on route) a journey greater than that from Moscow to London, and from the Siberian base the Russians would then work hundreds of kilometres out into the forest, bargaining with the tribes for furs and wintering in simple huts through temperatures 40°C or more below freezing point.

With the Cossacks often pioneering the routes, they sailed up the rivers, dragged their heavy boats over long portages and took the next favourably oriented valley to pursue the route eastwards. In winter, the frozen rivers and lakes provided travel conditions often better than the summer, when other perils and hindrances from rapids to mosquitoes took their toll. They penetrated beyond the Yenisey into eastern Siberia and, another

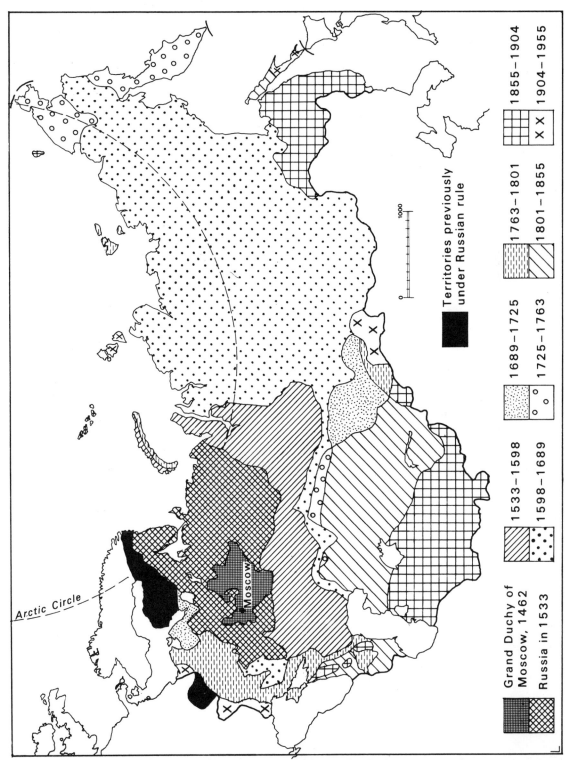

Fig. 1.2 The expansion of the Russian Empire. Some simplification has been necessary in the interests of clarity, especially in respect of gains and losses of territory in the European areas

thousand miles on, founded Yakutsk in 1632 on the Lena, and, penetrating the last mountain barriers, reached the Pacific Ocean in 1648. On the sea of Okhotsk they set up more trading posts and went on to explore the vast area that still lay between them and the northern seas.

The eighteenth century saw colonisation of Kamchatka, a peninsula which looks insignificant on the map of the USSR, yet is as big as Great Britain. After earlier setbacks, the Russian fleet under Bering proved the existence of the straits named after him and paved the way for later Russian colonisation of Alaska. The Tsars had acquired a vast empire wrapped round a third of the globe. They were not very much interested in it, except for the wealth it could provide—furs, salt, gold and other minerals.

A medieval tower in Baku, Azerbaydzhan, used as a refuge when raiders came across the Caspian Sea. Parts of the Soviet city can be seen behind the old Moslem town

After the strong reign of Ivan the Terrible, Russia suffered severe problems of succession. Ivan had killed his own son in fit of rage and for thirty years Moscow was the scene of plot and counter-plot to secure the throne. The Poles supported pretenders to the Russian throne and actually took command in Moscow, only to be ejected by a local uprising. Eventually a youth of 16, to whom there were fewer objections than to any other claimant, was elected Tsar. He was Michael Romanov, and thus began the line that was to hold the Russian throne until the revolution, 304 years later.

RUSSIA UNDER THE ROMANOVS

Despite the great advances to the east, the Romanovs were most concerned with their position in the west, where the boundaries of Russia met those of other powerful states. It was in western Europe that the great advances in science and technology were being made and it was to the west that Russia turned for help in its own modernisation. Peter I came to the throne in 1689 already aware of western progress, and visited Prussia, Hanover, Holland and England to acquire practical knowledge of new techniques and recruit foreign engineers, artisans, surgeons and other specialists. When he returned he had a new city built on the marshy land near the Baltic, on which the Russians had gained a precarious hold against Swedish power, and called it his 'window on the west', St. Petersburg. He transferred the capital to the new city in 1712 and from its foundation it was an important port. In a few decades it was a large industrial city, yet distinguished for the charm of its planned layout and the beauty of its buildings. Moscow was to be eclipsed as a capital for over 200 years, but with its central position in European Russia and the momentum of its past it continued to grow, though at a rate reduced by the loss of its functions as a capital.

Peter initiated many reforms including systematic organisation of the provincial governments, subordination of the nobility and clergy, currency reform and educational developments ranging from introduction of a system of elementary education to the foundation of the Academy of Sciences. The effects were in some cases slow to permeate the economy but industrial development was aided by the experts from western countries.

Petrodvorets, the summer palace of Peter the Great near Leningrad. The spacious gardens, now available to all, are noteworthy for their large number of varied fountains

Factories were set up, encouraged by the state, not only in Moscow and St. Petersburg but also in the Ural region, where iron ore was available. Shipyards and artillery works were set up or modernised to provide the basis of a reformed army and navy.

Wars were fought against Turkey and Sweden. The Russians had great successes in the north, enabling Russian rule to be extended over Karelia, Estonia and other areas, so consolidating the Russian position on and near the Baltic Sea. Still, however, Russia lacked access to a warmer, ice-free sea, and Peter's failures to defeat the Turks left this a problem to be tackled in the latter half of the century by Catherine the Great. For over 30 years under Catherine (1761–96), Russia made appreciable territorial advances, acquiring the Black Sea steppes, absorbing the lands of the Cossacks and, eventually, most of the Ukraine and the Crimea. Although the Bosphoros–Dardanelles passage from the Black Sea to the Mediterranean

was to cause trouble with Turkey and the western European powers right through to the twentieth century, Russia now had access to warm-water ports. Odessa, it is true, does freeze up for about a month but St. Petersburg was closed for about five months and Arkhangelsk even longer. Also, the communications with the Mediterranean countries were economically as well as strategically valuable, though not until the Suez canal was opened did the full benefit of the Black Sea possession become evident. Meanwhile, however, foreign trade was facilitated and within the country internal customs duties were abolished and roads improved. A notable achievement was the completion in 1773 of the Yakutsk Track from Irkutsk to Yakutsk, linking with the Yakutsk–Okhotsk track, so strengthening Russian power in the Far East.

On the fluctuating western frontiers also, Russia made progress. In the dismemberment of Poland by the three partitions, 1772, 1793 and 1795,

Prussia, Austria and Russia each took over large tracts of territory. Russia also acquired Lithuania and Latvia, with the useful port of Riga, and in 1809, control of Finland, so consolidating her position on the Baltic, while Caucasian conquests still further strengthened her in the south. Garrison towns and fortified lines were constructed to police the new territories and these provided a base for further colonisation and settlement.

Russia was now a mighty European power and its image in the west was greatly strengthened when, under Alexander I, the Russian armies and the Russian winter defeated Napoleon during his retreat from Moscow in 1812 and opened the way for his final overthrow.

The revolutionary movement

Participation in the Napoleonic Wars was one factor which stimulated the dissatisfaction felt by many of the intelligentsia and aristocracy of Russia. Many of the officers who went to fight in western Europe saw how much more advanced other countries were in economic and political affairs. The French and American revolutions had already encouraged discontent with the autocracy of the Tsars; now the demand for a constitution setting out the rights of the people grew apace. The

matter flared up when Nicholas I came to the throne in December 1825 and a number of officers paraded their troops, demanding a constitution and an end to serfdom. They were crushed savagely and the leaders executed or exiled. Bitter represssion was extended to everyone suspected of liberal ideas and Russia became a police state.

During the nineteenth century the name of Siberia became increasingly associated with exile and imprisonment. It should not be overlooked that to many of those who had gone there to settle in the past Siberia had been a land of promise, of freedom. The serfdom, which had been tightened up step by step throughout the Romanov period, bound the serfs rigidly to the landowners' estates and made them, in effect, the property of the landlords, but if they could escape to Siberia, where serfdom was not fully established, they could become free. From the sixteenth century, however, the state had used Siberia as a place of exile. This had the double advantage to the tsars of removing their troublesome subjects from the cities and helping to exploit the resources of the area. Siberia itself, however, benefited from the presence of some of the political exiles who spent much time experimenting with crops and trying to improve the living conditions of the people among whom they were cast.

Dvortsovaya (Palace) Square, Leningrad, from the Winter Palace. The column commemorates Tsar Alexander I and the victory over Napoleon in 1812

Neither death nor exile could stamp out the reform movement. Liberal writers defied the censorship and intellectuals went to work among the peasants to try to ease their lot by taking to them some of the benefits of improving medical and technical knowledge. After the long-delayed and inadequate measures to emancipate the serfs, beginning in 1861, unrest became more violent because of disappointment at the smallness of the holdings created for the peasants and other terms of the emancipation and the general lack of progress. In 1881 the Tsar, Alexander II, was assassinated, ironically just as he was about to publish a constitution, which was promptly suppressed. Affairs went from bad to worse. The gospel of Marxism now spread to Russia. One of those who saw in it salvation for the masses was the embittered brother of a student executed for complicity in a plot in St. Petersburg. Under the assumed name of Lenin he was later to be the main figure in the foundation of the Soviet Union, but this was not until after the last of the Tsars, Nicholas II, had plunged the country into the horrors of the First World War and taken it to the brink of destruction.

The first half of the nineteenth century saw appreciable industrialisation (the first cotton mill in St. Petersburg was built in 1798) and corresponding improvement in communications. Canals were built, especially linking the north with the Volga, the St. Petersburg–Moscow highway was surfaced, and in 1837 Russia's first railway was opened. In 1851 St. Petersburg and Moscow were linked by rail and numerous lines were opened in the 1860s and 1870s. Lines from the Ukraine made possible large scale movement of grain to the growing industrial cities as well as for export, and also the movement of iron ore, fuel and finished iron goods, which enabled the Donbas to become Russia's principal iron-producing region before the end of the century.

The final phase of imperial expansion

After the debacle of the Crimean War (1853–6) Russian expansion in Europe was firmly blocked by the western powers. In the east, however, there was still largely a power vacuum between Russian settlement across the Siberian steppes and along the north Pacific coasts and, in the south, British power in India and the weak, but populous Chinese empire.

The seventeenth century exploration of Siberia and the Far East had been checked when the Russians, few in number, had come to the borders of the Chinese realm at the Amur River. In the Treaty of Nerchinsk, 1689, they had been forced to accept the Chinese claims to the Amur, which denied them access to this great river and the cultivable land much needed for the supply of their settlements so far from the western grainlands. During the Crimean war, Count N. N. Muraviev, the Governor-General of Siberia, decided to force a concession from the Chinese, and to show the strength of the Russians he took a flotilla down the Amur and was, in fact, just in time to repulse a British expedition against Kamchatka. The Chinese were duly impressed and by 1860 the Russians had taken possession of the Amur and Maritime Provinces, and founded Vladivostok as far south as possible. By no means all the Tsar's advisers were convinced about the desirability of extending the Far Eastern empire and Muraviev had to fight hard for his cause. Eventually the Russian position on the Asian mainland was consolidated but Russian interests in Alaska and California were sold to the United States. Pressure was successfully brought to bear on the Japanese to recognise Russian control over Sakhalin.

As a result of the efforts of another vigorous proponent of eastern development, Count Witte, the Trans-Siberian Railway was commenced in 1891. By treaty with the Chinese the final section was built across Manchuria to Vladivostok, thus avoiding the long and circuitous route of the Amur valley, which was developed later. Against the wishes of Witte, who believed in peaceful, commercial co-operation, other concessions were wrung from the Chinese as Russia belatedly sought to share in the scramble initiated by the western powers to exploit Chinese weakness by establishing ports under their own control. Russia obtained control over north Manchuria, the Liaotung Peninsula and Port Arthur. This brought them into conflict with the Japanese, at whose hands Russia suffered a humiliating defeat in 1904 and the loss of its Chinese gains, except the railway route.

During this period after 1860 the Russians also advanced into the central Asian deserts, which had long kept them at bay. The oases and montane valleys north and west of the Pamir, Tyan–Shan and adjoining mountain ranges were occupied by Turkic and largely Moslem peoples organised in khanates or sultanates, some with well developed agriculture, others with a nomadic way of life. This was the country of the old Silk Road to China, opened by Marco Polo in the fourteenth century. These ancient states, such as Samarkand and Bukhara, not only attracted the Russians who were bent on military control and trade development, but also gave them excuses to intervene because of the raiders who periodically came out of the desert to attack Russian settlements in southern Siberia.

The Russians began to advance from the Lake Balkhash area in the middle of the nineteenth century, building the new town of Alma Ata in 1854. Tashkent was taken in 1865, and Samarkand in 1868. During the 1880s a railway was built from the Caspian Sea to Samarkand. Little by little the whole of the area right up to the borders of Afghanistan was brought under Russian control, leading to considerable tension as the British felt their interests challenged. Eventually, after the Russian defeat in the Far East by the Japanese, the respective spheres of interest of the Russians and British in the Near East were delineated and the borders stabilised.

Thus, as the rivalry of the great powers deepened in the early years of the twentieth century, a rivalry which in other spheres led inexorably to the catastrophe of the First World War, the Russian Empire spread over much the same proportion of the globe as the British, with no other comparable territorial domination. It was, however, a land empire, one consolidated block, dependent on land rather than sea communications. But compared with Britain and other western European powers, Russia was weak, economically, militarily and administratively. It was still an autocracy and a police state. After the attempted revolution of 1905, which had followed the humiliation of the Russo–Japanese war and growing discontent among intellectuals, proletariat and peasantry, Nicholas II had conceded the formation of a parliament, the Duma, but kept control of it by periodic dissolution and rigging of the electoral machinery. When Nicholas declared war on Germany on the side of the western allies, he thought he would thereby strengthen Russia, the citadel of autocracy and the divine right of kings. No ruler ever made a greater mistake.

The economy under the tsars
The weakness of the Russian Empire in the war stemmed largely from lack of economic development and organisation in all sectors of industry—primary (agriculture, mining etc.,) secondary (manufacturing) and tertiary (including the transport network). It is true that industrialisation had been proceeding fairly steadily, mostly in the Moscow, St. Petersburg, Ural and Ukraine areas. Whereas iron-working in the Urals had developed early in the eighteenth century, based on local iron ores, charcoal and water power, in the nineteenth century Donbas coal attracted heavy industry to the south. Cotton and flax mills were built in the towns around Moscow as well as in Moscow itself. Moscow and St. Petersburg became centres of engineering. These cities, those in the Baltic provinces and other northern towns manufactured clothing, shoes, chemicals, rubber and other goods.

By 1913 a substantial industrial base had been built up, but it was small in relation to the size and needs of the country, and did not compare with the industrialisation of Britain, Germany, France or the USA. Agriculture lagged perhaps even more strikingly compared with the western countries. Though large quantities of grain were exported, these shipments were achieved often at the expense of shortages within Russia. Serfdom had been abolished but poverty and indebtedness remained rife in the countryside. Land reform came late and had progressed but little before the catastrophe of war denuded the countryside of its able-bodied men and laid it open to the ravages of invasion. The weakness of the transport system meant that even when harvests were good, food supply in the towns was an uncertain business.

Russia, at the outbreak of the First World War, was a giant invested with some of the trappings of expanding capitalism, but lacking efficiency and the knowledge with which to realise its own potential.

THE CREATION OF THE SOVIET UNION

The war soon revealed the weakness of Russia. Soon the Tsar's armies were falling back on all fronts. Incredible suffering was borne by the Russian troops, not worse than that endured by those fighting in the horror-landscapes of Ypres, Verdun, Passchendaele and the Somme but on an even larger scale. The Russians, promised a quick victory, grew more disillusioned as the years went by. Successes were few and defeats many. The supply position grew worse. The railways became

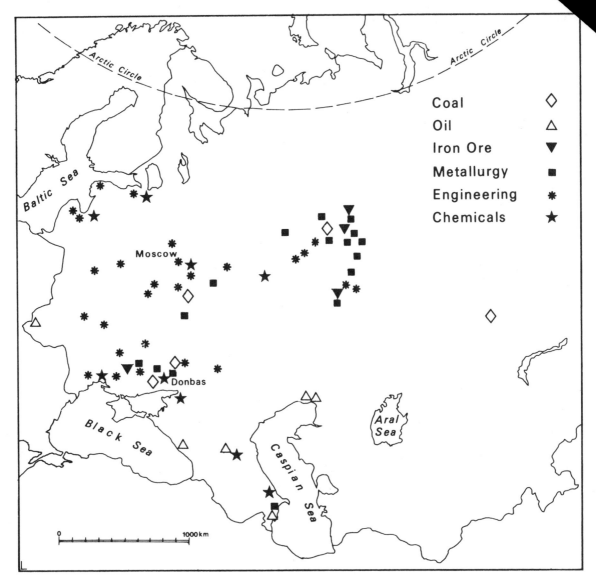

Fig. 1.3 The principal locations of heavy industry in Russia in 1913. The main industrial regions were the Donbas and Ural areas, while manufacturing industries were developed near Moscow and the capital, St. Petersburg (now Leningrad). Textile industries (not shown on the map) were particularly important near Moscow. Food processing industries were more widely scattered. There were also a few industrial plants in Siberia, mostly located beside the Trans-Siberian Railway

less and less reliable for want of maintenance and replacements, the farms, increasingly depleted of manpower, produced less, and it became more and more impossible to supply either the fighting troops or the armaments workers in the towns.

January 1917 was a terrible month, with temperatures well below freezing and the capital foodless. The leader of the Kadet Party, a liberal group in the Duma, had already said that the government's incompetence boardered on high treason. February saw the consolidation of opposition, and in March the workers took things into their own hands. A wave of strikes began in Petrograd, as St. Petersburg had been renamed, and Moscow. Processions came out with banners carrying slogans such as 'Down with the war' and

17

Troops were ordered out, but
themselves mutinied. The Tsar
mpt to return from the front,
one to take personal command
is, was prevented, and was forced
to abdicate.

The 300-year rule of the Romanovs was ended
and a Provisional Government was formed by the
Duma. Its authority was challenged from the
beginning by the Petrograd soviet (council) of
workers and soldiers which formed an executive
committee of leaders of the socialist parties. Lenin
returned from abroad to take the leadership of the
Bolshevik party, then in a minority position in the
soviet. An abortive rising by the Bolsheviks in July
was suppressed and Lenin and other prominent
Bolsheviks went into hiding. The Provisional
Government, however, failed to pursue its advantages and dissipated much of its energies in
trying to continue the war. On the night of 7
November (25 October by the Julian calendar then
in use in Russia) the Bolsheviks struck and took
control.

The new government set up by the Bolsheviks
lost no time in seeking a peace treaty with
Germany, though it resulted in great losses of
territory. Opposition mounted within the country
and the state of the economy worsened still
further. The Germans occupied the Ukraine and
the Donets region and anti-Bolshevik armies were
created in the north Caucasus and Transcaucasus.
Russia's former allies, dismayed at being left to
continue the war without an eastern front to split
the German effort and by the rise of communism,
themselves invaded the country in a number of
areas in the north and south while the Japanese
established a puppet state in the Far East.

Counter-revolutionary 'White' armies gained
control over large areas but the new Red Army
gradually recovered most of the former tsarist
empire and the civil war was virtually over by early
1921. Finally, the Japanese were expelled from
Siberia in 1922.

Although the Bolsheviks had preached international revolution and communism, when they
came to power in Russia they soon revealed
strongly nationalistic tendencies. One demon-
stration of this was the movement of the capital
from Petrograd back to Moscow. This symbolised
a return to the traditional Russian centre as well as
providing a base more secure from attack. One of
the 'planks' in their election programme was

recognition for national minorities and they soon
set to work to give large minorities separate
republics. Attempts by several, notably the
Ukraine, to achieve complete independence were,
however, resisted and all were finally incorporated
into the Union of Soviet Socialist Republics,
which was the name adopted for the new state in
1922.

The aim of the new government was the establishment of communism as early as possible.
This involved nationalisation of all land, factories,
transport facilities and other means of production,
previously privately owned, so that they could be
developed on behalf of the people as a whole.
Much of this was not, however, to the liking of the
people, especially the peasants who wanted to
possess their own land and who had supported the
revolution thinking they would thereby gain it
when the landlords were overthrown. To recover
their support and to stimulate production generally during the crisis period, Lenin proclaimed in
March 1921 the New Economic Policy, which
recognised the right to private production and
profit. Later, when Stalin had secured power after
Lenin's death, a policy of forced collectivisation of
farmland was introduced, and by 1931 over half of
the peasants had been brought into the collectives.
Many of those who resisted suffered the fate of
their forbears under the Tsars, being exiled to
work in labour camps in Siberia and other regions.

The Second World War
Stalin distrusted the western powers, for which
perhaps he had some justification in view of the
allied intervention against the Bolsheviks after
their withdrawal from the war. After negotiations
for a non-aggression pact with the British and
French he swung over in 1939 to concluding a pact
with Hitler, with the result that Russia was again
caught in an unprepared state when the Germans
invaded the USSR in 1941. Once again the
Russian armies had to fall back almost to
Moscow, but they held on tenaciously to
Leningrad which was besieged for two years. The
Russians pursued a 'scorched earth' policy to
hinder the German advance and evacuated people,
factories and livestock to the eastern regions. This
aided the development of the Ural, Siberian and
Central Asian regions. The retreat in the south was
finally halted at Stalingrad (now Volgograd) in
1942 where great battles through the winter finally
forced the surrender there of the German Sixth

Lenin, principal Bolshevik theorist and first head of the Soviet state, is commemorated in the USSR in every possible way. Here his portrait and name dominate a Moscow intersection

Army on 30th January 1943. It was another 28 months before the Germans were finally defeated and the Soviet losses amounted to close on 30 million dead and missing, and countless wounded.

Emergence from the war on the victorious side enabled the Soviet Union to play a major part in redrawing the boundaries of eastern Europe. They now obtained a boundary with Poland nearer to the line suggested by Lord Curzon on ethnic grounds than they had previously been given at the settlement in 1920, while Poland received compensation by being given districts that had previously been held by Germany. The USSR reincorporated Estonia, Latvia and Lithuania and other small additions were made at the expense of

the defeated countries. These included several important strategic areas such as Kaliningrad, a former East Prussian naval port, and parts of the Carpathians. In the east, the Tuva area, near Lake Baykal, became part of the USSR after having been at one time occupied by Russia, when nominally Chinese. The southern part of Sakhalin, which had been held by the Japanese since 1915, and the Kurile Islands were added to Soviet territory.

Thus, by 1945 the Soviet Union had, with some minor differences which approximately cancelled each other out in terms of area, regained virtually all the territory of the former Russian Empire, except for Finland.

COMECON

Following the defeat of Germany the Soviet Union proceeded to protect itself and secure its frontiers against further possible attacks by establishing control over the eastern European states between itself and the western powers. Intense political support was given to the 'patriotic fronts' and communist parties of the countries or, as in the case of Germany, the part of the country which had been occupied by Soviet military forces, the political activity being backed up by the continued presence of Soviet forces. Bourgeois and capitalist political parties were forced out and Soviet-type economies imposed. When, in 1947, the US Secretary of State, George Marshall, put forward the European Recovery Programme, under which the USA would supply raw materials, goods and capital to the devastated countries, the USSR rejected this as an 'instrument of dollar imperialism'. The following year the Organisation for European Economic Co-operation began to distribute the ERP funds and in 1949, in opposition to the Marshall Plan and the OEEC, the Soviet Union drew the eastern European states together in the Council for Mutual Economic Assistance. (CMEA or COMECON)

Through CMEA, the USSR and Poland, the German Democratic Republic, Czechoslovakia, Hungary, Rumania and Bulgaria co-ordinate their economies, with a high degree of industrial planning for mutual interdependence, especially through exchange of Soviet minerals and other raw materials for manufactured goods from the other countries. Following the creation and enlargement of the European Economic Community in the west the Soviet Union has sought to strengthen COMECON in all possible ways. The organisation has not been limited entirely to eastern Europe, Cuba having been admitted to membership in July 1972. The USSR, as the dominant power in COMECON, can thus be said to exercise a high degree of control over most of eastern Europe and to have formal means of co-operation in economic matters with Cuba. In addition Soviet influence is now widespread in south-east Asia, Africa and other parts of the world through trade and the granting of economic and military aid to countries of the Third World.

BIBLIOGRAPHY

Armstrong, T. (1965), *Russian settlement in the north*, CUP, Cambridge.

Brown, A. and Kaser, M. (eds.) (1978), *The Soviet Union since the fall of Khrushchev*, Macmillan, London.

Cohen, S. F., Rabinowitch, A. and Sharlet, R. (eds.) (1980), *The Soviet Union since Stalin*, Macmillan, London.

Crisp, O. (1976), *Studies in the Russian economy before 1914*, Macmillan, London.

Dobb, M. (1966), *Soviet economic development since 1917*, Routledge and Kegan Paul, London.

Fallenbuchl, Z. M. (ed.) (1975), *Economic development in the Soviet Union and Eastern Europe*, 2 vols., Praeger, New York.

Florinsky, M. T. (1953), *Russia: a history and an interpretation*, 2 vols., Macmillan, New York.

French, R. A. (1963), The making of the Russian landscape, *Advancement of Science*, **20**, 44–56.

Gilbert, M. (1972), *Soviet history atlas*, Routledge and Kegan Paul, London.

Hanson, P. (1968), *The consumer in the Soviet economy*, Macmillan, London.

Lyashchenko, P. I. (1949), *History of the national economy of Russia to the 1917 revolution*, trans. L. M. Herman, Octagon Books, New York, 1970.

Munting, R. (1982), *The economic development of the USSR*, Croom Helm, London.

Nove, A. (1975), *Stalinism and after*, Allen & Unwin, London.

Parker, W. H. (1968), *An historical geography of Russia*, University of London Press, London.

Pethybridge, R. (1974), *The social prelude to Stalinism*, Macmillan, London.

Portal, R. (1962), *The Slavs*, Weidenfeld and Nicolson, London.

Rozman, G. (1976), *Urban networks in Russia, 1750–1800, and premodern periodisation*, Princeton University Press, Princeton, New Jersey.

Shaw, D. J. B. (1977), Urbanism and economic development in a pre-industrial context: the case of southern Russia, *Journal of Historical Geography*, **3**, 107–122.

Sumner, B. H. (1961), *Survey of Russian history*, Methuen, London.

2 Physiography

One of the most striking facts about the USSR is its very great size. With a total area of 22.4 million km², the Soviet Union is, by a large margin, the biggest country in the world. From the western frontier to the Bering Strait is a distance of more than 9000 km and the greatest latitudinal extent, from the Arctic Ocean to the borders of Afghanistan, is well over 4000 km. Within this vast territory there is an enormous variety of geographical conditions, and this applies to structure and relief as to other aspects. At the same time, however, the major physiographic units of which the country is composed are themselves very large, giving a general uniformity of physical conditions over wide areas within each of these major units.

Figure 2.1 divides the Soviet Union into major structural units, which serve as a starting point for more detailed discussion of landforms and relief. Fundamental to the whole arrangement of structural elements are two Pre-Cambrian 'continental platforms', one underlying most of the country to the west of the Urals, the other occupying central Siberia between the Yenisey and Lena rivers. Between these two platforms lies a broad area which, in Paleozoic times, developed as a geosyncline and received vast quantities of sediment derived from the denudation of the adjacent stable blocks. The sediments were affected by Paleozoic fold movements during both the Caledonian and Hercynian orogenic periods, but the resultant structures are visible only in two areas, the Ural mountains and the Kazakh uplands. In both the west Siberian and Caspian–Turanian lowlands, Paleozoic fold structures lie deeply buried beneath great thicknesses of younger sedimentary rocks. Caledonian and some Hercynian structures are also visible in the present-day landscape to the south of the Siberian platform in the Altay – Sayan and Baykalia regions, and there are Hercynian elements in the Central Asian mountain systems.

In this brief listing of the main structural elements, we should also note the presence of complex fold mountain ranges, of Mesozoic and Tertiary origin, which lie to the south and east of the pre-Cambrian, Caledonian and Hercynian structural provinces. These ranges occupy a relatively narrow and discontinuous strip of territory along the southern edge of the Soviet Union as far east as Lake Baykal, but beyond the lake they swing round towards the north and north-east to cover virtually the whole area between the river Lena and the Pacific coast.

While a division of the Soviet Union into the units just described helps us to understand the basic structure of the country, it must be realised that, over very large areas, there is no direct or simple correlation between the present-day relief and the underlying structures. The surface configuration of the land is best described on the basis of the physiographic regions mapped in Fig. 2.2. The relation of these to the structural divisions in Fig. 2.1 is indicated in Table 2.1.

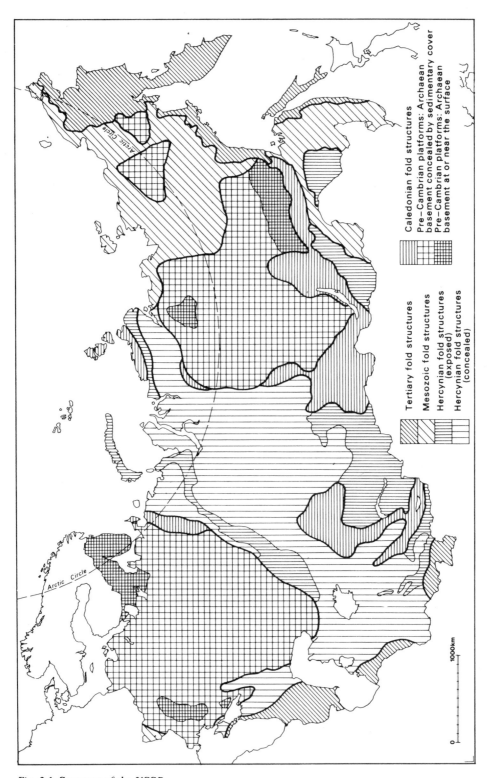

Fig. 2.1 Structure of the USSR

TABLE 2.1: PHYSIOGRAPHIC REGIONS AND THEIR RELATION TO STRUCTURE

Physiographic region	Structure
East European plain	Pre-Cambrian East European Platform, largely buried by sedimentaries of many different ages; platform exposed mainly in Fennoscandia and on a smaller scale in the Ukraine.
Ural mountains	Uplifted section of the Hercynian zone; Hercynian fold structures exposed
West Siberian lowland	Hercynian fold structures deeply buried by later sedimentaries
Central Siberian plateau	Siberian platform, largely buried by later sedimentaries
Kazakh upland	Caledonian and Hercynian fold structures, planated, re-elevated and exposed
Caspian – Turanian lowland	Caledonian and Hercynian fold structures, buried by younger sedimentaries
Mountains of the south and east	Varied structures
(a) Carpathians, Crimea and Caucasus	Tertiary fold mountains
(b) Central Asia	Caledonian, Hercynian and Tertiary fold structures
(c) Altay–Sayan	Caledonian and Hercynian fold structures
(d) Baykalia	Shield fragments, Caledonian, Hercynian and Mesozoic fold structures, much block faulting
(e) Amur-Maritime	Mesozoic and Tertiary fold structures with some Hercynian structures in basins
(f) North-east Siberia	Predominantly Mesozoic fold structures with older buried massifs
(g) Kamchatka	Part of the Pacific ring of Tertiary fold mountains.

PHYSIOGRAPHIC REGIONS: (A) THE PLAINS AND PLATEAUS

As the accompanying maps clearly demonstrate, plains together with hill lands and low plateaus, generally less than 1000 m above sea level, are the dominant elements. Such features occupy virtually the whole of the Soviet Union west of the Yenisey river with the exception of the narrow Ural ranges and the mountains of the southern frontier zone.

The East European Plain

The stable block of the east European platform occupies the whole of the USSR west of the Ural mountains and north of the Black and Caspian Seas, but the ancient crystalline materials of which it is composed outcrop only in two rather limited areas (see Fig. 2.4). The larger of these lies in the extreme north, in Karelia and the Kola peninsula, and is part of the Baltic or Fennoscandian shield. The smaller Ukrainian shield lies some distance north of the Black Sea, crossing the Dnepr river between Dnepropetrovsk and Zaporozhye.

Between these two areas, the ancient basement rocks are completely hidden beneath a cover of sedimentaries. These cover rocks are relatively undisturbed, having been protected from folding by the stability of the block on which they lie, but the latter has been subjected to a good deal of warping and faulting so that its surface is uneven and the thickness of the sedimentaries varies considerably. Between Kursk and Voronezh, for example, an upfaulted horst block brings the basement rocks very close to the surface, while between this block and the Ukrainian shield there is a deep structural trench in which a great thickness of sediments, including the Donbas coal measures, has been preserved.

The sedimentaries that underlie the bulk of the east European plain contain representatives of nearly every geological period and there is a general tendency for progressively younger rocks to appear at the surface in a transect from northwest to south-east, the oldest Paleozoics outcropping along the Baltic coast and the youngest Quaternaries around the Caspian Sea.

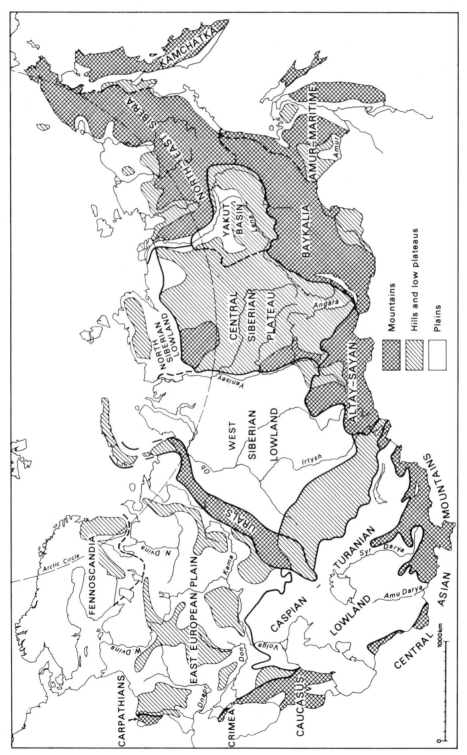

Fig. 2.2 Physiographic regions of the USSR

It will be appreciated that, as a result of the situation just described, the structure of the east European platform has little or no direct effect on the detailed relief of the east European plain, which is much more influenced by the nature and arrangement of the sedimentary cover. In addition, more than half this physiographic region has been affected by the events of the Pleistocene glaciation, during which the Fennoscandian shield was a zone of ice dispersal and much of the remainder of the plain was a region of glacial deposition. There is ample evidence in contemporary landforms of at least two major ice advances, which are known to Russian scholars as the Dnepr–Don and Valday glaciations. These were probably contemporaneous with the Riss and Würm advances in central Europe*. The earlier of the two, which was also the more extensive, sent tongues of ice down the valleys of the Dnepr and Don to within 200 km of the Black Sea. The more recent Valday ice sheet advanced a shorter distance, reaching only to a line running near Minsk, Smolensk and Moscow. As a result, the east European plain carries a very complex assortment of glacial, fluvio-glacial and post-glacial deposits, which add greatly to the intricacy of the region's landforms. The plain as a whole is a very low-lying region. Only in a few places does the surface rise more than 300 m above sea level and at least half the area is below the 200 m contour. Under these circumstances, quite small differences in height assume great local importance, and the landforms of glacial deposition may appear as 'major' local relief features.

A clearer picture of the physiography of the east European plain requires a more detailed description of its component parts. The Russian section of the Baltic shield, occupying the Kola peninsula and the territory of Karelia, between Finland and the White Sea, is a barren land, where expanses of bare, ice-scraped rock alternate with shallow,

drift-filled hollows, often occupied by lakes or marshes. Apart from one or two summits in the Khibin mountains (1)[†], which rise to nearly 1200 m, the greater part of this region is less than 300 m above sea level.

Beyond the faulted trough which marks the southern limit of the Baltic shield and contains the Gulf of Finland, Lake Ladoga and Lake Onega, the rocks of the shield disappear beneath the drift-covered sedimentaries of the plain. North of the latitude of Moscow, these sedimentary rocks dip south-east and eastwards towards basins developed between Moscow and the upper Kama, and denudation has given rise to a rudimentary scarp and vale topography. The main escarpments are developed on the Silurian limestone, which backs the southern coast of the Gulf of Finland, and the Carboniferous limestone forming the Valday Hills (2). The latter, which run in a north-east to south-west direction from the southern end of Lake Onega to the boundary of the Belorussian republic, are capped with one of the moraines of the Valday glaciation and reach 300–325 m in places. This relatively insignificant line of hills is one of the major watersheds of the European plain, separating the Volkhov, Western Dvina and other streams flowing to the Baltic from the southward-draining Volga system.

Another important morainic feature, probably marking the maximum extent of the final ice advance, is the Smolensk–Moscow ridge (3), which forms a traditional route from the western frontier to the capital. This northern section of the plain, between Moscow and the Baltic Sea, is one in which, since glaciation is relatively recent, the landforms of glacial deposition have been only partially removed by post-glacial erosion. The numerous moraines and other features are well-preserved and form well-marked relief features. The presence of moraines and other low hills provided ideal situations for the development of pro-glacial lakes during the Pleistocene period and many large, flat-floored, ill-drained depressions remain, some still carrying sizeable lakes such as Lake Ilmen (4) and Lake Beloye (5).

The zone between the limit of the Valday glaciation and that of the Dnepr–Don advance is somewhat different. The boulder clay from the latter is believed to have been rather thin and many of the features resulting from glacial deposition during this phase have either been re-

---

* Students of the Pleistocene Ice Age in central Europe conclude that it involved four major advances of the ice, separated by interglacial periods when the ice sheets withdrew from Europe. These four advances have been given the names of Gunz, Mindel, Riss and Würm, respectively. In the case of European USSR there is some doubt as to whether the area was affected by the first two advances. There is, however, strong evidence for at least two advances, the Dnepr–Don, contemporaneous with the third, and most extensive, Riss advance in central Europe, and the Valday, contemporaneous with the last, Würm advance.

† A number in brackets after the name of a relief feature refers to the relief map (Fig. 2.3).

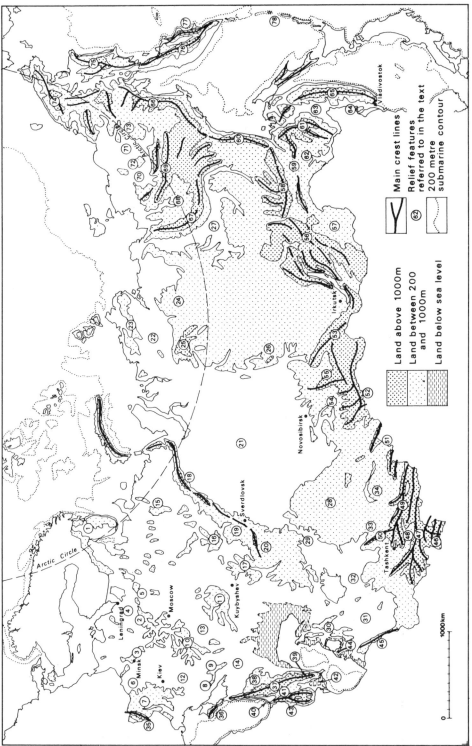

Fig. 2.3 Relief of the USSR

Erosion scars on the sides of valleys cut into the loess of the southern Russian steppes near Rostov-on-Don

moved by post-glacial action or covered by fluvio-glacial materials. The latter are most widespread along the upper valleys of the Dnepr and Don, where large depressions developed in which the glacial meltwaters accumulated. Parts are still very badly drained, particularly the area of the Pripyat (Pripet) marshes or Polesye (6). In the more southerly parts of this zone, where the ice sent tongues down the major valleys but did not succeed in over-running the interfluve areas, the pre-glacial relief is more clearly visible. This involves an alternation from west to east of low plateau uplands, often sharply dissected, and broad valley plains. Much of the western Ukraine is occupied by the Podolsk–Volyn uplands (7), which reflect the presence, at or close to the surface, of the Ukrainian shield. The highest point in this area is 472 m and the general level declines towards the Dnepr but rises again to the east of the river in the small upland of the pre-Azov heights (8), which reach 325 m. To the north-east of the latter are the Donets heights (9), rising in places to about 350 m, which represent the sediments of the Donets trench folded against the edge of the Ukrainian massif.

The south-western edge of the Moscow basin is marked by the beginning of the central Russian elevation (10), which runs southward between the Dnepr and the Don, terminating at the northern edge of the Donets valley. It is separated by the Oka–Don lowlands from a third upland, the pre-

Volga heights (11). All three uplands carry an extensive loess cover, while the plains of the Dnepr (12) and Don (13) are characterised by broad terraces at various heights connected with post-glacial changes in the level of the Black Sea. Where the Dnepr crosses the Ukrainian massif, however, its valley is sharply incised and there were rapids before these were drowned by the construction of the Dneproges hydro-electric barrage at Zaporozhye.

South of the Ukrainian massif, broad, gently-sloping plains, developed on Tertiary sediments with a patchy loess cover, occupy the southern Ukraine and the northern Crimea. In the Azov–Caspian depression (14), Hercynian structures are concealed beneath a sedimentary cover with Quaternaries at the surface.

The north-eastern section of the east European plain has so far received little attention and can be dismissed quite briefly. The terrain in this region is a good deal more monotonous than in the areas already discussed. Uplands are confined to the much-eroded Timan range (15), which runs north-westwards from the northern Urals to the Arctic Ocean, and the Perm (16) and Ufa (17) plateaus on the west flank of the Urals. The remainder of this part of the plain is composed of near-horizontal sedimentaries, among which the Permian is the most widespread outcrop. Glacial and fluvio-glacial deposition adds some variety to the landscape.

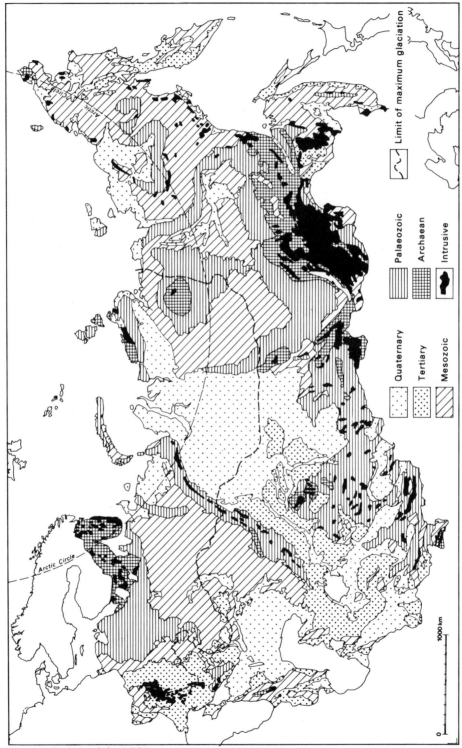

Fig. 2.4 Geology of the USSR

The Ural Mountains

While the fold structures of the Ural ranges are of Hercynian origin, the present height of the area is due to much more recent uplift. The original Hercynian mountain ranges, produced by orogenic movements at the end of the Paleozoic era, occupied the whole area between the European and Siberian platforms. This extensive mountain system was subjected to a long period of sub-aerial denudation, which reduced the area to a peneplane by the beginning of the Tertiary era. Late Tertiary uplift raised the eroded stumps of the old Hercynian ranges in the area now forming the Urals, thus initiating a new cycle of erosion which has carved out the present relief. As a result, the Ural mountains consist of a central belt of metamorphic and intrusive materials, which are very rich in minerals, flanked on either side by belts of tightly-folded Paleozoic sedimentaries.

Relief in the Urals consists of low, parallel, north-south ridges, broken in many places by cross-faulting. The bulk of the region is between 200 and 1000 m above sea level and the highest summits reach only 1500–1900 m. Despite their traditional role as the boundary between Europe and Asia, the Urals offer no really serious barrier to movement between Europe and Siberia. The region may be divided into three rather different parts. The northern Urals (18) extend approximately as far south as latitude 61°N and contain the highest peak in the whole system: Mount Narodnaya (1894 m). The mountains are at their narrowest here, consisting of two broken parallel ridges which coalesce into one north of the Arctic Circle, curving first north-west and then northeast through the tundra wastes to the Yugorskiy peninsula and thence into Novaya Zemlya. The central Urals (19), between latitudes 61° and 55°N, are wider but a good deal lower, the highly resistant rocks which make up the main range in the north being poorly represented here. This central section, with its subdued relief, lies mainly below 500 m, and the more important transport routes, including the Trans-Siberian Railway, cross the Urals in this section, which is also the site of the region's largest cities. Southward from Chelyabinsk, in the southern Urals (20) the ranges fan out and the system reaches its maximum width of 150–200 km. Heights of 1500 m or more are reached in several of these ranges which, in the extreme south of the region, open out to form a broad, dissected plateau, not unlike that of the adjacent Kazakh upland.

The West Siberian Lowland

Beyond the Urals and stretching more than 1500 km to the Yenisey and western edge of the Siberian platform, is the west Siberian lowland (21), quite the most striking single relief feature in the whole of the Soviet Union. Throughout this vast area of some $2\frac{1}{2}$ million km^2, the land is nowhere more than 200 m above sea level, and at least half the area is below the 100 m contour. The Paleozoic basement, with its Hercynian structures, lies buried beneath 1500 m or more of sedimentary rocks. Surface outcrops are entirely of Tertiary and Quaternary materials, the latter being more widespread.

In the extreme north, the surface deposits are the product of a post-glacial marine transgression, while south of these, to about 60°N, they are the result of glacial deposition and include both boulder clay and outwash materials. Beyond the limit of the maximum ice advance is a zone some 300 km wide where fluvio-glacial deposits predominate, south of which there is a belt of territory in which loess is widespread and overlies both Tertiary and Quaternary sediments. The rather drier and slightly more elevated zone in the south contains the bulk of the settled area and the region's farmland.

This enormous lowland is drained mainly by the Ob and its tributaries the Irtysh and Tobol; the Yenisey, which runs along the eastern edge, has a much smaller catchment area. These great rivers, which are among the biggest in the Soviet Union, have extremely gentle gradients and thus flow very slowly, carving out huge flood plains which may be as much as 100 km across and yet may lie only 10 or 20 m below the interfluve surfaces. Under these circumstances, flooding is a common occurrence, particularly during the spring thaw when it is intensified by the fact that the upper reaches of the rivers melt first while the lower parts are still frozen and water thus spreads out over great areas. Most of the region is very poorly drained and contains some of the world's largest swamps, notably the Vasyuganye swamp, between the Ob and Irtysh rivers, which is roughly the size of England.

Features similar to those of the west Siberian lowland are carried eastward around the northern edge of the central Siberian plateau in the north Siberian lowland or Khatanga depression (22), in which Hercynian structures are buried at depth and the surface is composed of Quaternary marine sediments. Hercynian and Caledonian fold structures are exposed in the Byrranga mountains (23) of the Taymyr peninsula, which forms a dissected plateau between 300 and 500 m above sea level, with occasional peaks rising to 1200 m.

The Central Siberian Plateau

The territory between the Yenisey and Lena rivers is occupied by the central Siberian plateau, a region which covers the greater part of the Siberian platform. Within the area of the plateau, the ancient basement rocks are exposed only in the relatively small northern section known as the Anabar shield (24). Elsewhere they are covered by sedimentary rocks, mainly of Paleozoic and Mesozoic age. These are thinnest in a central zone running south towards Lake Baykal, in which only the Paleozoics are preserved. To the east and west lie the Lena and Tunguska structural basins, in which the sedimentary rocks are very thick and include large quantities of Carboniferous material, containing huge coal reserves, though the surface outcrops are mainly of Mesozoic age.

The relief of the plateau, however, bears little relation to this structural arrangement and consists of a series of dissected erosion surfaces cut indiscriminately across Archaean, Paleozoic and Mesozoic rocks alike at heights varying between 300 and 800 m. In a few places, particularly resistant materials give uplands which stand out above the general summit level, as in the Putoran mountains (25) in the north-west, which reach 1700 m, or the Yenisey range (26) (1104 m) in the south-west. The plateau is a region of considerable relief since it has been vigorously dissected by tributaries of the Yenisey such as the Angara, Stony Tunguska and Lower Tunguska, and also, to a lesser extent, by those of the Lena. The Lena itself, however, and the lower reaches of its main tributaries, the Aldan and Vilyuy, flow in a broad structural trough between the eastern edge of the Siberian platform and the Mesozoic fold ranges. The sedimentary rocks which fill this trough form a triangular lowland, some 800 km across, known as the Yakut basin (27).

A comparison of the map of physiographic regions (Fig. 2.2) with that showing structure (Fig. 2.1) will indicate that the central Siberian plateau occupies only about two-thirds of the Siberian continental platform and that the latter extends further south to include most of the territory between the upper Lena and the Manchurian border. In this region, labelled Baykalia in Fig. 2.2 the Pre-Cambrian structures are exposed but have been broken by a series of roughly parallel faults to give a mountainous terrain. Consequently the southern part of the Siberian platform is described later, along with other southern mountain areas to which it is physiographically, though not structurally, more akin.

The Kazakh Upland

The Kazakh upland (28) borders the west Siberian lowland on its southern side and separates the latter from the Caspian–Turanian plains of Soviet Central Asia. The region was affected by fold movements in both Caledonian and Hercynian orogenic periods, but the resultant complex structures, like those of the Urals, have been planated and re-elevated in more recent times. Consequently the upland now consists of an alternation of plateaus and shallow depressions, and for the most part stands between 500 and 1000 m above sea level, with a maximum elevation of 1565 m roughly in the centre of the region. In several places the depressions preserve Mesozoic and Tertiary sedimentaries, but the greater part of the surface is composed of Paleozoic rocks together with Archaean metamorphic and igneous materials which are very rich in minerals. The upland is a region of dry steppe and semi-desert with arid landforms and permanent streams are confined to the northern half of the region.

The Caspian–Turanian Lowland

Like the west Siberian lowland, to which it is connected by the narrow, Quaternary-floored corridor of the Turgay Gate (29), the Caspian–Turanian lowland is part of the Hercynian structural province in which the Paleozoic structures are deeply buried and the surface rocks are entirely of Tertiary and Quaternary age.

Around the Caspian Sea is an area now some 30 m below world sea level. Quaternary plains marking the former extent of the Caspian stretch nearly 500 km northwards from the present shoreline. Over the Turanian lowland as a whole, the general arrangement is one in which low plateaus with steep, scarped edges, developed on Tertiary rocks, overlook the plains developed on Quaternary sediments. The most prominent of these plateaus is the Ustyurt (30), which rises to heights of 150–200 m between the Aral and Caspian Seas.

The Caspian–Turanian lowlands are, of course, an area of inland drainage. Apart from relatively small sections in the west and east, which drain towards the Caspian and Lake Balkhash respectively, drainage is towards the Aral Sea. Since this is a desert region, the only permanent watercourses are those which originate in the high mountains to the south and only two of these, the Amu Darya and Syr Darya, reach the Aral Sea; the remainder, including some sizeable rivers such as the Chu and Sarysu, as well as a number of smaller ones from the north, peter out in the desert. The arid landforms which are the characteristic of the region include large expanses of sand desert: the Karakum (31) between the Caspian and the Amu Darya, the Kyzylkum (32) between the latter and the Syr Darya, the Muyunkum (33) to the east of the Syr Darya and the Taukum (34) on the southern side of Lake Balkhash. In contrast, there are large stretches of clay desert and many ribbons of alluvium derived from ancient and modern rivers. The large number of abandoned river courses suggests that many of the landforms of this region are derived from a wetter period during the Pleistocene. Today most of the region is arid and, over large areas, agriculture is impossible without the aid of irrigation. The most productive soils are those of the piedmont zone along the southern edge of the desert, where loess has accumulated.

The regions so far discussed occupy approximately three-quarters of the land surface of the Soviet Union. Throughout that entire area there are only a handful of places at which the land rises above 1500 m and at least half is below the 200 m contour. These plains and low plateaus, which are dominant from the western boundary to the Lena river, take the form of an amphitheatre facing north to the Arctic Ocean and bounded on its eastern, southern and south-western sides by high mountain ramparts. Only in the west, through the 500 km-wide corridor between the Carpathians and the Baltic, and in the extreme south-east, where her territory overlaps the mountain rim and has a frontier with China along the Amur and Ussuri rivers, is the Soviet Union in easy overland contact with her neighbours. Elsewhere, her frontiers are the mountains or the sea.

PHYSIOGRAPHIC REGIONS (B) THE MOUNTAINS OF THE SOUTH AND EAST

The remaining quarter of the Soviet Union is occupied by a complex series of mountain systems which, although in a broad sense forming a single major physiographic unit, in fact have a great variety of structural origins and include pre-Cambrian, Caledonian, Hercynian, Mesozoic and Tertiary (Alpine) elements. The oldest fold structures, those of Pre-Cambrian age, now form the European and Siberian platforms, around which are arranged the later orogenic belts. Caledonian structures occur mainly around the southern edge of the Siberian platform, in Baykalia, but are also present in the Altay–Sayan district and in parts of Central Asia. Traces of Hercynian folding are to be found in Central Asia and the district between the Siberian platform and the Amur. The most widely developed mountain systems, however, are those associated with more recent folding in Mesozoic and Tertiary times, these young fold ranges occurring in the Carpathians, Crimea, Caucasus and parts of Central Asia as well as throughout the Soviet Far East.

There are fairly important contrasts between the Mesozoic and Alpine fold ranges on the one hand and those formed in Caledonian and Hercynian times on the other. The latter have, in most cases, undergone long periods of sub-aerial denudation and owe their present height mainly to recent block uplift, often taking the form of a series of basins and ranges. Mineral-rich metamorphic and intrusive core zones are often exposed in these ranges. The young fold mountains, however, particularly those produced by the most recent, Alpine, orogeny, have not been denuded to such a degree, though they have often been deeply dissected by fluvial and glacial erosion so that steep slopes and sharp crest-lines abound.

For the sake of clarity, the mountain zone will be discussed under the headings provided by the regional nomenclature in Fig. 2.2.

Carpathians

In the extreme west, the Soviet Union now contains a small section of the Carpathian mountains (35) and a small foothold in the plains of the Danube. This situation, which has considerable strategic significance, results from the annexation

Limestone ranges of the Crimea, a vineyard in the foreground

in 1945 of the former Czechoslovak province of Ruthenia, now known as the Sub-Carpathian Ukraine. In this district, the Carpathians take the form of a series of parallel ridges some 100 km wide with peaks between 1000 and 1800 m above sea level.

Crimea

The bulk of the Crimean peninsula is a continuation of the Tertiary plains of the southern Ukraine, but in the extreme south there is a narrow zone of Alpine folding about 30 km wide. There are three parallel ridges (36), of which the southernmost is the highest and rises a little above 1500 m. The shelter from northerly winds provided by these mountains gives a moderate climate along the Crimean coast, reflected in its specialised agriculture and its popularity as a holiday area.

Caucasus

This is a much larger and more complex mountain system, also of Tertiary origin, which occupies the isthmus between the Black and Caspian Seas.

With a length approaching 1000 km, the Caucasus are equivalent in size, height and structural complexity to the Alps of central Europe and Soviet geographers distinguish a large number of physiographic sub-divisions. We will consider this region in three sections: the Greater Caucasus, the Transcaucasian depression and the Lesser Caucasus.

The Greater Caucasus, or main Caucasian range (37) is a major anticlinal feature which stretches right across the isthmus from Novorossiysk on the Black Sea to the Apsheron peninsula on the Caspian, and is structurally continuous both with the Crimean ranges and the mountains of Soviet Central Asia. In the west, the anticline has been breached to expose the igneous and metamorphic rocks formed at depth during the mountain-building process and this core zone is flanked on either side by zones of tightly-folded Mesozoic sedimentaries. The main crest-line exceeds 3500 m over much of its length and there are several peaks above 5000 m, the highest of all being Mt. Elbrus (5642 m), one of a number of volcanoes which were active here in late Tertiary times. On the northern flank of this western section of the main Caucasian range, a zone of Tertiary sediments extends northwards between the Quaternary plains of the Terek and Kuban. This is the Stavropol plateau (38), a dissected platform which in places reaches 800 m above sea level but lies for the most part between 200 and 300 m, and is particularly important as a source of natural gas.

The eastern half of the main Caucasian anticline has not been breached so that Mesozoic rocks, among which Jurassic limestones are the most widespread, extend right across it. Karstic landforms are especially widespread in Dagestan (39). The crest-line in this eastern section is somewhat lower than in the west, but a number of peaks rise above 4000 m. The whole of the main Caucasian range has, of course, been vigorously dissected by normal erosion, especially in the west, where rainfall is higher. The upper slopes have been affected by ice action and still carry a number of small glaciers. The barrier presented by these mountains to northerly climatic and human influences does much to account for the distinctive character, both physical and human, of the Transcaucasian region.

The Transcaucasian depression itself falls into three parts. In the west is the small Kolkhida or Colchis lowland (40), developed along the lower reaches of the Rioni river. This triangular plain extends about 100 km inland from the Black Sea and is floored with Tertiary and Quaternary sediments. Heavy deposition of material eroded from the Caucasus ranges has given a flat alluvial plain, much of which has required artificial drainage. The lowland is terminated on its eastern side by the granitic Suram massif (41), through which the only route is the Suram Pass, a narrow defile with a summit at 850 m. Beyond this obstacle is the Kura basin (42), which stretches some 500 km eastwards from Tbilisi to the Caspian. Like the Rioni basin, that of the Kura is infilled with Tertiary and Quaternary sediments. The former occur as low hills and plateaus at heights of 200–600 m around the edge of the basin. The Quaternary deposits are ill-drained in their lower parts and the large Kura delta has much swampland despite its near-desert climate.

The Lesser Caucasus is an area of complex structure and falls into two main parts. North-east of a line running north-west to south-east through Lake Sevan, the rocks are sedimentaries of Mesozoic age, compressed into folds by the Alpine earth movements, and there are several peaks above 3000 m. The western part of the lesser Caucasus, however, consists mainly of the lava plateaus of Armenia (43), which stand at heights of 1000–2000 m. Within these plateaus are several down-faulted troughs, such as the one containing Lake Sevan and that which carries the Araks river along the Turkish frontier. Above the level of the plateaus rise numerous volcanic peaks, of which the highest is Mt. Aragats (4090 m). The lava plateaus continue into eastern Turkey, where Mt. Ararat (5165 m) overlooks the Araks valley from the south-western side.

The Mountains of Soviet Central Asia

West of the Amu Darya river, in the Turkmen republic, the system of mountain ranges is quite simple and only the Alpine orogeny is represented. The anticline of the main Caucasian range is continued across the Caspian into the Bolshoy Balkhan mountains (44), which reach 1880 m, and thence south-eastwards to the Kopet Dag (45) range. The latter, which rises to a maximum height of 2942 m near Ashkhabad, forms the northern edge of the Iranian plateau and marks the boundary between Iran and the USSR.

To the east of the Amu Darya, a much more varied and complex series of mountain systems is

Snow covered peaks in the Gissar mountains, Tadzhikistan, tower above a glaciated valley in which rapid deposition is now occurring as the glacial river brings down eroded material

to be found, involving structures from the Alpine, Hercynian and Caledonian orogenic periods. The youngest, and also the highest, of these fold ranges are the Pamir mountains (46), which occupy the eastern half of the Tadzhik republic. These ranges constitute the 'Pamir knot', a focal zone in the Eurasian alpine fold system whence chains of young fold mountains fan out to the south-west (Hindu Kush), south-east (Himalayas) and north-east (southern Tyan Shan). The Pamirs contain the highest peaks in the Soviet Union, notably Lenin Peak (7134 m) and Mt. Communism (7485 m). Below the main crest lines, which carry glaciers and extensive permanent snowfields, are large plateau areas at heights around 4000 m which are deeply dissected by narrow river gorges.

The northern limit of the Tertiary fold system of the Pamir mountains is marked by the deep-set valley of the Surkhob river. To the north of this valley, the Alay ranges (47), a series of re-elevated Hercynian blocks, run eastwards from Samarkand to the Chinese border. The main crest-lines exceed 3000 m over most of their length and carry several active glaciers. Subordinate ranges run off towards the south in western Tadzhikistan, separating the deep valleys of the Amu Darya's north-bank tributaries, while north of Samarkand low ridges finger out into the Kyzylkum desert.

The Alay ranges in turn give way northwards to the Fergana basin (48), the most impressive of several down-faulted Hercynian basins in this region. 300 km long and 160 km across, the Fergana basin is surrounded on all sides by mountain ranges save in the west, where there is a gap some 10 km wide, through which the Syr Darya makes its exit. The centre of the basin is a flat desert plain, while around the edges are a series of terraces and alluvial fans, backed by low, loess-covered hills composed of Tertiary and Quaternary sediments. The Fergana basin thus displays, in a relatively compact area, all the landforms which are associated with the Central Asian hill-foot zone, between the great desert and the southern mountain ranges.

North of the Fergana basin, the succession of east-west trending mountain blocks and troughs continues. The Tyan Shan system (49) is a broad complex of parallel ranges which includes both Caledonian and Hercynian structural elements and extends eastwards from Tashkent to and beyond the Chinese border. Crest-lines rise well above 3000 m and several peaks in the east top the 5000 m contour. In the north-west, several low ridges, such as the Karatau range, (50) finger out into the desert. Over most of its length, the northern face of the Tyan Shan system is very abrupt, dropping along fault lines to a loess-covered pediment zone at heights between 500 and 1000 m. Beyond this lie the desert basins of the Chu river and Lake Balkhash, which separate the fold mountain systems from the Kazakh upland. The Balkhash basin narrows eastwards but is joined to the Sinkiang province of China by the narrow Dzhungarian gate (51), which has for centuries been a routeway between Turkestan and the Asian interior.

The Altay–Sayan Ranges

The basin of the upper Irtysh river marks the north-eastern limit of the Kazakh upland, and beyond this a complex zone of Hercynian and Caledonian mountain ranges extends as far as Lake Baykal. These fall into two main groups, the Altay (52) and the Sayan (53), the division between them coinciding with the valley of the upper Yenisey.

Of the two systems, the Altay is the more complex with an intricate pattern of ranges which have a predominantly east-west trend in the south and important north-south elements in the northern part. In particular, the northward-protruding Salair and Kuznetsk Alatau ranges enclose the Kuznetsk basin, or Kuzbas (54), with its deep cover of Carboniferous rocks and its valuable coal measures. The Minusinsk basin (55) on the upper Yenisey is similarly enclosed between the Kuznetsk Alatau and Sayan ranges. The Altay system as a whole has undergone a good deal of block faulting so that high, dissected plateau uplands alternate with enclosed basins and valley troughs. A number of peaks close to the Mongolian border exceed 4000 m.

The Sayan consists of western and eastern ranges which trend south-west to north-east and north-west to south-east respectively, both with crest-lines above 2500 m, and these enclose the high basin interior of the Tuvinian ASSR.

Baykalia

Around and beyond Lake Baykal, in the region marked 'Baykalia' on Fig. 2.2, there is a very great variety of structural elements including Caledonian and Hercynian folds and a large exposed section of the Siberian platform, known as the Aldan shield. In the area between Lake Baykal and the Yablonovyy range (56), which forms the watershed between the Arctic and Pacific drainage

Lake Baykal, which occupies a major tectonic depression in southern Siberia, is the deepest lake in the world

basins, the landscape displays a distinct south-west to north-east grain imparted by large-scale block faulting. This is *horst* and *graben* country on a massive scale, with a great altitudinal range between the summits of the uplifted mountain blocks, which are often between 1500 and 2000 m above sea level, and the floors of the down-faulted troughs which are often below 800 m. One such trough is occupied by Lake Baykal, a water body some 640 km long and 45 km across. While the mountains on either side reach 2000 m, the bottom of the lake is 1300 m below sea level, a total height range of 3300 m. Baykal is the world's deepest lake, with a maximum depth of 1752 m.

Between the Yablonovyy ranges and the Manchurian border is the high-level basin of Dauria (57), in which Hercynian structures are buried beneath Mesozoic sedimentaries, and where low hill ranges alternate with broad, open plains.

The Aldan shield section of Baykalia is a massive upland, much less broken by faulting than the area closer to Lake Baykal, and has extensive summit plateaus above 1500 m. The watershed between the Pacific and the Arctic is carried eastwards across this zone by the Stanovoy range (58), the rounded summits of which exceed 2500 m. To the south of the Stanovoy and parallel to it, the Tukuringra and Dzhagdy (59) ranges lead off into the Amur-Maritime region. At its eastern end, the Stanovoy range runs into the coastal Dzhugdzhur mountains (60), composed mainly of Mesozoic volcanics, which mark the limit of the north-east Siberian region.

The Amur-Maritime Region
This region occupies the entire area south of the Stanovoy mountains and between the Manchurian border and the Pacific, and consists of an alternation of fold mountain ranges, Hercynian in the west, Mesozoic and Alpine in the east, and broad, open lowlands. The Dzhagdy range approaches within 100 km of the Pacific, where it merges with the Bureya mountains (61). The latter have a north-east to south-west trend and fall away towards the Amur, beyond which they are continued by the Hsiao Khingan of Manchuria. Within the enclosing arc of the Dzhagdy and Bureya ranges is the large Zeya–Bureya plain (62). Here, Hercynian structures are partially concealed beneath younger sedimentaries, which have been carved into terraces at various heights by the Amur, Zeya and Bureya rivers.

On the south-eastern side of the Bureya range is the lower Amur plain (63), which extends from the Amur–Ussuri confluence to the sea. The floor of the plain is mostly about 50 m above sea level and a great deal of it is poorly drained. Broad, open sections with well-developed terraces alternate with narrow stretches where the river has cut through the ridges which cross its course. The latter, composed mainly of Mesozoic rocks, rise to heights varying between 400 and 1000 m. Running southwards from the Amur–Ussuri confluence to the sea near Vladivostok is the Khanka–Ussuri plain (64). This is a fault-bounded depression, the Quaternary floor of which is some 50 m above sea level, and in Quaternary times was a sea strait separating the Sikhote Alin from the mainland. The Amur and Ussuri lowlands are of particular importance in that they contain the bulk of the settlement and agricultural land of the Far Eastern region.

The Sikhote Alin ranges (65) are among the youngest fold mountain systems in the USSR and include both Mesozoic and Tertiary structures. There are seven or eight parallel mountain chains, the peaks of which vary in height from about 1800 m in the centre to 1300 m at the northern and southern ends. Two more parallel ridges of Tertiary age, separated by a down-faulted, flat-floored depression, make up the island of Sakhalin.

North-East Siberia
North-east Siberia is one of the most remote, thinly settled and little explored parts of the Soviet Union, and knowledge of its geology and structure is still incomplete. The region comprises a complex system of Mesozoic fold ranges, between which there are large median masses. Some of these have been uplifted to form high plateaus, while others are represented by low-lying basins with a cover of Quaternary materials facing out to the Arctic Ocean.

The Dzhugdzhur range (60) backs the Pacific coast as far as Okhotsk, beyond which a more broken coastal upland leads eventually to the Gydan (or Kolyma) range (66). From these coastal ranges, a series of mountain chains run off north and north-westwards to the Arctic Ocean. Of these, the most clearly marked is the Verkhoyansk range (67), which forms a continuous barrier more than 1500 m high, with numerous peaks above 2000 m, immediately east of the Lena lowlands. The Verkhoyansk range is separated by the much-dissected Yano–Oymyakon plateau (68) from the Cherskiy (69) mountain system. The latter consists of a series of rather short, broken ranges, the summits of which rise to heights of 2000–2500 m. Between the Cherskiy and Gydan ranges, large median masses underly the Indigirka (70) and Kolyma (71) lowlands and the Alazeya (72) and Yukagir (73) plateaus. In the extreme north-east, the Chukotka range (74) forms the backbone of the Anadyr peninsula.

Kamchatka

The Mesozoic ranges described in the last few paragraphs are separated by a narrow, broken lowland corridor, floored with Tertiary and Quaternary sediments, from the Tertiary folds of the Koryak-Kamchatka-Kurile arc, part of the Pacific zone of alpine folding. The Koryak range (75) consists of a series of roughly parallel ridges rising to 2000 m with numerous extinct volcanoes and extensive lava flows. This fold system is continued into the Sredinyy range (76), with several peaks above 2500 m, running down the centre of the Kamchatka peninsula. To the west of this central mountain system is a broad, rather poorly drained coastal plain, while to the east, beyond the valley lowland of the Kamchatka river, lies a highly distinctive volcanic zone (77). This consists of lava plateaus between 500 and 1000 m above sea level. High above these plateaus rise 20 or 30 volcanic cones of which about a dozen are still active. Klyuchevskiy Peak, the most impressive of all, reaches a height of 4750 m. This volcanic zone is continued southwards through the Kurile Islands (78) to northern Japan.

CONCLUSION

Within the space available, it has been possible to give only a very general picture of the great variety of structure, rock-type, relief and landforms to be found within the vast territory of the USSR. In particular it has been possible to identify only the major physiographic regions and to name only a few of the most important relief features. It will no doubt be realised that, within each region discussed, and indeed within each 'feature' named, there is a great deal of variety and each could be further subdivided. It is an inevitable result of the great size of the Soviet Union that any first-stage regional break-down of the country gives regions which are themselves often very much larger than, say, the individual countries of western Europe.

The USSR, then, is a land of enormous contrasts in the nature of its physical geography and, in this respect, as in its sheer size, is more akin to a continent. At the same time, however, the individual physiographic units which go to make up the Soviet Union are in many cases so large that they give rise to monotonous uniformity of relief over wide areas. The east European plain, the west Siberian lowland or the Caspian–Turanian lowland, for example, are crossed by road or rail in journeys involving days rather than hours, and the traveller would notice little change in the relief or landforms over distances measured in hundreds of miles. In such areas it is aspects of the physical environment other than relief, notably climate, soils and vegetation, which are the most important influences on the whole complex of human geography. Paradoxically, however, on a local scale, quite minor relief features, involving very small changes in altitude, may be of great significance. A difference of a few metres in part of the east European plain, for example, may make all the difference between virtually useless swamp and moderately productive farmland or, in Central Asia, between irrigable flood plain and waterless sand desert.

Our hypothetical traveller across one of the great lowlands of the USSR would, therefore, be struck not only by the monotony of the landscape but also, if he were sufficiently observant, by the fact that this monotony was the product of the constant repetition of a small number of physiographic elements rather than the result of complete uniformity. A further point is that, were he to travel from north to south across one of these plains, he would also perceive a slow change in the nature of the landscape and in agriculture, resulting from changes in climatic conditions and associated variations in soil and vegetation types, factors which, in the lowland regions, are much more important than relief alone.

Quite different is the situation in the mountains of the south and east. Here, and only here, do we find those great contrasts in relief and landforms over short distances and the associated variety of human response which are commonplace in central and western Europe, and this serves to emphasise still further the contrast between these regions and the bulk of the USSR.

BIBLIOGRAPHY

Berg, L. S. (1950), *Natural regions of the USSR*, Macmillan, London and New York.

Bogdanoff, A. (1957), 'Traits fondamentaux de la tectonique de l'URSS,' *Revue Géog; Physique et Géol. Dynamique*, 2me. série **1** (3), pp. 134–65.

Fiziko-geograficheskiy atlas mira (1964), Moscow. A key in English to this atlas appears in *Soviet Geography, Review and Translation*, **6** (5–6), 1965, pp. 1–403.

Krasny, L. I. (ed.), *Structure géologique de l'URSS*, CNRS, Paris.

Markov, K. K. and Popov, A. J. (eds.), (1959), *Lednikovyy period na territorii evropeyskoy chasti SSSR i Sibiri*, Moscow.

Nalivkin, D. V. (1960), *The geology of the USSR*, Pergamon, Oxford.

Nalivkin, D. V. (1973), *Geology of the USSR*, Oliver and Boyd, Edinburgh.

Parker, W. H. (1969), *The world's landscapes: 3, The Soviet Union*, Longman, London.

Rikhter, G., Preobrezhenskiy, V. and Nefedyeva, V. (1976), The Soviet land revealed, *Geographical Magazine*, **48**, (5), 266–272.

Suslov, S. P. (1961), *Physical geography of Asiatic Russia*, Freeman, San Francisco and London.

Tushinskiy, G. K. and Davydova, M. I. (1976), *Fizicheskaya geografiya SSSR*, Moscow.

Velitchko, A. A. (1979), 'Soviet glaciers were late developers,' *Geographical Magazine*, **51**, (7), 472–478.

3 Climate

The Soviet Union is the most thoroughly continental as well as the largest of the nation-states, being virtually surrounded by other lands or by partly frozen seas. Nearly half of the Soviet Union to the north of its broadly settled belt is fundamentally unsuited to permanent human occupation owing to lack of heat, and into this agricultural wasteland, Great Britain could be fitted 40 times. In addition, to the south of the generally settled belt in the Soviet Union is an area of desert and inland drainage at least as large as Australia's.

Thus human settlement has become more or less channelled, over the centuries of expansion of the Russian Empire, into an elongated triangular area, with its base on the European frontier and its apex around Lake Baykal, forming a wedge between the cold northern forests and the deserts of Central Asia (Fig. 10.3).

Although the climate seems to exercise a decisive influence on the general pattern of population distribution in the Soviet Union, we must beware of ascribing to it an absolutely 'determining' power over the activities of man and even his psychology and degree of civilisation. The control of man's activities by climate is to be looked at through the medium of costs in the broadest sense. For instance, there are risky and expensive climates for farming but very few impossible ones; with enough financial subsidy all sorts of fruits and vegetables can be grown on the Arctic coast, but probably will not be if they can more cheaply be grown elsewhere, and transported to the north. In other words, the climate is a persuasive but not a compelling director of human affairs. However in these days of increasing competitive regional specialisation and more efficient transport, it seems likely that natural factors are becoming more, rather than less, influential in modern farming operations.

On the other hand, urbanisation has profoundly modified the significance of climate in the life of the Soviet people. Before the 1930s, the great majority of Russians were peasants and were effectively immobilised for long periods during the severe winter when there was little or no work, followed by a hectic pace of work in the short summer. However, today the average Russian is an industrial urbanite working indoors throughout the year, and although he may gravitate to cities with a somewhat better climate, amenities in the broad sense, like housing and education, are usually more important to him.

SALIENT FEATURES OF THE SOVIET CLIMATE

Together with its extreme continentality, already noted, the high latitudes in which most of the Soviet Union lies should be kept in mind. Transferred to the southern hemisphere at the same latitudes, most of the Soviet Union would lie well out in the Southern Ocean and into Antarctica. But the most meaningful comparison is with North America, and here it appears that some four-fifths of the Soviet area, and about nine-tenths of that part of the country which receives adequate moisture, are in the latitudes of Canada rather than of the United States. Moscow itself is further north than Edmonton, Alberta (the most northerly city of any real importance in Canada) while Leningrad, the second city and former capital, is in the latitudes of southern Alaska. Whereas no part of the coastline of the continental USA ever becomes frozen, almost all the Soviet coastline is subject to varying periods of freezing in winter.

A strong sense of climatic uniformity over large areas of the Soviet Union in any one season is gained from considering a few facts. In January it would be possible to skate on the rivers and canals from the Arctic to the Caspian Sea or sledge from the Polish border to the Pacific, while in July it is comfortably warm almost everywhere. Of course there are exceptions, such as the cool Arctic coast in summer and some warm sheltered parts of the Black Sea coast in winter.

A feature of the Soviet climate often overlooked but no less significant is its dryness. All of Britain receives at least 500 mm of precipitation in the year and well over half the United States is so favoured, but less than a quarter of the Soviet area comes up to this level. Even allowing for differences in evaporation, the USSR is more similar to Australia in this respect than to any other important country although Australia is, taken all round, much more arid.

The Pressure Systems

Because of the very large mass of land at relatively high latitudes, marked seasonal differences in pressure conditions occur, resulting largely from the profound and rapid changes in the prevailing temperatures.

During the frigid winter there develops over Siberia and Central Asia a high pressure system of an intensity unique in the inhabited world at any season. In the windless centre of this system radiation leads to the accumulation of dense air which drains into certain enclosed valleys, especially in north-east Siberia, as noted below, bringing the coldest temperatures recorded on earth (outside Antarctica). This outflowing air from the Siberian centre of high pressure extends also, less intensely, over European Russia and occasionally crosses the North Sea to paralyse eastern England, but throughout this western peripheral region its dominance is challenged by the inflowing air from the Atlantic.

Spring is a fleeting season in most of the Soviet Union, bringing rapidly rising temperatures, and spreading from across the country in a generally north-easterly direction from the south-west Ukraine, about March, to the mouth of the Lena in late June. The heating of the land and the consequent ascending air soon leads to the replacement of the winter high pressure system by one of low pressure, which opens the way for the inflow of moist oceanic air. The rise in temperature also promotes convectional activity with locally heavy thunderstorms in summer. In the Soviet Far East, the tail end of the Asian monsoon is experienced in August and September, though with far less intensity than further south. With the abruptly falling temperatures in October, the Siberian high pressure system builds up again and the seasonal cycle recommences.

The Burden of Winter

When considering the negative features of the Soviet climate, the length and severity of winter occupies a dominant position. Over half the area of the country experiences more or less continuously freezing temperatures and snow cover for over half the year.

Compared with North America, which lies open to tropical air masses from the Gulf of Mexico, the Soviet Union is cut off from the air from the Indian Ocean by an almost continuous mountain rim. The general westerly airstream makes the Atlantic, not the Pacific, the tempering influence, and both continentality (i.e. annual range of temperature) and winter severity and length are intensified from south-west to north-east.

Thus, almost all of Siberia has average winter temperatures below $-18°C$, i.e. colder than any part of the United States, let alone Britain, and almost all of European Russia has average temperatures below freezing point. The coldest places in winter, averaging $-51°C$ in January, are in north-east Siberia (Verkhoyansk and Oymyakon), relatively close to the Pacific coast. Some idea of the intensity of the winter in the eastern half of the country may be gained from the fact that most of the ground is permanently frozen ('permafrost' or *merzlota*)—a phenomenon which acts as a severe deterrent to all kinds of human activities.

The only part of the Soviet Union which has a January mean temperature more than a few degrees above freezing point is the south-eastern corner of the Black Sea (the Kolkhid lowlands) but even this area suffers from occasional killing frosts.

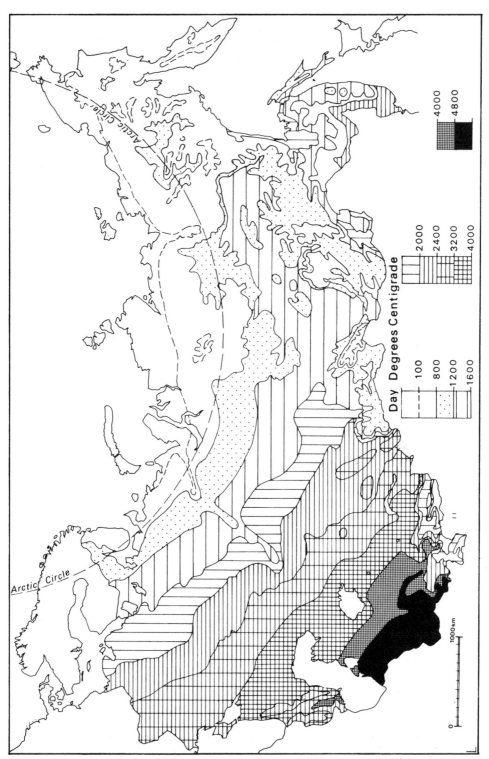

Fig. 3.1 Accumulated temperatures above a threshold of 10°C

The Heat and Water Budget

Annual precipitation figures and mean temperature values are only moderately significant for estimating the effect of climatic elements on man. As far as permanent settlement, fundamentally agricultural, is concerned, two values have been of overwhelming significance. These are 'accumulated heat', measured by 'day-degrees' above the threshold at which plant-growth begins, about 10°C, and 'effective moisture', that is, precipitation minus evaporation. In general, because of the sharp seasonality of the temperature and rainfall regimes (most rain comes in the summer) the most valuable comparisons to be made are again with North America.

Unfortunately the outstanding reservoir of accumulated heat (Fig. 3.1) in the Soviet Union is the Central Asian desert and semi-desert, which have heat and moisture balances comparable to most of the southern parts of the USA, but where economic farming depends on the availability of water for irrigation. The traditionally most intensively farmed land in the country, in the northern Ukraine, as well as the vast area of virgin lands in western Siberia and Kazakhstan, ploughed up in the late 1950s, have a heat budget similar to that of the prairie lands of the Dakotas and Minnesota. The region around Moscow, which was all the Russians were able to occupy for centuries, has a heat budget similar to that of the poorer parts of the Canadian prairies or north-west Europe. But even in the northern half of the country (mostly covered by coniferous forests) which has a shortage of heat, there are a few sheltered valleys—including the coldest in the world in January—which accumulate just enough heat for some passably successful agriculture in the short summer. Average figures for accumulated temperatures for different areas are given in the regional descriptions of agriculture in Chapter 7.

The moisture balance is described in greater detail in Chapter 5. Here it may simply be noted that for the distribution of 'effective moisture' (Fig. 3. 2), the most important fact is that most of the lands which have a 'surplus' are at least marginally deficient in heat. Of the regions of superabundant moisture, the only area where it is accompanied by ample heat is the very small basin of the western Transcaucasus, facing the Black Sea. Somewhat drier regions, but where the moisture is everywhere adequate, comparable to Britain or USA east of the Mississippi, include

European Russia north of Kiev and Kuybyshev and the Far Eastern monsoonal area of the Amur Valley. The large dry zone of inland eastern Siberia is to some extent ameliorated by the fact that the permanently frozen subsoil acts to conserve the limited moisture in the topsoil, preventing normal percolation.

In summary, it may be said that south of a line from Odessa to Lake Baykal (excepting the tiny anomaly of the western Transcaucasus), shortage of moisture is something of an obstacle to agricultural progress. The lands along this line may be compared to the western extensive wheat-growing margins of the North American Great Plains or Australia, which similarly fade into semi-desert ranching country and eventually desert.

Thus it can be seen that a major tragedy for the Soviet Union lies in the lack of broad geographical coincidence of its endowments of heat and moisture. There is nothing quite comparable to the great mass of the eastern United States where adequate supplies of both necessities coincide geographically.

THE IMPACT OF THE SOVIET CLIMATE

The Creation of 'Natural Zones'

Apart from the various direct influences exercised by climate on human activities—and on simply living—we must not forget its most basic indirect action in playing the dominant role in the creation of the prominent system of 'natural zones' in the Soviet Union. The Russian landscape is in a very real sense stamped in the image of its climate. The distinctions in the landscape which meant most to man as he strove to colonise these lands were not the mountains and the valleys, but the forests and the grasslands in their various forms. (See maps in Chapter 4)

In the geologically recent formative period following the pleistocene period, the low and subdued nature of the relief over the vast areas of the Russo-Siberian plains enabled climate to use a 'broader brush' in the creation of continuous, fairly homogeneous latitudinal 'natural zones' of soil and vegetation than anywhere else in the world. These and the soil-forming processes involved will be described in detail in Chapter 4. It will therefore be enough to say here that heat and water are the active elements in creating a soil and

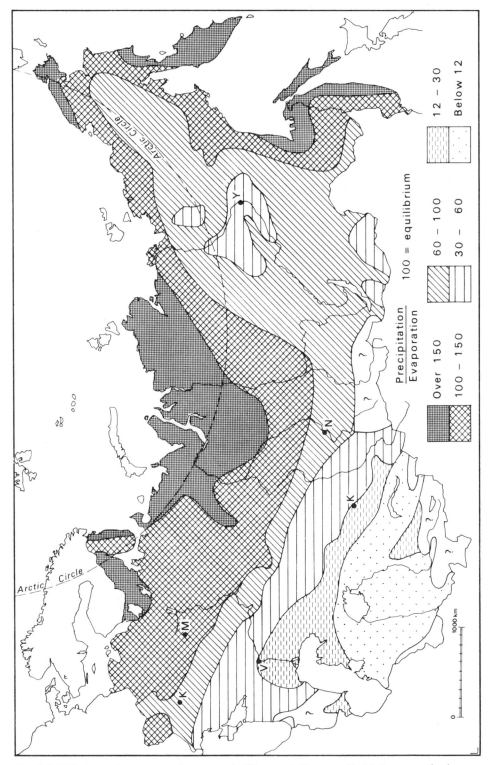

Fig. 3.2 Effective moisture, annual averages (millimetres). Sources: N. M. Ivanov and others

allowing a certain vegetation and animal life to live in it and give fertility and character to it. Thus the relative amounts of heat and water, considered above, are the key elements in creating and maintaining a distinctive soil-vegetation character and therefore the broad 'natural zones' become, to a significant degree, faithful reflectors of their climatic conditions. To the north of the wooded steppe zone there is adequate moisture but inadequate heat, the soils (mainly podzols) are leached and acidic, and trees dominate the scene roughly as far as the Arctic Circle. To the south where, except for some Black Sea lowlands, there is enough heat but not enough moisture, the soils (most notably the black earth or chernozem) are rich in humus in the more humid areas and in salts in the more arid, with grasses and drought-resisting shrubs (not trees) as the characteristic vegetation.

The climatic emphasis is reflected in the fact that the Soviet Union has a much greater proportion of tayga (coniferous forest) and tundra than has North America, slightly more grassland and desert and very much less well watered and heated forest land. This pattern has had incalculable effects on the history and character of colonisation and the wealth of the nations concerned, and indicates the fundamental significance of the climatic factor.

Climate and Farming

The influence of climate on agriculture seems obvious, but can easily be over-simplified if the historical, economic and technological circumstances are not kept in mind throughout. For instance, although over two-thirds of the Soviet arable area is now on black-earth soil (chernozem), the Russians, throughout most of their agricultural history, until the eighteenth century, were largely prevented from using it by non-Russian people who did not themselves till it.

It is true that the present distribution of population, urban as well as rural, has come, over the centuries, to coincide more or less with the distribution of arable land, and that there has been a natural tendency for farmers to move from poorer to better land. However, as in other industrialised countries, accessibility to the urban markets often transcends the normal disincentives of a poor agricultural climate, e.g. around

Moscow or Leningrad, and influences the type of farming practised. Location, traditions, comparative costs and general government policy may be just as important as any 'pure' climatic factor in deciding the distribution and specialisation of farming.

All the same, an important effect of the development of a national market and improved communications in large countries like the Soviet Union or the United States is, or should be, to make climatic factors more rather than less important in regional farm specialisation. In practice this process is frequently delayed in the Soviet Union by the Government's ambivalent attitude to regional self-sufficiency in agriculture, or overloaded transport lines or compulsory purchase orders for crops which neglect regional disadvantages.

There is some evidence that the Soviet government has recently come to realise that attempts to extend agriculture towards the climatic margins, instead of intensifying investment in optimum areas, while not by any means physically impossible, can be very expensive. Consideration of the heat and water budget leads to the conclusion that the fairly narrow zone of overlap of adequate heat and moisture in the European black-earth wooded steppe region and neighbouring areas is likely to yield the best return on investment for most of the widespread crops (and animals) in the country. Even here the crops are frequently devastated by a scorching wind (*sukhovey*) which causes rapid wilting of plants through excessive transpiration. The strain of coping with a short growing season or unreliable rainfall on the margins, say in Siberia or the virgin lands, not only means uncertainty about harvests, but ties up large quantities of equipment and labour which are only in use for a small part of the year. Even in the *relatively* well-favoured subtropical Caucasus regions, which receive only occasional killing frosts, the question arises whether it would not be cheaper in the long run to import the nation's needs of citrus fruits from Italy, Cuba or even Australia or the South Pacific.

There is not really much difference between the total area of climatically usable agricultural land in the United States and the Soviet Union. However, the significant difference lies in the fact that much more of the Soviet land is climatically marginal and therefore an unduly risky investment. Recently there have been moves toward a thorough appraisal of the essential quality of Soviet farmland with the aim of intelligently maximising specific long-term environmental assets. Although there is no doubt that the virgin lands extension which took place in western Siberia and Kazakhstan in the 1950s has effected an indispensable, massive and permanent shift of the centre of gravity of grain production to the east, the yields are low and vulnerable to climatic misfortunes. The realistic conclusion may well have been reached that intensive investment in proven good quality farmland is necessitated by the costly climatic marginality of much of the rest.

Climate and the Transport System
From what has been written already it will not be surprising that heavy climatic burdens are placed on the movement of people and goods during much of the year. From more temperate countries, where occasional natural hazards such as slips on the road, flash-floods or high winds at sea form the chief obstacles to movement, it is difficult to imagine the range of prolonged and paralysing problems imposed by the Russian winter.

A pass in the Pamir mountains in May. The road has just been opened after the winter closure

Until a century or so ago, most of the Russian freight was handled by the rivers, almost all of which are obstructed by ice for several months, followed by destructive floods and finally by dangerously low water in late summer. Transport on the large north-flowing rivers of Siberia is particularly limited because their lower reaches are still frozen while the upper reaches are in their spring flood. Almost all the seaports are troubled by ice and apart from the inactivity, considerable damage is done to bridges, port facilities and the like, on rivers, lakes and seas. Further, the presence of permafrost under nearly half the area of the country makes it difficult and expensive to build permanent railways or roads.

On land, the roads were (and in many cases still are) more impassable in the quagmire conditions of the spring thaw and early summer than in the winter, when sledging was relatively easy. The very cold weather sometimes causes metals to become brittle and makes lubrication and motor operation very difficult, apart from snow blockage and damage to electrical machinery, including transmission lines. For further details see Chapter 11.

New technology, whether on the railways, in the air, or in building the much overdue highway network, is gradually reducing the extent of the chaos which regularly prevailed and making it more feasible to plan in terms of regular, large-scale interregional trade. But the climate still adds high overheads to the operation of the Soviet transport system, compared with that of most modern countries, quite apart from the human discomfort, not to say hardship, involved.

Climate and everyday living
In addition to the almost crippling climatic disabilities under which certain specific essential economic activities labour, there remains the pervasive general effect upon everyday life, migration and even the state of mind of the Soviet people. The Soviet climate, in general, is something hostile to be wrestled with, or at least taken very seriously.

Throughout their history, the Russians, as distinct from the Georgians, Tadzhiks or other southerly-dwelling peoples who were conquered by them in the nineteenth century, have lived in a climate which must be considered rather miserable by most standards. Since the majority of them were, until quite recently, rural dwellers (the urban segment became a majority of the Soviet population only in 1962), they have lived close to nature. The forced winter inactivity, where peasants, if they could, frequently passed the time in a lethargic, and sometimes drunken state, has sometimes been blamed for supposed ingrained and unfortunate habits of mind in Russia. Ellsworth Huntington thought that the Russian peasants should be shipped south to sunnier Mesopotamia for the winter, for the good of their souls. Clearly, since the present Soviet population is largely an urban and an indoor, industrially-oriented one, the climate is being placed at further remove for more and more people. On the other hand, problems of winter in the rural areas are not rendered less by reduction of numbers; food still has to be produced, and moreover winter in the city also has its hardships.

A wistfulness for 'southern climes' has long been present among the Russians, as it has among other 'northern' peoples. A passage from Peter Kropotkin, the nineteenth century Russian philosopher-geographer, on his first journey to western Europe in mid-April, may be indicative:

'And the contrast of climate! Two days before, I had left St. Petersburg thickly covered with snow, and now, in middle Germany, I walked without an overcoat along the railway platform in warm sunshine, admiring the budding flowers. Then came the Rhine, and further on Switzerland bathed in the rays of a bright sun, with its small, clean hotels, where breakfast was served out of doors, in view of the snow-clad mountains. I never before had realised so vividly what Russia's northern position meant, and how the history of the Russian nation had been influenced by the fact that the main centres of its life had to develop in high latitudes. Only then I fully understood the uncontrollable attraction which southern lands have exercised on the Russians, the colossal efforts which they have made to reach the Black Sea, and the steady pressure of the Siberian colonists southward, further into Manchuria.'

There were, of course, many more primary reasons than the search for the sun for the persistent southerly movement of Russians in the last two centuries or so, notably the promise of improving farmland and colonial enrichment. However, now that these aims have been achieved and consolidated and the Soviet population has become more urban, mobile and better educated, the question of climate as an 'amenity' is beginning to make itself felt and modify significantly the population map.

Snow cover in the south of the USSR is of short duration on low ground but attracts large numbers of skiers to the mountains. Here a chair lift gives access from the Dombai valley in the Caucasus to the ski-field

The 1959 Census recorded a massive displacement of the Soviet population towards the harsher climates of the east, especially to the Urals, Siberia and Kazakhstan. Much of this can be attributed to the Second World War and Stalin's enforcement of labour movement to new factories in the eastern regions, but much also to Khrushchev's grandiose virgin lands campaign—probably the last major extension of the Russian 'pioneer fringe'.

But since the late 1950s, as discussed in Chapter 6, there has been clear evidence of a substantial net outflow from Siberia, where the climate is indeed very severe, in spite of a disproportionately high government level of investment and new discoveries of industrial resources. These 'losses' are officially admitted, but commentators are at pains to stress the importance of the relative lack of other amenities, like good housing and education, in addition to the climate. On the other hand, the more southerly regions, notably Soviet Central Asia, the north Caucasus and the southern Ukraine (including Crimea) have recorded a considerable degree of net in-migration from the north. Although articles in the Soviet press frequently deplore the movement to these areas, where there is already a labour surplus (Central Asia and Caucasia have a natural increase which is much higher than the national average) and the exodus from Siberia and north European Russia, they still continue. This indicates a considerable degree of personal freedom of migration decision-making compared with the recent past, but it is difficult to avoid the conclusion that one important component in the recent southerly drift is that of climatic attraction. There is some evidence that the Soviet government will accept these trends, locating 'foot-loose', labour-intensive industries in these new reception areas, while encouraging mainly resource-oriented, automated industry in areas which cannot retain labour, thus obviating the need for costly subsidies to unattractive areas.

The southern areas attract holidaymakers in large numbers not only in summer but also for winter sports as the Caucasus ranges provide better climatic conditions than the other ranges and are also relatively easy of access from the main centres of population.

CLIMATE AND MAN IN PARTICULAR PLACES

Up to now, we have examined broad patterns and general connections between the climate of the Soviet Union and various activities and needs of its people. But since geography does not entirely come into its own until it focuses on the integration of man and his environment in particular places, we will attempt to bring out some significant features of the climate-man complex at selected points across the Soviet map. These points are necessarily cities, but they will be assumed to include the surrounding rural districts (Fig. 3.3).

Kiev

The first Russian city of any wealth and consequence was Kiev, in the wooded-steppe region of what is now the northern Ukraine, and although this success was mainly due to trade in furs, a sizeable population of farmers developed in the vicinity. Although by west European standards the winter in this region is severe (about three months with freezing temperatures) the growing season is long enough and warm enough for the safe cultivation of most of the European grains (including maize), vegetables and animals. Kiev is

in the narrow region of overlap of adequate moisture (with a summer maximum) and adequate heat and sunshine, with a quite fertile type of black or grey earth and a fairly easily cleared mixture of open grassland and deciduous trees producing mild humus. By comparison with most of the USSR today, it is a mild and well-watered region and is one of the most intensively farmed as well as being relatively well regarded as a living-place for urban workers. The apparent regional trends in both agriculture and industry in the Soviet Union seem to favour the long-term growth of the Kiev area (quite apart from its importance as the capital of the Ukraine and a historico-cultural centre). From many viewpoints, the climatic factor in the future of Kiev is increasingly favourable in the Soviet context.

Moscow

When the city-state of Kiev was sacked by Batu's Mongol Hordes in 1240, the Slavic remnants had to regroup in the watery, forested region between the Upper Volga and Oka rivers, centred on Moscow. Although on the broad scale of the Soviet Union the two areas have a not very dissimilar climate, the marginal differences are, in fact, significant enough to produce differences in the total environment which must have been painfully noticeable to the early escapees from Kiev. Moscow's climate is generally damper, cooler and more cloudy than Kiev's with twice as much snow, lying for five months instead of three, and appreciably less accumulated heat, sunshine and, thus, evaporation. This leads to a more water-logged landscape, a predominance of coniferous rather than deciduous trees and a more podzolic, less humus-rich soil. Costs of items like snow clearance are heavy.

The traditional crops were the hardy rye, oats, flax, potatoes, cabbages and other vegetables and the competitive position of the area's grain farming has been suffering ever since the infiltration again of the better lands south of the Oka by Russian peasants several centuries ago. The current presence in its midst of the largest urban market in the country has promoted dairying and market gardening and saved the physically somewhat marginal farmland from continued decline. As far as the large urban population is concerned, the unique metropolitan amenities undoubtedly make up for the somewhat dismal climate.

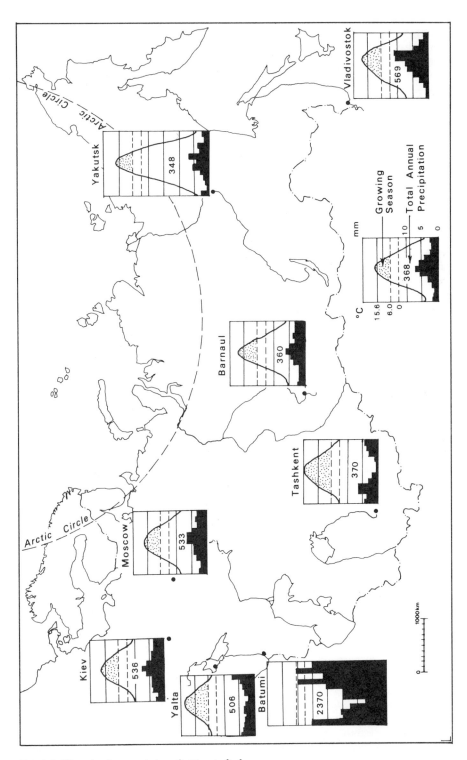

Fig. 3.3 Climatic characteristics of cities studied

Barnaul

Barnaul lies in the Altay Steppe, near the eastern end of the continuous zone of wooded steppe, black-earth and optimum overlap of heat and water, just before it is brought to an end by the mountains and permafrost which characterise eastern Siberia. During the first incursions of peasants into Siberia in the eighteenth century, the Altay Steppe was perhaps the most coveted, in spite of being the most distant, of the good lands and still today, for Siberia, it is one of the most reliable and productive farming areas.

However, a climatic comparison with Kiev, on the western end of this long strip of wooded steppe, may be illuminating. Barnaul is distinguished by much colder winters, a significantly shorter growing season, and less accumulated heat, although the mid-summer temperatures are much the same. Although Barnaul has less precipitation in the year, it is more concentrated in the spring and summer when it is needed and evaporation is less, so that the average supply of effective moisture is much the same in both cases.

The severity of the winter means that crops like wheat have to be sown in the spring, rather than the autumn as in the Kiev region, and this places a greater strain on equipment and labour and makes the farming routine more hectic and rather more limited in range of crops and livestock. In common with the rest of Siberia, the length and severity of the winter, when coupled with shortcomings of other amenities, makes retention of people increasingly difficult. However, the climatic conditions for permanent agriculture in this region are better than one can find anywhere in that half of the Soviet Union which lies to the east of it. In fact, it is likely to continue to be one of the most densely populated agricultural communities of any size in Siberia.

Yakutsk

Yakutsk, on the bend of the Lena river in northeast Siberia, has much the most severe continental climate of any of these chosen case-studies and is the only one situated on permanently frozen ground. The mean January temperature is about $-40°C$ compared with a mere $-18°C$ at Barnaul and, of course, much lower actual temperatures are recorded. Since little snow falls in this centre of the winter high pressure system, permafrost several hundred feet thick is formed and maintained, and the danger of frostbite is acute during even a

short walk in the town. However, although snow lies for seven months and night frosts may occur in any month except July, circumstances have accorded this region a warmer summer (warmer than Moscow in July) and a longer growing season—about three months—than is normal for this latitude. Therefore, although relatively unimportant nationally this region is the only notable outlier of agriculture in the great wilderness of Siberia, north of the closely settled belt. Frost-resistant strains of wheat and other crops are grown for local use. Rainfall is light, and although the great majority of it falls in summer, and the permafrost conserves the surface water, irrigation is usually needed. But the permafrost, which is potentially unstable at its upper edge, presents constant problems for building, transport and urban life in general.

This is an extremely severe environment by any standards and, were it not for the fact that it is the centre of a huge area where there are valuable mineral workings and also the focal point of a vigorous native group, the Yakuts, the hardships would be too difficult, or too costly, to bear.

Vladivostok

The southernmost Soviet port on the Pacific, Vladivostok has a severe winter for its latitude and

Collapse of part of an apartment house in Yakutsk following subsidence caused by melting of permafrost

position on the sea, since it is under the influence of strong outflowing Siberian winds. It has freezing temperatures for about five months and its excellent harbour has to be kept open by ice-breakers, while new, virtually ice-free ports, Nakhodka and Sovetskaya Gavan, on the open sea, have been developed. Although the growing season is long enough for normal European or north Chinese agriculture, the rainfall maximum comes in late summer, at the tail end of the Asian monsoon, when ripening crops may be damaged, while irrigation is often needed in the early summer. The humidity in late summer can be uncomfortable and clouds of biting insects add to the discomfort. Thus an unfavourable climatic 'comfort index', added to isolation and a limited amount of second-class farmland, conform to the common Siberian pattern as far as human attractiveness is concerned.

Some Southern Exceptions

All of the stations discussed so far have much more severe winters than are ever experienced in England or Australasia and a more or less restricted growing season. They represent about four-fifths of the total area and the total farmland of the Soviet Union, and therefore can be said to typify the most common range of climatic problems. On the other hand, the next three to be considered, although anomalous in Soviet terms, are basically much more akin to stations in New Zealand and the southern parts of Australia or the United States, in whose latitudes they lie, with their warmer summers and winters and a growing season which lasts at least three-quarters of the year.

Tashkent

In the centre of the Asian landmass, Tashkent has long hot, and dry summers, with accumulated heat values similar in amount to those of Arizona, inland California or inland southern Australia. As in those places, irrigation is necessary for intensive farming of cotton, fruit and vegetables, while away from the irrigated areas only extensive dry-farming techniques and ranching are possible. Actually Tashkent has a higher rainfall, concentrated in the winter, than much of the semi-desert to its west, owing to the fact that it is at the foot of the mountains which intercept the rain-bearing depressions. The fertile loess soil, common to this piedmont strip, is easily blown about so that the summers are hot, dry and dusty.

Provided that an adequate supply of irrigation water continues to be forthcoming, the hot, long growing season and the increasing demand for cotton and fruits in the USSR will ensure the continued importance of the area, but the supply of water, as well as fertile soil, is strictly limited. The summer heat does not seem to deter the immigration of Russians into Tashkent, any more than it does Americans to Arizona. In addition, the native people of the region have a much higher rate of natural increase than the country as a whole, and do not tend to leave the area. Thus, the water limitation will probably be the crucial long-term problem in the man-land equation here.

Batumi

On the shores of the Black Sea, Batumi, with the Kolkhid lowlands to the north of it, are climatically unique in the Soviet Union in several respects. It is the only part of the country where the January mean temperature is over 6°C, and correspondingly higher day temperatures, giving a year-round growing season. However, occasional killing frosts do occur and threaten the citrus fruits. Secondly, it is the only part of the Soviet Union which has abundant rainfall as well as adequate year-round heat. In fact, draining of excessive water has been the major prerequisite to developing the land for tea and other plants which need abundant water but also good drainage. The swamps were also breeding-grounds for malaria-carrying mosquitoes until recently. Thirdly, it is the only Soviet area with a very heavy total rainfall and a winter-autumn maximum—although it receives a good deal in the summer as well.

All of this gives the area a luxuriant sub-tropical vegetation, with tree-ferns, eucalyptus and plants from sub-tropical China, Japan and India—altogether a most untypical situation in the Soviet Union. Since this is the only practicable area of the country for the growth of frost-sensitive crops like citrus fruits and tea, it has received special attention from the government. Because of topographical and local frost difficulties the area which is really well suited to commercial growth of these exotic crops is quite limited and, were it not for the autarchic traditions of Soviet agriculture, might well be better employed growing less exotic crops like maize or rice.

Yalta

Yalta is the centre of a string of tourist resorts

Seaside crowds at Yalta in the Crimea, vessels for tourist trips in the foreground

along the very narrow southern coastal strip of the Crimean peninsula, backed by steep mountains protecting the coast from the cold northern winter winds. After the Russians had conquered the Crimea in the late eighteenth century and found this sheltered coast to have no regular freezing period and abundant winter sunshine, the nobility soon began to build palaces there as an escape from Moscow or St. Petersburg—they are mostly converted to sanatoria today. The January temperatures—averaging about 3°C—are appreciably cooler than at Batumi and there is a brief plant resting period. The rainfall regime is a partial Mediterranean one, with a winter maximum but much less heavy than at Batumi and with more sunshine. The summers are relatively dry and sunny, again much less humid than Batumi. On a year-round basis this is probably the pleasantest climate in the Soviet Union which fact, combined with its natural beauty, explains the concentration of tourist and medical establishments. Most of the very limited area not taken up by resorts is given over to growing vines and other fruits. Altogether it presents a climatic scene not unlike many coastal places in the northern Mediterranean, southern Australia, or California, but one which is quite unique in the Soviet Union.

CLIMATIC COSTS, BENEFITS AND ADAPTATIONS

The Soviet climate has been analysed in terms of how it appears to the inhabitants who have to live in it, how it affects their activities, and how this compares with the climatic lot of people in other parts of the world, notably North America, Britain and Australasia. By way of summary, a balance sheet of the costs, benefits and trends will now be presented.

Costs

(*a*) The length and severity of the winter effectively rules out at least half the country's area, in the north and east, for normal agriculturally-based settlement. It incidentally causes most of this area to be permanently frozen underground and to have poor vegetation and soil conditions. Transport operations are severely restricted and made expensive, and so are all economic activities, like mining, which have to be carried on in the non-agricultural areas. Labour is also expensive and difficult to attract and retain in these winter-bound areas.

(*b*) The generally drought-ridden character of parts of the country which are not severely crippled by the winter places a serious extra cost-burden on the national economy. Irrigation development in Central Asia in the very dry areas as well as heavy investment in equipment and men, coupled with a high risk of drought failures in the drier parts of the black-earth belt, add to the costs of farming enterprises.

(*c*) The lack of a broad overlapping zone of the large areas which have *either* enough moisture *or* enough heat is a major tragedy compared, say, with the situation of the United States. The fact that the relatively small overlap zone is in relatively high latitudes compared with that of the USA or much of Europe is an additional misfortune and cost.

Benefits

It is difficult to discover really positive, large-scale benefits accorded to the Soviet people by their climate, but certain silver linings to the clouds may be pointed out. In other words, things could have been worse!

(i) In spite of the narrowness of the zone of overlap between heat and water in relation to the country's total area, the vast size of the Soviet Union ensures that, in absolute terms, the generally productive land is extensive enough given good management and enough investment, to feed the population adequately in the foreseeable future.

(ii) The low rainfall totals are significantly ameliorated by the fact that most of the year's precipitation is received in the growing season and most of the rest is kept in cold storage until the spring.

(iii) At least there are some areas of sub-tropical climate, however small, which constitute just as much psychological and recreational assets as strictly economic ones.

Adaptations

It has often been implied in Soviet government pronouncements since the time of Lenin that general policy was to develop all regions of the country regardless of comparative costs. Indeed there has been a considerable extension of the cultivated area, culminating in the massive virgin lands scheme of the 1950s. However, in recent years, the evidence seems to indicate a new recognition of the climatic limitations and the cost of failing to pay close attention to them—largely, but by no means entirely, with reference to farming.

In general, the geographical directions of change seem to be towards the west and south rather than to the east and north as in previous decades. This results from a recognition of (*a*) the fact that an increase in food production can be obtained more economically from the already more intensively farmed and climatically well-endowed parts of the European black-earth zone than from further extension at the climatic margins, and (*b*) that, with a more mobile, educated and affluent population, a significant migration is under way from the areas generally considered climatically 'difficult' to live in, towards those that are easier—given the presence of other amenities and employment.

BIBLIOGRAPHY

Berg, L. S. (1950), *Natural regions of the USSR*, Macmillan, London and New York.

Borisov, A. A. (1965), *Climates of the USSR*, Oliver and Boyd.

Budyko, M. I. (1974), *Climate and life*, English edition, D. H. Miller (ed.), Academic Press, New York and London.

Fiziko-geograficheskiy atlas mira (1964), Moscow. A key in English to this atlas appears in *Soviet Geography, Review and Translation*, 6 (5–6), 1965, pp. 1–403.

Gibson, J. R. (1969), *Feeding the Russian fur trade*. University of Wisconsin Press.

Hooson, D. J. M. (1966), *The Soviet Union*. University of London Press, London.

Lydolph, P. E. (1978), *Climates of the Soviet Union, World survey of climatology*, Vol. 7, Elsevier.

Lydolph, P. E. (1959), 'Federov's complex method in climatology.' *Annals Association American Geographers*, **49**, pp. 120–144.

Lvovich, M. I. (1963), *Chelovek i vody*, Moscow.

Parker, W. H. (1968), *Historical geography of Russia*. University of London Press, London.

Rogers, J. A. (ed.) (1962), P. A. Kropotkin *Memoirs of a Revolutionist*. Doubleday, N. Y., p. 178.

Shashko, D. I. (1962), 'Climate resources of Soviet agriculture', in Akademiya Nauk SSSR (1962), *Pochvenno-geograficheskoye rayonirovaniye SSSR*, trans. by A. Gourevitch, *Soil-geographical zoning of the USSR (in relation to the agricultural usage of lands)*, IPST, Jerusalem, 1963.

Suslov, S. P. (1961), *Physical geography of Asiatic Russia*, Freeman, San Francisco and London.

4 Biogeography—the Vegetation, Soils and Animal Life

The vegetation and soil constitute two of the principal natural renewable resources of the USSR, as they form the basis of her agriculture and of the supply of many kinds of organic raw materials. There is a close inter-relationship between the type of vegetation and the character of the soil, and both are strongly influenced by climate, relief and other factors. Plants and soils are two of the principal components of the natural biological systems or ecosystems. Plants are the producing components as their green foliage converts solar energy, water and atmospheric carbon dioxide into food material by photosynthesis. Animals form the consuming element, whether as herbivores they eat plant material directly, or as carnivores they derive food energy by predation upon other animals, or like man they may take both forms of food. Animals also influence the spread and growth of plants and the development of plant communities and contribute to the fertility of the soil. Soils control the nutrient supply to the plants; some of this comes from the weathering of the underlying parent rock, but an essential contribution is derived from the decomposition of dead plant and animal matter by the soil fauna and microflora, a complex process producing the soil humus and releasing nutrients such as nitrates which are absorbed by plant root systems. In a biotic community such as a forest, all the organisms present are interdependent and they interact with each other in varying degrees. Changes in any one factor can thus produce important and often unpredictable effects on other components of the ecosystem, as exemplified by man's power of changing ecosystems by replacing natural vegetation by crop systems and creating changes in the character of the soil, animal life and climate.

During the advance of continental ice-sheets in the Quaternary period there was an almost complete obliteration of the natural vegetation of northern Eurasia. As the climate became warmer during the post-glacial period, a succession of communities of plants occupied the area which is now the USSR. These became the 'climax' communities, that is, each represented a relatively stable vegetational response to the changes of climate and the development of soils of the post-glacial period. The influence of natural selection thus brought into existence a cover of vegetation characterised by communities of major plant types, species of which were closely adapted to climate and soils in growth form or habit. Such communities of dominant plant types are known as plant formations; they are widely distributed over very large areas of the Soviet Union which are hence substantially uniform in vegetational character. Each formation is associated with a distinctive soil type and with various animal groups ranging in size from soil micro-organisms to large mammals. Each formation thus represents a major ecosystem or life-zone. Human development and exploitation of the zones have resulted in widespread changes in their character, although the basic relationships between the environment and the biotic communities are still functionally important.

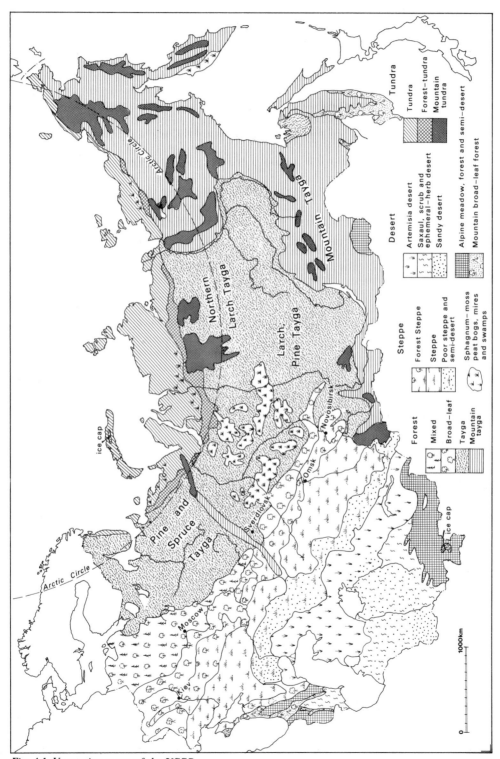

Fig. 4.1 Vegetation zones of the USSR

As there is a north-to-south gradation in temperature, precipitation and other climatic features, there is a corresponding change in the type of plant formation, so that several distinct west-east zones are distinguished (Fig. 4.1). In the far north are the treeless cold deserts or tundras; farther south, the higher temperatures and longer growing seasons have produced various kinds of forest vegetation, the latter still forming the most characteristic scenery of many rural areas of the Soviet Union. The forests are succeeded southwards by open steppes or temperate grasslands which are the vegetational response to the sub-humid conditions unsuitable for tree growth in these areas. In turn the steppe grasslands grade to the south with increasing aridity to the semi-deserts and deserts. This succession becomes modified where mountains produce a more rapid climatic zonation and hence a vertical zonation of biotic communities; and it is much less evident in east Siberia and the Far East. Sub-tropical conditions occur only in relatively small areas in the far south, such as in Georgia, where highland barriers exclude the chill of continental winters.

Modern soil science owes much to the pioneer researches of the great Russian pedologists, Dokuchayev and his associates such as Kostychev and Glinka. Dokuchayev stressed the interaction and the interrelationships of all natural phenomena of the earth's surface. His views were developed by the geographer Berg who, in the context of the Soviet Union, advanced the concept of the geographical landscape, the latter being a combination or grouping of objects and phenomena in which features of relief, climate, water, soil, plant cover and animal life and also human activity combine into one harmonious whole typically repeated throughout a given area of land. More modern work has emphasised the functioning together of living communities and their non-living environment so as to form an ecosystem. The terms biocoenosis and biogeocoenosis are terms often used in European and Russian literature and are equivalent to community and ecosystem respectively.

Within these natural communities, soil is a principal component. Five factors may be distinguished in the development of soil: they consist of the parent rock material, the relief of the land, the climate, the living organisms both plant and animal, and the time involved. The interaction of these factors gives rise in a mature, undisturbed

soil to several distinct layers or horizons, collectively called the soil 'profile' and observed if a vertical section is exposed. The latter is usually divided into three main horizons from the surface downwards and corresponding to the surface soil, the subsoil and the substratum of parent rock material. Taken together the horizons contain the four constituents of soil, namely mineral matter, organic matter, soil air and water.

Climate is of particular importance in soil development; it plays an important role in the chemical and physical disintegration of the parent rock and, mainly through the interplay of temperature and precipitation, also determines the type of vegetation. The latter provides the soil's main supply of organic matter in the form of leaf litter or root debris; this material is broken down by bacteria, fungi and the soil fauna thus producing the soil humus. The latter is of great importance as it improves the texture, the moisture-holding property and the nutrient-producing capacity of the soil; it provides energy-rich food for soil organisms so that nutrients are released for absorption in solution by plant roots.

As large areas of the Soviet Union are lowlands, substantially uniform topographically and geologically, the influence of the two major soil-forming factors of climate and vegetation upon the soil geography is emphasised. Soil types therefore correspond closely to the zones of vegetation established by the interaction of climatic elements and consist of broad zones or belts trending from west to east, except in areas of strong relief where altitude causes rapid changes in climate, vegetation and hence of soil type.

The vegetation formations and their associated soil types in the main climatic regions are shown in Table 4.1. Beneath the conventional name of the soils are the names recently given to soil units on the maps published by FAO/UNESCO (1972). The map (Fig. 4.2) illustrates the distribution of the soils. This should be compared with the map (Fig. 4.1) showing the natural vegetation.

The Tundra
The Arctic tundra or cold desert covers almost all of the extreme north of European and Siberian USSR, north of the forested zone and including island groups; a closely related type of vegetation, the Alpine tundra extends southwards into mountainous areas such as the northern Urals or highland areas of Siberia and the Far East.

TABLE 4.1 VEGETATION, SOIL TYPE AND CLIMATIC RELATIONSHIPS IN THE USSR

Vegetation	Soil type	Climate
Tundra	Tundra soils (Gleysols)	Arctic
Boreal Forest	Podzols (Podzols)	Sub-arctic
Mixed forest	Brown podzolic (Cambisols)	Cool temperate continental
Broad-leaf forest and wooded steppe	Grey forest soil (Orthic luvisols)	
Steppe	Black earths (Chernozems)	Continental semi-arid
Poor steppe	Chestnut soils (Kastanozems)	
Desert and semi-desert	Grey desert soils (Xerosols and Yermosols)	Arid continental
Mountain	Mountain soils	Mountain climates
Warm-temperate forests	Red podzolic soils (Acrisols)	Humid sub-tropical.

Tundra plants are adapted to severe Arctic type climates and to unfavourable soils, conditions which exclude tree growth. They consist of the hardiest of all green plants, the mosses and lichens, together with species of perennial herbs such as grasses, sedges and rushes and also dwarfed woody shrubs. During the prolonged, cold and dark winters they remain dormant but burst into active growth during the few weeks of summer. Even in July, the warmest month, temperatures average only 10°C, but the vegetation benefits from the long period of daylight in midsummer allowing growth, flowering and fruiting to take place within a short time. The accumulated food reserves built up in summer are stored in extensive rooting systems, ready for use for resumption of growth in the following spring; above ground, however, the plants are stunted, with foliage lying close to the soil surface where it obtains some protection from cold and the drying effect of winds.

A gradual decrease in climatic severity southwards is accompanied by change in the type of vegetation, defined by the sub-zones recognised by Soviet geographers, namely the Arctic tundra, the typical or shrubby tundra, and the forest-tundra. The Arctic tundra is a desolate northernmost strip found mainly along the Arctic coastlands of Siberia where there is much bare, stony ground interspersed with patches of vegetation consisting of species of the primitive plants, algae, mosses and lichens. Farther south is the typical tundra. Here the vegetation is richer, forming a more continuous cover and includes woody shrubs such as the dwarfed birch, willow and alder species, together with flowering herbaceous perennial plants, mosses and lichens. The mosses form extensive *Sphagnum* peat bogs in the south of this zone, which grades into the forest-tundra, a transitional belt occupied by plant types of both the tundra and the boreal forest to the south. The trees are usually stunted birch, alder and coniferous

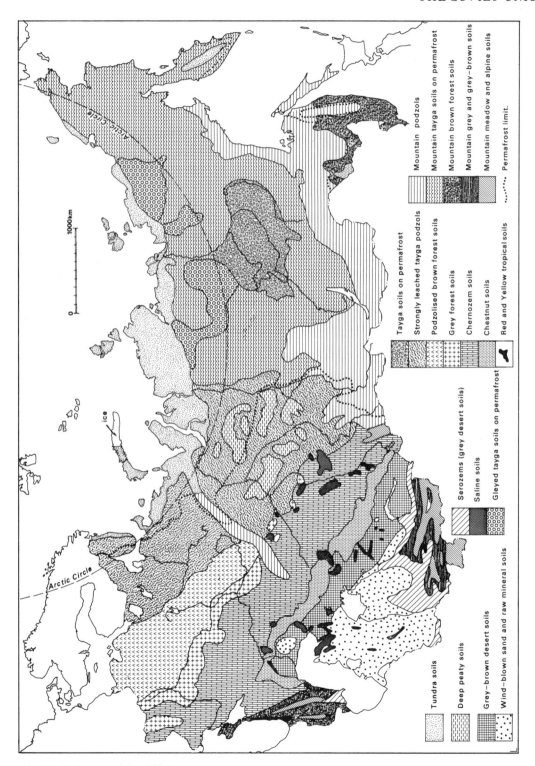

Legend:

Mountain podzols
Mountain tayga soils on permafrost
Mountain brown forest soils
Mountain grey and grey–brown soils
Mountain meadow and alpine soils
Permafrost limit.

Tayga soils on permafrost
Strongly leached tayga podzols
Podzolised brown forest soils
Grey forest soils
Chernozem soils
Chestnut soils
Red and Yellow tropical soils

Serozems (grey desert soils)
Saline soils
Gleyed tayga soils on permafrost

Tundra soils
Deep peaty soils
Grey–brown desert soils
Wind–blown sand and raw mineral soils

1000 km

Arctic Circle

ice

Fig. 4.2 Soil zones of the USSR

larch or spruce species, occupying more sheltered habitats whereas the higher and more exposed situations carry typical tundra vegetation.

Apart from the broad regional changes described, tundra vegetation displays marked local varieties, usually associated with micro-relief and drainage. The glaciation of the area has produced a varied topography and soil parent material, each of which affects soil drainage and micro-climate, reflected in differing patterns of plant life. Thus there are swampy depressions carpeted with *Sphagnum* and other mosses or stretches of open water fringed by sedges and rushes; exposed ridges carry a discontinuous cover of mosses or lichens, but sheltered spots with sunny exposures bear grasses, shrubs or brightly-flowering herbs.

The character of tundra vegetation is strongly influenced by the soil and subsoil. Underlying the shallow surface soil is the permanently frozen subsoil, or *permafrost*. It occurs in the greater part of the Soviet northlands, lying beneath all the tundra and much of the coniferous forest, attaining a depth of 600 m at Nordvik, in the north of Siberia. In winter the ground becomes frozen solid right up to the surface but the warmth of spring and summer thaws the upper few centimetres, forming the *active layer*. All rooted plants must grow within this thin active layer, for the permafrost below it is impenetrable and sterile. Yet even the active soil layer is a poor rooting medium as it is usually swampy and waterlogged; moisture from thawed ice or precipitation cannot drain away owing to the permafrost layer beneath and the presence of water excludes air. Hence the action of bacteria and fungi in breaking down organic matter is very slow, inhibiting the release of nutrients such as calcium and nitrogen.

Thus a typical tundra soil consists of a surface layer composed of raw, peaty, dark-brown organic matter and humus, the remains of the surface vegetation of mosses, lichens, shrubs or herbs. Below this, in place of the usual subsoil horizon, is a layer of mottled blue and brown clayey mineral material, deficient in oxygen and seasonally flooded with meltwater; this is termed the gleyed layer. Below it is the permafrost.

However, the development of horizons in tundra soils is commonly prevented by the upheavals caused by alternation of freezing and thawing which forces lower material up to the surface. This includes assorted rock fragments and the latter accumulate upon the surface in defined patterns, usually circular or polygonal in shape. The 'spotty tundra' and 'hummocky tundra' described by Soviet geographers are of this origin. On sloping land, solifluction causes the active soil layer to slide downhill and the patterns take the form of parallel lines or 'stone stripes'. Soil disturbances of this kind are injurious to plant life which becomes buried or suffers damage to roots or stems. The total area of tundra soils in the USSR is about 7.7% of the total land area.

Soviet tundras, like those of North America, attract a rich animal life which conservationists are anxious to protect from the impact of increasing economic development. Many birds and mammals are migrants, spending the summer in the tundra where there is food and an absence of disturbance from humans, and returning southwards with the approach of winter. Residents during the winter include the lemming, the arctic fox, the ermine, the snowy owl and the ptarmigan; some, like the arctic fox, yield valuable pelts. But populations of this and other animals of the tundra are subject to wide fluctuations in number; thus fox numbers depend upon numbers of lemming, their chief prey, which in turn are affected by the abundance of pasture plants. The Soviet arctic tundras provide pastures for about 2.5 million domesticated reindeer; controlled systems of management of the grazings are applied to ensure preservation of the natural ecosystem; overgrazing may cause irreversible damage of the plant cover as the lichens and other herbage require several or many years for regeneration in the severe climate. In natural conditions of the ecosystem, predation by wolves controls the numbers of reindeer, so that overgrazing is avoided. Protection of the herds and hence of an important source of meat is ensured by a campaign of wolf extermination by means of aviation and chemical pest killers.

The Northern Forest Zone
The extent of the forested area may be seen from Fig. 4.1 which shows that it occupies more of the surface of the USSR than any other vegetation formation, although the widespread clearances for economic and urban development that have occurred, particularly in the south-west, are not shown on this map.

As there are considerable variations in climate and soil within this vast area, three subdivisions are necessary. The main area is the *tayga* or boreal coniferous forest, occupying much of the north-west in Europe, but also extending across Siberia and reaching the Pacific Ocean. To the south-west the tayga grades into the *mixed forest*, consisting of a mixture of coniferous and broad-leaved deciduous trees, with the latter becoming pre-dominant in the south; in the Soviet Far East the tayga is replaced by a species-rich *broad-leaved deciduous forest*, many species of which have Manchurian and Japanese affinities.

The Soviet tayga contains the world's greatest reserve of softwood timber and yields each year the largest volume of lumber cut for industrial purposes. Apart from its economic importance, the tayga is of great global significance in its favourable influence on atmospheric conditions and in its regulation of stream flow and soil moisture reserves; it also provides recreational and scenic resources and gives food and shelter for wild animal species.

The tayga is separated from the tundra proper by a belt of transition, the *forest-tundra*, where associations of the flora of tundra and boreal forest are intermingled according to site con-ditions. Among the dominant needle-leaf coniferous species, pine (*Pinus*), and spruce (*Picea*) are the most valuable economically and cover large areas west of the Ural mountains, their distribution usually influenced by variations

in the soil character. This is determined by the irregular distribution of glacial material and the sandy areas carry stands of pine, with spruce often dominant on loams and clays. In Siberia, the tayga attains its greatest extent, approaching 1600 km from north to south, its composition changing in accordance with regional climatic, soil or other conditions; thus in western Siberia the dominant pine, spruce and larch (*Larix*) species are absent over large areas where very poor drainage has resulted in the formation of huge peat bogs and swamps. But in central and eastern Siberia the forest type becomes influenced by the varied relief and the extreme continentality and dryness of climate; east of the river Yenisey the Dahurian larch becomes dominant, rooted in the thin active soil layer above the permafrost and forming rather open forests with subordinate shrub, herb and moss layers in the undergrowth. Within the tayga, areas of highland give rise to subalpine or mon-tane formations of conifers; these are replaced by montane grasslands or tundras beyond the treeline. The tayga also contains widespread areas of deciduous trees such as the light-loving birch and aspen which commonly replace the conifers after the latter have been destroyed by forest fires or lumbering operations.

Many animals are dependent upon the vegeta-tion; few of them migrate, in contrast to those of

A riverside clearing in the Siberian tayga

the tundras, despite the cold and heavy snow of winter; some adapt by living beneath the snow or by hibernation, others remain active. Rodents such as the squirrel and the chipmunk live on needles, berries, seeds and buds which also feed birds such as the crossbill and members of the grouse family. These animals are the food of the valuable fur-bearing predators, the marten, ermine, fox and polecat. Beaver and muskrat are common where there is water. Such animals suffered from overhunting until the Soviet government took urgent steps to preserve a number of species; hence populations have somewhat recovered and fur is an important product of the forest, though the number of hunters has declined. But changes in the ecosystem of the forest zone arising from forest fires and logging have an unfavourable effect on several valuable species of sable and pine marten.

To the west and south of the tayga, the more oceanic climate of the central part of the European plain of the USSR allows the dominance on richer soils of broad-leaved deciduous trees such as oak (*Quercus*) and elm (*Ulmus*); conifers such as pine and spruce, however, occupy poorer soils. Much extension of agriculture has taken place in this mixed forest region, following clearance of the more favourable soils and the draining of marshes and peat bogs. Near the Ural mountains, this type of vegetation disappears as a result of increasing continentality of climate and it is replaced in Siberia by a narrow transitional belt of birch which separates the tayga from the semi-arid steppe and wooded steppe region.

In the extreme south-east of the tayga, in the Soviet Far East, the sub-arctic boreal forest is replaced in lowland areas by vegetation of temperate type, analogous to that of the European mixed forest. The monsoonal climate with warm, humid summers in this area is associated in the valleys of the Amur and Ussuri with species-rich broad-leaved forests of deciduous oak, lime (*Tilia*) and ash (*Fraxinus*). The variety of species is particularly large in the Ussuri area where the flora is enriched by elements from Manchurian and Japanese sources. As in Europe, however the demands of economic development have reduced the cover of natural vegetation.

THE FOREST SOILS

As we have pointed out, the soil mantle is formed by the interaction of such factors as geology, the vegetation and animal life, and the climatic elements such as temperature, precipitation and evaporation. In the forested regions of the USSR, the cold winters, heavy snowfall and short summers create soil conditions in which the loss of moisture through evaporation and transpiration is much less than the input resulting from precipitation. Hence there is a predominantly downward movement of moisture through the profile, transferring material derived from the surface towards the lower layers. This is the process of podzolisation; it affects a large proportion of the soil cover of the Soviet Union, including both lowland and highland areas, and amounting to about 52% of the total area of the country.

Podzolisation is most pronounced in the tayga where a layer composed of decaying plant debris or 'litter' accumulates on the surface of the soil. Acids are formed in this horizon as it undergoes decomposition by bacteria and fungi, so that a layer of acid humus is developed immediately beneath it, the humus layer. The acids from this layer increase the solvent powers of percolating rainwater so that minerals are washed out or 'eluviated' from the upper horizon of soil producing a white or ash-coloured bleached layer of the characteristic podzol (*zola* is the Russian word for ashes), composed largely of insoluble silica. Farther down the profile, oxides and mineral colloids are precipitated, forming the subsoil horizon of illuviation, usually reddish-brown and rich in iron and aluminium, but also acid in reaction, and often containing an actual thin layer of iron which may impede drainage or penetration of plant roots. Beneath it is the layer of parent material, often till, sand or other material of glacial origin.

Such soils are of low agricultural productivity and their capacity for cropping decreases rapidly unless they are treated with applications of organic and mineral fertilisers and intensive liming. Some types of podzol become gleyed in their lower layers as a result of seasonal flooding by ground water, with the development of deep peat near the surface; in this case cultivation, or conversion to pasture is possible only after drainage.

Soils associated with deciduous forests are common in the mixed forest zone. The litter of deciduous trees is richer in nutrients than the needles of conifers and produces a less acid humus in which earthworms and other soil fauna can live. Leaching occurs but the process is reduced in conditions of greater evaporation resulting from the warmer summers; the eluviated lower surface horizon and the darker illuviated subsoil horizon are present but the distinction is much less apparent as material from each horizon is mixed by the activity of the abundant earthworms and other soil fauna. The subsoil is a brown loam or clay, moderately acid. Such soils are the brown podzolic soils, commonly developed from clayey glacial drift or shaley or limestone parent materials. Although moderately fertile, their continued productivity requires applications of lime to counteract acidity together with a farming system that includes crop rotation and animal husbandry.

The Steppe Zones

Southwards of the forests, in both the European and west Siberian areas of the USSR, gradual climatic changes give rise to several distinctive belts or zones of vegetation and soils. The climate is characterised by an increase to the south and south-east in summer temperatures and evaporation but a decrease in rainfall, so that aridity becomes progressively increased. The dominance of climatic influence upon the vegetation and soil is emphasised by the uniformity of relief and of soil parent material, the latter consisting predominantly of wind-blown loess which has a high potential fertility.

Separating the forests from the open steppe grasslands is a belt of transition, known as *forest-steppe*, formed of stands of deciduous woodland alternating with open grasslands. Each type of vegetation is associated with a different but related soil type: the deciduous woodland with grey forest soils and the steppe grassland with chernozem (black-earth) soils. Both types are now much modified by the development of agriculture, resulting from the fertility of the soils which, though occupying only about 15% of the area of the USSR, make a very important contribution to food production.

The tracts of woodland of the European forest-steppe are dominated by oaks, but in Siberia where climatic conditions are more severe, the arboreal vegetation is represented by birch with an admixture of aspen and willow. The trees indicate the advance of deciduous species from the north into the grassland zone during a period of increased precipitation in post-glacial times and prior to the commencement of agriculture, and consequent disturbance of the natural vegetation and soil, by man. Associated with the wooded areas are grey

forest soils consisting of an upper grey organic horizon above an eluviated layer depleted of clay and organic matter. Below this leached layer is a subsoil horizon enriched with clay and humus. The lowest horizon comprises a little-altered parent material of loess or loess-like loam.

The forest-steppe gives way southwards to the true steppe, the open, treeless grassland which forms a wide, rolling plateau extending from the Carpathian mountains across the Ukraine to central Siberia, broad in European USSR but narrowing east of the Urals. The entire area is subject to drought and the effective rainfall in the zone is insufficient for tree growth as the light spring rains moisten only the top horizon of the soil and the strong winds promote evaporation and transpiration of moisture from vegetation.

The natural vegetation consisted of drought-resistant perennial and annual herbaceous plants, dominated by various grass species, green and lush in the spring and early summer but turning yellow and brown in the droughts of late summer when prairie fires were common. For many centuries the steppes were grazed by herbivorous animals— herds of antelope and wild horses together with many types of small burrowing rodents which were the prey of wolves and eagles; the steppes were also the grazing territory of nomadic herdsmen but were gradually brought into cultivation during the expansion of the Russian state.

The grassland changes in composition from north to south with the gradual reduction in soil moisture in that direction. The steppes richest in plant species occupy a northern zone, formed of meadow steppes where the grasses are mixed with many types of flowering herbs such as legumes, daisies and irises. Southwards in drier conditions the proportion of the latter is reduced and the vegetation is dominated by tussocks of narrow-leaved feather grasses, accompanied by herbs having deep roots allowing them to tap the deeper layers of soil. Both types of steppe are developed upon chernozem soils. Beyond them to the south, the semi-arid conditions give rise to the poor steppe where there are open communites of scattered plants separated by bare soil. Here the tussock grasses are accompanied by dwarfed drought-resistant shrubs, together with many annual plants which flower quickly during spring rains and then die or remain dormant in the form of seeds. Halophytes, or plants tolerant of saline soils are also common. This poorer type of vegetation occupies the zone of the chestnut soils.

THE STEPPE SOILS

The soils of the richer steppes are the famous chernozems, named after the layer of black or dark-grey organic matter forming the surface horizon. This is the product of the decay of the dense network of roots of the grasses, together with the activity of the abundant earthworms and other soil fauna which mixes the organic matter throughout the upper soil profile. Intense activity of bacteria in the moister conditions of spring releases nitrogen, calcium and other plant nutrients, and the latter remain close to the surface as leaching is counteracted by the strong evaporation and transpiration. Some leaching of the profile does occur in the northern part of the zone, where precipitation is greater, producing the soil called 'leached chernozem.' The former advance of forest trees on to the steppe by depositing leaf litter on to the surface and by reducing evaporation has promoted leaching and the formation there of the grey forest soils.

Steppe soils are derived from a parent material of loess, an aeolian deposit rich in lime, providing a reservoir of nutrients. They sustain much of the Soviet Union's cereal production, but their natural fertility is often reduced by the frequency of droughts or by strong dessicating winds. They are also affected by wind or water erosion unless an adequate plant cover is maintained. These adverse influences have given rise to the policy of planting drought-resistant trees to serve as windbreaks or 'shelterbelts'.

Within the zone of the chernozems, subdivisions are applied according to soil depth and degree of leaching; the 'deep' and 'normal' chernozems have a humus horizon up to one metre in depth, but increasing aridity southwards is accompanied by a shallower humus layer in the 'southern' chernozems; these grade into the chestnut soils of the poor steppe.

These grassland soils of the USSR have undergone major changes in the type of land use since 1954 as a result of the increase in the area of arable land and a reduction in the area of hay, pasture and uncultivated land. About 21 million hectares of the soils are today under the plough, and of these 10 million hectares are chernozem and grey forest soils and 11 million hectares are chestnut soils. Further extension of cultivation of the soils is considered possible but only if accompanied by measures to combat erosion or the application of irrigation or of specialised techniques.

The chestnut soils, like the chernozems, have a wide distribution and are found in the south of the Ukraine and along the western shores of the Caspian Sea, extending from there into western Siberia and Kazakhstan, forming a transition between the chernozems and the desert soils. They take their name from the chestnut-brown colour of the upper horizon. As the natural vegetation of the zone is sparser than in the richer steppes, the supply of organic matter is reduced and the upper horizon is much shallower. There is little leaching because of the strong evaporation and low precipitation so that soluble materials remain in the upper part of the soil profile, and a layer rich in lime just below this. Such soils are much less fertile than the chernozems and crop production in them is frequently reduced by drought.

The poorest soils of this zone are the *solonchak* and the similar *solonets* soils whose names are derived from the Russian word for salt. They commonly develop in depressions or in valleys without continuous drainage. Solonchak soils form snow-white patches in the landscape in areas where ground-water containing dissolved salts rises by capillarity to the surface and evaporates, forming a crust of sodium sulphate or other salt. Solonets soils are derived from solonchaks under conditions of increased precipitation or during the application of irrigation water to the solonchak; this produces limited leaching at the surface and salts are moved down the profile. The result is a thin, greyish, friable upper horizon overlying a distinct lower horizon, darker in colour, with a strongly alkaline reaction. Neither solonchak nor solonets soils are of much value for cultivation because of their unfavourable physical and chemical properties.

The Desert and Semi-Desert Zone

Desert or semi-desert conditions extend southwards of the poor steppe and chestnut soil zones and cover the great basin of inland drainage between the Caspian Sea and the highlands of Soviet Central Asia in the Turkmen, Uzbek, Tadzhik and Kazakh republics. The great heat of summers, the cold winters and the low and irregular rainfall, and the presence of large expanses of loose sand or of salt-encrusted soil all form adverse environments for plant and animal life which exhibit characteristic desert adaptations.

Among the commonest forms of plant life in the region are the true xerophytes, plants able to endure long droughts and to utilise the scanty rainfall by means of long roots which reach supplies of moisture situated at great depth in the soil. Above ground the plants are low shrubs or small trees with reduced, spiny or otherwise modified leaves so that moisture losses through transpiration are minimised. Examples include the artemisias, low perennial shrubs, common in such deserts as the Betpak-Dala, and the saxauls, which are small trees tolerant of shifting sand and of saline soils, frequent in the Karakum. Artemisia shrubs are the main fodder of the northern desert pastures and support sheep flocks.

Short-lived or ephemeral plants are also abundant in the Soviet deserts, particularly in the southern foothills area, where the scanty spring rains support a variety of shallow-rooted herbaceous species. These are present in the soil as dormant seeds but germinate after sufficient rain and flower rapidly in a short vegetative period of a few weeks. The soil becomes covered by sedges, grasses, poppies, crowfoots and other herbs which wither and die as the soil dries in the heat of summer. Such temporary vegetation provides good pastures for livestock.

The desert environment gives rise to adaptations by the fauna as well as by its plant life; its unique animal world contains only those species able to adapt to high air and soil temperatures and lack of water. Many of the smaller animal groups avoid midday heat by retreat into burrows, exemplified by the jerboas, and also by many kinds of reptile, such as snakes and lizards, emerging for feeding after sundown. The large hoofed herbivores include the saiga antelope and the gazelle, animals that were once abundant, but are now much fewer because of hunting or loss of habitat to agriculture.

THE DESERT SOILS

These soils cover about 9.5% of the area of the USSR. They are derived from loess parent material or from mainly unconsolidated sands, the latter of alluvial, subaerial or fluvio-glacial origin. Soils of the sandy deserts such as the Karakum and the Kyzylkum are associated with localised areas where there is sufficient moisture for plant life, such as in depressions between sand dunes; for the root systems of plants not only stabilise shifting sand but add organic matter which conserves moisture. But large areas without vegetation have a layer only of raw mineral material.

The most valuable soils of the desert zone are those of the extensive southern foothill belt. These are moistened by light spring rains and carry a vegetation of desert ephemeral plants. Such soils are the *serozems* or grey desert soils; they become very fertile when watered and have been in cultivation for many centuries in the numerous oases in this area, where cotton is an important crop. Serozems are developed upon loess; the surface horizon is grey in colour with a low content of organic material; the soil is rich in calcium carbonate with poorly defined horizons, although some leaching of soluble salts takes place.

The Sub-tropical Zones

Sub-tropical lowland forest occurs only in a relatively small region, in Transcaucasia. The hot summers, warm winters and abundant all-season rainfall give rise to dense woodland of great luxuriance and variety, although most has been cleared for settlement and agriculture. Marshy lowland areas have forests of oak, hornbeam and beech, with climbing plants such as ivy and grapevine. Evergreen trees are also represented, including holly and box, and large tree-ferns grow in some areas. The eastern part of the area, however, in Azerbaydzhan has a drier climate, colder in winter; in the lower Kura valley is a natural poor steppe and semi-desert area where the alluvial grey desert soils require irrigation for crop production.

Mediterranean conditions, characterised by a mild winter with a moderate rainfall and a hot, dry summer, occur in a very limited area in the Soviet Union, where protection from cold influences by relief occurs, together with influences from the Black Sea and the Mediterranean Sea. Along the coast of the Crimean peninsula this environment is associated with xerophytic woodland areas of oak and juniper with groves of pine at higher altitudes. The woodland undergrowth contains evergreen shrubs typical of the Mediterranean such as rockrose, laurel and myrtle. Many types of fruit tree flourish in this region including peach, pomegranate and olive; vineyards are prominent in the landscape in the Yalta area.

The characteristic soils of the humid sub-tropics are yellow and red earths. They occur on the lower slopes of the north-west Caucasus in the Kolkhid valley, where heavy all-season rainfall is combined with hot summers and warm winters. They are clay soils that have developed largely from igneous rocks and the weathered soil mantle is relatively deep, often several feet in depth. They are leached soils, reddish in colour in their lower layers owing to the presence of residual iron-oxides, but the upper horizons contain plenty of organic material. These soils, when cleared of forest, yield crops of tea and citrus fruits.

The Highland Zones

The vegetation and soils of highland areas are extremely varied and reflect the local variations of slope, parent rock, exposure, temperature and precipitation. As a result of soil movement by forces of gravity, horizon development is often prevented or modified, particularly where the vegetation cover has been disturbed, allowing soil erosion and downhill movement of materials. The nature of the various vertical zones of vegetation and soils which accompany the changes in climate produced by altitude depends upon the latitude of the highland areas and on the regional climates.

As exemplified by the Caucasus, these high Alpine-type mountain ranges rise to well over 5000 m (Elbrus, the highest peak in Europe is 5642 metres). As they form an important climatic divide, there are great contrasts between the north and south facing slopes, well exemplified by the Great Caucasus range which separates poor steppe and semi-desert environments to the north from the humid sub-tropical conditions to the south.

On the south side, the warm-temperate forests give way upwards at about 1000–1500 m to forests of beech, developed on brown forest soils; above these at about 1200–1800 m are dark coniferous forests. These grow in cool, humid conditions and their soils are podzolic, resembling those of the northern tayga. Above the limit of tree growth, alpine and sub-alpine meadows extend upwards to the zone of permanent snow and glaciers; mosses, lichens, dwarf-shrubs and flowering herbs constitute the natural vegetation, which is used for summer pasturage. The soils are often shallow, stony and subject to gravitational movement; a peaty upper layer may be present.

All the highland areas of the USSR show conspicuous vertical vegetation/soil zones, analogous to those of the Caucasus. In the higher latitudes the belts occur at lower altitudes: thus in north and north-east Siberia, the tree-line is much lower and in highland areas such as the Verkhoyansk and Kolyma mountain ranges there are forests of larch, birch and pine and above these are tundra areas of lichens, mosses and sedges. An important feature of the Altay, the Sayan mountains and other highlands along the southern border of Siberia is an extensive area covered by mountain steppe. In the Altay ranges the lowest zone consists of a rich grassland rising in places to over 1000 m and it is used for pasture and for crop production. Forests usually succeed the grassland with increasing altitude but are replaced above the tree limit by alpine-type tundras or alpine meadows where the vegetation closely resembles that of the northern polar tundras; plants are dwarfed woody or herbaceous perennials, often bearing bright flowers such as the gentians, the saxifrages and the edelweiss. Mosses and lichens occupy the most exposed habitats.

The Altay ranges show the characteristic zonation of animal life associated with the belts of vegetation, and both flora and fauna include many species that are endemic to the area. The high alpine tundras at about 2400 m in the south are the habitat of ptarmigan, dotterel and other mountain birds. Somewhat lower, within the sparse forests near the upper tree-line are the large herbivores, the Siberian ibex, the stag and the musk deer; the ibex is the favoured prey of the rare and beautiful snow leopard. Some of the mountain animals move to lower altitudes in winter but many of the smaller species such as the rodents hibernate or store food. At these lower altitudes of the Altay, dense forests of larch and pine occur; they contain a varied animal life, providing seeds and fruits for herbivores like chipmunks and nutcrackers and harbouring also carnivores such as wolves and bears. But man's actions have reduced the forest cover, extending meadowland in the interests of cattle grazing or cultivation and reducing wild animal populations.

THE CONSERVATION OF VEGETATION AND SOILS

The Soviet social system and planned management of the economy appears to embody great potential for the rational use of the natural resources. But in the drive to achieve industrialisation, urbanisation and an adequate food supply there has in fact been as much neglect of the need for environmental protection as in any of the capitalist countries. This need is recognised but there are still substantial shortcomings in the matter of conservation. This is pointed out in the Conservation Laws of the RSFSR.

The extension of cultivation has, of course, involved widespread deforestation and also the conversion of natural grassland to pasture or arable land. Great areas have been made productive by drainage of waterlogged land or by the irrigation of dry land; natural animal communities have been modified or destroyed by overhunting or by loss of habitat. These environmental changes have also involved important changes in the character of the soil, not always with favourable results.

The Wetlands

In the more humid western regions, glaciation has resulted in a morainic type of undulating landscape with very extensive low-lying tracts where the soils are affected by impeded drainage, poor aeration and the formation of gleying in their lower horizons. Other very large areas have developed a soil cover which is purely organic in composition, consisting of a deep layer of peat, being composed of the remains of swamp, bog or mire vegetation such as reeds, sedges and mosses. Originally, such plants formed the littoral or aquatic vegetation of glacial lakes. When these soils are drained, the aeration is improved and in time nutrients within the peaty soils become available to agricultural crops, and high yields of, for example, animal foodstuffs may be obtained from them, or they can be made to produce valuable timber. Peat is also used as a fuel for electric power stations.

A notice at a conservation park (Zapovednik) in the Caucasus mountains, organised in 1936 to protect the 'unique natural complex'

Drainage is especially important in the Baltic countries, in Belorussia, in the northern Ukraine and in other European areas where such wetlands abound. In pre-revolutionary Russia gradual progress was made in draining large swampy lands such as the Polesye, that is, the basin of the river Pripyat and middle Dnepr and the Meshchera depression in the Oka valley, south-east of Moscow. However it is estimated that excessively wet land even today still comprises at least 25 % of these western areas where the land is either unusable or seasonally waterlogged. Soviet agronomists have commented upon the relatively high crop yields obtainable from drained land in the area but have stressed the inadequacy of the measures being taken at present for further reclamation.

The most extensive areas of such land are in western Siberia and it is estimated that at least one half of the great river Ob lowland area is subject to mire or peat-bog formation. Some of the swamps cover areas of 10 000 km² or more; the great Vasyuganye bog, the largest in the world, covers an area of about 53 000 km² and the intensity of bog-forming processes there is greater than similar processes known anywhere else in the world, and they affect all the natural zones from tundra to wooded steppe regions.

The bogs contain very large peat reserves, estimated at about 104 billion tons. They overlie rich mineral-bearing areas and their future development poses an important problem for conservation of the environment; some investigators believe that bogs should be drained. Thereafter the land could be converted to agricultural use. Yet it is only in the southern region of the west Siberian plain that the physical conditions appear to be favourable for such use. It is also considered that the great mires of the area should be used as the basis for the construction of power stations and chemical industries, making use of peat as fuel and raw material. But conservationists believe that peat bogs should not be disturbed as they represent the evolution of natural processes continued for many thousands of years and still in progress, as evidenced by the fact that there is competition between the forests and the mires. Drainage may affect the adjacent regions and reduce total precipitation in the neighbouring southern areas where even in present conditions drought is a problem.

At the present time west Siberian peat is used

both as fuel (e.g. in the Tyumensk thermal power station) and as a fertiliser (in the Tomsk and Omsk regions). The development of oil and gas fields in the area has required the construction of roads across the mires and the wells are often sited in them. This leads to the disturbance of the natural conditions of the mires, although the damage is considered not to constitute a real danger to the environment. Future utilisation appears to depend upon the determination of which mires should be preserved for their scenic and scientific value, and which should be turned into productive forest lands and used as a source of timber, with areas set aside for recreation and hunting. In the tundra and forest-tundra, the drained bogs would provide pasturage for deer farming.

Forest depletion

One of the principal renewable resources of the Soviet Union is the forest, the bulk of which forms the great northern tayga and consists mainly of coniferous softwood species. Maintenance of adequate forest reserves is vital on the grounds of both the economy and the environmental quality.

Forests fulfil an essential protective role; they protect the land and the soil from erosion, deflation and waterlogging; a forest cover shields the soil from the direct impact of rain and increases the absorptive property of the soil so that runoff is regulated. Riparian forests lessen the turbulence of rivers and the loss from evaporation, and near towns are of recreational and cultural significance. Runoff develops from the entire area of drainage and can be regulated only by a uniform distribution of forests over the watershed. If, however the basin is completely cleared of forests, runoff is unchecked, gullies and ravines are formed, allowing soil to be carried into the main river causing silting and damage to fish populations.

Despite the immense area of the forests and the seemingly inexhaustible nature of the resource, the adverse effects of long-continued heavy exploitation are apparent. Most of this has in past years been in the more accessible forests of the European part of the RSFSR where there is now an increasing shortage of good timber and hence an increasing dependence upon the reserves situated east of the Urals. But in the tayga as a whole, inadequate replacement of trees removed is evident; of the 3 million hectares of timber cut annually, only 30–75% is currently restored and 10–15% is not afforested at all so that there are large barren cut-

over areas in the forest; such clearings soon become invaded by secondary deciduous trees consisting of birch, aspen or scrub species which replace the more valuable stands of pine or spruce.

The development of the timber industry in Siberia has resulted in widespread clearances, as for example in the Irkutsk area. This depletion has been the result of the non-intensive use of timber resources and the wasteful discarding of material. Under Siberian conditions timber grows slowly so that the period of renewal of commercial reserves is prolonged. In western Siberia the expansion of the timber industry has had a considerable impact upon the forest ecosystem. As the cut-over area along the newly-built Ivdel-Ob railway has increased, followed by the expansion of settlement, there has been excessive trapping and poaching among the local beaver and sable populations. Because of their limited reproductive capacity the two species are now threatened with extinction in the area. Lumbering operations in the drainage basins tend to disturb runoff and the regime of the beaver streams, with adverse effects on the ecology of the beaver habitat. It is considered that as lumbering expands into the forest animal reserves in the Sosva river basin excessive trapping will cause the sable and other animals to disappear from some of the more accessible areas.

In addition to the losses of forest through logging, extensive tracts of the forest have been destroyed during the flooding of river valleys such as the Volga for the creation of the great reservoirs supplying water to the hydro-electric stations. Losses have been particularly great in Siberia as a result of the construction of huge projects such as that at Bratsk, requiring the destruction of river-bank forests of high productivity. In the basins of southern rivers inundation frequently destroys the only forests in existence. The total loss of timber is estimated at more than 1000 million cubic metres.

In the future, further forest clearances will be required, however, in response to the demand to extend agriculture upon suitable forest soils. In north-western USSR such soils play an important part in the production of milk, vegetables, flax and potatoes. The aim is to preserve some integration of forestry with the needs of agriculture so that farm settlements may have a sufficient amount of forest maintained for a supply of timber, for the shelter of the farm land and for recreational needs. Forest and woodlands have also an increasingly important role in the creation of green belts and

Accelerated soil erosion on the slopes of a valley, Tadzhikistan, where the dry climate results in soil being easily removed when occasional rain occurs, with wind an added threat

parks around cities, as in the case of the forest-park belt which surrounds Moscow.

Soil erosion

Soil erosion in the USSR has in recent years caused great concern among environmentalists. The processes of soil erosion are initiated by misuse of the land by man after removal of the protective cover of the natural vegetation. The formation of a mature soil may take many thousands of years yet it may be torn away right down to the parent rock material within a short time by erosion. Agriculture, the chief cause of erosion, is of course seriously affected, but other branches of the economy are usually also damaged: floods occur in river valleys resulting from the rapid runoff, and rapid silting takes place in river channels and in reservoirs. It has been estimated that the total area of the USSR subject to soil erosion is about 50 million hectares of which 30 million hectares are arable land. The degree of liability to erosion differs according to conditions, especially climatic conditions (Fig. 4.3).

Running water and wind are the chief agents of soil erosion and both of these have caused serious soil losses in the USSR. Sheet, rill and gully erosion are the types associated with running water. Initially, water moving as a sheet or film uniformly down a slope becomes concentrated into small channels or rills which become deepened and widened into small ravines or gullies. The latter develop branching systems and their coalescence removes the entire soil cover including humus, nutrients and micro-organisms so that a wasteland is produced. Wind erosion (deflation) is common in arid or subhumid regions where the soils are light-textured such as sandy loams. Strong winds carry away the upper layer of the soil, killing crops by blowing them away or by burying them under dust. The dust accumulates on fields, on roads or on sources of freshwater or settlements.

Study of gully formation in the steppe and wooded steppe areas of the European USSR has shown that most gullies have been formed as a result of ploughing of land over a period of 150 to 300 years and can therefore be assumed to be the result of human activity. Gully development has been initiated by the destruction of the protective cover of vegetation followed by the deep ploughing of steeply sloping land and the formation of dirt tracks by farm vehicles.

The problem of soil loss through gullying is present also in the central region of the USSR (west Siberia, Kazakhstan and Central Asia). Within this great area the contrasts in climate, relief and agricultural use influence the character

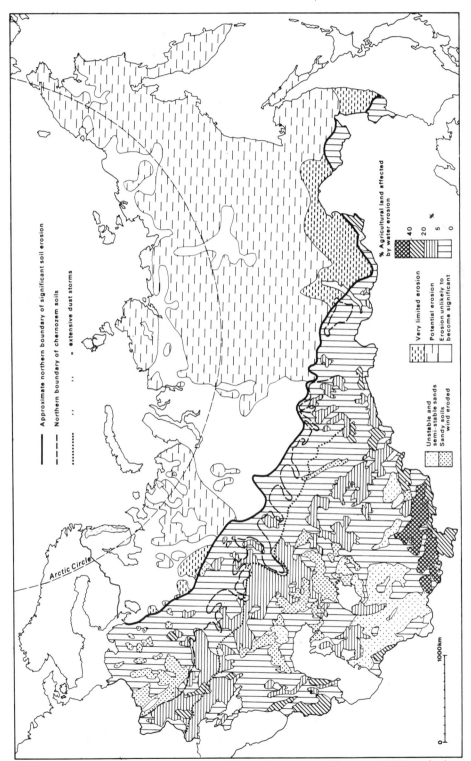

Fig. 4.3 Soil erosion   *Sources: Atlas sel'skogo khozyaystvo, Silvestrov (1971) and others*

and the intensity of the erosion. It occurs in the areas subject to permafrost because running water tends to have a thermal impact on the upper layers of frozen ground, thus reducing its resistance to erosion. In the wooded steppe and steppe areas the hazard is serious because of the friable nature of the subsoil and the intensity of the runoff following heavy showers of rain. Gullying is however less likely in the forested zones and also in the deserts unless irrigation is applied.

With regard to wind erosion, this form of soil damage has been characteristic particularly of the steppe region, affecting the chernozem and chestnut soils, often in circumstances where the natural cohesion of soil particles has been lost through overcropping. The strong dry winds or *sukhovey* which affect the open plains create formidable dust storms and 'dust bowl' conditions. The Ukraine suffered such storms after the cultivation of the steppe grassland in Tsarist times but these were intensified after the collectivisation campaign so that 5 oblasts lost one million hectares of soil between 1950 and 1960. Khrushchev's decision to plough large areas of the virgin lands of western Siberia and Kazakhstan, which took effect from 1954, resulted in frequent and destructive dust storms in those areas. Published data indicate the extensive scale of wind erosion in the USSR. In 1952 dust storms destroyed about 18% of the agricultural area of the Bashkir ASSR and

thousands of hectares of crops in the Kuban region. In Pavlodar oblast in 1955 nearly 170 000 hectares of crop land were damaged and about 127 000 hectares of crops were destroyed; in 1956, much the same occurred. Again in 1955 in Omsk oblast, deflation destroyed 20% to 58% of the sown grain. In the 1950s, an estimated 5–6 million hectares of sown land in the steppe areas were subjected annually to deflation and of this, up to 1.5 million hectares were completely destroyed.

Conservation measures are being applied to the problem of soil damage by the various union republics; they include rotation systems of different crops so that exposure of bare soil to damage by water or wind is avoided; contour ploughing, or ploughing along the slope; controlled grazing of pasture land; the planting of shelterbelts of trees which lessen surface runoff of water and also break the force of the wind. This last measure is of particular importance in the sparsely wooded steppe region where it is considered that the protective function of forestry has not been given adequate scope in erosion and deflation control. Plans for large-scale planting of shelter strips have been only partially fulfilled and many areas still require protection of this kind.

The soils of the semi-arid and arid zones of the USSR are potentially productive as the high summer temperatures and long growing season of these areas make them ideal for cotton and other

Accelerated erosion in the Caucasus mountains resulting from deforestation and overgrazing

sub-tropical crops; irrigation is however necessary and irrigation brings its own problems in soil management. Irrigation practices on such soils can improve or impair their usefulness as crop soils; problems of salt accumulation are commonly encountered, produced by the evaporation of saline groundwater at the soil surface, which is damaging to crops. Excess irrigation raises the watertable, leading to soil damage through waterlogging.

Conservation of the northern areas

The economic development of the Soviet north has led to an increasing concern among conservationists for the protection of the wilderness areas of the tundra and the northern tayga. These ecosystems are extremely vulnerable to disturbance and recent research has indicated that man's activities have been affecting the environment in many ways.

The soil and vegetation cover has been altered in distribution and composition. As a result of man's impact, which started many centuries ago, combined with natural processes, the northern boundary of the tayga is retreating southwards, allowing the forest-tundra sub-zone to advance in that direction, increasing its total area by an estimated 0.5% every year. This recession of the forest margin has resulted from economic development of the area with settlements, road and railway building and mining, all of which have been accompanied by forest fires. However, an important additional factor is the migration of great herds of reindeer across the forest boundary twice yearly as they move from winter quarters in the forest towards their summer grazings on the tundras. They exert grazing pressure on the vegetation by eating leaves, young shoots and trampling plants, and the herds are tended by large numbers of reindeer herders who use bushes and trees for fuel; this often results in forest fires.

An intensive development of thermokarst-erosion relief coincides with the first arrival of heavy vehicles on the tundra, destroying the delicate moss/herb cover. This removes the insulating cover of vegetation so that the depth of the thawed layer increases. Depressions of the surface are thus formed which become marshes, ponds and lakes, or they lead to the formation of erosion channels. Caterpillar tractors are particularly destructive of tundra plants, and the use of these vehicles promotes this type of damage to the environment. Studies in the tundras of the Yenisey basin in Siberia have shown that lichens are among the most important plants to be destroyed by human activity as they provide winter forage for the reindeer herds.

Areas where there is intensive industrial and mining development are characterised by other types of impact. Around Vorkhuta there is atmospheric pollution by gases such as sulphur dioxide which is injurious to plant life, causing the disappearance of lichen growth and altering the species composition of the moss cover. Waste water discharged from pits, together with sewage from settlement, causes damage to fish, invertebrate populations and plant life of streams and lakes. Similarly, the smelting of non-ferrous metals at Monchegorsk in the Kola peninsula produces emissions of sulphur dioxide damaging to trees, mosses and lichens in the area.

BIBLIOGRAPHY

Averyanov, S. F., Minayeva, E. N. and Timoshkina, V. A. (1971), *Increasing agricultural productivity through irrigation and drainage*, in Gerasimov *et al.* (eds.), 1971, pp. 131–160.

Borzhonov, B. B., Borozdin, E. K., Dyachenko, N. O. and Zabrodin, V. A. (1976), 'The domestic reindeer industry, influence on the flora and fauna of the tundra of the USSR,' in symposium, *Geography of polar countries*, XXIII International Geographical Congress, Leningrad, pp. 134–135.

Conservation Law of the Russian Republic. *Pravda* 28 Oct. 1960, p. 2, translated in *Current Digest of the Soviet Press*, Vol. XII, No. 44, 30 Nov., 1960.

Cox, C. B. Healey, I. N. and Moore, P. D. (1976), *Biogeography, an ecological and evolutionary approach*, London.

Doncheva, A. V. and Kalutskov, V. N. (1977), Prediction of the environmental impact of mining and metallurgical production in the tayga zone, *Soviet Geography*, **18**, pp. 223–229.

FAO/UNESCO (1972), *Soil maps of the world.* UNESCO, Paris.

French, R. A. (1964), 'The reclamation of swamp in pre-revolutionary Russia.' *Trans. Inst. Br. Geogr.*, **34**, pp. 175–188.

Gayel, A. G., Doskach, A. G. and Trushkovskiy, A. A. (1961), O pylnykh buryakh v marte-aprele 1960, *Isvestiya AN SSSR Seriya Geogr.*, 1961, No. 1.

Gerasimov, I. P. and Glazovskaya, M. A. (1965), *Fundamentals of soil science and soil geography.* Trans. IPST, Jerusalem.

Gerasimov, I. P., Armand, D. L. and Yefron, K. M. (eds.) (1971), *Natural resources of the Soviet Union, their use and renewal*, translation ed. W. A. D. Jackson, Freeman, San Francisco.

Goldman, M. I. (1972), *The spoils of progress, environmental pollution in the Soviet Union*, MIT Press, Cambridge, Mass.

Kosov, B. F., Zorina, Ye. F., Konstantinova, G. S. and Lyubimov, B. I. (1977), 'The gullying hazard in the Midland region of the USSR in conjunction with economic development,' *Soviet Geography*, **18**, pp. 172–178.

Kryuchkov, V. V. (1976), The change of the northern environment as a result of its use, in symposium, *Geography of Polar Countries*, XXIII International Geographical Congress, Leningrad, pp. 129–131.

Medvedkova, E. A. and Malykh, G. I. (1973), 'Cartographic evaluation of the use of timber resources in the Irkutsk oblast.' *Soviet Geography*, **14**, pp. 184–194.

Neishtadt, M. I. (1977), 'The world's largest peat basin, its commercial potentialities and protection,' *Bulletin, International Peat Society*, No. 8, pp. 37–43.

Osakov, Yu. A., Kirikov, S. V. and Formozov, A. N. (1971), 'Land game,' in Gerasimov *et al*, 1971, pp. 251–292.

Ponomanev, G. V. (1973), 'Changes in the wildlife population in the Sos'va section of the Ob basin as a result of human activity in the tayga,' *Soviet Geography*, **14**, pp. 356–362.

Proshchenko, V. F. (1965), 'Pyl'naya burya zimoy,' *Priroda*, 1965, No. 2.

Shelkunova, R. P. (1976), 'The lichen cover change caused by the human activity at the north of the Yenisey basin,' in symposium, *Geography of Polar Countries*, XXIII International Geographical Congress, Leningrad, pp. 136–137.

Silvestrov, S. I. (1971), 'Efforts to combat the processes of erosion and deflation of agricultural land,' in Gerasimov *et al*, 1971, pp. 161–183.

Sukachev, V. and Dylis, N. (1964), *Fundamentals of forest biogeocoenology*, Edinburgh.

Suslov, S. P. (1961), *Physical geography of Asiatic Russia*, London.

Uspensky, S. M., Vekhov, N. V., Kuliyev, A. N. and Lobanov, V. A. (1976), 'Protection of natural complexes of the Arctic and Sub-Arctic,' in symposium, *Geography of Polar Countries*, XXIII International Geographical Congress, Leningrad, pp. 126–129.

Vasilyev, P. V. (1971), 'Forest resources and forest economy,' in Gerasimov *et al*, 1971, pp. 187–215.

Walter, H. (1973), *Vegetation of the earth*, London.

Zorina, Ye. F., Kosov, B. F. and Prokhorova, S. D. (1977), 'The role of the human factor in the development of gullying in the steppe and wooded steppe of the European USSR,' *Soviet Geography*, **18**, pp. 48–55.

5 Water Resources

The vast area of the USSR allows her to claim a very large share of the global supply of moisture termed the hydrosphere. Her water resources include the maritime water of coasts and seas, the freshwater of rivers, streams and lakes, the moisture supply of the soil and the ground water contained in rock formations. Of these, it is the freshwater supply, derived mainly from rain and snow, that forms her most precious natural asset, for unlike most other resources, freshwater has no substitute. Water therefore occupies a unique place among the nation's renewable resources. Yet demands upon it are constantly increasing, for adequate water supplies are essential for almost all kinds of economic development.

The Soviet government has acknowledged these aspects of the water resource in the law of the Conservation of Natural Resources in the RSFSR (1960); all the sources of water are affected by it and emphasis was laid upon the need for planning and conservation of water supplies for the expansion of agriculture and forestry.

The Water Balance

The relationship between the supply of freshwater from precipitation and the subsequent losses of moisture from the land is shown in Table 5.1. Two fifths of the precipitation in the USSR (3340 km^3) are carried back to the sea by gravity and surface runoff (S). The most important part of the water balance is the volume of water absorbed by the land, the total soil water supply (W). This water either remains in the upper soil layers where it may evaporate, or it is utilised by vegetation in growth and in transpiration from leaf surfaces (E). A proportion of the soil water, however, moves downward beyond the reach of plant roots where it becomes the ground water; here it migrates through water-bearing rocks into rivers as underground runoff (U), or is retained in the rocks as a valuable subterranean reservoir. Hence, $W = P - S = E + U$.

TABLE 5.1 ANNUAL WATER BALANCE OF THE USSR

	km^3
Precipitation (P)	8,480
Total runoff	*4,220*
Underground (stable) runoff (U)	880
Surface runoff (S)	3,340
Total soil water supply (W)	5,140
Evaporation (incl. transpiration) (E)	4,260

Source: M. I. Lvovich *et al.*

A glance at a map of the river systems of the Soviet Union seems to indicate a country very well endowed with water resources, yet these are not nearly so favourable as they appear to be at first sight. Table 5.2 shows features of their distribution and individual characteristics. By far the greater proportion of the river flow to the sea passes through sparsely peopled regions, exemplified by the Ob and other great Siberian rivers which drain northwards to the Arctic Ocean; however the greater part of the Soviet population and the economic activity are clustered in the European area of the country. In contrast to the 155 000 rivers in Siberia there are only 45 000 in the European part, and in terms of quantity of water, the European inhabitants, who form about 70%

of the population, have to share only about 18 % of the water.

To this unsatisfactory geographical distribution of water we must add also the fact that there is an uneven seasonal distribution; 60 % of the rainfall comes in the spring and summer, so that spring flooding of the rivers is widespread, followed by low-water periods later in the year, and then a long period of freezing when surface flow ceases completely. There are also considerable annual fluctuations in precipitation which affect the water supplies. An alternation of cycles of high and low

TABLE 5.2 CHARACTERISTICS OF SOVIET RIVERS

Name of river	Drainage area (thousands of sq km)	length (km)	Average flow (thousands of m³/s)
Ob	2990	3650	12.5
Yenisey	2580	3487	17.5
Lena	2490	4400	15.5
Amur	1855	2824	11.5
Irtysh	1643	4248	3.0
Volga	1360	3531	8.0
Angara	1039	1779	4.2
Aldan	702	2240	5.2
Kolyma	647	2513	3.8
Kama	507	1805	3.8
Dnepr	504	2201	1.7
Amu Darya	309	1415	1.5
Syr Darya	219	2212	1.2
Northern Dvina	357	744	3.5
Pechora	327	1790	4.1

Sources: Atlas SSSR; Lavrishchev (1969).

water years occurs in different regions; an increase in river flow in the European area and in western Siberia frequently coincides with a decrease of flow in eastern Siberia; in the 1930s the opposite variation favoured eastern Siberia with a sharp decrease in river flow in eastern Europe, the Kazakh steppe and western Siberia. The Soviet Union also has 513 lakes with an area of 20–1000 km² and 24 lakes with an area of more than 1000 km² each.

The distribution of water resources
There are marked contrasts in the water resources of different regions of the Soviet Union resulting

from the regional variation in climate, relief and other factors of physical geography. In European Russia the rivers flow radially from upland watersheds situated centrally in the Russian plain, but the dominant directions are either northwards to Arctic waters or southwards to the Black Sea or the Caspian Sea. In spring, the thawing of the deep snow cover produces high flood levels in these rivers. The southward flowing rivers such as the Volga and the Dnepr leave their moist, forested source areas where they receive large tributaries and then cross the open treeless prairie grasslands where the higher summer temperatures, and the hot, dry winds and lower rainfall result in a reduction in surface runoff. Intense evaporation occurs, much increased in recent decades by the additional water surface area created by large storage reservoirs. The northern river basins represented by that of the Northern Dvina are endowed with extensive water resources. Divided from the Volga drainage by a long, low morainic ridge, the rivers meander slowly over the undulating, glaciated surface of the lowland. However, ice closes them for many winter months; navigation is impeded by ice at the mouth of the Pechora for about nine months of the year, but freezing is less severe in the upper courses so that navigation can begin some time before the lower reaches are open. There are widespread floods in spring, but much of the flood water is retained in the countless bogs, swamps, depressions and large lakes. Evaporation is less than in the case of the lower Volga and Dnepr as the climate is cooler in summer and there is a dense cover of coniferous forest; the geological structure also favours water regulation and retention by the many aquifers so that almost one-third of the runoff is in the form of an underground component.

Spring flooding also characterises the great rivers of Siberia. The Ob, the chief river of the west Siberian lowland, drains a vast basin and has a huge annual discharge (12 500 m³/s in its lower course). With its tributaries it is fed by ground water and by the steady flow from its vast watershed peat bogs and swamps as well as from innumerable lakes. As the west Siberian rivers are mostly fed by melting snow and ice they have a clearly pronounced spring flood period, but high water levels continue into the summer as the break-up of ice begins in the south and gradually advances northwards. Warm water in spring, coming from the southern Siberian steppe region, overflows the ice which is still obstructing navigation in the north and raises the level of the Ob and other rivers in the middle of summer. The spring ice flow on the Ob and the Irtysh is often accompanied by numerous ice jams, causing erosion of the river banks and damage to riverside installations.

In eastern Siberia the presence of permafrost becomes an important factor in the water regime of the rivers. The two longest rivers, the Yenisey and the Lena have average discharge rates greater than $15\,000\,\mathrm{m^3/s}$ so that they rank among the greatest in the world. But the intense cold of winter freezes them for long periods (Fig. 11.2), the ice becomes exceptionally thick and some rivers freeze right down to their bottoms. The spring runoff comprises the melting of snow, ice and rainfall, almost all of which is surface water, as the impermeable layer of permafrost prevents the infiltration of water to the subsoil. Ground water contribution to the runoff is thus minimal, but surface runoff is intense, and 90–95 % of the annual discharge occurs in the warm spring and summer months when river levels some 20 m above the normal cause extensive flooding. The small ground discharge is usually the primary source of water in early winter, but it stops completely when the active soil layer becomes frozen down to the permafrost. All the rivers are lowest in winter and highest in summer when their period of spate varies from one basin to another, depending upon local conditions of temperature and snow depth. Among the southern tributaries of the Yenisey, the powerful Angara is unique, as its source is Lake Baykal, a natural reservoir and one of the world's largest lakes. This endows the Angara not only with abundant water but with the most uniform discharge of all the eastern Siberian rivers.

WATER RESOURCES IN CENTRAL ASIA
The water balance has a critical importance within the great arid or semi-arid Turan lowland area east of the Caspian Sea, for its agriculture is almost entirely dependent upon irrigation. Here, the greatest area of land irrigated for arable crops in the Soviet Union is in the Central Asian republics and the southern part of Kazakhstan, where there are fertile soils within access of copious water supplies from streams originating in the abundant precipitation of the lofty mountain systems to the south of the region, the Tyan Shan, the Hindu

Kush and the Pamir–Alay. Most rivers from these highlands become dry as they emerge on to the hot, arid plains, but the two principal rivers, the Amu Darya and the Syr Darya, maintain their flow for the whole year, and after traversing the deserts of Kyzlkum and Karakum, enter the Aral Sea, a large brackish-water lake. These two rivers thus have immeasurable economic importance for the whole area, and the many irrigated oases within their basins have some of the highest rural population densities in the Soviet Union.

Central Asia has a closed hydrological cycle and is an inland drainage system without any stream connection to the ocean. The incoming water supply of the arid lowlands or piedmont areas is provided mainly by surface runoff from the mountains with some groundwater complement flowing within alluvial fans in the foothills. Most streams form expanses of swamp in the piedmont areas or are broken up into distributaries for irrigation and end in an intricate fan of irrigation canals. Intense evaporation of surface water occurs.

The Amu Darya and the Syr Darya, however, have a continuous heavy flow as they rise above the snow line in the mountains at or above a height of 3500 metres. They have two high-water periods: in spring (April–May) from the melting snow in the mountains, and in the summer (June–July) when glaciers begin to thaw. These rivers are the chief source of irrigation water. Rivers of snow-feeding such as the Angren, rising at lower latitudes, have a more variable discharge.

Nurek Lake, high in the Pamir Mountains, supplies water to the giant Nurek hydro-electric scheme, one of the greatest in the USSR, and especially valuable to a region in which water is scarce

The Amu Darya is the largest river of Central Asia. It rises on the north slopes of the Hindu Kush and is fed by vigorous tributaries, such as the Vakhsh, coming from high glaciers and snowfields which provide abundant melt-water in spring and summer. The lowest discharge is in January and February, the highest is in July, so that the regime is very favourable for irrigation as water becomes available at the start of the growing season in spring and the supply reaches its maximum in the summer months, just at the time of greatest need for irrigation. Apart from their inestimable value in supplying water for irrigation, Central Asian rivers carry, in suspension and solution, vast quantities of mineral material. The Amu Darya transports twice as much suspended alluvium as the Nile, most of which is taken up during the increased flow in summer. Deposited on bottomlands and terraces this alluvial soil is exceptionally productive, being rich in plant nutrients such as lime, potassium and phosphates.

Like the rivers of Central Asia, those of the Caucasus and the Soviet Far East have a maximum discharge during the summer months. The principal drainage basin of the Far East is that of the Amur. It receives substantial rainfall from warm monsoon winds from the Pacific Ocean and the rapid runoff produces flood levels of 10–15 m along the Amur and smaller rivers may flood after every intense downpour. At Khabarovsk the water level is highest between May and September but winter and spring levels are low as the winter snowfall of the region is light, although temperatures are severe enough to freeze the river for five months. The Amur is important for navigation and has considerable potential for more intensive use of its waters.

THE USE OF RIVER RESOURCES

In common with other industrialised countries, the Soviet Union has a vast and rapidly increasing consumption of river water for many essential requirements: for domestic supplies of drinking water and sewage disposal; for the production of electric power; for irrigation, and for the transport of passengers and freight. Estimates of the increase suggest that from 1965 to 1985 the use of water for the population will have increased fourfold, and for industry and agriculture, threefold (Oziranskii 1968). The increases are particularly heavy in the European part of the Soviet Union, where, as we have seen, there is least water available; industrial needs in the more developed areas will rise to 300–320 km³ each year. Many modern products make heavy demands upon water supply: thus cotton textile factories use about 250–300 m³ of water per tonne of fabric, and in the production of synthetic rubber, each tonne requires about 2,000 cubic metres of water; again, the refining of petroleum and the production of some metals uses a great amount of water.

Irrigation and drainage

An urgent need in the Soviet Union at the present time is a marked and permanent expansion of agricultural output from the southern steppe and poor steppe regions where the precipitation is variable and marginal for cropping; and also from the arid deserts and semi-deserts of Central Asia farther south. In both these areas climate and soils are favourable for development, but this is totally dependent upon the provision of additional supplies of water for irrigation. However, at the opposite end of the moisture spectrum are those areas where soils are waterlogged and drainage is required to make them productive. These are mainly in western European USSR and have been referred to in Chapter 4.

In 1980, Soviet irrigated land totalled over 17 million hectares, of which nearly half was in the Central Asian republics, traditionally an area of irrigated agriculture. Further developments are planned for this area. Much development of irrigation is also in progress in the Ukrainian and Siberian prairie regions of the USSR, where a considerable proportion of the Soviet cereal production is grown but where droughts are frequent. Small areas of irrigated land have been created in the Far East near the border with China.

IRRIGATION IN SOUTH-EAST EUROPEAN USSR
Rapid increases in irrigation have taken place in the Ukrainian SSR, the Volga region and the north Caucasus region of the RSFSR (Fig. 5.1). Water has been taken from the main rivers along canals leading from large reservoirs impounded behind dams. Seasonal floodwater has thus been controlled and stored, both for irrigation and for the generation of hydro-electric power, with facilities for river navigation. In the entire region, precipitation decreases from west to east (600–800 mm along the lower Dnepr to 100–200 mm

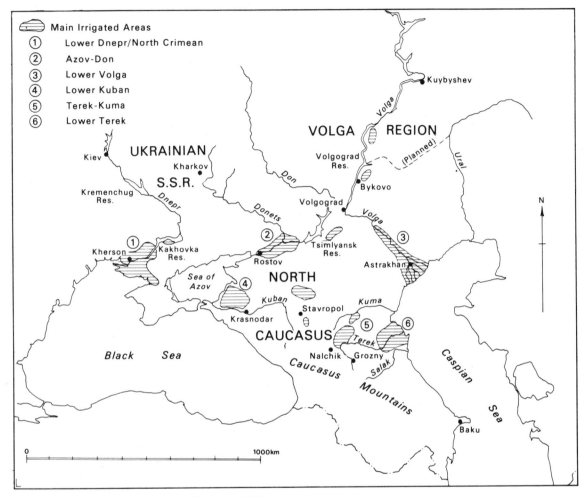

Fig. 5.1 Irrigation schemes, southern European USSR

along the lower Volga) so that the need for irrigation of crops becomes more and more essential eastward. Hence the north Caucasus region contains the largest concentration of irrigated land (1.3 million hectares) in the area, most of it along the lower Kuban and Don rivers. As an example of this development, the spring floodwater runoff of the Kuban River (which rises in the snowfields of Mount Elbrus, the highest of the Caucasus peaks) has been diverted so that part of the water irrigates a large area of the arid Stavropol steppe in two separate sections and also provides hydro-electric power for industrial development in the Stavropol kray. To the southeast, two other mountain streams from the north slopes of the Caucasus, the Terek and the Kuma, are the basis of an irrigation system which includes two canals, the Terek–Kuma Canal and the Kuma–Manych Canal. These bring water to large tracts of the arid Nogay steppes in the south and to the Black Land poor steppes farther north.

Farther west, the lower Dnepr is the source of much recent irrigation. Water from the Kakhovka reservoir on the Dnepr irrigates large areas of the lower flood-plain and the plain of north Crimea, forming a system larger than any other in Europe with an area of 1.5 million hectares; further development is expected to double this area, and eventually will extract 61 % of the river's average discharge.

The most intensely utilised of all the rivers of the Soviet Union is the Volga. A cascade of vast reservoirs extends along the river and its tributaries from the vicinity of Moscow in the upper basin to Volgograd on the lower course. Designed primarily for power generation, industrial and urban water supply, flood control and added benefits for navigation, these reservoirs now have an important role in supplying irrigation water where the river crosses the steppe and semi-desert zones along its lower course. Crop failures have been common in this area as a result of droughts, which in some years reduced wheat production to a fraction of that of the more favourable years. Hence extended irrigation systems now bring Volga water to the dry lands lying to the east of the middle and lower parts of the river in the Kuybyshev, Saratov, Volgograd, Uralsk and other adjacent oblasts. This has resulted in greatly improved spring-wheat yields. The construction of the Volga-Ural Canal began in 1975 and will continue beyond 1985. This is a huge undertaking, linking the two rivers, Volga and Ural, and planned to irrigate eventually 2 million hectares. The later stages of this scheme are, however, dependent on the addition of water to the Volga by a diversion of northern European rivers and lakes.

Water being piped to a Crimean vineyard. Irrigation is essential in this southerly area for intensive agriculture

IRRIGATION IN CENTRAL ASIA AND
KAZAKHSTAN

This extensive area has a long history of irrigation. Before the Soviet period the supply of water from the rivers was controlled by feudal landowners and distributed through a network of small channels to a dense mosaic of tiny peasant holdings, worked by native farmers with the aid of draught animals and primitive implements. After the collectivisation of agriculture in Soviet times, the water supply was placed under the control of the state and study was begun on the problems of reclaiming lands which had become useless for agriculture because of salt accumulation in the soils. Large reservoirs were built to improve the water supply and long canals constructed to convey water to the land.

One of the earliest and most ambitious of Soviet water-management projects was the building of the Great Fergana Canal in the Fergana valley in Uzbekistan and Tadzhikistan. In 1939 this canal initiated irrigation of the fertile loess soils on a major scale, by bringing water from the upper Syr Darya (the Naryn River) along the southern side of the valley, intersecting the several separate irrigated alluvial fans there and adding to their water supply. It also produced a much more uniform distribution of water, permitting the better irrigation of more land, including some of the unused land towards the centre of the valley. Subsequently, two other large canals were completed, the North Fergana in 1940 and the Central Fergana in 1970. A fourth canal, the Great Namangan Canal, is in course of construction.

Syr Darya water is also utilised in the irrigation of the Golodnaya (Hungry) Steppe, south-west of Tashkent. Completion of the Farkhad Dam near Bekabad in 1948 gave storage facilities for the irrigation of a very large area of nearly 400 000 hectares, much of which is producing cotton. The tenth Five Year Plan (1975–80) provided for the construction of the South Golodnaya Steppe Canal and for the possibility of doubling the irrigated area. Farther to the east, the Chu river, an intermittent feeder of the Syr Darya, is used in an extensive irrigated area centred upon the city of Frunze; Alma Ata and Kurgan are associated with important irrigated areas based on river systems flowing into Lake Balkhash (Fig. 5.2).

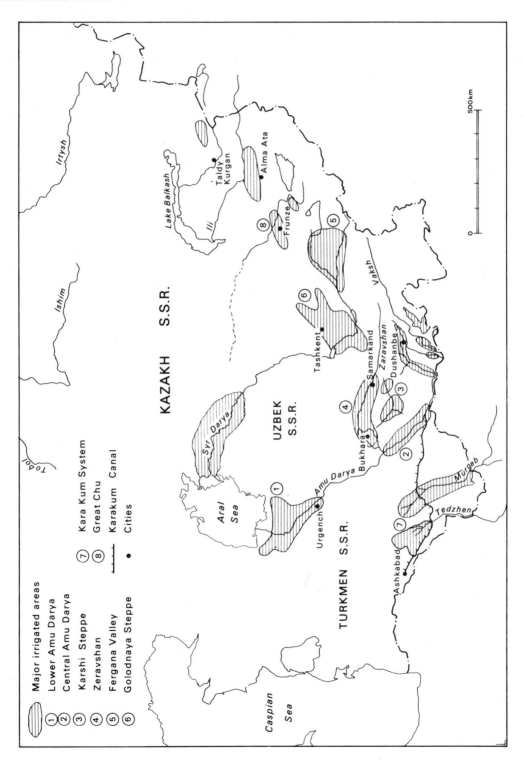

Fig. 5.2 Irrigation schemes in Central Asia

Water power in Uzbekistan, an old water wheel with a hydro-electric plant in the distance

The largest irrigation projects of Central Asia are associated with water from the Amu Darya. The most spectacular of these is the irrigation of the piedmont areas of arid southern Turkmenistan by the Karakum Canal. This structure takes water from the Amu Darya at Kerki and runs westwards through farmlands formerly dependent upon intermittent rivers such as the Murgab and the Tedzhen. The area irrigated from the canal had reached half a million hectares by 1975 but this is to be greatly increased as the canal is extended westwards to the Caspian, withdrawing more and more water from the river, eventually to amount to 1400 m³/s, a figure representing 70% of the Amu Darya's average annual discharge at Kerki. At completion the canal will be 1450 km in length, the longest canal of any type in the world and nine times the length of the Suez Canal. However, the Amu Darya water is required also to irrigate other lands along its course; its upper tributaries, the Vakhsh and the Surkhandarya rivers, are involved

in supplying projects such as that of the Sherabad Steppe; farther downstream is the Karshi Steppe system which draws water from the Amu Darya to supplement the limited water resources of the Kashkadarya River. The Zeravshan, rising from the large Zeravshan glacier is so intensely utilised for irrigated agriculture that in some years it fails to flow into the Amu Darya. The delta region of the Amu Darya is also a complex network of canals conveying water and fertile alluvium to bottomland farms.

In south-west Siberia, water from the Ob river is being diverted via the Kulunda Steppe Canal for irrigation of the dry steppe of Siberia and neighbouring Kazakhstan.

Problems of irrigation

There is an urgent need in the Soviet Union not only for additional supplies of water for irrigation but also for a much more efficient use of water supplies for this purpose. There is evidence of considerable wastage of the present supplies through inefficient techniques, causing water loss by evaporation and also causing soil damage by the accumulation of harmful salts. In the Soviet Union water is provided free of charge and is classed as an inexhaustible resource, an attitude that has led to waste of water, particularly in the application of irrigation on farmland. The efficiency of the systems is low; techniques require improvement and water is lost from canals through seepage as waterproof linings are not widely used (Askochensky, 1962; Kuznetsov and Lvovich, 1971). However, progress is being made in the reconstruction of older irrigation facilities, including extended lining of canals, the installation of water measuring and regulating equipment, and the use of sprinkler watering systems. With the latter, water is sprayed on the soil from a rotating tube on a pivot thus watering a circular area with a radius up to 450 m. Stress was laid upon such improvements in the tenth Five Year Plan (1975–80).

Soil salinisation, common in other arid or semi-arid parts of the world has been a particularly acute problem in the Soviet Union. The excessive watering of soils there has contributed to this condition. Secondary salinisation, as it is termed, is produced when the groundwater level rises because too much water is applied to crops and the surplus seeps downwards to the watertable, or because water escapes from irrigation canals. Salt accumulations in the subsoil cause the groundwater to become highly saline, and when this approaches the soil surface, drawn upwards by capillary action, evaporation of the water allows a saline crust to form in the soil. Waterlogging by saline water also occurs. In the late 1960s land abandonment because of salinisation in the irrigated oases of Central Asia was equal to the area of newly irrigated land (Gerasimov, 1968). In the Murgab oasis in Turkmenistan, the increased water supply from the Karakum Canal has allowed a great expansion of irrigation, but crop yields have been reduced by the rise of saline groundwater (Kornilov and Timoshkina, 1975).

Reclamation of saline soils depends upon flushing away the salts from the upper layers of soil by heavy applications of water (up to 300 000 m³/ha). This water, with its dissolved salts, has then to be removed by the installation of adequate drainage facilities. Salt-absorbing crops such as rice are also employed. These measures are now being widely applied in the Soviet Union's irrigated areas.

In addition to improvement in the efficiency of irrigation, supplies of water are available from underground sources. The geological structures in the Turan lowland are highly favourable for the supply of groundwater; the rock formations contain a series of water-bearing layers, containing abundant artesian water. The source of the latter is the heavy precipitation, snow and glaciers of the southern mountain ranges. At the limits of the Turkmen republic, many underground water sources of varying mineralisation are found in the area of Alpine folding, associated with a great artesian basin north of the Kopet Dag and this water comes to the surface near Tashkent.

Although this water is important for the supply of drinking water for the flocks and herds in the region, the groundwater reserves are under-utilised, supplying less than 10 % of the withdrawals. This is particularly the case in Central Asia and southern Kazakhstan where many areas are under irrigation but where the groundwater reserves are enormous. Kazakhstan alone has supplies estimated at over 5000 km³, much of which is situated in the southern part of the republic. However, the use of this groundwater has not been greater than 2.5 km³ each year in this area (Vendrov and Dyakonov, 1976). Certain problems in its use are its depth from the surface and its slow rate of recharging and although it is brackish it could be desalinised.

Other additions to the water supply in the Turan lowland could be provided by the utilisation of Caspian Sea water for irrigation. The salinity of this water is much lower than that of sea water and experiments with its application to crops have shown that it will promote the growth of winter wheat, barley, sunflowers and lucerne. Water is also wasted in the drainage of irrigation systems, which has created large shallow lakes in the Aral basin. These evaporate large quantities of water and could be eliminated by returning the drainage water to the main rivers.

Water projects and the environment

Various ministries and departments in the Soviet Union are responsible for the management of the water resources. Major decisions are made by the Party and contained in the Five Year Plans, but the technical operations are implemented through organisations existing at national and republican levels, where there has been inadequate attention to the needs of conservation. Priority has almost always favoured the requirements of industry for water supplies and for hydro-electricity and the undesirable consequences of river projects have not been given sufficient consideration.

The impoundment and storage of large bodies of freshwater is a capital-intensive and long-term operation, basic to water control and regulation projects, but is itself accompanied by adverse environmental modifications. In lowland areas broad and shallow reservoirs are formed, flooding farms, forests and settlement sites; the large surface area of the water in relation to depth leads to great losses from evaporation and there are further inevitable losses from seepage and also soil damage by waterlogging beyond the flood level. For the USSR as a whole, about $7\frac{1}{2}$ million hectares of all categories of land have been inundated by hydro-electric reservoirs of which about 25 % has been land capable of agriculture (Pryde, 1972). Although the provision of water for irrigation has allowed the cultivation of more land, it is believed that the areas irrigated from most reservoirs are less than the lands flooded by them. A further type of environmental disturbance is the relocation of towns and villages removed from the vicinity of the reservoir: the Tsimlyansk reservoir linking the Don and the Volga required the removal of 159 towns, villages and hamlets; the Rybinsk reservoir likewise needed the shifting and relocation of 600 villages and farms; the Kuybyshev reservoir alone flooded approximately 277,000 ha of agriculturally useful Volga riverside land (Fig. 5.1). As regards evaporation losses, 5 cubic kilometres are lost annually from the Volga–Kama reservoirs and 4 cubic kilometres from those of the Dnepr; the water lost in this way would be adequate to irrigate 3–4 million hectares of steppe lands.

THE CASPIAN AND ARAL SEAS

The most serious effects of the withdrawal of water from rivers for irrigation and hydro-electric projects have been shown by the fall in the level and reduction in size of the great inland seas of the Soviet Union, namely the Caspian Sea and the Aral Sea. The case of the Caspian Sea is most important (Micklin, 1972; Vozresenskiy et al, 1975). It is the world's largest lake; it is a major fishery and waterfowl habitat; it plays an important role in transport with major ports such as Astrakhan along its shores; its great size influences regional climates.

There have been climatic and other physical factors influencing past fluctuations of the Caspian Sea; the most recent of these has been a fall in precipitation in the 1930s arising from a reduction in the number of moist cyclones from the Atlantic. However the main cause of the fall in level has been a reduction of the runoff from the River Volga which provides 80 % of the discharge into the Caspian Sea. Great quantities of water have been withdrawn from the 1930s onwards for the initial filling of the several huge reservoirs along the Volga, followed by increasing use of the water for irrigation of the semi-arid steppe lands and for industrial and municipal use in the towns and cities. The withdrawals had reached 20–24 km^3 in the late 1960s and may rise to 60–65 km^3 in the future; these, together with the losses arising from evaporation from reservoirs, have caused a fall in level of the sea by 2.5 m since 1929.

The economic and environmental consequences have been very serious. The fishing industry has been severely damaged by reduction of the marginal shallow-water areas which provide a spawning ground for some species and feeding grounds for valuable fishes such as salmon and sturgeon; migration of fishes along the Volga to spawning grounds has been prevented by river regulation. Increasing pollution of the water by oil and other substances has also contributed to the decline in catches of the more valuable species, although numbers of low-value species such as sprats are increasing. The retreat of shorelines has affected access of shipping to the ports; in the area of the Volga delta the shore has extended outwards by 25–30 km and the shallowing of the water has necessitated dredging to allow ships to reach ports such as Astrakhan and Krasnovodsk. Wharves have been made unusable and some fishing collectives have lost all connection to the sea as it has retreated. The oil industry has been affected by loading difficulties at ports. Agriculture has suffered in the lower Volga area as the water levels have declined. There has also been increased salinity and the precipitation of unwanted salts.

The future of the Aral Sea is also causing increasing public concern in the Soviet Union. Its level was relatively stable from 1911 until 1960, but dropped by nearly 3 m by 1975 (Gerasimov et al, 1976). This fall in level reflected not only the dry climate of that period but the more intensive use of the water by management projects within the basin based upon the two main feeders, the Amu

Darya and the Syr Darya. The sub-surface inflow, once thought to be considerable, has been found to be negligible. Evaporation from the river and floodplain surfaces and transpiration from the abundant aquatic vegetation growing along both main rivers are also causing substantial losses of water entering the sea. Further extensive withdrawal from the rivers for irrigation is planned and could reduce sea levels by another 3.5 m by 1985 and an additional 5 m by the year 2000, causing the area of the sea to shrink to one quarter of its size in 1960. Already fish catches have declined by 50 % as a consequence of increasing salinity and a continuation of this trend may endanger existing biological species (Kuznetsov, 1977; Micklin, 1978). The eventual conversion of the sea into a residual brine lake as more and more water is drawn from the rivers is considered to be quite likely and this result would adversely affect the climate of the area by reducing precipitation; and there would be the added danger of salt deposits from the dried margins being blown on to adjacent agriculturally productive land. Measures to moderate the negative impact of the drying out of the Aral Sea have been proposed by Borovskiy (1980).

Water pollution

The question of an adequate supply of freshwater is only one aspect of the problem of adequate management of the water resources of the Soviet Union; of even greater importance than quantity is the maintenance of its quality. But in this respect, despite the much greater control exercised by the Soviet state on the development of natural resources than in the West, the situation shows no amelioration. Industrial and urban expansion, so spectacular in the Soviet Union during the past 50 years, created a deterioration of water quality that became catastrophic in some regions and continues to be serious; the waters of the Volga, Kama, Oka, Belaya, Ural, Northern Donets and other rivers have lost or are losing their valuable natural properties. The discharge of toxic effluent from industrial enterprises and domestic sewage from towns and cities into these rivers increased almost 20 times during the period 1930 to 1970 and lakes have been affected in the same manner. (Kuznetsov and Lvovich 1971).

Poisons in solution occur in the effluents of many kinds of modern industry. They include acids and alkalis, phenols and cyanides from chemical industries and mines; the commonest poisonous inorganic substances are chlorine, ammonia and hydrogen sulphide and the salts of many heavy metals such as copper, lead, zinc, chromium and mercury, very small amounts of which can remove all animal life from streams. Organic matter such as human sewage or wastes from pulp and paper mills has a polluting effect related to the amount of oxygen consumed by bacteria in bringing about the decomposition of the material. When large quantities of dissolved oxygen in the water are used up by bacteria in the process of decomposition, the water becomes devoid of oxygen and this causes the death of many forms of plant and animal life. Deep, slowly flowing rivers such as those of the Soviet lowlands have naturally low oxygen levels, but this condition is accentuated when they are polluted by large quantities of organic matter rich in nitrate and phosphate; these nutrients cause abundant algal growths which decay and are then consumed by bacteria. Over-enrichment (or eutrophication) also results when rivers receive runoff from fertilised farm land with similar results on oxygen levels. Water returned to rivers and lakes in a heated state (as from thermal power stations) is also harmful to aquatic organisms such as fish, as their life cycle may be delicately adjusted to the temperature of the water.

Such pollution of inland water bodies fatally affects both the quantity and the quality of fish. Many rivers (the Tom, Ufa, Belaya, Kama and others) where fishing was formerly prosperous have now completely or partially lost their commercial importance. Even in the new large reservoirs there is massive destruction of commercial fish, and the annual loss incurred by the fishing industry from pollution is assessed at several hundred million rubles (Vinogradov et al, 1971).

Lake and reservoir water is particularly subject to these influences as it is static or has only a feeble through-flow, so that an accumulation of pollutants may occur within it, markedly affecting the water quality of even extensive bodies of water. The lakes Onega, Baykal, Balkhash and the Ivankovo and Kama reservoirs have been affected by effluent from pulp and paper mills and other industrial plants along their shores. The great size of the Caspian Sea has not saved it from serious contamination by wastes of, for example, the oil industry; until recently waste oil was deposited directly into the water from the oil refineries at

Baku, and tankers were allowed to discharge their ballast overboard; oil also escaped from offshore drilling operations.

LAKE BAYKAL

In Siberia, the unique flora and fauna of Lake Baykal have been threatened by the effects of the development of industry in the area, arousing public concern and protest. The waters of the lake are particularly clear and deep (1620 m) and form the habitat of endemic plants and animals of great scientific interest. Despite widespread objection that industrialisation near the lake would destroy the quality of its water, two paper mills were built and plans for additional mills have been discussed. Soil erosion near the lake resulting from increased logging required to supply the needs of the mills also gave concern for the ecology of the lake, as the climate of the area allowed only a slow natural recovery of the forest and soil cover.

Conservation measures

A government decree of 1969 declared the entire Lake Baykal area a water conservation zone, prohibited logging and ordered the treatment of industrial and urban wastes, including effluent from the paper mills. Further regulations have been imposed to safeguard the lake, but doubt remains whether these will be completely effective. As on previous occasions, economic advantage has tended to be placed before concern for the environment and regulations for the protection of the latter are often not effectively enforced.

However, efforts in the Soviet Union to correct the advanced state of pollution of freshwater have had some positive results. Factories in the Volga basin are installing facilities for waste water purification; one example is the Saratov oil refinery which repeatedly uses waste waters containing oil and such circulating systems reduce pollution significantly. Factories along the Kama and in the Donbas are now extracting many compounds from their waste products, reducing pollution and utilising valuable substances and many cities such as Moscow and Kuybyshev have built sewage treatment systems. There is evidence of firmer supervision by regulatory bodies on the concentration of pollutants that may be present in discharges of waste water. If their concentrations exceed standards now set by the state, heavy penalties of large fines or imprisonment are prescribed for those responsible (Gassilina, 1978).

Moscow's water problems

Particular problems arise in the supply and disposal of water to very large cities, notably in the case of Moscow, and its surrounding industrial area. There is a high population density (about 300 per km^2) and a high level of industrialisation; agriculture also makes demands upon the freshwater supply for the irrigation of pastures and of vegetable crops for consumption within the area. However the region is not favourably situated as it is near the divide of the Volga basin where the water resources are relatively limited.

The conditions within the Soviet capital are characteristic of very large cities. Moscow receives a 10 % higher precipitation than surrounding non-urban districts. In summer, showers produce a very high runoff from the impermeable surfaces of streets and buildings, but much of this is lost in evaporation (57 %) and only about 16 % reaches the subsurface. The remainder drains into the Moscow River, which with its tributaries and reservoirs formed the original principal source of supply of water to the entire city. In winter, snow is cleared systematically from the impermeable surfaces and brought to temporary dump areas such as ravines where it is melted artificially. Although Moscow is a conspicuously clean city, runoff from its streets inevitably becomes polluted.

Water consumption per person is about 650 litres each day (this figure includes water used in industry), and is supplied by the Moscow River together with water from the Volga, brought to the city by the 129-km Moscow Canal since its completion in 1937. The canal is part of a system including regulating reservoirs and power stations and forms a navigable waterway linking the capital to the sea. In spite of efficient treatment of Moscow's effluent, its volume became relatively large compared with the discharge of the Moscow River; however, in 1978 additional dilution became possible with the diversion of the Vazuza River into the Moscow River. The Vazuza is a tributary of the Volga and supplies water at a rate of about 30 cubic metres per second.

The discharge of city sewage could be decreased by using it for the irrigation and fertilisation of forage crops and studies are being made in the area of this possibility (Lvovich and Chernogayeva, 1977). Sewage contains nutrients in a form that is easily assimilated by plants and the yield of forage crops irrigated with sewage has been shown· to be increased by three to four times.

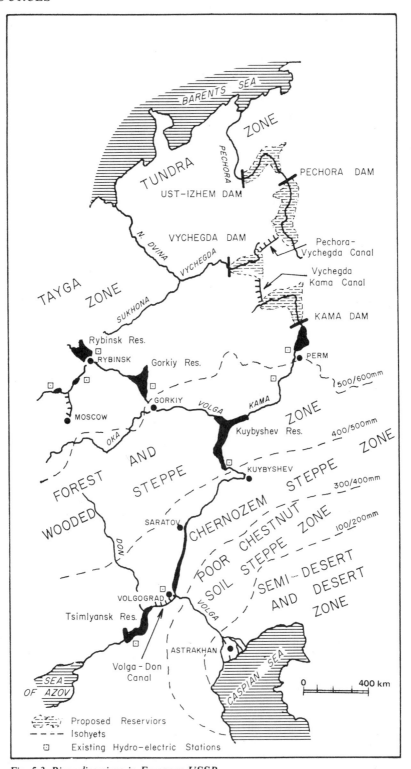

Fig. 5.3 River diversions in European USSR

Water diversion proposals

The contrast in the Soviet Union between the vast water surpluses in the northern sparsely-peopled areas and the water deficiences of the more fertile and highly-developed southern steppes and irrigated oases is keenly perceived; it has given rise to proposals that the great northern rivers might be diverted southwards to the advantage of irrigated agriculture and of other forms of economic development. Such inter-basin transfers have already been achieved on a smaller scale, such as the supply of water to Moscow by means of the Moskva–Volga Canal and the Karakum Canal; and the apparent success of these schemes has made much larger projects seem feasible.

The various schemes now under serious consideration for major water transfers in both the European and the Siberian regions have been reviewed by Lvovich (1977). In Europe the north-western project would transfer 31 km³ a year from the Sukhona and Onega rivers and Lake Onega into the Rybinsk reservoir. In the north-east, it is proposed to transfer 34 km³ a year from the Pechora and Vychegda rivers to the Kama river. Both transfers benefit the Volga–Kama system which would gain 65 km³ a year at first, increased later by an additional 20 km³. The level of the Caspian Sea would be maintained by the additional water which would be released from three reservoirs connected by canals. But such a body of water would inevitably be detrimental to the northern vegetation and soils and would affect groundwater levels, local climates and ice regimes. Farther south, another European scheme would involve the lower Danube, taking about 30 km³ of its water to benefit the southern Ukraine. These European schemes have been considered to be likelier for early implementation than those concerning diversions from Siberia to Central Asia (Vendrov, 1976) (Fig. 5.3).

In the latter case, western Siberian water would be diverted southwards in two stages, amounting at first to 25 and later to 60 cubic kilometres. Three alternative projects for the two stages are proposed: (1) withdrawal of water from the lower Irtysh, the Tobol and the Ob below the confluence with the Irtysh at Belogorye; (2) withdrawal of water from the Chulym and Tom rivers as well as from the Novosibirsk reservoir on the Ob, with the transfer of water through a canal to a proposed reservoir at Yamyshevo on the Irtysh and onward by canal to Kurgan; (3) a combi-nation of the first two, with withdrawal of water from the Novosibirsk reservoir on the Ob river and transfer by canal to the Yamyshevo reservoir on the Irtysh as well as withdrawal from a proposed reservoir on the Tobol.

All three alternatives then propose a southward trunk canal to convey the water in a north–south direction through the Turgay trough towards the interfluve between the Syr Darya and the Amu Darya; the canal would be 2000–2500 km long and its annual streamflow would be about equivalent to that of the Dnepr River. There is also an Asian–European alternative which suggests the transfer of water from the lower Ob river across the Ural mountains to link up with the Pechora–Kama diversion and thence to the Volga (Fig. 5.4).

The effect upon the Siberian lowland of substantial withdrawals of water is problematical. There is an immense water surplus in the area, as evidenced by the enormous extent of the mires, bogs and swamps, estimated to cover 800 000 sq km and they are expanding at the rate of 100 sq km each year. A reduction of the runoff would facilitate their reclamation. The first stages of swamp reclamation are already being taken in connection with the west Siberian oil and gas development and a gradual continuation of this process is envisaged, with probable conversion of the land to agriculture or forestry, a process in which the Soviet Union has much experience and expertise. Moreover, the great depth of peat over large areas would provide useful thermal-electric power. The lowland mires occurring in the southern part of the west Siberian plain can be used in agriculture. However the problem of the west Siberian swamps, mires and bogs is difficult because of their vast distribution over the entire territory and also because of the presence of numerous different types of bogs with respect to latitudinal geographic zonality; there are also variations in the type of peat deposits and the quality of the peat. Further study of the deposits is required in order to determine which bogs should be left untouched as reserves and as examples of natural ecosystems.

Climatic changes might follow swamp reclamation, as the great area of the west Siberian bogs and swamps affects the precipitation regime. Thus about 5000 km³ of atmospheric moisture which move annually over west Siberia from west to east, consist largely of the evaporation of the swamp

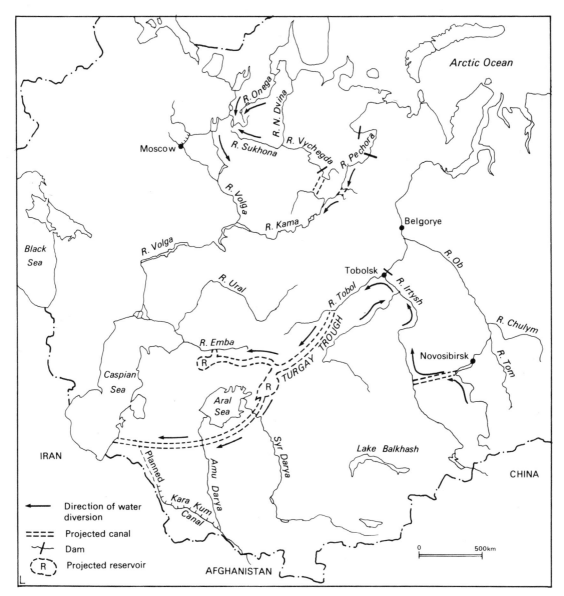

Fig. 5.4 Proposed diversions of river water including projects transferring water from Siberia to Central Asia
Sources: M. I. Lvovich, Micklin (1977) and others.

area and this moisture supply would certainly diminish with drainage of the swamps. If the rivers are diverted from the Arctic Ocean then its waters will become more saline and will therefore freeze less readily and may cause cyclones from the Atlantic to follow a more northerly path; this could be unfortunate for the mid-latitude areas of eastern Europe as they would receive less precipitation. Increased aridity of the Soviet steppe areas would be the result. However the introduction of large quantities of Siberian water southwards would be likely to add moisture to the atmosphere of Central Asia. The prevailing westerly air flow in the region causes moisture to condense in the mountains of that region and therefore the runoff of the mountain rivers would be increased, a highly desirable prospect.

Much of the tayga is swampland, with an excess of water useless for cultivation because of the low temperatures that prevail

These and other factors need to be taken into account before final decisions are reached; a broad geographical perspective is required in predictions of the potential impact of the projects before vast capital investment is committed to the schemes.

BIBLIOGRAPHY

Ashkochensky, A. N. (1962), 'Basic trends and methods of water control in the arid zones of the Soviet Union,' in *The problems of the arid zone*, UNESCO, Paris, pp. 401–410.

Atlas SSSR (1969), Moscow, 2nd ed.

Bogomolov, G. V. (1961), 'Conditions of formation of fresh waters under pressure in certain desert zones of North Africa, the USSR and South-West Asia,' in *Salinity problems in the arid zones*, UNESCO, Paris, pp. 37–41.

Borovskiy, V. M. (1980), 'The drying out of the Aral Sea and its consequences,' *Soviet Geography*, **21**, pp. 63–77.

Central Intelligence Agency (1974), *USSR agriculture atlas*, Washington DC.

Dreyer, N. N. (1969), Water resources of the major economic regions of the RSFSR, and the other Union Republics. *Soviet Geography*, **10**, pp. 137–145.

Gassilina, N. (1978), 'Systems of water pollution control in the USSR,' Paper read to Inst. Water Pollution Control, 1978 conference.

Gerasimov, I. P. (1968), 'Basic problems of the transformation of nature in Central Asia.' *Soviet Geography*, **9**, 6, pp. 444–458.

Gerasimov, I. P., Armand, D. L. and Yefron, K. M. (eds.) (1971), *Natural resources of the Soviet Union, their use and renewal*, translation ed. W. A. D. Jackson, Freeman, San Francisco.

Gerasimov, I. P. *et al* (1976), 'Basic problems in the transformation of nature in Central Asia,' *Soviet Geography*, **17**, pp. 235–245.

Goldman, M. I. (1972), *The spoils of progress; environmental pollution in the Soviet Union*, MIT Press, Cambridge, Mass. and London.

Hynes, H. B. N. (1970), *The biology of polluted waters*, Liverpool.

Kornilov, B. A. and Timoshkina, V. A. (1975), 'The impact of Karakum on the environment,' *Soviet Geography*, **16**, pp. 308–314.

Kovda, V. A. (1961), 'Principles of the theory and practice of reclamation and utilisation of saline soils in the arid zones,' in *Salinity problems in the arid zones*, UNESCO, Paris, pp. 201–213.

Kuznetsov, N. T. (1977), 'Geographical aspects of the future of the Aral Sea,' *Soviet Geography*, **18**, pp. 163–171.

Kuznetsov, N. T. and Lvovich, M. I. (1971), 'Multiple use and conservation of water resources,' in Gerasimov *et al* 1971, pp. 11–39.

Lamb, H. H. (1970) 'Climatic variation and our environment today and in the coming years', *Weather*, **25**, pp. 447–453.

Lappo, G., Chikishev, A. and Bekker, A. (1976), *Moscow, capital of the Soviet Union*, Moscow.

Lavrishchev, A. (1969), *Economic geography of the USSR*, Moscow.

Lvovich, M. I. (1977), 'Geographical aspects of a territorial redistribution of water resources in the USSR,' *Soviet Geography*, **18**, pp. 557–574.

Lvovich, M. I. and Chernogayeva, G. M. (1977), 'Transformation of the water balance within the city of Moscow,' *Soviet Geography*, **18**, pp. 302–312.

Micklin, P. P. (1972), Dimensions of the Caspian Sea problem, *Soviet Geography*, **13**, pp. 589–603.

Micklin, P. P. (1977), NAWAPA and two Siberian water diversion proposals, *Soviet Geography*, **18**, pp. 81–99.

Micklin, P. P. (1978), Irrigation development in the USSR during the 10th Five-Year Plan (1976–1980). *Soviet Geography*, **19**, pp. 1–24.

Neishtadt, M. I. (1977), The world's largest peat basin, its commercial potentialities and protection. *Bulletin*, International Peat Society No. 81, Helsinki, pp. 37–43.

Oziranskii, S. (1968), Plata za vodnye resursy, *Planovoe khozyaystvo*, September.

Pryde, P. R. (1972), *Environmental pollution and environmental quality in the Soviet Union*, CUP, London.

Shabad, T. (1978), 'Progress report on big interbasin diversion projects,' *Soviet Geography*, **19**, pp. 215.

Suslov, S. P. (1961), *Physical geography of Asiatic Russia*, London.

Thiel, E. (1957), *The Soviet Far East*, London.

Vendrov, S. L. (1976), 'Problems in the spatial redistribution of streamflow,' *Soviet Geography*, **17**, pp. 415–420.

Vendrov, S. L. and Dyakonov, K. N. (1976), *Vodokhranilishcha i okruzhayushchaya prirodnya sreda*, Moscow, pp. 119–25.

Vinogradov, L. G. *et al* (1971), Fisheries resources, in Gerasimov *et al* 1971, pp. 303–335.

Volgyes, I. (ed.) (1974), *Environmental deterioration in the Soviet Union and Eastern Europe*, Praeger, New York.

Vozresenskiy, A. N., Gangardt, G. G. and Gerardi, I. A. (1975), 'Principal trends and prospects of the use of water resources in the USSR,' *Soviet Geography*, **16**, pp. 291–307.

6 Population

ETHNIC COMPOSITION

As has been described in Chapter One, the present territory of the USSR was inherited, in 1917, from its political forerunner, the Russian Empire which, by a process of expansion lasting some 400 years, had spread out from its original nucleus around Moscow to cover vast areas of eastern Europe and northern Asia. Like the other European-dominated empires established in the same period, the Russian Empire came to include, in addition to the Russians themselves, a large and varied collection of other peoples, so that the Soviet Union, inheriting the lands of the Empire, also inherited its extremely diverse population. Thus, the peoples of the present-day USSR differ from each other in their racial, cultural, historical and religious backgrounds and in the languages they speak.

The Soviet census of 1979 recognised no fewer than 92 distinct national groups within the population of the USSR. Many of these groups were very small: 16 had fewer than 10 000 members each and 39 were between 10 000 and 250 000 strong. This leaves 37 larger nationalities, ranging in size from 287 000 to 137 million, which together accounted for 98.7% of the Soviet population (Table 6.1).

TABLE 6.1: THE LARGER NATIONALITIES OF THE SOVIET UNION POPULATION (000S) AT THE CENSUS OF 1979 (PERCENTAGE OF TOTAL POPULATION IN BRACKETS)

Russians	137 397	(52.42)	Bashkirs	1371	(0.52)
Ukrainians	42 347	(16.16)	Mordovs	1192	(0.45)
Uzbeks	12 456	(4.75)	Poles	1151	(0.44)
Belorussians	9 463	(3.61)	Estonians	1020	(0.39)
Kazakhs	6 556	(2.50)	Chechens	756	(0.29)
Tatars	6 317	(2.41)	Udmurts	714	(0.27)
Azerbaydzhanis	5 477	(2.09)	Mari	622	(0.24)
Armenians	4 151	(1.58)	Osetins	542	(0.21)
Georgians	3 571	(1.36)	Avars	483	(0.18)
Moldavians	2 968	(1.13)	Koreans	389	(0.15)
Tadzhiks	2 898	(1.11)	Lesghians	383	(0.15)
Lithuanians	2 851	(1.09)	Bulgars	361	(0.14)
Turkmen	2 028	(0.77)	Buryats	353	(0.13)
Germans	1 936	(0.74)	Greeks	344	(0.13)
Kirgiz	1 906	(0.73)	Yakuts	328	(0.12)
Jews	1 811	(0.69)	Komi	327	(0.12)
Chuvash	1 751	(0.67)	Kabardins	322	(0.12)
Latvians	1 439	(0.55)	Karakalpaks	303	(0.12)
			Dargintsy	287	(0.11)

Source: Vestnik Statistiki 1980 (2), 24–5, Moscow.

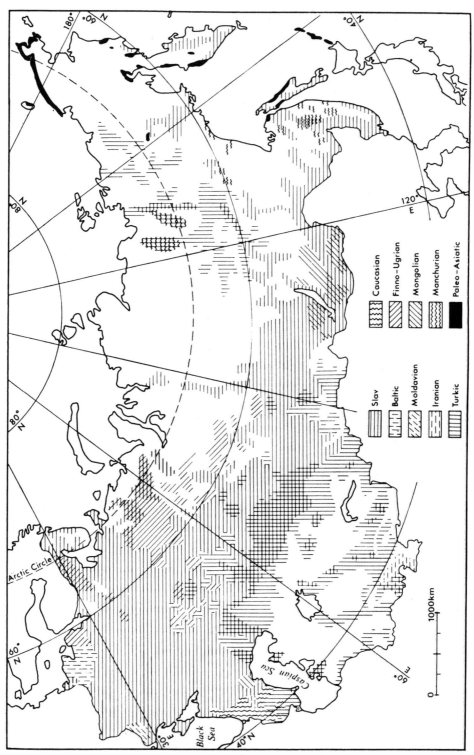

Fig. 6.1 Distribution of major ethnic groups. Unshaded areas are very thinly populated, mainly by small tribes

The 92 nationalities defined in the 1979 census fall into some 10 major ethnic groups, the distribution of which is illustrated in Fig. 6.1. It should be realised that there has been a great deal of migration within the Russian Empire and Soviet Union by members of these groups. They have thus become intermingled to a progressively greater extent and there are now relatively few areas inhabited by a single group to the exclusion of all others. Nevertheless, each ethnic group has an area or areas in which it forms the majority of the local population or in which the bulk of its members are to be found.

Since language is the main criterion by which the Soviet Union distinguishes its national groups, the distribution of these groups is best described on a linguistic basis. The USSR contains representatives of two of the world's major language families, the Indo–European and the Ural–Altaic, both of which originated in the Eurasian interior in remote prehistoric times. Languages of the Indo–European family, which is much the larger of the two, are indigenous over a zone extending from the Atlantic in the west to northern India in the east. Ural–Altaic languages have spread to Siberia and the Pacific in one direction and to eastern Europe and the Middle East in the other. Within the Soviet Union there are several areas in which languages belonging to each family are spoken by peoples living in adjacent districts.

Indo–European ethnic groups
By far the largest sub-division of the Indo–European family found in the USSR is the Slav group of tongues, spoken by roughly three-quarters of the population. Dominant among the Slavs are the 137 million *Russians* proper, or Great Russians, who make up some 52 per cent of the inhabitants of the Soviet Union. The traditional home of the Russians is the mixed forest zone of the USSR, centred on Moscow, and it is here that the bulk of them are still to be found. As the dominant force in the growth of the Empire, however, they played a leading role in migration eastwards into Siberia, which has been going on since the seventeenth century. Owing to the small size of the indigenous population of Siberia, Russians are now in a majority over the greater part of the inhabited zone, where they are now found not only in urban areas but also forming the bulk of the rural population wherever settled agriculture has been established. Russians have

also moved in large numbers into Kazakhstan, where they now outnumber the indigenous Kazakhs. In the other four Central Asian republics, however, they are largely confined to urban areas and make up only about 15 % of the total. A somewhat higher proportion of Russians is found in the Ukraine, particularly in the eastern part, where they assisted in the industrialisation of the Donbas. Russians have also moved in appreciable numbers into Latvia and Estonia since 1945, and account for 28 % of the population of those republics. Areas with relatively few Russian settlers, less than 10 % in each case, include Lithuania and the Transcaucasian republics of Georgia and Armenia.

The *Ukrainians*, of whom there are more than 42 million, are the second largest national group, both among the Slavs and in the Soviet population as a whole. Speaking a language closely allied to Great Russian, the Ukrainians originated as a distinctive group in the wooded steppe and steppe lands of the European south, where they were much affected by the Tatar invasions of the medieval period. Like the Russians, the Ukrainians carried out widespread colonisation in Siberia, where they are to be found in considerable numbers, particularly in the west and in the extreme far east.

The third major Slav group, the *Belorussians*, is much smaller (9 million) and is largely confined to the western part of the country. As a result of this location, they were subject to Lithuanian and Polish influences and many Belorussians became Roman Catholics in contrast to the predominantly Orthodox Russians and Ukrainians.

The *Poles* form a Slav minority group of considerable size in the western parts of Belorussia and the Ukraine, areas which were at various times under Polish control and where the population remains very mixed.

The *Lithuanians* and *Latvians* speak Baltic languages which, though remotely related to Russian, are quite distinctive, employing Roman as distinct from Cyrillic script. These two groups, numbering about 4 million, have been much affected by western contacts; the Lithuanians, as a result of their long connection with Poland, adopted Roman Catholicism, while the Latvians received the Lutheran form of Christianity from German immigrants.

In addition, there are several non-Slav Indo–European groups within the European USSR.

These include the 3 million *Moldavians* of Bessarabia, who speak a Romance language allied to Rumanian. The Teutonic sub-division is represented by 1.9 million *German*-speakers, descendants of farmers and artisans who entered Russia from the eighteenth century onwards, often as refugees from religious or political persecution. Before the Second World War, they were mainly concentrated along the west bank of the Volga, where they had their own Volga–German Autonomous Republic, but during the war this was abolished and the population dispersed to Central Asia and Siberia. The number of *Jews* in the Soviet Union (1.8 million) is much below the pre-war level owing to the effects of the German occupation and some recent emigration. Although a Jewish Autonomous Oblast was established in the Far East as long ago as 1934, it has failed to attract many settlers and is the home of only one per cent of Soviet Jews. The majority are found in the European part of the country, but there are also a number of very ancient Jewish communities in Central Asia. Most of the 344 000 *Greeks* live in old trading cities along the Black Sea coast.

Finally, among the Indo–European peoples, we must note the presence of Indo–Iranian groups, speaking languages allied to Persian, in Central Asia (*Tadzhiks*) and the Caucasus (*Osetins* and numerous smaller groups), most of whom are Moslems.

The Caucasus, and particularly Transcaucasia, is a region of very great ethnic diversity. In addition to a number of Indo–European groups, the region contains the Turkic-speaking *Azerbaydzhanis* who belong to the Ural–Altaic family. Two large groups, the *Georgians* (3.6 million) and *Armenians* (4.2 million), have their own separate languages which are related neither to the Indo–European nor to the Ural–Altaic, nor to each other. Each has its own highly distinctive script, quite different from both Roman and Cyrillic. The Georgians are Orthodox Christians and the Armenians follow the Gregorian rite. The region has many other mutually unintelligible languages spoken by such peoples as the *Chechens*, *Lesghians* and *Kabardins*; many of the smaller Transcaucasian groups adhere to Islam.

Ural–Altaic ethnic groups

There are at least four main sub-divisions of the Ural–Altaic language family represented in the Soviet Union: the Finno–Ugrian, Turkic, Mongolian and Manchurian.

Finno–Ugrian peoples are distributed over a broad zone which embraces much of western Siberia and the northern half of the European USSR, where they were present before the arrival of the Russians. Over large areas they have been assimilated into the Slav majority but there are several areas where Finno–Ugrian languages are still spoken by the majority of the population. One such zone is in the extreme north-west of the Soviet Union, where the one million *Estonians*, much influenced by cultural contact with the Germans, and Protestant in religion, form a compact block of Finno–Ugrian speech. The 138 000 *Karelians* are closely related to the neighbouring Finns, but are now heavily outnumbered in their homeland by Russian settlers. A second zone in which Finno–Ugrian groups can be identified lies immediately west of the Urals, extending from the Arctic Ocean to the middle Volga. In the extreme north are the *Nentsy* reindeer-herders (30 000) and the *Komi* (327 000), many of whom are now employed in mining, lumbering and farming. Between the Volga and the Urals live the *Mordovs*, *Udmurts* and *Mari*, who together number 2.5 million. These groups are culturally more advanced than their northern neighbours: they have adopted Orthodox Christianity and settled agriculture and are now involved in the industrial development of their territories. Finally, to the east of the Urals, the west Siberian lowland, a wilderness covered by swamps and forests, is thinly occupied by the *Khanty* (21 000), *Mansi*

Armenian children in the uniform of the Pioneers, the communist party organisation for young children. In the background is Baku bay

(7 700) and other small Finno–Ugrian tribes.

Turkic-speakers, who number about 40 million and thus constitute some 15 % of the Soviet population, are the largest non-Slav element and are widely distributed in the regions east of the Volga. 23 million Turkic-speakers belong to the four major groups of Soviet Central Asia: the *Uzbeks, Kazakhs, Turkmen* and *Kirgiz.* The Uzbeks are by tradition settled farmers, engaged mainly in irrigated oasis cultivation, and have been much influenced by Persian culture. The Kazakhs were predominantly nomadic pastoralists but, since the Revolution, have for the most part been settled. Turkmen have included both pastoralists and farmers. The Kirgiz, like their Indo–Iranian Tadzhik neighbours, have a background of mountain stock-rearing but also include valley cultivators. All these groups are Moslem, and Islamic culture is dominant throughout this part of the Soviet Union, especially in rural areas. Most of the towns however, many of which are of very ancient origin, now have large communities of Russian settlers. The *Azerbaydzhanis* (5.5 million), on the west side of the Caspian, form an extension of this Central Asian Turkic zone and are quite distinct from the adjacent Georgians and Armenians.

Further large Turkic groups living between the Volga and the southern Urals include over 6 million *Tatars,* 1.8 million *Chuvash* and 1.4 million *Bashkirs.* Smaller nationalities speaking Turkic languages occur in various parts of Siberia, but do not amount to much more than 650 000 people in all. Most important are the *Yakuts* (328 000) of the Lena basin, the *Tuvinians* (166 000) of the Sayan Mountains and the *Khakass* (71 000) of the Altay.

Peoples of Mongolian origin form a small minority of the population of Siberia, rising to a majority in a few southern areas, the most important group being the *Buryats* (353 000) of the Lake Baykal region. These people are Buddhists, as are their cousins the *Kalmyks* (147 000) who reached the steppe to the west of the lower Volga in the eighteenth century.

A number of small Manchurian groups live in various districts of eastern Siberia and the Far East. The largest of these, the *Evenki,* number only 25 000. The *Koreans,* once an important minority near the border with Manchuria, now live mainly in Soviet Central Asia, though a few are still to be found in the Amur lowlands.

Paleo–Asiatic peoples

Probably pre-dating the arrival of the Ural-Altaic groups are a number of small, rather primitive tribes who live in the extreme north-east of the country. These Paleo–Asiatic peoples, each numbering only a few thousand, include the *Chukchi* of the Anadyr peninsula, who are related to the American Eskimo, the *Koryaks* of Kamchatka and the *Ainu* of Sakhalin and the Kurile Islands. The *Aleuts* of the Komandorskiye Islands, off the east coast of Kamchatka, had the distinction of being the smallest national group (441 people) recorded in the 1970 census.

The larger national groups retain their own languages for official purposes and newspapers and books are published in them. Russian is, however, taught in all schools and is the second language of all educated members of the minority groups. Several of the less important languages, spoken only by small numbers of people, are dying out and being replaced by Russian. In 1970, 76 % of the Soviet population claimed the ability to speak Russian as either their first or second language, including about half the people of non-Russian nationality. Ability to speak Russian was highest among dispersed groups such as the Jews (95 %) and Germans (92 %) and among the peoples of the Volga–Ural zone, such as the Chuvash (71 %), Mordovs (88 %) and Udmurts (81 %). At the other end of the scale, ability to speak Russian was lowest among the Moslems of the south; less than 20 % of the Uzbeks, Tadzhiks, Turkmen, Kirgiz and Azerbaydzhanis spoke Russian. It should be noted that in many areas where Russians are in a minority they are often to be found in positions of influence, and Russians play a leading role in the affairs of the Soviet Union to an even greater extent than their numerical superiority suggests.

POPULATION DISTRIBUTION

The total population of the Soviet Union as revealed by the last census, taken in January 1979, was 262 440 000. Only two countries, China (950–1000 million?) and India (623 million), have larger numbers. The population of the USSR exceeds that of the USA (217 million) by 18 % and is 4.6 times that of the United Kingdom (56 million). In relation to the size of the Soviet Union, however, its population is a good deal less impressive. The USSR has an area of 22.4 million square kilometres (8.6 million square miles) and covers one-sixth of the world's land surface but it contains only one-fifteenth of the world's population. Its area is about two-and-a-half times that of the United States (9.4 million sq km) and China (9.6 million sq km), more than six times that of India (3.3 million sq km) and no less than 92 times that of the United Kingdom (245 000 sq km). Thus the average population density of the USSR (11.7 people per km²) is much lower than in any of the other countries mentioned: UK 229, India 182, China 88, USA 23 per km². These comparisons emphasise the fact that the Soviet Union is a thinly settled country; closer examination reveals that vast areas are virtually uninhabited, contrasting vividly with the relatively limited areas of densely settled territory.

The situation is illustrated in Fig. 6.2, which shows the distribution of the Soviet population among the various republics and economic regions (see also Table 6.2). Of the 262.4 million inhabitants of the USSR, 181.1 million or 69 % live in the European part of the country, which accounts for only 24.4 % of the national territory. This relatively densely settled area is continued southward into the Transcaucasian republics, whose population of 14.1 million represents 5.4 % of the total living in 0.8 % of the area. A further

TABLE 6.2: POPULATION OF THE USSR, 1979, BY REPUBLICS AND MAJOR ECONOMIC REGIONS*

Region or Republic	Area 000 km²	%	Population 000	%	Density per km²
USSR	22 402.2	100.0	262 442	100.0	11.7
RSFSR	17 075.4	76.2	137 552	52.6	8.1
North-west	1 661.8	7.4	13 275	5.1	8.0
Centre	485.2	2.2	28 947	11.0	59.7
Volga–Vyatka	263.2	1.2	8 343	3.2	31.7
Black Earth Centre	167.7	0.8	7 797	3.0	46.5
Volga	680.0	3.0	19 393	7.4	28.5
North Caucasus	355.1	1.6	15 487	5.9	43.6
Ural	680.4	3.0	15 568	5.9	22.9
West Siberia	2 472.2	10.8	12 959	4.9	5.2
East Siberia	4 122.8	18.4	8 158	3.1	2.0
Far East	6 215.9	27.8	6 819	2.6	1.1
Ukraine	601.0	2.7	49 757	19.0	82.8
Donets–Dnepr	220.5	1.0	21 045	8.0	95.4
South-west	269.8	1.2	21 578	8.2	80.0
South	110.7	0.5	7 134	2.7	64.4
Baltic	189.1	0.8	8 192	3.1	43.3
Lithuania	65.2	0.3	3 399	1.3	52.1
Latvia	63.7	0.3	2 521	1.0	39.6
Estonia	45.1	0.2	1 466	0.6	32.5
†Kaliningrad oblast	15.1	0.1	806	0.3	53.4
Transcaucasia	186.1	0.8	14 075	5.4	75.6
Georgia	69.7	0.3	5 016	1.9	72.0
Azerbaydzhan	86.6	0.4	6 028	2.3	69.6
Armenia	29.8	0.1	3 031	1.2	101.7
Central Asia	1 279.3	5.7	25 480	9.7	19.9
Uzbekistan	449.6	2.0	15 391	5.9	34.2
Kirgiziya	198.5	0.9	3 529	1.3	17.8
Tadzhikistan	143.1	0.6	3 801	1.4	26.6
Turkmeniya	488.1	2.2	2 759	1.1	5.7
Kazakhstan	2 715.1	12.1	14 685	5.6	5.4
Belorussia	207.7	0.9	9 559	3.6	46.0
Moldavia	33.7	0.2	3 948	1.5	117.2

* For the boundaries of these regions, see Fig. 1.1.

† Figures for Kaliningrad oblast are also included in RSFSR totals.

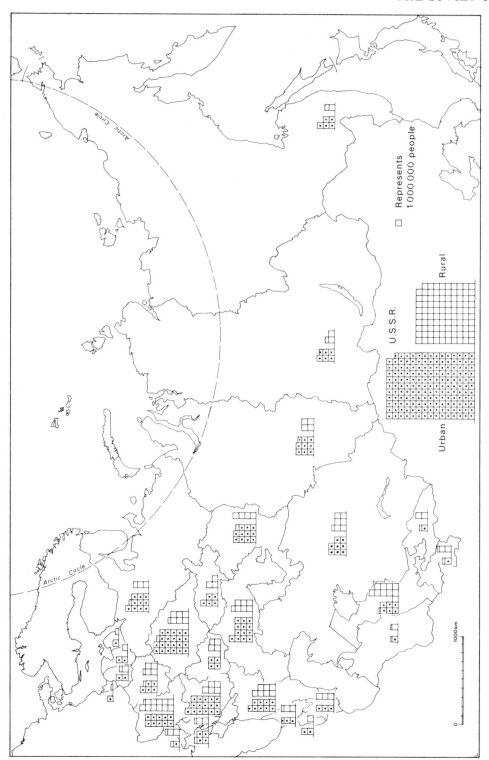

Fig. 6.2 Distribution of the Soviet population in 1979, by republics and major economic regions. Each small square represents one million people, 0.38% of the total population

40.2 million, 15.3 per cent of the population, live in Kazakhstan and the four Central Asian republics which together constitute 17.8% of Soviet territory. All these regions, and particularly the European USSR, are in striking contrast to Siberia and the Far East. These vast territories make up 57% of the land area but have only 10.6% of the population; in some 12.8 million km² there are only 27.9 million people. Most striking of all is the Far East region, an area as large as Europe with a population roughly equal to that of Switzerland.

Fig. 6.3 shows in some detail variations in population density throughout the USSR, and from this map it is possible to identify areas in which density is significantly above or below the national average. Immediately apparent is the relatively restricted area falling into the 'above-average' category. This includes what may be termed the main settled zone, a triangular area with its base along the western frontier and its apex in the Urals. There is a southward extension of this zone into the North Caucasus and Transcaucasian regions. Outside these areas, districts with above-average density are small and discontinuous. One such covers parts of south-west Siberia and continues eastward in a narrow belt along the Trans-Siberian Railway to the Pacific at Vladivostok; another occurs in parts of Soviet Central Asia. For a fuller picture of the situation and of the factors at work, this pattern must be discussed on a regional basis.

European USSR

The location of the main settled zone of the Soviet Union is indicated by densities above 25 people per km². The most densely populated districts of all (over 100 people per km²) are in and around the major cities: Moscow, Kiev and the Donbas industrial complex, for example, stand out clearly on Fig. 6.3. However, very high densities (by Soviet standards) are also recorded in some predominantly rural areas where conditions are especially favourable for agriculture, as in the western Ukraine. The agricultural productivity of the Ukrainian steppe and the wooded steppe as a whole is reflected in a broad belt of territory where densities are between 50 and 100 people per km², despite the fact that the urban proportion rarely exceeds the national average of 63% and is often well below that level. As an example we may note the Cherkassy oblast, with an area of 20 900 km² and a population of 1.5 million of whom 860 000 are classed as rural, giving an overall density of 74.1 people per km² and a rural density of 41.1 people per km². Rural densities are lower in the eastern Ukraine but overall density is raised by the presence of major industrial cities; thus the Donetsk oblast has an area of 26 500 km² and a population of 5.2 million, 89% urban; its rural density is only 17.4 people per km², but the overall figure is 195 people per km², one of the highest in the country.

Away from this high-density zone, densities diminish both northwards into the mixed forest and southwards into the drier parts of the steppe, though in the grainlands of the North Caucasus economic region high densities are common. North of a line from Leningrad to Perm, there is an abrupt change to areas where the average density is below 10 per km² and in many places below 1 per km². In these northern districts, agriculture is of little or no importance and the dominant activities are lumbering and mining. Consequently, the urban proportion is abnormally high. An extreme example is provided by the Murmansk oblast. This has an area of 144 900 km² and a population of 965 000, giving an overall density of 6.7 per km². However, 89% of the population is urban, 381 000 living in the port city of Murmansk alone, with a rural population of only 102 000 and a rural density of only 0.7 per km².

Eastwards towards the Urals, the densely settled zone becomes narrower as the negative areas of tayga and tundra to the north and dry steppe and desert to the south become wider with increasing continentality. A pocket of densities in the 25–50 people per km² range marks the position of the main industrial area of the central Urals. Here again, agricultural potential is limited and the rural population is small. In the Sverdlovsk and Chelyabinsk oblasts, 6.6 million out of a population of 7.9 million are classed as urban and the rural density is only 4.5 people per km².

The Caucasus

The main Caucasian range forms a narrow belt of thinly settled territory on either side of which are productive lowlands where population density is several times the national average. This applies particularly to Georgia and Armenia, which have densities of 72.0 and 101.7 people per km² respectively. Highly productive sub-tropical agriculture in western Georgia supports rural densities exceeding 100 people per km² in places.

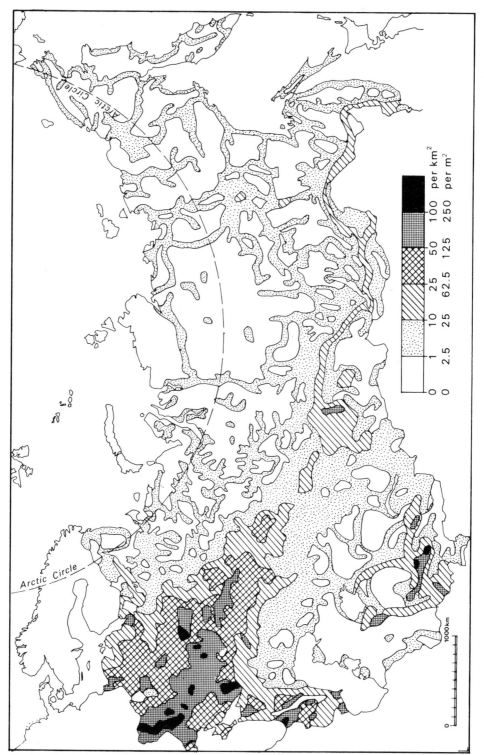

Fig. 6.3 Population density. White and stippled areas have densities below the national average

Kazakhstan and Central Asia

In the steppelands of northern Kazakhstan, despite the expansion of the cultivated area achieved under the virgin lands scheme of the 1950s, overall densities are generally well below 10 people per km^2 and rural densities less than 5 people per km^2; for example the Tselinograd oblast has 6.5 persons per km^2 but a rural density of 2.8 persons per km^2. Populations are predominantly rural save in the Karaganda oblast where there has been large scale industrial development but conditions are too dry for productive farming (86 per cent urban, rural density 2 people per km^2, overall density 14.7).

South of the Kazakh steppe lie the vast expanses of the Turanian desert, where densities are below 1 person per km^2 over large areas. Beyond the desert is the densely-populated mountain-foot zone where, although there are a number of large and ancient cities, some 60 % of the population is rural and very high rural densities, based on irrigated farming, are common. In the Fergana basin, for example, live more than 4 million people, of whom 2.8 million (68.6 %) are classed as rural, giving a rural density of 146 people per km^2. Narrow belts of high density also extend out across the desert along the valleys of the Amu Darya and Syr Darya rivers.

Siberia and the Far East

As already indicated, these are the most thinly settled regions of the USSR. West Siberia, East Siberia and the Far East have overall densities of 5.2, 2.0 and 1.1 persons per km^2 respectively. Only in West Siberia is there a zone of appreciable size in which densities exceed 10 people per km^2; this embraces the Kuzbas industrial area and the agriculturally more productive parts of the Altay kray and the Novosibirsk and Omsk oblasts. Despite recent developments in oil and gas production, the central and northern parts of the West Siberian lowland are very thinly populated indeed; covering most of this region is the Tyumen oblast which has an area of 1 435 000 km^2 but a population of only 1.9 million, giving an average density of only 1.3 people per km^2.

In East Siberia and the Far East, densities rise above 10 people per km^2 only in a narrow belt along the Trans-Siberian railway. Away from this zone, settlement is mainly confined to river valleys and coastal fringes, between which there are vast areas of virtually uninhabited territory. The Taymyr and Evenki autonomous okrugs, for example, have a population of only 60 000 in an area of 1.6 million km^2 (0.04 people per km^2); one person to every 25 km^2 of land. Over many of these sparsely populated areas of northern Siberia, the urban proportion is very high; in Magadan oblast, for example, 365 000 out of a total population of 466 000 (78 %) are classed as urban.

The striking regional variations in population density outlined above are to a large degree the result of physical factors. The low densities prevailing in the Siberian tundra and tayga and in the deserts of Central Asia are obvious cases in which the nature of the physical environment is hostile to the development of a large population. At the same time, historical and economic factors are also of major importance. The long-established role of the European part of the country as its agricultural and industrial heartland has been responsible for the fact that it contains nearly 70 % of the Soviet population. A great potential for future economic development exists in the Asiatic parts of the Soviet Union, particularly in Siberia, and despite the physical difficulties there are many areas which can, and no doubt eventually will, support much large numbers than at present. Indeed, the movements of people from the European to the Asiatic parts of the country is a persistent theme in the history of population change in the USSR, even though counter movements occur.

POPULATION CHANGE

This topic will be discussed in two stages: a brief general statement of developments in the period up to the census of 1959, and a more detailed examination of recent trends as exemplified by the changes which have occurred since that date.

Population change 1897–1959

To give precise data on the growth of the Soviet population during the present century is by no means a simple task, for a variety of reasons. In the first place, complete censuses have been carried out on only six occasions: in 1897, 1926, 1939, 1959, 1970 and 1979. For years other than these, it is necessary to make use of estimates from a variety of sources, not all of which are wholly reliable. Secondly, there have been major changes in the boundaries of the Soviet Union. Following the First World War, large areas, including Finland, the Baltic states, Poland and Bessarabia, were detached from the USSR; parts but not all of these territories were recovered during and after the Second World War when the Soviet Union also gained additional territory from Germany and Czechoslovakia. In addition, the two World Wars, the Revolution and the Civil War which followed it, together with other internal upheavals, had a profound effect on population growth. These events not only caused a large number of extra deaths but also resulted in reduced fertility so that the number of births was much smaller than that of more normal times. It has been estimated that, had it not been for these setbacks, the population of the USSR would now be in excess of 350 million as against an actual

total of 262 million in 1979. Thus the figures given in Tables 6.3 and 6.4 are, for years prior to 1959, only approximate; nevertheless they give a reasonably good impression of the changes which have occurred since the late nineteenth century.

Prior to the First World War, the population of the Russian Empire was steadily increasing at a rate of about 1.6% per annum. Fertility was still very high, but this was largely offset by high mortality. Despite this somewhat primitive demographic régime, there was an increase of nearly 35 million (27.8%) in the 16 years between 1897 and 1913. In marked contrast, the next 13 years (1913–26) saw a net gain of only 5.8 million (3.6%) and

TABLE 6.3: POPULATION CHANGE, 1897–1979
(ALL FIGURES REFER TO THE PRESENT TERRITORY OF THE USSR)

| Year | Population (millions) | | | Change (%) | | |
	Total	Urban	Rural	Total	Urban	Rural
1897	124.6	18.4	106.2	—	—	—
1913	159.2	28.5	130.7	+27.8	+54.9	+23.1
1926	165.0	33.0	132.0	+ 3.6	+15.8	+ 1.0
1940	194.1	63.1	131.0	+17.6	+91.2	− 0.8
1950	178.5	69.4	109.1	− 8.0	+10.0	−16.7
1955	194.4	86.3	108.1	+ 8.9	+24.4	− 0.9
1960	212.3	103.8	108.5	+ 9.2	+20.3	+ 0.4
1965	229.2	121.7	107.5	+ 8.0	+17.2	− 0.9
1970	241.7	136.0	105.7	+ 5.5	+11.8	− 1.7
1975	253.3	153.1	100.2	+ 4.8	+12.6	− 5.2
1979	262.4	163.6	98.8	+ 3.4	+ 6.9	− 1.4

Sources: Narodnoye khozyaystvo SSSR (Moscow, various years); Bond, A. R. and Lydolph, P. E.; 'Soviet Population Change and City Growth, 1970–79,' Soviet Geography, 20, (October 1979).

TABLE 6.4: VITAL RATES 1913–1975
(ALL FIGURES PER 1000 OF THE POPULATION)

Year	Birth Rate	Death Rate	Natural increase
1913	47.0	30.2	16.8
1926	44.0	20.3	23.7
1940	31.2	18.0	13.2
1950	26.7	9.7	17.0
1955	25.7	8.2	17.5
1960	24.9	7.1	17.8
1965	18.4	7.3	11.1
1970	17.4	8.2	9.2
1975	18.1	9.3	8.8
1979	18.2	10.1	8.1

Source: Narodnoye khozyaystvo SSSR za 60 let, (Moscow, various years).

an annual growth rate of barely 0.3%. These figures indicate the disastrous results of war, revolution and civil war. Had the pre-war rate of natural increase continued down to 1926, the population at that date would have been about 193 million. In fact it was only 165 million, indicating a 'population deficit' of 28 million for the period. This deficit comprised 16 million extra deaths, a shortfall of 10 million births and a net migration loss of 2 million.

Officially-published data for the inter-war period, exemplified by the figures for 1926 and 1940 in Tables 6.3 and 6.4, provide conflicting evidence of population trends. The total increase of 29.1 million (17.6%) in fourteen years indicates an average annual growth of about 12 per 1000, yet the natural increase rate was 23.7 per 1000 in

1926 and 13.2 per 1000 in 1940, this decline being due mainly to a fall in the birth rate. The fact that the average rate of population growth between 1926 and 1940 was lower than the natural increase rate at the beginning and end of the period can only mean that, at some time during this period, the rate of natural increase was well below the 1940 level. This situation may be attributed to the effects of forced collectivisation and low agricultural production which in some areas led to famine in the early 1930s. By the eve of the Second World War, these difficulties had been overcome and the Soviet population was expanding at a rate much more rapid than that of any west European country.

The Second World War proved a setback to Soviet population growth even more serious than that of 1913–26. Between 1940 and 1950 there was an actual decline of 15.6 million (8%) and, since this decade included five post-war years of rapid growth, the decline during the war must have been very much greater, possibly in the region of 30 million. Once again it is revealing to compare the actual situation, this time in 1950, with what might have been expected had there been no war. Even allowing for a continuation of the decline in birth rates visible before the war, the population of the USSR should by 1950, have reached 224 million. Instead, it was only 179 million, indicating an enormous wartime deficit of 45 million. No detailed figures of their war losses have been published by the Soviet authorities, but close examination of the age and sex data in the 1959 census suggests that the deficit of 45 million involved 10 million deaths in the armed forces, 15 million extra civilian deaths (11 million men and 4 million women) and a deficit of births, resulting from low fertility and high infant mortality, of 20 million.

These events have had fundamental effects on the composition of the Soviet population in the post-war years, some of which are shown by the age-sex pyramids in Fig. 6.4. These effects were most marked in 1959 but were still visible in the 1970s. The Soviet population has a large excess of females over males. In 1959 there were 114.8 million women, but only 94 million men, a ratio of 122 women to every 100 men. By 1979 the position had improved considerably, but there were still 114 women to every 100 men and it will be some years before a more normal sex-ratio is achieved. This lack of balance between the sexes is visible in all age-groups born before 1940 and reaches its maximum among those born between 1910 and 1924, the majority of whom were of military age during the Second World War. Among those aged between 45 and 59 in 1970, there were only 60 men to every 100 women, 167 women to every 100 men. Low fertility during the war years is reflected in the small numbers of both sexes in the 25–29 age group in 1970, while the large numbers aged 10–19 indicates accelerated natural increase in the early post-war years. The inset at the base of the pyramid reflects fertility decline in the 1960s (see below). As a result of these factors, the Soviet population is a relatively youthful one, though less so than 20 years ago. In 1970 there were about 70 million people (29%) below the age of 15.

A further general point is that, in common with most other countries, the USSR is becoming increasingly urbanised. The proportion of the population classed as urban rose steadily from the very low level of 15% in 1897 to 48% at the 1959 census. The landmark of 50% urban was passed in 1961 and 62.3% was reached in 1979. The rural population is now declining in numbers but remains very much larger (98.8 million in 1979) than is the case in other developed countries.

With the publication of the 1959 census results, an assessment of change over the previous 20 years became possible and the regular publication of demographic data in Soviet statistical handbooks permits a more detailed examination of more recent trends. Between 1939 and 1959, the total population of the USSR grew by only 18.1 million or 9.5%, an annual growth rate of little more than 0.4%. This overall change involved a large decline during the war and a rapid growth in the post-war years. Rural population declined in many areas and, over much of the European part of the country, more than offset the urban growth of the period, giving a net decline in places of 10% or more. Total growth well above the national average, however, occurred in the Asiatic regions. The population of Kazakhstan, for example, grew by 50.8% and that of the Far East by 69.7%. Natural increase in the early post-war years rose well above that of the inter-war period; while the birth rate declined from 31.2 per 1000 in 1940 to 24.9 per 1000 in 1960, the death rate fell dramatically from 18.0 to the remarkably low level of 7.1 per 1000 at the latter date. Thus the natural increase rate throughout the 1950s was around 1.75% per annum, half as much again as in the inter-war years.

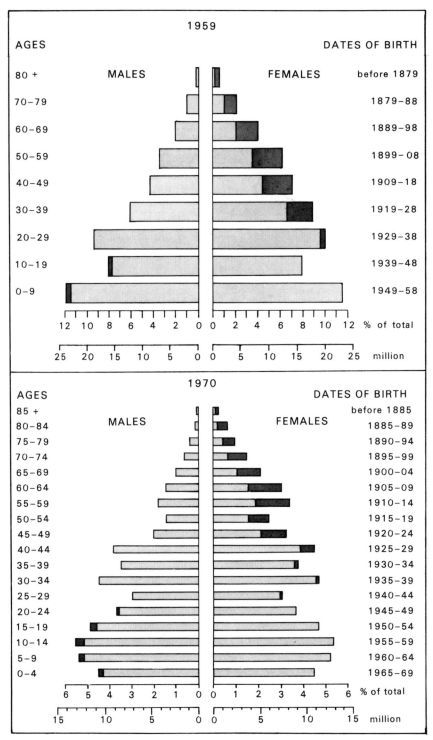

Fig. 6.4 Age and sex structure of the Soviet population in 1959 (top) and 1970 (bottom). The shaded portion of each age-group bar indicates an excess of one sex over the other: male surplus on the left, female surplus on the right

The net result of these trends, combined with large-scale migration from European to Asiatic areas, was a further increase in the proportion of the Soviet population living in Siberia, the Far East, Kazakhstan, Central Asia and the Transcaucasus. Between 1939 and 1959, the population of the European USSR rose by only 2.9%, while that of Transcaucasia grew by 18.4%, Central Asia by 29.8%, Siberia and the Far East by 36.9% and Kazakhstan by 50.8%. The European share of the total fell from 78.9 to 74.1%, that of Asiatic areas rose from 21.1 to 25.9%. In terms of absolute numbers, there was an increase of only 4.3 million in the population of the European sector, whereas the population of the Asiatic USSR grew by 13.8 million.

Population change 1959–1979

Detailed data for the period 1959–1979 are displayed in Tables 6.5 and 6.6. Over this twenty-year period, the Soviet population grew by 53.6 million or 25.7%, an average annual increase of about 1.2%. These figures denote a slower rate of population growth in the 1960s and 1970s compared with that of the 1950s, mainly as a result of diminished fertility. Until about 1960, the birth rate was declining relatively slowly and this trend, combined with a continuing reduction in the death rate, gave an accelerating natural increase, which reached a peak of 17.8 per 1000 in 1960. Since that

date, however, the death rate has edged slowly upwards owing to an increase in the proportion of old people and the fall in the birth rate has become more rapid. Thus, by 1969, the rate of natural increase had fallen to 8.9 per 1000, a level significantly below that of the inter-war years and precisely half that of 1960. In the early 1970s there was a slight recovery in the birth rate, due mainly to the fact that the large birth cohorts of the late 1940s were now producing children, but the death rate also rose and the natural increase rate in 1976 was again 8.9 per 1000. This has meant an actual reduction in the number of people added to the Soviet population each year. Between 1950 and 1960, this annual increment averaged 3 380 000, with a peak of 3 900 000 in 1959. During the 1960s the average was 2 940 000 and fell again to an average of 2 302 000 in the period 1970–1979. Any forecast of future trends presents considerable difficulties, but a further reduction in fertility seems likely, at least in those Asiatic areas now characterised by exceptionally high birth rates. At the same time, mortality will probably show a further slow increase as the population continues to age. Thus it seems likely that, within the next decade, the rate of natural increase in the Soviet Union will decline still further, possibly even to west European levels.

Within these general trends, there are marked regional contrasts as well as differences between

TABLE 6.5: BIRTH, DEATH AND NATURAL INCREASE RATES (PER 1000) BY REPUBLICS 1950–1979

	Birth Rate			Death Rate			Natural Increase		
	1950	1965	1979	1950	1965	1979	1950	1965	1979
USSR	26.7	18.4	18.2	9.7	7.3	10.1	17.0	11.1	8.1
RSFSR	26.9	15.7	15.8	10.1	7.6	10.8	16.8	8.1	5.0
Ukraine	22.8	15.3	14.7	8.5	7.6	11.1	14.3	7.7	3.6
Lithuania	23.6	18.1	15.2	12.0	7.9	10.2	11.6	10.2	5.0
Latvia	17.0	13.8	13.7	12.4	10.0	12.7	4.6	3.8	1.0
Estonia	18.4	14.6	14.9	14.4	10.5	12.3	4.0	4.1	2.6
Belorussia	25.5	17.9	15.8	8.0	6.8	9.5	17.5	11.1	6.3
Moldavia	38.9	20.4	20.2	11.2	6.2	10.5	27.7	14.2	9.7
Georgia	23.5	21.2	17.9	7.2	7.0	8.3	15.9	14.2	9.6
Azerbaydzhan	31.2	36.6	25.2	9.6	6.4	7.1	21.6	30.2	18.1
Armenia	32.1	28.6	22.9	8.5	5.7	5.6	23.6	22.9	17.3
Kazakhstan	37.6	26.9	24.0	11.7	5.9	7.7	25.9	21.0	16.3
Uzbekistan	30.9	34.7	34.4	8.8	5.9	7.0	22.1	28.8	27.4
Kirgiziya	32.4	31.4	30.1	8.5	6.5	8.3	23.9	24.9	21.8
Tadzhikistan	30.4	36.8	37.8	8.2	6.6	7.7	22.2	30.2	30.1
Turkmeniya	38.2	37.2	34.9	10.2	7.0	7.6	28.0	30.2	27.3

Source: Narodnoye khozyaystvo SSSR v 1965 godu, . . . v 1979 godu Moscow, 1966, 1980.

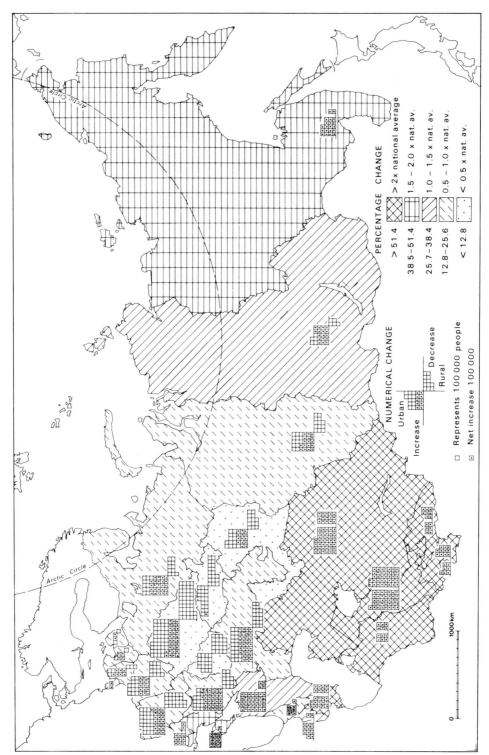

Fig. 6.5 Population change, 1959–79, by republics and major economic regions. The small squares show numerical increases (above the line) and decreases (below the line) in urban (left) and rural (right) populations for each area. Squares with dots indicate net increase. The shadings show percentage increase in relation to the national average of 25.7%

urban and rural populations. These contrasts are illustrated by Fig. 6.5 as well as by Tables 6.5 and 6.6. Over the country as a whole rapid urban growth continued, the urban population increasing by well over 60% in 20 years. The rural population, on the other hand, showed a net decline of 9.2%, compounded from decreases exceeding 35% (Central and Volga–Vyatka economic regions) and increases of more than 65% (Uzbek, Tadzhik and Turkmen republics). Table 6.6 shows clearly the basic contrast between Europe and Siberia on the one hand and the southern Asiatic regions on the other, as regards rural population change. In the former group, all regions except the North Caucasus, the Far East, Moldavia and the South showed large-scale rural

decline, whereas rural populations increased throughout Kazakhstan, Central Asia and the Transcaucasus. Table 6.7 summarises numerical and percentage changes and shows that the net addition to the Soviet population between 1959 and 1979 was almost equally divided between the European and Asiatic sections of the country.

By 1979, the proportion of the Soviet population living in Europe had fallen still further, to 69.2%, compared with 73.2% in 1959, 78.6% in 1939 and 82.1% in 1913. Migration played an important role in bringing about this change, but regional variations in the rate of natural increase were also of major significance as a closer examination on a regional basis clearly illustrates.

TABLE 6.6: *POPULATION CHANGE 1959–1979 BY REPUBLICS AND MAJOR ECONOMIC REGIONS*

Region or Republic	Numerical Change (000) Urban	Rural	Total	Percentage Change Urban	Rural	Total
USSR	+63 613	− 9 998	+53 615	+ 63.6	− 9.2	+25.7
RSFSR	+33 764	−13 746	+20 018	+ 51.6	−24.6	+17.0
North-west	+ 3 530	− 1 120	+ 2 410	+ 50.3	−29.2	+22.2
Centre	+ 7 393	− 4 164	+ 3 229	+ 48.4	−39.9	+12.6
Volga–Vyatka	+ 1 981	− 1 890	+ 91	+ 61.6	−37.5	+ 1.1
Black Earth Centre	+ 1 948	− 1 920	+ 28	+ 92.0	−34.0	+ 0.4
Volga	+ 5 381	− 1 963	+ 3 418	+ 73.2	−22.8	+21.4
North Caucasus	+ 3 535	+ 351	+ 3 886	+ 71.3	+ 5.2	+33.5
Ural	+ 2 723	− 1 339	+ 1 384	+ 30.7	−25.2	+ 9.8
West Siberia	+ 3 044	− 1 338	+ 1 707	+ 53.2	−24.2	+15.2
East Siberia	+ 2 191	− 506	+ 1 685	+ 64.2	−16.5	+26.0
Far East	+ 1 816	+ 169	+ 1 985	+ 55.6	+10.8	+41.1
Ukraine	+11 369	− 3 481	+ 7 888	+ 59.4	−15.3	+18.8
Donets–Dnepr	+ 4 618	− 1 339	+ 3 279	+ 41.1	−20.5	+18.5
South-west	+ 4 732	− 2 181	+ 2 551	+ 87.1	−16.0	+13.4
South	+ 2 019	+ 40	+ 2 059	+ 81.9	+ 1.5	+40.6
Baltic	+ 2 137	− 558	+ 1 579	+ 65.0	−16.8	+23.9
Lithuania	+ 1 016	− 328	+ 688	+ 97.1	−19.7	+25.4
Latvia	+ 552	− 124	+ 428	+ 47.0	−13.5	+20.4
Estonia	+ 346	− 77	+ 269	+ 51.2	−14.8	+22.5
†Kaliningrad oblast	+ 222	− 27	+ 195	+ 56.2	−12.5	+31.9
Transcaucasia	+ 3 432	+ 1 138	+ 4 570	+ 78.7	+22.1	+48.1
Georgia	+ 888	+ 84	+ 972	+ 51.8	+ 3.6	+24.0
Azerbaydzhan	+ 1 433	+ 897	+ 2 330	+ 81.1	+46.5	+63.0
Armenia	+ 1 111	+ 157	+ 1 268	+126.0	+17.8	+71.9
Central Asia	+ 5 590	+ 6 208	+11 798	+117.1	+69.7	+86.2
Uzbekistan	+ 3 621	+ 3 651	+ 7 272	+132.7	+67.7	+89.6
Kirgiziya	+ 670	+ 793	+ 1 463	+ 96.3	+57.9	+70.8
Tadzhikistan	+ 678	+ 1 143	+ 1 821	+105.0	+85.7	+91.9
Turkmeniya	+ 621	+ 622	+ 1 243	+ 88.6	+76.3	+82.0
Kazakhstan	+ 3 854	+ 1 536	+ 5 390	+ 94.8	+29.4	+58.0
Belorussia	+ 2 781	− 1 278	+ 1 503	+112.1	−22.9	+18.7
Moldavia	+ 909	+ 155	+ 1 064	+141.6	+ 6.9	+36.9

† Figures for Kaliningrad oblast are also included in RSFSR totals.

Soviet citizens and tourists watch the guard leaving Red Square after the changing-over ceremony at Lenin's tomb. In the background is GUM, the State Universal Store which occupies a pre-revolution building

EUROPEAN USSR

As already indicated, this part of the country has experienced a rate of growth appreciably below the national average; between 1959 and 1979 its population increased by only 17.2%. This was the result of a relatively slow natural increase, due mainly to low fertility, combined with emigration to other parts of the country. European USSR includes three regions, the Centre, Urals and Donets–Dnepr, which have throughout the Soviet period contained the bulk of the country's industrial capacity and about a quarter of its population. All three had rates of growth below the national average between 1959 and 1979. This applied even to their urban populations, indicating that industry in these areas, while still expanding, was doing so a good deal less rapidly than in areas of more recent industrial development such as the Volga region. The highest rates of urban growth were in fact recorded in such regions as the Black Earth Centre, Belorussia, Lithuania and Moldavia, formerly industrial backwaters which,

during the 1960s and 1970s, were the scene of numerous industrial developments.

European USSR is also characterised by a very marked decline in rural populations. This reached its extreme in the Centre and Volga–Vyatka regions, long the most densely settled parts of the mixed forest zone, and was considerable not only in regions of low agricultural potential, like the North-west but also in highly productive agricultural regions such as the Black Earth Centre. Indeed in the Volga–Vyatka and Black Earth Centre regions, though urban growth was up to the national level, total population has shown practically no growth since 1959. Rural depopulation also occurred, though to a less marked degree, in the Ukraine, the Baltic republics, Belorussia and the Urals. Three European regions provide exceptions to this general picture of rural decline. The South (i.e. the southern Ukraine) received a small addition to its rural population, despite a low natural increase. Practically the whole of this occurred in the Crimea and must

TABLE 6.7: POPULATION CHANGE, 1959–1979 BY MAJOR GEOGRAPHICAL DIVISIONS

	Urban 000	%	Rural 000	%	Total 000	%
European USSR	+43 686	+ 58.7	−17 207	−21.7	+26 479	+17.2
Asiatic USSR	+19 927	+ 77.8	+ 7 209	+76.4	+27 136	+49.3
Siberia and Far East	+ 7 051	+ 56.8	− 1 673	−16.5	+ 5 378	+23.8
Kazakhstan	+ 3 854	+ 94.8	+ 1 536	+29.4	+ 5 390	+58.0
Central Asia	+ 5 590	+117.1	+ 6 208	+69.7	+11 798	+86.2
Transcaucasia	+ 3 432	+ 78.7	+ 1 138	+22.1	+ 4 570	+48.1
USSR	+63 613	+ 63.6	− 9 998	− 9.2	+53 615	+25.7

have involved immigration into that area. The North Caucasus had a larger rural increase, which may have involved some migration gain but was also due to a high natural increase among non-Slav minorities. Moldavia, a region of intensive and prosperous agriculture, was also favoured by a high birth rate.

SIBERIA AND THE FAR EAST
These regions show trends very different from those of earlier periods. Much of their population growth over the past 100 years has been the result of immigration from the European USSR and the high fertility associated with a youthful immigrant population. Thus their rate of increase in the inter-war years was twice, and that between 1939 and 1959, five times, the national average. Since 1959, however, their growth rate has been slightly below that of the USSR as a whole. Indeed in West Siberia it was only 15.2 %, barely two-thirds of the national average. The present growth rate in Siberia and the Far East as a whole represents an annual addition to the population of these vast territories (56 % of the land area of the USSR) of only about 260 000. Such a slow build-up of population presents serious problems in the development of the regions' vast natural resources.

Despite important agricultural developments, notably the virgin lands scheme in south-west Siberia, there was a decline of 1.7 million in the rural population of Siberia and the Far East between 1959 and 1979. Furthermore, despite major industrial developments, urban growth has been slightly below the national average and can be accounted for largely by natural increase and rural-urban movement. From published data and from numerous comments in the Soviet press, it appears that, since the labour controls character-istic of the Stalin period were relaxed, the rate of

migration to the eastern territories has declined drastically and the Soviet authorities are finding it increasingly difficult to maintain in these regions a permanent labour force large enough to carry out plans for their economic development. Furthermore, the natural increase, which until 1960 was well above the national average, mainly because of high fertility, has also undergone a marked decline. In 1950, birth rates in Siberia and the Far East were well above the national average; today they are little above those of European areas.

KAZAKHSTAN AND CENTRAL ASIA
These five republics provide a strong contrast with the areas discussed so far, for their populations are expanding more rapidly than those of any other part of the Soviet Union. Between 1959 and 1979,

An Uzbek taxi driver eating shashlick (roast mutton)

the population of Kazakhstan and Central Asia rose by 75%, from 23 to 40 million. In these regions there is no question at present of rural population decline; in fact, since 1959, increase in rural numbers (7.7 million) has not been very far behind urban growth (9.4 million) overall, and has actually exceeded urban growth in the four Central Asian republics. This unique situation may be attributed mainly to the high rate of natural increase which, throughout practically the whole of the region, is double and in places three times the national average. The underlying cause is simple: while death rates have been brought down to levels similar to those prevailing in other parts of the Soviet Union, birth rates remain extremely high and, except in Kazakhstan, have shown little or no decline over the last 30 years. The fact that these regions are inhabited mainly by non-Slav peoples is the prime reason for this situation. High fertility is part of the unique, essentially non-European culture which prevails, at least in rural areas, throughout Central Asia. Even so, natural increase alone cannot account for the very high rate of population growth, averaging 3% per annum. There has, in addition, been considerable immigration from other parts of the country, mainly to urban areas but, in Kazakhstan at least, to rural areas as well.

Kazakhstan shows somewhat different trends from the other four republics yet, at the same time, clearly illustrates the factors at work in the region as a whole. Between 1959 and 1979, the population of Kazakhstan rose by 58.0%, the urban element increasing by no less than 94.8% and the rural by 29.4%. Its birth rate was much lower than those of the other four republics, reflecting the fact that Russians are the largest ethnic group, and the rate of natural increase declined from 3% in 1960 to 1.7% in 1975. Only large-scale immigration to the virgin lands and to Karaganda and other industrial complexes can account for this situation. The other four republics still have birth rates well above 30 per 1000 and natural increase rates of 2.2–3.0% per annum.

Thus Kazakhstan and Central Asia have experienced not only rapid natural increase but also, in some years at least, a sizeable net migration gain. As a result, their share of the total Soviet population rose from 8.6% in 1939 to 11% in 1959 and 15.3% in 1979. Since rapid natural increase is found mainly among non-Slav groups, it follows that their relative size is also increasing.

TRANSCAUCASIA

Transcaucasia shows a rate of population growth second only to that of Central Asia, with a 48% rise between 1959 and 1979, including 22.1% rural and 78.7% urban increase. In this case, however, rapid natural increase among predominantly non-Slav populations, particularly those of Azerbaydzhan and Armenia, accounts for practically all the increase, and immigration has played only a minor role, taking place mainly to oil-producing districts. The Transcaucasus has fewer Slavs among its population than any other major region of the USSR. Total numbers are, of course, quite small, but the economic importance of Transcaucasia is indicated by its high density and rapid growth and the fact that it contains twice as many people as the whole Far Eastern region.

Types of population change

Regional contrasts in the nature and scale of recent population trends are further illustrated by the typology of population change shown in Fig. 6.6, where 27 areal units—the republics and major economic regions which constitute the USSR—have been allocated among seven types according

TABLE 6.8: TYPES OF POPULATION CHANGE IN THE USSR, 1959–1979

1. *Total increase above average; urban increase above average; rural increase*: Tadzhik SSR, Uzbek SSR, Turkmen SSR, Armenian SSR, Kirgiz SSR, Azerbaydzhan SSR, Kazakh SSR, Southern region (Ukraine), Moldavian SSR, North Caucasus region (RSFSR).
2. *Total increase above average; urban increase below average; rural increase*: Far Eastern region (RSFSR).
3. *Total increase above average; urban increase above average; rural decrease*: East Siberian region (RSFSR).
4. *Total increase above average; urban increase below average; rural decrease*: Kaliningrad oblast (RSFSR).
5. *Total increase below average; urban increase above average; rural decrease*: Lithuanian SSR, Belorussian SSR, Volga and Black Earth Centre regions (RSFSR), South-western region (Ukraine).
6. *Total increase below average; urban increase below average; rural increase*: Georgian SSR.
7. *Total increase below average; urban increase below average; rural decrease*: North-western, Central, Volga–Vyatka, Ural and West Siberian regions (RSFSR), Donets–Dnepr region (Ukraine), Latvian SSR, Estonian SSR.

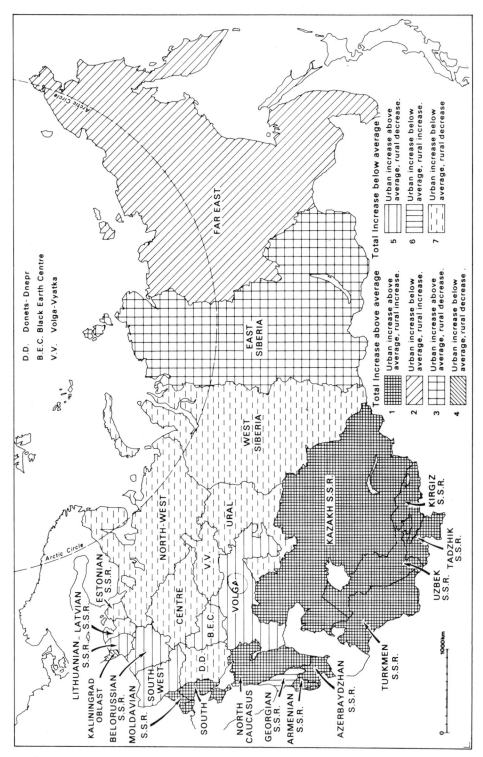

Fig. 6.6 Types of population change, 1959–79

TABLE 6.9: DATA FOR THE SEVEN TYPE-REGIONS IDENTIFIED IN TABLE 6.8

		1	2	3	4	5	6	7	Total
Total (000)	1959	47,998	4,834	6,473	611	53,538	4,044	91,327	208,827
share (%)	1959	23.0	2.3	3.1	0.3	25.6	1.9	43.7	100.0
Total (000)	1979	75,793	6,819	8,158	806	61,726	5,016	104,124	262,442
share (%)	1979	28.9	2.6	3.1	0.3	23.5	1.9	39.7	100.0
Total change (000)	1959–79	+27,795	+1,985	+1,685	+195	+8,188	+972	+12,797	+53,615
Total change (%)	1959–79	+57.9	+41.1	+26.0	+31.9	+15.3	+24.0	+14.0	+25.7
Urban (000)	1959	19,556	3,265	3,414	395	18,426	1,713	53,209	99,978
Urban (%)	1959	40.7	67.5	52.7	64.6	34.4	42.4	58.3	47.9
share (%)	1959	19.6	3.3	3.4	0.4	18.4	1.7	53.2	100.0
Urban (000)	1979	38,007	5,081	5,605	617	34,284	2,601	77,396	163,591
Urban (%)	1979	50.1	74.5	68.7	76.6	55.5	51.9	74.3	62.3
share (%)	1979	23.2	3.1	3.4	0.4	21.0	1.6	47.3	100.0
Urban change (000)	1959–79	+18,451	+1,816	+2,191	+222	+15,858	+888	+24,187	+63,613
Urban change (%)	1959–79	+94.3	+55.6	+64.2	+56.2	+86.1	+51.8	+45.5	+63.6
Rural (000)	1959	28,441	1,569	3,059	216	35,112	2,331	38,117	108,845
Rural (%)	1959	59.3	32.5	47.3	35.4	65.6	57.6	41.7	52.1
share (%)	1959	26.1	1.4	2.8	0.2	32.3	2.1	35.0	100.0
Rural (000)	1979	37,786	1,738	2,553	189	27,442	2,415	26,728	98,851
Rural (%)	1979	49.9	25.5	31.3	23.4	44.5	48.1	25.7	37.7
share (%)	1979	38.2	1.8	2.6	0.2	27.8	2.4	27.0	100.0
Rural change (000)	1959–79	+9,345	+169	−506	−27	−7,670	+84	−11,389	−9,998
Rural change (%)	1959–79	+32.6	+10.8	−16.5	−12.5	−21.8	+3.6	−29.9	−9.2

to their rates of total, urban and rural population change in relation to the average values of the Soviet Union as a whole. The seven types, and the areas belonging to each, are listed in Table 6.8, and selected data are given for each type in Table 6.9.
Type 1. Between 1959 and 1979, the ten areas in this category recorded a total increase of 27.8 million (57.9%) which, in numerical terms, constituted slightly more than half the entire growth of the Soviet population. Both rural and urban elements grew rapidly, the former by 32.6 and the latter by no less than 94.3%. Most of this growth occurred in the essentially non-Slav areas of Central Asia and the Transcaucasus, supported by high rates of natural increase and, in Central Asia at least, by a sizeable net migration gain. Growth was less rapid in southern areas of the European USSR, particularly in the case of the rural population, and in these areas migration gain was an important element. Rapid urban growth in regions still characterised by rather low levels of urbanisation was combined with continuing agricultural development. The trends in these regions represent

a distinct southward shift of the centre of gravity of the Soviet population. Type 1 regions' share of the total rose from 23% in 1959 to 29% in 1979.
Type 2. The only region to fall into this category was the Far East. Urban growth below the national average reflects the rather slow pace of industrial development; the 'rural' population rose by more than 10%, but much of this growth occurred in non-agricultural settlements too small to be placed in the 'urban' category.
Type 3 applies only to the East Siberian region, where pronounced rural decline combined with urban growth marginally above the national average to give total population growth very slightly in excess of the rate for the USSR as a whole.
Type 4 also contains only one area, namely the Kaliningrad oblast, a detached section of the RSFSR. Such a combination of growth rates can occur only in highly urbanised districts—the oblast was 65% urban in 1959 and 77% urban in 1979. Other such cases would no doubt be visible from an analysis of data at the oblast level.

Type 5. The areas in this group suffered a rural decline of 7.7 million (21.8%) between 1959 and 1979 and thus, along with those in Type 7, constituted a zone of marked rural depopulation. This process affected not only regions of low agricultural potential like Lithuania and Belorussia, but also some of the most highly productive agricultural areas such as the South-west and the Black Earth Centre. Urban growth, however, was rapid, amounting to 86% for the group as a whole and as much as 92% in the Black Earth Centre and 112% in Belorussia. This rapid urban growth was associated with low levels of urbanisation at the beginning of the period. Type 5 regions had only 34% of their populations living in towns in 1959; by 1979 the figure was 55.5%.

Type 6. The Georgian SSR was the only area of this type. Along with the rest of Transcaucasia, the republic continued to experience rural growth, though at a much slower rate than in Azerbaydzhan and Armenia, while urban growth, in contrast with that of the other two republics, was well below average. As Table 5 shows, Georgia has a low rate of natural increase and there is little immigration.

Type 7. In 1979 some 40% (104.1 million) of the Soviet population lived in Type 7 regions, a significant reduction from the 44% living in the same regions in 1959. This group contains many of the most densely settled and heavily industrialised parts of the country; 74.3% of the population lived in towns by 1979. Particularly striking is the fact that this zone of slow growth, with its low rate of natural increase and overall net migration loss included not only the main areas of nineteenth-century economic development, such as the Centre and Donets–Dnepr regions, but also the Urals and West Siberia, which were areas of particularly vigorous economic growth prior to 1959. Type 7 regions had a higher rate of rural depopulation and a lower rate of urban growth than any other category. As a result, total growth, at 14%, was only a quarter as rapid as that of Type 1 regions, which had a numerical increase (27.8 million) more than double that of Type 7 (12.8 million). Despite their 44% share of the Soviet population in 1959, Type 7 regions have contributed less than a quarter of total growth since that date.

Summary of trends

To summarise, we may note the following main points:

(i) The population of the Soviet Union is still expanding at a significant rate but, since the early 1960s, there has been a marked falling off in the rate of growth, which is now very close to that of the United States and may well, in the not-too-distant future, approach that of the majority of countries in Europe. The slowing down of population growth is now presenting serious problems to Soviet economic planners, and these are likely to become greater with the passage of time. In particular, the size of the annual addition to the labour force is now beginning to decline and economic expansion will depend to an increasing extent on improvements in labour productivity more than on increases in the numbers at work.

(ii) There are pronounced regional contrasts in the rate of population growth which are due, to a large degree, to differences in the birth rate between the Slavs and the other Soviet peoples. As a result, the latter, though still very much in a minority, are becoming a progressively larger proportion of the total.

(iii) Migration movements also play a very important role. Throughout the country, there is large-scale movement from the countryside towards the towns, so that urban populations are growing more rapidly than rural almost everywhere. At the same time, there are major inter-regional movements, mainly from the European to the Asiatic section of the country, though the direction of these movements has changed. Until the 1950s, migration on a massive scale took place to Siberia, but movement in this direction in the 1960s and 1970s has been on a much smaller scale and has taken second place to movements into Kazakhstan and Central Asia.

(iv) The combined effects of natural increase and migration have produced a clear regional dichotomy within the USSR. Central Asia, Kazakhstan, most of Transcaucasia and a few southern parts of the European USSR have high natural increase rates, a net migration gain and rapid growth of both rural and urban populations. The greater part of the European USSR, together with much of Siberia, have low fertility, net migration loss, rural depopulation and relatively slow urban growth.

(v) Urbanisation continues at a rapid pace, but the rural element, though now declining in absolute as well as in relative terms, remains much larger than in most other industrially-developed countries.

(vi) For a long time now, the population of the Asiatic regions has grown more rapidly than that of the European zone. Nevertheless, the European USSR remains overwhelmingly predominant in population as it is in industrial and agricultural production, and this balance is changing only slowly. One major problem now facing Soviet economic planners is that of establishing, and maintaining, in Siberia and the Far East, a population large enough to permit the development of the vast resources of those eastern regions.

BIBLIOGRAPHY

Azrael, J. R. (ed.) (1978) *Soviet nationality policies and practices*, Praeger, New York.

Anderson, B. A. (1977) 'Data sources in Russian and Soviet demography' in Kosinski, *op. cit.*

Baldwin, G. (1973) *International population reports: estimates and projections of the population of the USSR by age and sex; 1950–2000*, US Dept. of Commerce, Bureau of Economic Analysis, Washington DC.

Ball, B. and Demko, G. J. (1978) 'Internal migration in the Soviet Union,' *Economic Geography*, **54**, pp. 95–113.

Bond, A. R. and Lydolph, P. E. (1979) 'Soviet population change and city growth, 1970–79: a preliminary report.' *Soviet Geography* **20**, pp. 461–488.

C.S.P.P. (Centre for the Study of Population Problems, University of Moscow) (1973) *Problemy narodonaseleniya*, Statistika, Moscow.

Czap, P. (1977) 'Russian history from a demographic perspective,' in Kosinski, *op. cit.*

Demko, G. J. (1977) 'Demographic research on Russia and the Soviet Union,' in Kosinski, *op. cit.*

Demko, G. J. and Casetti, E. (1970) 'A diffusion model for selected demographic variables: an application to Soviet data,' *Ann. Assoc. Amer. Geogr.*, **60**, pp. 533–539.

Desfosses, H. (1977) 'The USSR and the world population crisis,' in Kosinski, *op. cit.*

Dewdney, J. C. (1971) Population changes in the Soviet Union, 1959–1970, *Geography*, **56**, pp. 325–330.

Dewdney, J. C. (1974) 'Inquiry into people: the USSR,' *Geographical Magazine*, **46**, pp. 350–354.

Feshbach, M. (1979) 'Prospects for outmigration from Central Asia and Kazakhstan in the next decade,' *Soviet Economy in a Time of Change*, US Govt. Printing Office, Washington, DC.

Feshbach, M. and Rapaway, S. (1976) 'Soviet population and manpower trends and policies,' *Soviet Economy in a New Perspective*, US Govt. Printing Office, Washington, DC.

Field, N. C. (1963) 'Land hunger and rural depopulation in the USSR,' *Ann. Ass. Amer. Geogr.* **53**, pp. 465–478.

Garry, R. (1962) 'Réflexions sur l'évolution de la population sovietique de 1939 a 1959,' *Rev. Canadienne Géog.*, **16**, pp. 3–12.

Grandstaff, P. J. (1977) Estimates of USSR population by republics, 1951–73, *Soviet Geography*, **18**, pp. 258–261.

Harris, C. D. (1970) *Cities of the Soviet Union*, Rand McNally, Chicago.

Harris, C. D. (1970) 'Population of cities of the Soviet Union in 1897, 1926, 1939, 1959 and 1967,' *Soviet Geography*, **11**, whole issue.

Harris, C. D. (1971) 'Urbanization and population growth in the Soviet Union, 1959–1970,' *Geographical Review*, **41**, pp. 102–124.

Kosinski, L. A. (ed.) (1977) *Demographic developments in Eastern Europe*, Praeger, New York.

Kovalev, S. A. (1976) Farewell to the rural scene, *Geographical Magazine*, **48**, pp. 427–432.

Kovalev, S. A. and Kovalskaya, N. Ya (1971) *Geografiya naseleniya*, University of Moscow.

Krotki, K. J. (1977) 'Fertility and KAP surveys in eastern Europe and the Soviet Union,' in Kosinski, *op. cit.*

Kvasha, A. and Kiseleva, G. P. (1973) 'The impact of age structure on the growth of population in the USSR,' in *CSPP op. cit.*

Larmin, O. V. *et al* (1972) 'Social-demographic aspects of urbanization in the USSR,' *Soviet Geography*, **13**, pp. 99–108.

Lewis, R. A. (1969) 'The post war study of internal migration in the USSR,' *Soviet Geography*, **10**, pp. 157–166.

Lewis, R. A. and Rowland, R. H. (1969) 'Urbanization in Russia and the USSR, 1897–1966,' *Ann. Assoc. Amer. Geogr.* **59**, pp. 776–796.

Lewis, R. A., Rowland, R. H. and Clem, R. S. (1976) *Nationality and population change in Russia and the USSR: an evaluation of census data, 1897–1970*, Praeger, New York.

Listengurt, F. (1976) 'Soviets seek the city lights,' *Geographical Magazine*, **48**, pp. 492–496.

Lorimer, F. (1946) *The population of the Soviet Union – history and prospects*, League of Nations, Geneva.

Lydolph, P. E. (1972) 'Manpower problems in the USSR,' *Tijdschrift voor Econ. en Soc. Geografie*, **63**, pp. 331–344.

Lydolph, P. E., Johnson, R. and Mintz, J. (1978) 'Recent population trends in the USSR,' *Soviet Geography*, **19**, pp. 505–539.

Lydolph, P. E. and Pease, S. R. (1972) 'Changing distribution of population and economic activities in the USSR,' *Tijdschrift voor Econ. en Soc. Geografie*, pp. 244–261.

Matthews, M. (1972) *Class and society in Soviet Russia*, Lane/Penguin, London.

Mickiewicz, E. (1973) *Handbook of Soviet social science data*, Free Press (Collier–Macmillan), New York.

Moiseyenko, V. M. (1973) 'The role of migration in the formation of urban population in the USSR,' in CSPP, *op. cit.*

Parker, W. H. (1973) *The Russians*, David and Charles, Exeter.

Perevedentsev, V. I. (1965) 'The influence of ethnic factors on the territorial redistribution of population,' *Soviet Geography*, **6**, pp. 40–50.

Perevedentsev, V. I. (1969) 'Contemporary migration in the USSR,' *Soviet Geography*, **10**, pp. 192–208.

Pokshishevskiy, V. V. (1963) 'Prospects of population migration in the USSR,' *Soviet Geography*, **4**, pp. 13–25.

Pokshishevskiy, V. V. (1971) *Geografiya naseleniya SSSR*, Prosveshcheniye, Moscow.

Pokshishevskiy, V. V. (1972) Evaluation of the Soviet population census, 1970, *Geoforum* **9**, pp. 3–60.

Pokshishevskiy, V. V. *et al* (1964) On basic migration patterns, *Soviet Geography*.

Rapaway, S. (1979) 'Regional employment trends in the USSR, 1950 to 1975,' *Soviet economy in a time of change*, US Govt. Printing Office, Washington DC.

Roof, M. K. and Leedy, F. A. (1959) 'Population redistribution in the Soviet Union,' *Geographical Review* **49**, pp. 208–221.

Rybakovskiy, L. L. (1975) 'Inter-regional migration analysis,' *Soviet Geography*, **16**, pp. 435–452.

Shabad, T. (1975) 'Intercensal migration', *Soviet Geography*, **16**, pp. 466–472.

Shabad, T. (1977) 'Soviet migration patterns based on the 1970 census data,' in Kosinski, *op. cit.*

Shabad, T. (1979) 'Preliminary results of the 1979 Soviet census,' *Soviet Geography*, **20**, pp. 440–456.

Shabad, T. (1980) 'Ethnic results of the 1979 Soviet census,' *Soviet Geography*, **21**, pp. 440–487.

Slater, P. B. (1975) 'A hierarchical regionalisation of RSFSR administrative units using 1966–69 migration data,' *Soviet Geography*, **16**, pp. 453–465.

Smith, H. (1976) *The Russians*, Sphere Books, London.

Sokoloff, A. N. (1972) 'Rural and urban society in the USSR,' *FAO Monthly Bulletin of Agricultural and Economic Statistics*, **21**.

Stanley, E. (1968) *Regional distribution of Soviet industrial manpower, 1940–60*, Praeger, New York.

Thomas, C. (1972) Urbanisation and population change in Russia, *Scottish Geographical Magazine*, **88**, pp. 196–207.

Urlanis, B. Ts. (1974) *Problemy dinamiki naseleniya SSSR*, Nauka, Moscow.

Valenti, D. I. (ed.) (1973) *Narodonaseleniye: prikladnaya demografiya* Statistika, Moscow.

Vinnikov, Yu. R. and Kozlov, V. I. (1962) 'Changes in the numerical strength and settlement patterns of the peoples of the USSR,' *Soviet Geography*, **3**, pp. 28–31.

Wädekin, K. E. (1966) 'Internal migration and the flight from the land in the USSR, 1939–59,' *Soviet Studies*, **18**, pp. 131–52.

7 Agriculture

Agriculture has been practised in lands now included in the Soviet Union since very early times, the oases of central Asia having supported sedentary farming while stock rearing was carried out in the mountain lands, both long before farming spread about 5000 BC from the Mediterranean and Near East lands to southern Europe. Early cultivation in the afforested lands was based on forest-fallow methods in which natural or re-grown vegetation was burnt to clear it and fertilise the ground with the ashes, and seeds sown with the aid of digging sticks to turn the soil. After a few crops the land would be allowed to revert to rough pasture or scrub while fresh clearings were prepared. Similar methods were used in the more open country where the burning of the grass would precede cultivation, but the exposure of the steppes of Russia to the invasions of successive waves of nomads, described in Chapter 1, delayed the development of agriculture in those areas.

Thus it was in the forest-steppe area, somewhat more protected from raids than the steppes, and possessed of easily worked loess soils, that agriculture prospered more steadily, based on primitive wheats, peas, lentils and flax, oxen, sheep and pigs. Throughout the Neolithic Age, as already noted (Chapter 1) and the Bronze Age (roughly 3000–2000 BC) there was a slow diffusion of improvements, especially in the southern European areas. The light plough or *ard* of the Bronze Age was followed in the Iron Age of the last millenium BC by a wide range of iron tools, the use of which spread also from southern Europe into the interior. By the second century AD such

improvements had been carried as far as western Siberia, so that diffusion of farming had spread in a great semi-circle from the eastern lands in southerly latitudes and back round to the east in more northerly and harsher climates, but with new technology added on the way. The continuing evolution of agricultural methods in Kievan Rus and further north in the forest lands has already been mentioned (Chapter 1), leading to the establishment of the typically Russian form of rural organisation centred on the commune or *mir*, in which land use was managed on a co-operative basis. The elders of the commune regulated the use of meadows, forests, rivers and other resources as well as supervising the strip cropping in the arable fields, including periodical rotation of the strips among the villagers, and the primitive rotation of crops. The latter involved mainly an autumn-sown cereal, which was wheat in the more southerly areas and rye elsewhere, and a spring-sown crop, barley.

It was only as serfdom was being gradually eliminated in western Europe that it became fully entrenched in Russia, following the granting by the tsars of increased powers and lands to favoured gentry in return for military support and colonisation, which required greater control and subjection of the peasantry. Serfdom was strengthened by successive rulers of Russia during the seventeenth and eighteenth centuries by, for example, giving owners the right to pursue and recapture runaway serfs, and by extending the practice into areas like the Ukraine where it had previously not prevailed. The landowners were legally required, from 1734, to assist their serfs through periods of famine, but the advantages of the system lay clearly with the owners, whose land was worked by the serfs. Two main forms of relationship between serf and owner evolved. Under the *obrok* system the serf made payments to the landowner in return for an allotment of land for his own use, whereas under *barshchina* the serf earned his allotment solely by labour. In either case the owner's land was cultivated by the serfs.

There were many rebellions, some of which, like that led by Pugachev (1773–75), threatened the whole fabric of the Russian state, but most were minor affairs, easily suppressed. Many serfs managed to escape to the freer lands of Siberia, or the southern steppes, where they joined Cossack bands, but there was little fundamental change until the latter half of the nineteenth century. The three-field system continued to prevail, the commune continued to regulate local affairs and the landowner continued to hold almost total power over his serfs or 'souls' as they were called. As the nineteenth century progressed, however, it became increasingly apparent to the more perspicacious landowners that serfs did not, and could not be expected to, provide efficient labour and that with increasing commercialisation, including opportunities for the export of crops abroad, as well as sales in the expanding industrial towns, their interest would be served by a change in the system. The entrepreneurs in the industrial towns had even more reason for wanting an end to serfdom, because it restricted the supply of labour to the towns.

Proposals for the emancipation of the serfs were eventually approved by Tsar Alexander II. The Emancipation Act of 1861 conferred legal freedom on the majority of the 47 million (out of a total population of 74 million) serfs and compelled the landlords to give up certain portions of their estates to the serfs. The areas of land allotted to the peasants were, however, too small to give them economic security and independence and many soon fell into debt to the landlords, or to neighbouring peasants who were more successful. Some of the latter were able to buy up holdings that fell vacant and become more prosperous, but even in 1917 about one third of the land remained in the hands of the gentry. Furthermore, the small holdings allotted to the freed serfs, who had to make payments for them against loans advanced for 49 years by the state, did not become the property of the peasants themselves—land titles were vested in the commune. The smallness of the holdings, the high valuation put upon them, and the vesting of the land in the commune made the peasants feel that they had been cheated out of the land which they felt should be theirs. Many left the land to seek employment in the growing industrial centres but many more remained to fall into debt to the landlords and the more successful peasants who developed into the *kulak* class which was later to become the chief target of the revolutionaries.

The reforms of 1906
Continued unrest led eventually to further reforms. The vigorous Prime Minister, Stolypin, brought in legislation to assist modernisation of farms in 1906. Stolypin's aim was to reduce the power of the commune and to divide up the land into compact holdings, for in most cases the land was still held by the commune in the three-field system, in which each peasant worked a number of strips of land scattered over a large area. Other reforms included making finance for development easier to obtain and migration easier, so that more holdings became available for sale to the more prosperous peasants. It is possible that Stolypin's reforms would eventually have resulted in a satisfactory pattern of agriculture but the entry of Russia into the First World War in 1914 soon placed an intolerable burden on the peasants, as on the rest of the country.

As the men were drafted to the fighting fronts, more and more of the struggle to keep up production fell on the women, children and old folk. Arrangements for transport and marketing grew steadily worse, and hunger in the big cities contributed materially to the rise in opposition to the Tsar and his conduct of the war.

The Revolution
When, in 1917, the February Revolution ejected the Tsar, the peasants widely assumed that the land would at last become theirs; but the Provisional Government postponed action on this vital question until a Constituent Assembly could be held, meanwhile continuing the war. The soviets, or councils of workers, soldiers and others constituted a rival authority. Those holding the Bolshevik point of view held that the war must be ended and the land distributed to the people at once. When the Bolsheviks carried out the October Revolution, which created the first communist state, the peasants again assumed that the land would finally become theirs and proceeded to

appropriate the estates. Without delay, the new revolutionary government nationalised all land and instituted strict controls to endeavour to restore food supplies to the starving cities. When the Red Army finally emerged victorious from the civil war, the countryside was largely devastated and its occupants utterly demoralised and bewildered. The peasants had assumed the land would finally be theirs after the revolution but there was great confusion and with the currency almost worthless those who were able to raise crops kept them for their own survival, so the position in the towns remained serious. Lenin's New Economic Policy gave greater freedom to trade and a measure of stability to the countryside, and for a time, it looked as if the Bolsheviks might be willing to accept a countryside of small, peasant farmers, but local soviets began to press for the establishment of communes. These communes bore limited resemblance to those of the historic Russian kind, which had, indeed, taken control again in many areas after the Revolution, but the emphasis was on the confiscation of the land and equipment of the former landowner and the wealthier peasant (*kulak*) for the benefit of the poorer classes. Hence, the Bolsheviks drew their main support in the countryside from the impoverished peasants. Voluntary collectivisation made progress in some areas, but in many cases the earlier communes were disbanded before full-scale collectivisation was ordered. Continuing difficulty with food supplies for the industrial towns, allied to the belief that the peasantry constituted a survival of conservative and capitalist forces, led to Stalin's decision in the late 1920s to enforce collectivisation.

COLLECTIVISATION

In 1928 there were about 25 million peasant holdings which averaged about 15 hectares in size. Initially, the collectivisation movement involved the grouping of typically about 75 such holdings into a collective farm (*kolkhoz*) administered by a chairman and his assistants. The members were required to devote half or more of their time to the collective enterprise and the rest they could spend on their personal plots of land or gardens, which were allocated on the basis of up to half a hectare per family. Collectivisation was bitterly resisted by the wealthier peasants, by the Cossacks with their traditions of independent frontiersmen, by the

semi-nomadic Kazakhs and by others who were opposed to agrarian communism. Many of the opponents were arrested and deported to labour camps. The peasants themselves destroyed crops and slaughtered livestock to prevent them falling into the hands of the collectives.

Nevertheless, there were, as in the earlier attempts at collectivisation, many peasants who genuinely believed in the movement. The power of the government and the Communist Party was behind these, so the transformation of the countryside went on in spite of opposition. By 1940, only about 3 % of the peasants remained outside the collectives, mostly in remote areas. Many of the original collectives had been amalgamated to form still larger units, and the average size had risen to about 500 ha of sown land averaging 81 households. In total there were 235 000 collective farms spread across the Soviet Union, with about 75 million people living on them. By this time, some of the advantages of collectivisation had become apparent, especially through the mechanisation programme. There had been hardly any machinery on the farms in 1928 and few of the peasants could have handled tractors. To assist in modernising the farm processes (and at the same time to provide cells of politically reliable socialist workers in the generally conservative or apathetic countryside), Machine–Tractor Stations were set up to handle all the larger and more complex mechanical operations and maintain the machines. In spite of many failings, the new system could carry out ploughing and sowing much more quickly, taking advantage of suitable weather conditions, and it was easier for trained specialists to influence the farming work in the direction of more up-to-date methods.

Just as the Stolypin reform programme was interrupted by the First World War, so the increases in production and productive resources under collectivisation were halted by the Second World War. During the war years, 1941–45, some 25 million Soviet people died and the peasants were called on to adopt a 'scorched earth' policy in front of the German armies to deny them food and shelter for as long as possible. After the war, it took about six years even to catch up with the production level of 1941, when the sown area had been 150 million hectares, compared with 113 million in 1928. The livestock numbers in 1941 had not recovered to pre-collectivisation levels and in 1945 the numbers of cattle and sheep were some

13 % less and the number of pigs was almost halved from the pre-war figure.

As in the early days of collectivisation, much improvisation was necessary during the years of post-war reconstruction. The supply of machinery was slow because factory production was overwhelmingly devoted to yet more urgent needs. Black market trade of farm produce for spare parts and materials was common. Slowly recovery was achieved. There were more tractors and combines in use in 1950 than in 1941, though the level of mechanisation remained far short of that in many western countries. Since that time there have been immense improvements in mechanisation, electrification and other aspects of modernisation though the overall pattern is still one of less sophisticated equipment available for working the land than in the more advanced countries of the capitalist world, and correspondingly more reliance on manual labour.

Collective and state farms (*kolkhozi* and *sovkhozi*)*

The land of a collective farm is, like all land in the Soviet Union, owned by the state, but is leased permanently by title deeds to the workers of the farm, who form an association governed by a farm committee. The chairman, a nominee of the Communist Party, occupies a powerful position and is responsible for ensuring that the farm operates in accordance with the annual targets of the national Five Year Plan, broken down into regional and local levels. Remuneration varies with the profitability of the farm but the state now guarantees regular cash payments. Wage rates vary considerably with the more responsible and technical jobs counting higher than ordinary manual labour. The farm is required to deliver to the state a stipulated amount of produce of various kinds at fixed prices. The remainder of the output can be used on the farm, sold to the state (usually at higher prices than for the compulsory deliveries), or sold in the kolkhoz markets which exist in most towns. Here too, the individual collective farm member can sell surplus produce from his personal plot to augment his earnings on the collective. The farm worker may own his own cow and calf, one or two pigs, up to 10 sheep, plus poultry, rabbits and beehives, and his house as

well as all personal possessions. Other resources are owned collectively by the kolkhoz and these now include all items of machinery, the Machine-Tractor Stations having been disbanded in 1958, when it was assumed that the farms could manage their own mechanical equipment. The farms have set up workshops for running repairs, but district maintenance stations do major jobs. These are run by a rural technical organisation (*Selkhoztekhnika*).

So far, description of the Soviet farm has been confined to the kolkhoz or collective farm, but the state farm or *sovkhoz* has become increasingly important. The workers on these farms are state employees and they usually earn more than do collective farm workers. State farms were set up to pioneer new methods and break in new land besides setting higher standards generally in the countryside, and they have been greatly extended in recent years. In 1940 there were only 4200 state farms (compared with 235 000 collectives) but by 1980 there were 21 057 state farms compared with 25 900 collective farms. Not only have some collectives been transformed into state farms but the collectives themselves have been amalgamated into larger and larger units so that they have fallen in numbers.

In 1980 the average size of the collective farms was 3700 hectares (9143 acres) of sown land, with over 1800 head of cattle, about 1100 pigs and 1750 sheep. The average number of households per farm was 492. The average size of state farms was still larger: 5300 hectares (13 096 acres) of sown

Grain silos on an Ukrainian farm

* Abbreviations for *kollektivnoye khozyaystvo* and *sovetskoye khozyaystvo*.

land, about 1900 cattle, 1100 pigs, some 3300 sheep and over 460 workers. These are averages for all types of farms, and farms specialising in grain production are often much larger, while sheep rearing farms with a large amount of pasture may have well over 100 000 hectares and tens of thousands of sheep. Even so the sovkhoz average sizes are rather smaller than they were a few years ago, partly because of the conversion of collectives into state farms.

Because of the great size of these farms they are divided into several units, and the labour force is organised into 'brigades' responsible for particular jobs, such as cultivation, livestock husbandry, and operation and maintenance of machinery. Each farm has several specialists, including economists and accountants, field and livestock specialists and veterinary surgeons. Most are large enough to have the amenities of a large village, such as a cinema, library and perhaps a ballet school, as well as ordinary educational facilities and a small hospital.

CLIMATE AND SOIL

Soviet farmers have to contend with some of the worst climates faced by farmers anywhere, and even the best areas suffer badly from long winters or frequent droughts. Such generalisations must, of course, be modified for different regions. The Baltic republics and adjacent parts of the RSFSR and Belorussia are relatively well endowed with moisture, reflected in the importance of dairying in their agriculture, but inadequate drainage poses problems. Southerly areas from the Ukraine to the Far East enjoy high summer temperatures but in few areas does summer rainfall offset high evaporation and transpiration, so that irrigation is necessary for intensive farming. Only in the so-called sub-tropical areas of Transcaucasia and in the Maritime kray in the Far East do high summer temperatures coincide with ample rainfall. Most areas have summer maxima of precipitation but only rarely is the total amount satisfactory for agriculture. (Figs 3.1 and 3.2)

Warmth, moisture and light are the principal components of the climatic resources available for agriculture, other climatic features, such as wind and cloudiness, being of subsidiary importance, weakening or reinforcing the effect of the fundamental components. These latter factors may assume dominant importance locally, when they become extreme, as do winds which cause or exacerbate drought and the removal of snow from the soil when its cover is needed, but warmth and moisture provide the basic indices used in agroclimatology and the delimitation of agricultural regions. (Shashko, 1962)

The importance of accumulated temperatures, ie the sum of daily temperature increments above 10°C in the growing season, is shown in Table 7.1, which gives the requirements of various crops.

Table 7.1 shows that the sum of temperatures required varies considerably according to the variety of crop and the objective for which the crop is being raised. The lower requirements for eastern Siberia and the Far East are explained by smaller fluctuations permitting finer limits and by the clearer continental conditions. In some cases, as in the sub-tropical crops, distribution is conditioned less by accumulated temperatures than by wind conditions. In general, the temperatures shown should ensure satisfactory results in nine out of ten years.

In addition to accumulated temperatures, the availability of warmth at critical periods of plant growth, the risk of damage from heavy frosts and the number of days available for growth are important aspects of temperature. Much depends on the combination of climatic elements in any given year, or of climate and the soil conditions described in Chapter 4.

The main area of agricultural land stretches from the western frontiers, (where the Soviet Union borders the Baltic Sea in the north, and then marches with Poland, Czechoslovakia, Hungary and Rumania) eastwards in a belt of gradually diminishing breadth across the southern parts of Siberia, overlapping the north of Kazakhstan and tapering out in the mountains of east Siberia (Fig. 7.1). Many of the basins in the mountains and the maritime areas beside the Pacific Ocean provide detached areas of temperate climates, while the oases and irrigated areas of Central Asia are particularly valuable for sub-tropical crops such as cotton. South of the main range of the Caucasus mountains is the one other area in the Soviet Union which has a nearly sub-tropical climate, and Transcaucasian specialities are grapes, citrus fruits and tea.

The temperate agricultural lands comprise, in Europe, the areas roughly south of Leningrad and extending southward to the Black Sea, and in Siberia, the narrower belt of south Siberia and

TABLE 7.1 CROP REQUIREMENTS IN ACCUMULATED TEMPERATURES (ABOVE 10°C) FOR RIPENING IN COMMERCIAL CONDITIONS

Crops	European USSR and western Siberia day-degrees C	Eastern Siberia and Far East day-degrees C
Vegetable crops on sheltered ground	400	400
Turnips, cabbage (e)	800	700
Barley (e), winter rye (e) in warmer locations	1000	800
Oats (e), barley (m)	1400	1200
Spring wheat (e), winter wheat, maize (m) for green feed, sugar beet for fodder	1600	1400
Spring wheat (l), sunflower (e) for seed, sugar beet for sugar	2000	1800
Maize for grain (e), beans (e), millet (l)	2200	2000
Maize (m-l) for grain, rice (m), grapes	3200	—
Soya beans (l), ground nuts (e) sorghum (l), figs	3600	—
Cotton (e), lemons, tangerines	4000	—
Cotton (m), rice (l), grapes (l)	4400	—
Olives, oranges, jute	4800	—

e = early, *m* = medium, *l* = late ripening varieties.
Sources: Shashko, D. I.; (1962), 'Climate resources of Soviet agriculture', *Akademia Nauk SSSR* pp. 378–445 and Davitaya, F. F., and Sapozhnikova, S. A.; (1969) 'Agroclimatic studies in the USSR', *Bulletin of the American Meteorological Society*, 50(2) pp. 67–74.

north Kazakhstan. These are devoted to various types of mixed farming, as will be described later in more detail. The climate of the more northerly areas makes it difficult to get high yields of grain but wheat, rye, barley and oats are grown either for human or animal consumption. The cool, relatively moist climate in the westerly parts favours root crops such as potatoes and green crops such as cabbage, as well as grasses and clovers. The podzolised soils require considerable dressings of fertilisers and, in some areas, extensive drainage networks. This is particularly true of the Belorussian lands which include the Pripyat marshes.

In the southerly parts of European Russia and the Ukraine, the physical conditions are reversed. Evaporation exceeds precipitation and, as noted in Chapter 4, the soils are of the chernozem type (Fig. 4.2). During the eighteenth and nineteenth centuries much of this black-earth land was ploughed up and developed as the main grain producing area of Russia.

Between the area of podzolised soils in the northerly areas and the chernozems of the south is the intermediate zone of the wooded steppe, in which the vegetation is also transitional from forest to grassland, which stretches eastward from about Kiev to Kuybyshev, and beyond the Ural mountains from Chelyabinsk to Novosibirsk.

Conditions for agriculture here are relatively favourable. Neither the frequency of droughts, nor the excess of cold and damp conditions encountered respectively to south and north hinder cultivation. Grains, including maize, sugar beet, sunflower and other oil crops, dairy cattle, pigs and sheep are among the principal products, but the range is very wide. Irrigation can boost production, but it is less essential than in the more southerly regions. The winter is less severe than further north, so that although snow lies on the ground for about three months, winter wheat can be sown in preference to spring wheat which yields less highly. This does not apply, however, east of the Ural mountains where conditions are drier and there is insufficient snow cover to protect the seed in the ground, or the snow may be blown away to expose the ground to the exceedingly severe frosts so that spring sowing is necessary.

In the Far East, along the Pacific Ocean coast and in the valleys of the Amur and Ussuri rivers, a modified kind of monsoonal climate prevails and, in this relatively mild and humid area, rice is one of the crops grown, along with a wide selection of temperate crops and fruits. The agricultural zone here is, however, narrow, because of the mountains which, as previously mentioned, dominate east Siberia. Summers are short, but cultivation can be carried out in the valley lands, even on

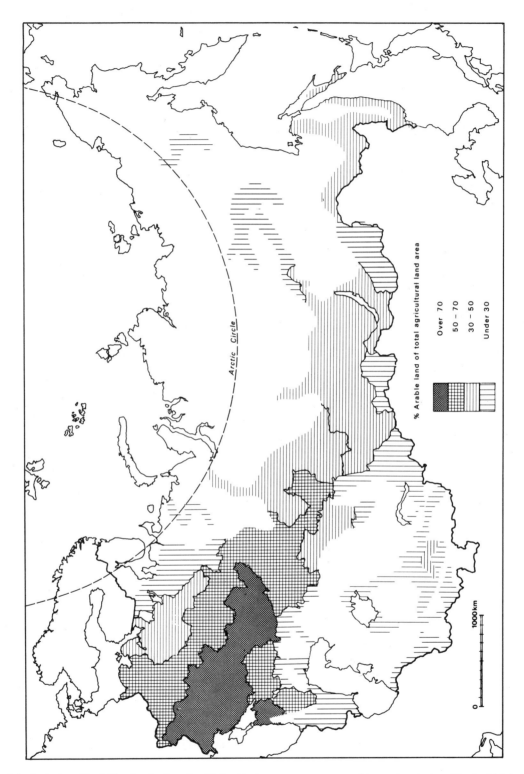

% Arable land of total agricultural land area

Over 70

50 – 70

30 – 50

Under 30

Arctic Circle

1000 km

Fig. 7.1 Agricultural land. The distribution of arable land is shown as a percentage of the total agricultural land, which includes pasture and land for hay. Arable land is that which is suitable for ploughing but the total ploughed in any one year may be substantially less in some areas

permafrost, where the surface of the soil thaws. Improved plant breeding has enabled agriculture to spread in the more favoured valleys right to the Arctic coasts, but production in such areas is necessarily limited to the hardier grains, grasses and livestock. Apart from this pioneer fringe of cultivation, most of the tundra lands are grazed by vast herds of reindeer, herded nowadays, at least in part, from the air. Yet, alongside the aeroplane and helicopter, the sledge hauled by dogs or reindeer is still invaluable as a means of transport in winter.

Land Amelioration

The difficult physical conditions that characterise the Soviet Union, together with Soviet belief in the ability of man to overcome problems posed by the environment, have led to much land improvement work, especially irrigation in water-deficient areas and drainage in humid areas. Before the Revolution, about 3.5 million ha were irrigated, mainly in Central Asia. By 1970, nearly 11 million ha were irrigated and additions have continued at the rate of about 700 000 ha per year, to make the total 17 256 000 ha in 1980. Almost one-half of this total is in Central Asia and Kazakhstan (Fig. 5.2), with the Ukraine and southern parts of the RSFSR (Fig. 5.1) notable among recent increases, there being increasing emphasis on irrigation of grain and fodder crops.

By contrast, lands requiring drainage are naturally to be found in the northern, moist areas where evaporation is low. Schemes to improve drainage are proceeding at a rate similar to those for irrigation, the total being almost 17 million hectares in 1980 compared with 10.2 million in 1970 and 8.4 million in 1956. The bulk of the work continues to be in Belorussia and adjacent areas of the Ukraine, RSFSR and the Baltic Republics. Drained lands actually in use agriculturally amounted in 1980 to 12.0 million ha, rather more than one-half (6.5 million ha) being under crops, and most of the remainder (5.2 million ha) under pasture and for hay.

For many years, addition to the cultivated area was the main concern of agricultural planners. Severe soil erosion, especially in the virgin lands, however, eventually became recognised and conservation measures were put into effect and excessive cropping has given way to more balanced land use policies, especially involving fodder crops. Marked erosion can, however, still be seen in mountainous, hilly and semi-arid areas and further measures are needed.

THE REGIONAL PATTERN OF AGRICULTURE

Climatic and associated soil conditions limit the types of agriculture that are practicable, but in any region large urban centres stimulate production of agricultural products for consumption in the towns. While climatic and soil conditions continue to limit the local specialisation to suitable products, the nearness to markets and consequent low costs of transport, as well as the reduced risk of fresh produce perishing on the way to market, make it practicable for such areas to incur higher costs of production. Thus, more may be spent on fertilisers, housing for dairy cows, glass and heating for greenhouses, and other requirements for intensive agriculture. In the Soviet Union, this is particularly true of the Central Industrial region, which includes Moscow and its surrounding towns, the Dnepr–Don industrial areas of the Ukraine, the Leningrad area, and the industrial regions of western and central Siberia. The Moscow area, especially, has a number of large state farms specialising in vegetable, fruit and dairy products. These interrupt the pattern of regions described below and illustrated in Fig. 7.2.

1. Reindeer rearing and hunting region

This most northerly region extends from Kola to Kamchatka and includes tayga, wooded tundra and tundra. Reindeer rearing has few links with true agriculture but is closely integrated with hunting of fur animals, fishing and catching of seals. The lands of two main natural zones are grazed—the tundra for summer pasture and the northern parts of the tayga as winter pasture, while in mountainous regions, the high unforested lands serve as summer pasture. To the south, reindeer become of subsidiary importance to other branches of agriculture. Scattered hearths (*ochagi*) of cultivation—mainly under glass—occur near mining and transport settlements.

2. Reindeer rearing, hunting and agricultural region

This region includes the northern part of the tayga zone in the European parts of the USSR and almost all the tayga zone in Siberia and the Far East. Accumulated temperatures range from 1000 to 1800 day-degrees. Some cropping and rearing of animals occurs in islands of cultivation in forest and marsh. Heavy dressings of fertilisers are

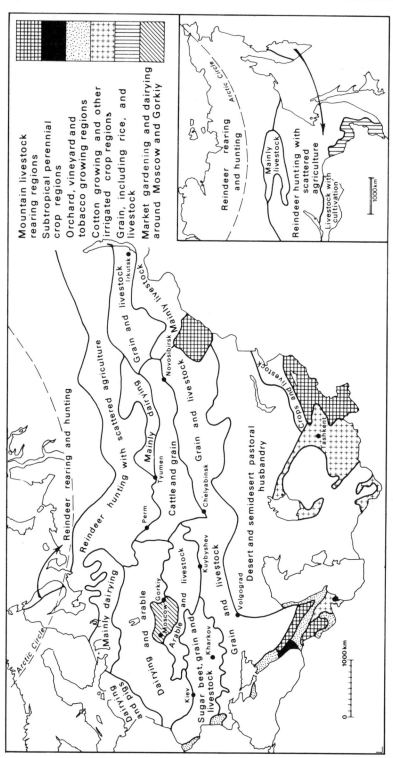

Fig. 7.2 Agricultural regions of the USSR. The regions shown are simplified, boundaries are very much generalised and regions normally merge gently into each other

needed. Agricultural work is commonly combined with forestry, fishing and hunting.

3. Northern dairying region

Within the tayga zone, a more developed form of agriculture is found in some European areas, notably near Leningrad and Murmansk and in west Siberian areas, with specialisation, generally, in cattle raising and dairying based on the natural fodder of water meadows and low-lying pastures. Cultivation is less important, but fast-growing and frost-resistant varieties of grain (mainly barley and rye) are grown, and a larger share of the arable area is occupied by potatoes and fodder crops. Extensive areas of marsh still exist.

4. Livestock rearing and cultivation region of Yakutia

In eastern Siberia more continental conditions prevail and soils are less leached. In the central Yakutia lowlands livestock are reared on natural pasture and hay found in forest clearings, but also crops can be grown at unusually high latitudes. Because of the winter drought only spring crops are practicable, barley, spring rye and spring wheat being predominant. The fodder available and the extensive nature of the husbandry result in a bias towards beef cattle, with dairying subsidiary.

5. North-central dairying and arable region

In the southern part of the tayga and the greater part of the zone of mixed forests from the Baltic republics to the Ural mountains, the cultivation of grains is not seriously restricted by the amount of warmth, accumulated temperatures being 1600–3200 day-degrees. The number of plants that can be raised is, therefore, much greater than in the previously described regions.

The podzolised soils require heavy dressings of lime and fertilisers, and there is still a high proportion of forest and marsh land as yet underdeveloped. Over the greater part of the region arable land varies between 20 and 40 % of the agricultural area.

Potatoes and grains (including maize and other crops for silage) are important crops. Roots are used for fodder and these restore fertility to the soils, but liming and fertilising are no less important in this region of surplus moisture and leaching. With their use and with drainage, sown pastures can be highly productive.

A good supply of pasture and fodder facilitates dairying with low costs, and also makes for a wider variety of livestock than in the more northerly regions. This region has been stimulated by large urban and industrial centres, including Moscow, and relatively good communications, which have promoted intensification of agriculture, particularly in dairy, pig and poultry and vegetable production. Pig rearing is based on potatoes, grain and the waste products from milk processing. Many large sovkhozes have been created in this region, especially around Moscow, in order to meet the demand for meat, milk, vegetables and fruit.

Further from industrial centres, farming combinations include grain and potatoes with livestock rearing, and this is the most important region for flax.

6. The Moscow–Gorkiy market gardening and dairying region

Immediately surrounding the capital and in a belt extending westwards to include Gorkiy is a region within which the influence of the urban markets is especially discernible. Specialised dairy farms are now numerous, with corresponding emphasis on fodder crops. Vegetable growing has become more specialised and output increased though less land is now devoted to field vegetables and potatoes, a traditional crop on the light soils of the Meshcherskiy area south–east of Moscow. Flax production has also been cut back sharply to make more room for the products required for food supplies in the urban areas.

7. Baltic dairying and pig rearing region

The greater part of the Latvian, Estonian and Lithuanian republics, the western part of Belorussia and the Kaliningrad oblast of the RSFSR, enjoy relatively moderate temperatures. Lithuania and the coastal belt around the Gulf of Riga have a frost-free period of more than 150 days. Accumulated temperatures range from 1600 to 2200 day-degrees C.

The chief crops are potatoes, fodder crops and bread grains. Potatoes are produced for industrial purposes and as a food crop, but above all for fodder. Natural pastures are less important, arable and permanent hay meadows more important, than in Region 5. Marshlands have largely disappeared under cultivation. Dairy cattle and pigs dominate livestock rearing, especially in Lithuania

A livestock farm in the Ukraine. Cattle are fed in the yard, the climate being unsuitable for reliance on pasture

where numbers of both have more than doubled since 1941 and are 50 % more than in 1966.

8. West-central sugar beet, grain and animal husbandry region

This region occupies the western parts of the wooded-steppe zone, and extends into the southern parts of the mixed forest and northern parts of the steppe zones, including the Central Chernozem and parts of the S. W. Ukraine and Donets–Dnepr economic regions. Pasture and hay meadows are found in moist lowlands, in river valleys and among the mixed forests, but the further south, the less the land that is occupied by forest, waste-lands and commons, and the more by arable use, which totals 75 to 80 % of the whole area.

The balance between precipitation and evaporation is better in this region than in the areas to the north (too humid) or to the south (too dry), but severe droughts occur once or twice in four years and so irrigation is valuable. Accumulated temperatures range from 2400 to 3000 day-degrees C. The soils, though rich, are easily washed or blown away and shelter belts are planted to provide protection from erosion.

The majority of farms have a mixed pattern of husbandry, with grain growing and livestock rearing dominant and sugar beet important in the west. In the north-western part, the rotation includes more than 60 % grains, especially winter wheat, esparto grass and clover, and sugar beet is the leading industrial crop, commonly occupying between 10 and 25 % of the sown acreage. Though sugar beet is restricted in frequency in any one field, it leads to intensive cultivation because it requires deep ploughing, frequent loosening of the soil between rows and heavy fertilising. The remaining crops of the rotation gain also from the weed-free fields. The main winter crop is wheat, but maize, for which good conditions prevail, has long been grown in the western part of the region.

Sugar beet regions have relatively high intensity livestock rearing. The mass of waste products of the beet processing, maize production and concentrates, together provide much of the fodder supply, and the region has become important for both dairying and pre-slaughter fattening. Whereas cattle from the pastoral fattening regions reach the slaughter houses predominantly in autumn, here the main fattening period is that of the beet processing, ie winter.

In the southern, drier parts, good crops of winter wheat require clean fallow in the rotation. The drought-resistant sunflower is an important crop, yielding both oil and animal fodder.

9. East-central region of arable and animal husbandry

This region is also within the wooded steppe and mixed forest zones, but further north and east than the preceding region, extending from the mid-Russian heights to the Ural mountains. The climate here is much drier with accumulated temperatures of 2100 to 2500 day-degrees C.

Crop rotation is based on bread grains, maize and potatoes. Grain crops occupy 50–60 % of the sown area. Formerly the main crops were winter rye, oats and 'groats crops'—millet and buckwheat. In recent years the emphasis has turned to wheat and fodder crops, particularly maize, to support cattle and pigs. Other characteristic crops of this area are potatoes and hemp, these being more important than sugar beet, in contrast to the position in the last region. In some parts of the region, sunflowers are grown. Fruits, especially apples, are also grown here.

Fodder crops yield coarse succulent and green feedstuffs as well as concentrated fodder and silage. On these, intensive livestock rearing is carried out, the most important branch being cattle, but with increasing attention to pig breeding and poultry keeping, which need less pasture.

10. South-central grain and animal husbandry region

In this region, in the steppe zone to the west of the Volga, extending from the Bashkir ASSR to the Black Sea and north Caucasus, the advantages of greater warmth are for many crops offset by the dryness so that yields per hectare tend to be less than in the wooded steppes.

There have, however, been great advances in overcoming drought: protective forest plantations, snow control, construction of ponds and reservoirs, irrigation from local streams and also from the great rivers—Don, Kuban and Dnepr. On the irrigated lands there has been development of cattle and sheep rearing, orchards, vineyards and, in places, rice growing.

This is one of the areas involved in the virgin lands developments in the late 1950s and early 'sixties resulting in increases of 70–80 % in the sown areas of some oblasts. Some reductions have taken place with the restoration of fallowing to offset soil erosion and depletion.

The main crops are wheat and other grains, which in all total about 50–70 % of the sown area, rising to 76 % in Orenburg oblast, with wheat occupying similar proportions of the total grain. In the less dry, western parts of the region, maize has been sown increasingly in connection with a swing towards intensive livestock husbandry, and wheat is mainly sown in winter. Eastward, the climate becomes harsher and spring-sown varieties progressively replace winter wheat. Sunflowers are the most important industrial crop except in the higher rainfall areas of the north Caucasus, where sugar beet predominates. Melons, grapes and other fruits are produced. In the eastern parts, however, unimproved steppe pastures remain over extensive areas and are used for stock rearing, with Stavropol kray notable for specialised sheep breeding.

11. Lower Volga grain and livestock rearing region

This is a drier region with dark chestnut soils, and there is more emphasis on grain crops and livestock rearing in generally less intensive agriculture, but vegetable crops, melons and mustard are important. The lower Volga valley provides a zone of fertile and intensively cropped soils separating semi-desert areas to east and west. Cattle, mainly beef, and fine-woolled sheep utilise the poorer lands. Large numbers of sheep from the neighbouring parts of the steppe zone are moved for winter grazing to the arid steppe pastures of the lowlands near the Caspian Sea.

12. Ural and west Siberia cattle and grain region

This region includes the plains and foothills rising to the Ural mountains on the European side, but is mostly in western Siberia. The European part is the more developed with a cattle and grain type of agriculture intermixed with forest areas. There is less forest land east of the Ural mountains, and the wooded steppe is used for dairying and grain husbandry. In some parts of the west Siberian lowlands large areas of marshes and saline soils hinder development, but they are partially used for dairy and beef cattle. Accumulated temperatures are 1800–2100 day-degrees C.

The better drained areas are in arable cultivation and the abundance of land led to major developments under the virgin land schemes, so that this became an important grain producing region with spring wheat as the chief crop.

13. North Kazakhstan and west Siberia grain and livestock rearing region

This region comprises, in the north, chernozem steppe, and in the south, dry steppe with mainly dark chestnut soils, accumulated temperatures ranging from 2100 to 2600 day-degrees C. Widespread development began only at the end of the nineteenth century, but between 1954 and 1960 it was the scene of the main development of virgin lands. Large areas were developed by new state farms being organised on land previously in pastoral use.

The region has developed the most specialised grain farming in the country with advanced mechanisation, although the climatic conditions result in sharp fluctuations in yields. Thus, in 1976–80, Kazakhstan supplied over 16 million tonnes of grain annually to the state purchasers. In 1977 only $8\frac{1}{4}$ million tonnes could be supplied but in 1980 it was 16.4 million tonnes. Livestock rearing has been intensified with significant dependence on root crops, but because in this vast area there are widespread occurrences of saline and other soils unsuitable for ploughing, large areas of natural pastures remain. This is especially true of the driest, most southerly areas of sheep and cattle rearing. Soil erosion is a serious problem (Fig. 4.3).

14. Pastoral husbandry region of the desert and semi-desert

With the transition to semi-desert conditions, Kazakhstan, Astrakhan oblast and the Kalmyk ASSR, natural pasture becomes the main form of land use in non-irrigated areas. In the southern parts of the region snow cover is light and of short duration so that pasture provides maintenance for livestock throughout the greater part of the winter, whereas in the northern part of the desert and semi-desert, between the Aral Sea and Lake Balkhash, stall feeding is necessary all the winter.

Large areas with sandy soils offer comparatively good pastures in spring, when the ephemeral plants are growing and retention of water in the sands makes possible continued grazing in the early summer, but the reservoirs tend to dry up and fodder supplies fall. Conditions improve again in autumn when absinthe and other plants yield large quantities of fodder.

Sheep rearing is generally dominant, but cattle are important in the semi-desert areas. Many are driven to the heights of the Mugodzhar, Kazakh foothills, Tarbagatay and Tyan Shan ranges in summer to graze on mountain meadow-steppe and meadow pastures.

In contrast to the former nomadic husbandry, the state and collective farms prepare hay in grazing areas and fodder concentrates are transported to the wintering places from arable regions. Water supply to pasture and irrigation of hayfields is frequently ensured by modern techniques, including utilisation of artesian water. The production centres of the farms and permanent settlements are usually located near the wintering places.

In the north and north-western regions of the semi-desert, specialisation in sheep breeding and fattening cattle is based on subsidiary cultivation of irrigated and non-irrigated lands. Hay-making is on a comparatively large scale and there is considerable stall feeding of cattle in winter.

In the southern desert zone, where the possibility of stall feeding is less, pastures less well supplied with water and fodder poor in summer, breeding of Karakul sheep for their valuable fleeces is important, but sheep rearing is here subsidiary to keeping camels.

15. Mountain livestock rearing region of the Caucasus

In the mountain regions, where cultivation is hindered by relief and shortness of the growing season associated with altitude, livestock rearing is dominant above 1500 m. and lower in exposed places. On the lower slopes forest and meadows are interspersed, with arable land in the valleys and on gentle slopes. Pasture land is less prevalent in the western, more forested and moister parts of the Caucasus than in the eastern drier parts.

Cattle are brought for summer grazing from the foothills and plains (cotton, grain, orchard-vineyard and tobacco regions) and, in addition, there are livestock-rearing kolkhozes based on the mountain lands themselves. Both forms of utilisation are necessary since the grazing capacity of the mountain lands is much higher in the three to four months of summer than in the rest of the year. In fact there is two-way interchange, livestock from the mountain kolkhozes being taken to the plains in winter. This seasonal exchange extends over a distance of 300–500 km. Sheep are involved in the furthest movement, being pastured in summer on the high, stony and less well grassed areas, while cattle are kept on the less steep and better lands.

Cultivation, using contour terraces to control erosion, on a Tadzhik hillside

16. Mountain livestock rearing region of Central Asia

This region includes the high mountain areas of the Kirgiz and Tadzhik republics, on both ridges and intermontane basins with altitudes above 1500 m. In contrast with the Caucasus, the livestock rearing is much more concerned with wool and meat than dairying. The orientation is explained by the character of the pastures, of steppe rather than meadow type, and the absence of winter precipitation in the intermontane basins, which limits fodder.

Wool output has been greatly increased as a result of the crossing of the formerly widespread Kurdish sheep with the fine-woolled Tyan Shan breed. On the Pamirs and in the highest intermontane valleys of the Tyan Shan, yaks are found as well as sheep and horses.

17. Mountain livestock rearing region of the Altay

In the inner parts of the Altay, shut off from the west and north by mountain ranges, the climate is dry, and the dominant vegetation is grassland of meadow-steppe, steppe and, in parts, even semi-desert types.

In the central, eastern and south-eastern regions of the Altay, pasture is overwhelmingly the main form of agricultural land use. Beef cattle and sheep, together with yaks, are reared. In the north and north-west, cattle take precedence and, while beef is the main product, cheese and butter factories have been established.

18. Orchard, vineyard and tobacco growing region

The conditions which encourage these crops include high accumulated temperatures, 3000–4000 day-degrees C., and a long frost-free period (190–250 days) with a mild winter. Whereas the relief would hinder cultivation for field crops, it helps towards freedom from frost, good soil drainage and a choice of differently exposed slopes for fruit cultivation. Fruit is also dominant on the flats among the foothills where the many mountain streams are used for artificial irrigation.

Apples, pears, cherries, peaches, apricots, figs, walnuts and grapes of both wine and table varieties are grown. Vineyards are a specialisation of the areas with drier summers. Tobacco is important on the wetter, leached soils of Transcarpathia, the Moldavian republic, the Crimea and western parts of the Caucasus.

In these areas fodder for cattle is limited. However, on hill slopes and in the dry areas of the eastern Transcaucasus and Dagestan, pastures are available and cattle and sheep rearing has developed with seasonal movement as necessary. Pigs are also kept, in some cases on forest pastures. Silkworms are important in some areas, the cultivation of the mulberry and feeding of silkworm caterpillars integrating well with the local intensive agriculture.

19. Region of subtropical perennial crops

This region includes the hilly Caucasian mountain foreland, which in places reaches to the sea, and the cultivated part of the Kolkhid lowlands. It is the principal region described in the USSR as 'subtropical', with 240–250 frost-free days, and the mildest winters, in which January temperatures average between 3 and 8°C. Accumulated temperatures in the vegetative period exceed 4000 day-degrees C. Annual precipitation is high, totalling between 1200 and 3000 mm.

The cultivated lands form only a low proportion of the total surface area, which includes both high mountains and marshy lowlands. Tea occupies first place among the crops on the hillsides up to about 800 m. and also over a considerable area on the plain. Citrus fruits are second in terms of area planted. They are tolerant of soil conditions but restricted climatically, particularly by winter minimum temperatures. Plantations of lemons, oranges and mandarins are located mainly near the sea and on steep slopes where the risk of frost is least, frequently on terraces. Mulberry plantations occupy third place. They are less frost-hardy than tea but more resistant than citrus fruits, and require less labour input.

Among annual plants, tobacco is important, its distribution depending on soil characteristics. Essential oils (chiefly geranium) are grown on the plains. Vegetables are grown to utilise the colder parts of the year and to be marketed earlier than those from other regions.

A tea farm near Sochi on the Black Sea coast. Tea is best grown on sloping land, as cold air drains to the valley bottoms

The chief field crop, and, on many farms, the only one, is maize. The climatic conditions permit two harvests of fodder crops. There is little land in pasture, but some collectives drive cattle to the sub-alpine and alpine pastures in the summer. Far more important in terms of value than ordinary livestock rearing, however, is the breeding of silkworms.

20. Regions of cotton and other irrigated crops

In these regions of Central Asia and Transcaucasia the frost-free period is 180–230 days and accumulated temperatures exceed 3000 day-degrees C. The summer is rainless, with a very high number of sunny days (up to 26 in July and 28 in August). The mountains provide water for artificial irrigation.

Within the zone climatically suitable there are regions of strong specialisation in cotton (including Fergana, the Hungry Steppe and the Zeravshan valley), and others with a considerable development of other branches of agriculture. Where irrigation provides sufficient water in the summer, cotton is given precedence, followed by lucerne in rotation with maize, rice and jute. Heavy applications of fertilisers are needed and both mineral fertilisers and manure are used, while the irrigation waters themselves deposit silts which contain nutrients.

The use of non-irrigated lands is in many cases integrated with the irrigated areas. In the foothills, many cotton collectives grow crops capable of using the abundant rain in early spring and finishing their growth by the onset of the dry season. Such crops comprise wheat (mainly winter varieties) and barley (spring and winter varieties) but also include flax, mustard and sesame.

Cropping of this type has great value to the farms for the supply of coarse and concentrated fodder. Livestock rearing in the cotton region is, in general, divided into two isolated types, that of the oases, based largely on the surrounding pastures, and that of the desert plains of Central Asia where herds are comprised predominantly of Karakul sheep.

Within the cotton area, a number of supplementary agricultural enterprises are found, including sericulture, fruit growing and vine cultivation. Vineyards are often relegated to lands unsuitable for field cultivation, but their produce and that of the orchards places them in the first rank for exports of fruit to the other parts of the Soviet Union.

The cotton growing region has great potential for development because of its reserves of land and sources of water from the great rivers, the Kura, Syr Darya and Amu Darya.

21. Central Asian regions of intensive crops and livestock rearing

North of the cotton region in Kazakhstan and Kirgizia, an area important for crops slightly less warmth-demanding than cotton extends from the foothills of the Tyan Shan down to about 400 m on to the plain.

Except where irrigated, land is largely desert or semi-desert pasture suitable for winter, spring and autumn grazing. On the foothills, above 500–800 m., hayfields are found, while higher yet is the zone of mountain pastures. These are used chiefly in summer but some are available for grazing also in winter, especially those in valleys and ravines sheltered from the north and west by mountain ranges and therefore little affected by snow. Settlements are commonly located in irrigated areas.

In all parts of these regions livestock have a large role, based on the seasonal availability of different pastures, alpine and sub-alpine in summer, desert and semi-desert in winter, though these involve movement of stock over considerable distances.

Cultivation of sugar beet is combined with grain and fodder growing, and livestock rearing on irrigated land and areas of horticulture occur where favourable climatic and soil conditions are found on the foothills, the most important being near Alma Ata.

22. Grain growing and livestock rearing region of eastern Siberia

A grain and cattle rearing region extends discontinuously along the southern parts of Siberia, including parts of the Buryat ASSR and Chita oblast, bordering on Mongolia and China. Agriculture is found in the warmer intermontane basins, separated by forest-covered heights, and these areas show fairly high degrees of continentality with intense cold and only light snow in winter and most precipitation in the relatively warm summer. Accumulated temperatures reach 2500 day-degrees C.

The character of the agricultural economy strongly reflects the great distance of these regions from the economically advanced and densely populated regions of the USSR. Their economy is founded on the supply of the most easterly regions with products for which there is a continuing demand. The emphasis is on grain, meat and dairy products, with little regional differentiation.

23. Livestock regions of east Siberia and the Far East

In the Sayan and neighbouring mountainous areas of Tuva ASSR and the Buryat ASSR cattle and sheep rearing is based mainly on pasture, of which there are considerable areas in the sheltered valleys. As snowfall is light, grazing can be prolonged late into autumn and even into winter, and semi-nomadic herding is still common. The hay area is considerable and all valleys have some cultivation, with artificial irrigation of hay and arable fields in the driest areas. Stall feeding is thereby facilitated. Cattle and sheep are the main livestock.

24. Grain, rice and livestock region of the Far East

This region occupies the lowlands of the Amur and Ussuri rivers. Accumulated temperatures reach 2400 day-degrees C. There is ample rainfall which falls mainly in summer, with a comparatively dry spring. These conditions suit warmth-loving and late-flowering crops, such as soya beans, maize and sorghum. Easy conditions for irrigation facilitate widespread rice growing.

The rapid industrialisation of the Far East and the distance from other regions make it important for it to become largely self-supporting in agricultural products. Today, a large part of the sown area is devoted to bread grains, especially spring wheat and oats. There are large areas of hay meadows and pasture and great potential for livestock development, especially cattle rearing.

PRODUCTION PROBLEMS

To meet the needs of the growing population of the Soviet Union—about 267 million in 1981—it is necessary to keep on increasing agricultural production. By world standards, output per hectare and per man employed in Soviet agriculture is rather low. This is partly explained by the severities of the climate and the large areas which are poorly endowed by nature for cultivation. It is also partly to be explained by shortages of machinery, fertilisers and other requirements for agriculture, which have persisted in spite of considerable improvements. The pace of investment in agriculture has, however, been stepped up within the last few years and better prices have been paid to farmers to encourage them to produce more.

As a result of these efforts, production has risen more rapidly of late. There have also been very substantial additions to the areas under cultivation. Most notable was the virgin lands scheme

which was at its height between 1954 and 1960. During this period some 35 million ha, mostly in the eastern parts of European Russia, beyond the Volga, and above all in north Kazakhstan and south Siberia, were converted from steppe grazing lands of very low productivity to arable lands producing spring wheat and other crops. Although harvests from these lands, where the annual rainfall and snowfall is very uncertain, have fluctuated greatly, on average about half the Soviet grain supply comes now from these eastern regions. This, in turn, has freed some of the Ukrainian and other western areas, which formerly were required to produce almost all the country's grain, for more varied production, including sugar beet and cattle rearing.

Analysis of Production

The areas of land under the principal crops and the total number of the main classes of livestock throughout the Soviet Union are given in Tables 7.2 and 7.4 with comparable figures for post-war years and for pre-revolutionary Russia.

Output of all grains was nearly 196 million tonnes in 1977, 237.4 million tonnes in 1978 but

TABLE 7.2 AREAS OF PRINCIPAL CROPS

Crop	Million ha						
	1913	1950	1967	1977	1978	1979	1980
Wheat, winter sown	8.3	12.5	19.7	20.7	23.1	18.7	22.6
Wheat, spring sown	24.7	26.0	47.3	41.3	39.8	39.0	38.9
Rye	28.2	23.6	12.4	6.7	7.7	6.5	8.5
Maize (for ripe grain)	2.2	4.8	3.5	3.4	2.5	2.7	3.0
Barley	13.3	8.6	19.1	34.5	32.7	37.0	31.6
Oats	19.1	16.2	8.7	13.0	12.1	12.2	11.8
Other grains	8.8	11.2	11.5	10.8	10.5	10.3	10.0
Total grains	104.6	102.9	122.2	130.4	128.4	126.4	126.6
Cotton	0.7	2.3	2.4	3.0	3.0	3.1	3.1
Sugar beet	0.7	1.3	3.8	3.8	3.8	3.7	3.7
Sunflower	1.0	3.6	4.8	4.6	4.6	4.4	4.4
Flax	1.2	1.9	1.4	1.2	1.2	1.0	1.1
Potatoes and vegetables	5.1	10.5	10.3	8.7	8.7	8.7	8.6
Fodder crops, including sown grasses	3.3	20.7	59.6	63.4	65.7	67.3	66.9
Other crops	1.6	3.1	2.4	2.6	2.8	2.7	2.9
Total sown area	118.2	146.3	206.9	217.7	218.2	217.3	217.3

To obtain the total agricultural area, fallow land, hay meadows and pasture lands must be added, these being in 1980 about 14 million, 35 million and 287 million ha respectively, making nearly 554 million ha, excluding reindeer pastures. Source: Narodnoye khozyaystvo SSSR v 1980 godu.

only 179.2 million tonnes in 1979, with about 92, 121 and 90 million tonnes of wheat respectively included in these figures.

The 1980 harvest of 189 million tonnes probably indicates an average achievement under present conditions. The average annual amounts of grain and other major products are given in Table 7.3 for representative periods. These are 1976–80 for recent years, 1966–70, 1946–50, when the recovery from the Second World War was beginning and 1909–13, representing the period before the First World War and the Revolution. These figures, divided by the population of the country for the periods concerned, give the amounts available (neglecting imports or exports) per head of the population.

It will be seen that for some years after the last war outputs of grains and meat *per capita* were below the pre-First World War level, and milk was no higher. All these commodities have since been increased in output *per capita* beyond the 1909–13 level by two-thirds or more, while the industrial crops, sugar beet and cotton, have been increased much more. The output of potatoes has increased less than the population has risen since the Second World War but was, in 1980, 67% above that of the pre-Revolutionary period. More alternatives are now available.

From Table 7.2 it will be seen that areas of crops as well as outputs have continued to fluctuate. In 1978 the winter wheat did well and there was little necessity for re-sowing with spring grains, which occurs after a winter with inadequate snow cover for the protection of the land. The barley area, however, fell, probably because of problems in the spring. An unfortunate combination of adverse climatic conditions in 1979 led to failure to complete the sowing on many farms and the season continued with droughts and bad weather

which led to a low harvest. Only purchase of grains from abroad enabled the livestock numbers to be maintained (Table 7.4).

Considerable emphasis is currently being placed on livestock production to provide for a higher standard of living. In the past, the livestock branches have been particularly weak, with low milk yields per cow, and poor meat yields, and they still have a long way to go to equal performances in advanced livestock-producing countries, but milk yields per cow have improved from 1853 kg in 1965 to 2222 kg in 1980 on both collective and state farms, with the greatest increases in production in the humid western areas and the developing Siberian regions. The overall growth in livestock numbers since pre-Revolution times is shown in Table 7.4 but vast fluctuations have occurred even in recent times.

The personal plots of the collective farmers and workers yield produce far more than proportionate to their areas. The cultivated land in personal use is only about 3% of the total sown area, but from these plots are produced (1980 figures) nearly two-thirds of all the potatoes, and one-third of the eggs, milk, meat and vegetables produced in the Soviet Union. Formerly the proportions were much larger, but increases in output from the collective lands and state farms have reduced the importance of the contribution from the personal plots. Also, as earnings have improved on the collectives, the members have had more incentive to work longer hours on the collective lands and to rely less on their plots. It should, in addition, be remembered that the proportion of produce from the personal plots which is offfered for sale is much smaller than from the collective and state farms, as a large part is consumed by the families or personal livestock of the owners. The large farms are more concerned

TABLE 7.3 OUTPUT OF MAIN AGRICULTURAL PRODUCTS

	Annual Averages of output (Million tonnes)				Output per head (kg)			
	1909–13	1946–50	1966–70	1976–80	1909–13	1946–50	1966–70	1976–80
Grains	72.5	64.8	167.6	205.0	450	360	707	788
Potatoes	30.6	80.7	94.8	82.6	190	450	400	318
Sugar beet	10.1	13.5	81.1	88.4	60	70	342	340
Meat	4.8	3.5	11.6	14.8	30	17	49	57
Milk	28.8	32.3	80.6	92.6	180	180	340	356
Cotton	0.7	2.3	6.1	8.9	4	13	26	34

Source: Narodnoye khozyaystvo SSSR, various years.

with providing a stable supply for the urban markets.

Development strategies

In order to increase production while releasing labour for work in other branches of the economy there has been great emphasis on the mechanisation and electrification of Soviet farms. In 1928 about one-third of all livestock fodder was required for draught animals and in spite of the creation of the Machine-Tractor Stations to serve the needs of the new collectives and a considerable emphasis on tractor production in the first and second Five Year Plans there was still heavy reliance on draught animals until after the Second World War. By 1965, however, 1.6 million tractors were in use, compared with 531 000 in 1940. The MTS had been disbanded and collectives and state farms made responsible for their own maintenance of machinery, with a new organisation, *Selkhoz-tekhnika* (Agricultural-technical service), providing major overhaul services and special contract work. Complaints about design of machinery and lack of spare parts were, however, rife, and these have by no means disappeared. However, numbers of tractors on the farm inventories had increased to nearly 2.6 million by 1980, and there were 722 000 grain combines compared with 520 000 in 1965 and 182 000 in 1940. Electrification now extends to virtually all farms, whereas in 1950 only 15 % used this form of power.

Another bottleneck to increasing production which has been, if not removed, at least greatly diminished in its effect, is the shortage of fertilisers. In 1940 only some three million tonnes of fertiliser were available for all Soviet agricultural land. The continuing shortages after the war was one of the factors in the decision to exploit the accrued fertility of the virgin lands during the

Mil-2 helicopter crop-spraying. Booms distribute chemical sprays, the hoppers on the sides are used for dusting land with granules such as fertilisers or seeds

period that was required for the construction of new fertiliser plants. In 1965, 27 million tonnes of fertilisers were delivered to farms, and by 1980 this figure was raised to 82.0 million tonnes. There has also been considerable improvement in the variety and grades of fertilisers available though there are still many complaints about quality and about erratic deliveries to farms.

The application of fertilisers as well as the spraying of crops against pests and diseases, defoliation of cotton to facilitate mechanical harvesting and other tasks are carried out to a considerable degree by aircraft. About 100 million hectares of land are treated from the air annually. The aerial application of fertilisers is especially valuable when fields are too wet from snow melting in spring for tractors to work on them so there has been a big increase in the use of aircraft in the north-west areas of the RSFSR and the Ukraine. In summer, several thousand aircraft are

TABLE 7.4 LIVESTOCK

| | Million head at 1st Jan. | | | | | | |
	1916	1951	1966	1979	1980	1981	1982
Cattle Total	58.4	57.1	93.4	114.1	115.1	115.1	115.7
of which, cows	28.8	24.3	39.3	43.0	43.3	43.4	43.6
Pigs	23.0	24.4	59.6	73.5	73.9	73.4	73.2
Sheep	89.7	82.6	129.8	142.6	143.6	141.6 ⎱	
Goats	6.6	16.4	5.5	5.5	5.8	5.9 ⎰	148.0
Horses	38.2	13.8	8.0	5.7	5.6	5.6	

Source: Narodnoye khozyaystvo SSSR, various years.

assembled in Kazakhstan and Central Asia for cotton defoliation.

Encouragement of the labour force has accompanied technological improvement with the introduction in the 1960s of guaranteed regular cash payments for collective farm workers to bring them close to the wages paid to state farm workers, and the payments made by the state for agricultural produce have been much improved. Nevertheless, in spite of all incentives, productivity on Soviet farms remains low compared with the more advanced agricultural systems of the western world. The labour force in agriculture amounted in 1980 to 26.1 million persons, a reduction from 1940 of little more than 16% Distribution of labour provides problems in that some traditional agricultural areas are still over-populated whereas regions such as the virgin lands and other parts of Siberia and the Far East suffer from severe labour shortages, especially at harvest time. To meet these needs large numbers of workers migrate from the European areas, but this sometimes upsets the balance in the areas from which they move, as it is the younger and more energetic who are most mobile. Hence, there is still considerable pressure on non-farming people to help with the harvests.

When the crops are harvested they still have to be transported to stores or markets and here again there have been severe strains on the system owing to the lack of vehicles, both road and rail. Many complaints have been registered concerning the deterioration of produce in transit, or while awaiting shipment, and much still needs to be done to eliminate wastage both in transit and from vermin and deterioration in store.

Prompt processing of produce intended for factories helps to eliminate waste and much attention has been given to building and modernising plants to handle fruit and vegetable crops, milk and other products. Over one-half of all agricultural produce is now destined for processing compared with under 30% in 1960. This development has played a large part in the development of new forms of enterprise in the Soviet countryside which accelerated during the 1970s. These enterprises include Sovkhoz Factories, Agro-Industrial Associations and Intercollective Farm Co-operative Enterprises. Sovkhoz Factories have the longest history and are mainly concerned with the processing of the produce of one state farm, usually fruit and vegetable, with wine production one of the traditional occupations. An Agro-Industrial Production Association consists of a group of farms and factories together with support organisations such as laboratories and supply chains. Viticulture is an example of a specialisation lending itself to such development, especially in the Crimea and Transcaucasus regions.

Though associated with processing and stimulated partly by the need to improve utilisation of produce, the Intercollective Farm Co-operatives appear now to be concerned mainly with the supply and building aspects. They are involved in the provision of workshops, electricity generation, fodder production and land improvement. Individual collective farms are shareholders in such enterprises but remain economically and organisationally independent. Similar organisations exist to link both collective and state farms with varying combinations of enterprises.

The total number of interfarm co-operative enterprises was 9638 in 1980 compared with 4554 in 1970. They involved 153 700 farms and enterprises. (68 721 in 1970) They are strongest in the Ukraine and European areas of the RSFSR, and neighbouring Belorussia. They are also important, relative to the sizes of the republics, in Moldavia and the Transcaucasian republics, and the Baltic republics, especially Lithuania, and less important, so far, in Central Asia. It is not possible to estimate as yet what will be the eventual influence of these developments on the organisational pattern of Soviet farming but their development undoubtedly indicates a recognition of the need to regard farming as an industry, and to promote its integration with the manufacturing industries upon which it is increasingly dependent and those that it supplies, as well as in the provision of necessary services.

BIBLIOGRAPHY

Akademiya Nauk SSSR (1962), *Pochvenno-geografich-eskoye rayonirovaniye SSSR* trans. by A. Gourevitch, *Soil-geographical zoning of the USSR (in relation to the agricultural usage of lands)* IPST, Jerusalem, 1963.

Anderson, J. (1967), 'An historical-geographical perspective on Khrushchev's corn program,' in Karcz (ed.), (1967), pp. 104–134.

Blum, J. (1961), *Lord and peasant in Russia from the ninth to the nineteenth century*, Princeton University Press, Princeton.

Bandera, V. N. and Melnyk, Z. L. (eds.) (1973), *The Soviet economy in regional perspective*, Praeger, New York.

Clarke, R. A. (1969), 'Soviet agricultural reforms since Khrushchev,' *Soviet Studies*, **20**, pp. 159–178.

Cohen, S. F. *et al* (eds.) (1980), *The Soviet Union since Stalin*, Macmillan, London.

Davies, R. W. (1980), *The socialist offensive: the collectivisation of agriculture, 1929–1930*, Harvard University Press, Cambridge, Mass.

Davitaya, F. F. and Sapozhnikova, S. A. (1969), 'Agroclimatic studies in the USSR', *Bulletin of the American Meteorological Society*, **50**, (2) pp. 67–74.

Dibb, P. (1969), *Soviet agriculture since Khrushchev, an economic appraisal*, Canberra, Australian National University.

Hahn, W. G. (1972), *The politics of Soviet agriculture 1960–1970*, John Hopkins University Press, Baltimore and London.

Jackson, W. A. D. (1959), 'The Russian non-chernozem wheat base', *Annals of the Association of American Geographers*, **49**, pp. 97–109.

Jensen, R. G. (1967), 'The Soviet concept of agricultural regionalisation and its development,' in Karcz (ed.) (1967), pp. 77–98.

Jensen, R. G. (1973), 'Regional pricing and the economic evaluation of land in Soviet agriculture,' in V. N. Bandera and Z. L. Melnyk (eds.), *The Soviet economy in regional perspective*, Praeger, New York, pp. 305–27.

Karcz, J. F. (ed.) (1967), *Soviet and East European agriculture*, California University Press, Berkeley and Los Angeles.

Khan, A. R. and Ghai, D., (1979), *Collective agriculture and rural development in Soviet Central Asia*, Macmillan, London.

Laird, R. D. (ed.) (1963), *Soviet agricultural and peasant affairs*, Univ. of Kansas Press, Lawrence.

Laird, R. D. and Crowley, L. (eds.) (1965), *Soviet agriculture; the permanent crisis*, Praeger, New York.

Lewin, M. (1968), *Russian peasants and Soviet power*, Allen & Unwin, London.

Lydolph, P. E. (1979), *Geography of the USSR; topical analysis*, Misty Valley, Elkhart Lake, Wisconsin.

McCauley, M. (1976), *Khrushchev and the development of Soviet agriculture: the virgin land programme 1953–64*, Macmillan, London.

Mathieson, R. S. (1975), *The Soviet Union; an economic geography*, Heinemann, London.

Millar, J. R. (ed.) (1971), *The Soviet rural community*, University of Illinois Press, Urbana.

Narodnoye khozyaystvo SSSR v . . . (various years), *Statisticheskiy ezhegodnik*, Statistika, Moscow.

Nove, A. (1978), 'Agriculture', in A. Brown and M. Kaser (eds.), *The Soviet Union since the fall of Khrushchev*, Macmillan, London.

Rostankowski, P. (1980), 'The nonchernozem development program and perspective spatial shifts in grain production in the agricultural triangle of the Soviet Union,' *Soviet Geography*, **21**, pp. 409–19.

Saushkin, Yu. G. *et al.* (eds) (1967), *Ekonomicheskaya geografiya Sovetskogo Soyuza*.

Shaffer, H. G. (1977), *Soviet agriculture: an assessment of its contribution to economic development*, Praeger, New York.

Shashko, D. I. (1962), 'Climate resources of Soviet agriculture', in *Akademiya Nauk SSSR*, pp. 378–445.

Smith, R. E. F. (1959), *The origins of farming in Russia*, Mouton, Paris.

Strauss, E. (1969), *Soviet agriculture in perspective*, Allen & Unwin, London.

Strauss, E. (1970), 'The Soviet dairy economy,' *Soviet Studies*, **21**, pp. 269–296.

Stroyev, K. F. (1975), 'Agriculture in the non-chernozem zone of the RSFSR', *Soviet Geography*, **16**, pp. 186–96.

Stuart, R. D. (1972), *The collective farm in Soviet agriculture*, D. C. Heath, Lexington, Massachusetts.

Symons, L. (1972), *Russian agriculture, a geographical survey*, Bell, London.

Volin, L. (1970), *A century of Russian agriculture*, Harvard University Press, Cambridge, Massachusetts.

Wädekin, K. E. (1973), *The private sector in Soviet agriculture*; trans. K. Bush, ed. G. Karcz, 2nd ed. University of California Press, Berkeley.

8 Minerals, Fuel and Power Resources

Of all forms of natural wealth, it has been the great richness of the territory of the Soviet Union in fuels and mineral ores that has provided the foundation of her rapid progress to her super-power status. At the present time, the increasing population, the rising standards of living and the political, economic and military commitments of the country all combine to place greater and greater stress upon the optimum development of these resources.

This wealth in minerals is related to the immense area of the country and the wide variety of geological formations that occur within its bound-aries. Although the initial geological survey has been completed, some of the deposits are still not completely known, and new discoveries are often being claimed. The widespread distribution of the mineral deposits, however, creates difficulties of exploitation; many are located in the more inaccessible parts of Siberia where inhospitable environments produce problems of mining, trans-port and labour supply and also hinder the establishment of a balanced economy in the various economic regions.

The close relationship between geological struc-tures and the occurrence of economic minerals may be illustrated by the case of the combustible minerals, such as coal, and the metal ores. Coal and the other fossil fuel deposits are, of course, organic in origin and are all associated with sedimentary rocks formed since the early Paleozoic era. These formations are associated mainly with the extensive lowland or plateau relief areas of the Soviet Union, in situations where they have been largely unaffected by intensive geo-logical folding or intrusion by igneous rocks. By contrast, many of the metallic mineral ores are found in areas where there has been great disturb-ance of the crust by folding or faulting or by the penetration of igneous material. For instance, many valuable non-ferrous metal ores such as lead, tin, silver and gold originate from intrusions of molten rock that in past ages have accompanied mountain-building crustal movements. This is exemplified by the Ural mountain area where great mineral wealth and variety have been associated with intense crustal disturbance; another source of such minerals, however, is the Pre-Cambrian buried platform or shield which underlies much of the sedimentary rock cover of the USSR. This ancient eroded mountain mass exposes its crystal-line rocks from beneath the overlying cover of younger sediments in certain places so that its ore deposits become accessible to mining operations as, for instance, in the Angara region of Siberia, or in Karelia, in north-western USSR.

THE SOVIET ENERGY SUPPLY

Coal dominated the energy supply of the Soviet Union during the great drive for industrialisation and electrification before the Second World War and for more than a decade after its end. Coal was the fuel that played a key role in the production of thermal electricity, in the development of the iron, steel and other forms of heavy industry and in railway transport. Relatively minor contributions to the energy mix came from hydro-electricity, peat, oil, and wood. In the early 1950s coal account-ed for as much as 66% of all fuel produced.

A marked change in emphasis appeared in the later 1950s in favour of the hydrocarbon fuels, oil and natural gas. This followed a belated appreciation by Soviet planners of the greater advantages of these fuels; these included their higher calorific energy, their ease of transport (by pipeline), the wide range of refinery by-products that became available for the petro-chemicals industry, and their cleanliness. Within 25 years oil and gas fuels had become the dominant fuel in thermal power stations accounting, in the early 1970s, for two-thirds of the fuel production. Oil and gas also became important Soviet exports, providing hard currency earnings and forming an important contribution to the economic development of satellite countries of eastern Europe.

However, it became apparent in the mid-1970s that some of the older oil and gas fields in the European territory of the USSR were failing to reach output targets and were nearing exhaustion; and in view of the vast reserves of solid fuels, especially coal, known to be available, this fuel was again to be given an important role in thermal power generation. Thus the annual production of coal in the Soviet Union, which had increased only slowly during the 1960s has now been stepped up again, despite such problems as those posed by conversion of some thermal power stations from the use of fuel oil to coal. Together with this new emphasis on coal went the decision to proceed with the rapid development of nuclear power, particularly in the European region which had become a fuel-deficient area and where the demand for electricity was constantly increasing.

Oil (Table 8.1)

There are marked contrasts in the oil production of various parts of the USSR. The vast Russian republic contains the principal oilfields and produces more than 80 % of the total output (87 % in 1977). The remainder is contributed mainly by Kazakhstan, Turkmenistan, Azerbaydzhan and the Ukraine.

Before the Revolution, most Russian oil came from the Baku field, near the western coast of the Caspian Sea, together with smaller outputs from a

Table 8.1 Geographical Distribution of Soviet Oil Production (millions of tonnes)

	1965	1970	1975	1979	1980	1981
USSR	343	353	491	585	603	609
RSFSR	200	285	411	527	550	
Europe	144	227	221			
Komi ASSR	2.2	7.6	11	(18)	25	
Tatar ASSR	80	102	104			
Bashkir ASSR	41	39	40			
Kuybyshev Oblast	33	35	35			
Urals	12	24	40	(43)	(45)	
Perm Oblast	9.7	16	22			
Orenburg Oblast	2.6	7.4	14			
Udmurt ASSR	—	0.48	3.7			
Siberia	3.4	33.8	150	(310)	(315)	
West Siberia	0.95	31.4	148	(305)	(310)	
Sakhalin	2.4	2.4	2.5			
Ukraine	7.6	13.9	12.8	(9)		
Belorussia	0.04	4.2	7.95			
Azerbaydzhan	21.5	20.2	17.2			
Georgia	0.03	0.02	0.26	(3.0)		
Kazakhstan	2.02	13.2	23.9	(26.0)		
Turkmenia	9.6	14.5	15.6	(15.0)		
Uzbekistan	1.8	1.8	1.4			
Tadzhikistan	0.05	0.18	0.27			
Kirgizia	0.31	0.30	0.23			

Figures in brackets are estimates.
Sources: Narodnoye khozyaystvo SSSR, RSFSR, various volumes and Shabad, T., (1978) *Soviet Geography,* **19,** pp. 273–293 and others.

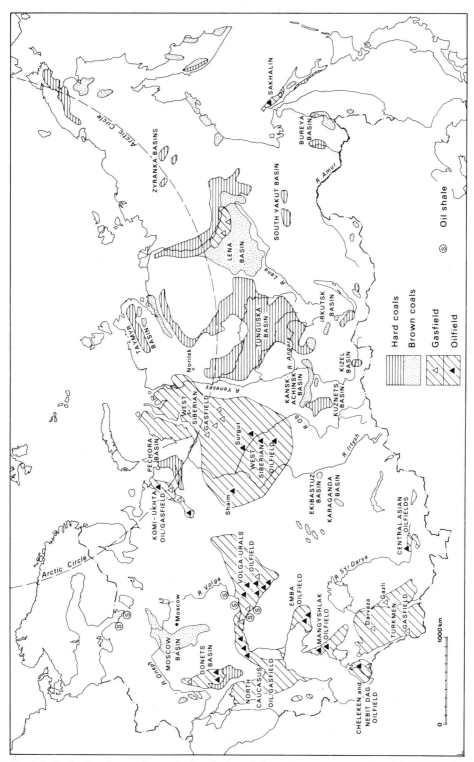

Fig. 8.1 Coal, oil and natural gas; the distribution of the major energy resources of the USSR

chain of separate oilfields extending along the north Caucasus piedmont region. This area continued to provide the bulk of the oil supply of the Soviet Union up to the time of the Second World War. However, a much larger oilfield had become known, occupying a huge area of Paleozoic sedimentary rocks extending east of the Volga as far as the Ural mountains. This oilfield, called the Second Baku or Volga–Urals field, was rapidly developed during and immediately after the war and by the early 1950s had surpassed the production of the Baku–north Caucasus area, most of the output coming from the Bashkir and Tatar Autonomous Republics, together with the Kuybyshev oblast. By the middle sixties the field accounted for almost three-quarters of the total crude-oil production, and reached a record peak in 1975 of 179 million tonnes, providing much of the fuel for the post-war economic recovery of the Soviet Union and of her satellite countries of eastern Europe. Today, reserves are diminishing in this field and the principal output of oil now comes from the vast new oilfields of western Siberia (Fig. 8.1).

The latter occur within a great sedimentary basin drained by the Ob river and its tributaries, an area characterised by difficult waterlogged terrain, extensive bogs, swamps, tayga forests and harsh sub-arctic climate. Rapid development from the 1960s onwards was achieved despite these conditions, with drilling teams being flown in by helicopter from permanent settlements, working a shift system for one or two weeks, then returning for a rest period. The settlements have grown from villages into towns or cities, the two principal oil towns on the Ob being Nizhnevartovsk (1981 population 134 000) and Surgut (1981 population 137 000). The oilfield consists of numerous separate fields, many of which are in the Tomsk and Tyumen oblasts; the giant field of Samotlor yielded 140 million tonnes of crude oil in 1977–8 but there are many others of giant capacity such as the Fedorovsk field and the Kholmogory field, both situated north of Surgut. Despite labour shortages the area of exploitation is increasing in a northward direction towards the gasfield of Urengoy, and also towards the Vasyuganye swamp area, from the Novosibirsk oblast. The importance of

Oilfield plant in the Siberian tayga, Tyumen in the Ob river basin

west Siberian oil is indicated by output figures of 215 million tonnes in 1977, representing 39 % of the total oil production of the USSR.

The smaller and mostly older oilfields of the USSR are declining in output. Ukrainian oil production has always been small (about 4 % of the total for the USSR) but its importance lay in its proximity to European industrial and urban areas and in its high quality, having a high yield of light distillates. Oil, together with natural gas, is extracted from the belt of sedimentary rocks forming the south-east area of the main Caucasus mountain range and in the foothills of the Lesser Caucasus. The main producing republics are Azerbaydzhan and Georgia.

Several oilfields occur east of the Caspian Sea. They include that of Emba on the north-east coast, and also the Mangyshlak field, both of which are in Kazakhstan. The latter field is the larger, though its 1978 output of 15 million tonnes represented a decline from an earlier peak; its crude oil is valuable for the chemical industry, having a high paraffin content and being non-tarry, but requires heating to maintain its flow through the pipeline to the refinery at Kuybyshev, 1600 km distant. Farther south are the deposits of Turkmenia where production began in the Cheleken peninsula in Tsarist times; geologically the oil-bearing strata are a continuation of those on the opposite shores of the Caspian Sea in the south-eastern part of the Caucasus and the Apsheron peninsula in Azerbaydzhan (where the oil centre of Baku is situated). The Transcaspian fields include the Cheleken, Kundag and Nebit Dag areas and part of the extraction is from offshore wells; but production figures of 15 million tonnes in 1978 had declined from a peak in 1973. Western Turkmenia also contains a new oilfield in the vicinity of Kotur–Tepeh.

In Central Asia, there are several oilfields of relatively minor importance in the Uzbek SSR, the Tadzhik SSR and the Kirgiz SSR. These are associated with large quantities of natural gas of which there are very large reserves.

Of the other oilfields those of the Komi ASSR in the far north of Europe are important, production having increased in recent years from the Ukhta, Usinsk and Vozey fields, reaching a total of 14 million tonnes in 1978. In the Far East, oil is extracted on the east coast of northern Sakhalin where the field was first exploited by the Japanese in the 1920s. The total production is modest and it satisfies only a fraction of the regional demand, yet is important in such a remote region.

The rapid development of hydrocarbon fuels in the Soviet Union since the 1950s has been accompanied by the construction of an extensive network of pipelines, for the transport of both oil and gas. Two separate systems are required for the fuels, differing in layout and in function.

The transport of oil

Prior to the pipelines, crude oil had been shifted from the oilfields mainly by rail and by water. The main direction of movement had been to the north or north-west from the Baku-north Caucasus oil-bearing areas in southern USSR to the consuming areas such as the Central industrial region. The Caspian Sea and the Volga played an important role in oil transport, allowing the fuel to be shipped from Baku to Astrakhan and then transferred to barges for transport upstream to refineries situated at rail crossings at Saratov and Gorkiy. From there it was taken by railway to consuming centres. In 1955 nearly one-third of the Volga freight tonnage was oil or oil products. Pipelines were used to link the various oilfields of the north Caucasus area to the Black Sea ports of Tuapse and Batumi where refineries were situated and the products shipped to the Ukraine.

Oil rigs in the Caspian Sea

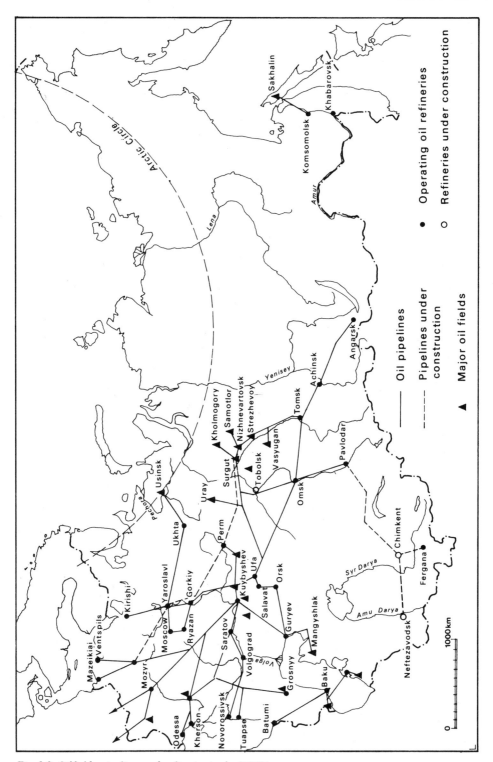

Fig. 8.2 Oilfields, pipelines and refineries in the USSR

With the development in the Volga–Urals field and the increasing demand for oil and oil products in the industrial and urban areas in the western USSR, the pipeline system grew rapidly, linking the new field with its markets in two dominant directions. Towards the west, oil was piped to Gorkiy, Ryazan, Moscow and Cherepovets, eventually reaching Leningrad. Another branch ran to Bryansk and thence to Polotsk, Riga and to the Latvian export terminal at Ventspils with an extension to Klaypeda in Lithuania. Crude oil was also pumped from Bryansk westwards along the 'Friendship' line to refineries at Plock (Poland), Schwedt (East Germany), Bratislava (Czechoslovakia) and to Szazhalombatta in Hungary. Another great artery of oil ran eastwards to serve the Ural manufacturing areas and continued across Siberia to Omsk, Novosibirsk, Krasnoyarsk and Irkutsk (Fig. 8.2).

Further extension and expansion of the pipeline network has followed the increasing production of oil from the new west Siberian fields since 1964. The objective has been to provide adequate pipeline capacity from the Siberian fields to refineries in the European USSR and to western oil-export terminals. The westward flow of oil from these fields in 1970 was only about 4 % of the total national production but by 1975, when the total Soviet output was 491 million tonnes, the flow had increased to 23 % of the national production. It was expected that by 1980 the Siberian fields would supply the western refineries with 240 million tonnes of crude oil, or 37 % of the total output of 640 million tonnes. Larger pipeline diameters have been necessary to carry these increasing loads.

Pipelines now run from the oilfield centres of Nizhnevartovsk, Surgut and Shaim, with the bulk of the flow directed south and west through Omsk and Kurgan, crossing the Urals via Chelyabinsk to Kuybyshev and then on to the Moscow region. A second outlet, under construction, runs further north from Surgut over the Urals near Perm to the refineries at Gorkiy, Ryazan, Moscow and Novopolotsk, and may reach the refinery being built at Mazeikiai in Lithuania or the oil-export terminal at Ventspils on the Baltic Sea. West Siberian crude oil is also being distributed to the east, south and south-west. The eastward flow runs from Nizhnevartovsk towards eastern Siberia through Krasnoyarsk to Irkutsk; this may be connected to the Baykal–Amur Mainline by a tanker train service to reach the Pacific coast. The south–westward flow is for the benefit of the Ukraine and runs from Kuybyshev to the refinery at Lisichansk in the Donets basin; an extension is in progress to reach another refinery at Kremenchug on the Dnepr and also to bring oil to the tanker terminal in Odessa on the Black Sea. A southward flow runs from Omsk into Kazakhstan and Central Asia; it reached Pavlodar in 1977 and the pipeline will eventually reach a new refinery at Chimkent and will be extended to Neftezavodsk in Turkmenistan and to Fergana in Uzbekistan.

Other important though less extensive pipeline systems are those linking the Caspian Sea oilfields, and also the Komi oilfield in the far north, to their respective markets; Emba oil on the Caspian is pumped to Guryev and Orsk where it is refined for use in the Urals; farther south, oil from the Mangyshlak oilfield is piped for refining northwards to Kuybyshev, although part of the production is shipped across the Caspian to Baku from Shevchenko. In Turkmenia, oil production from the Nebit Dag field is linked by pipeline to the refinery at Krasnovodsk on the Caspian coast. West of the Caspian, refining centres of the north Caucasus field such as Dagestan and Groznyy send oil to the Ukraine and to the Black Sea ports. Soviet Arctic oil is brought from fields such as the Vozey and the Usinsk fields to Yaroslavl and Moscow for refining. In the Far East, oil from Sakhalin is piped across the Strait of Tartary to Komsomolsk-on-Amur.

From the above details it is apparent that the distribution of the oil industry has undergone marked changes within the past thirty years; the Caspian–Volga waterway is no longer the principal artery, having been replaced by a great east-west pipeline complex brought about by the development of the two giant oilfields situated on both sides of the Urals. These now dominate the oil supply but the predominant movement of oil is still towards the western USSR where there are the largest cities and the principal industrial areas.

The character of the oil-refining industry has changed in response to these developments. Individual oilfields acquired their own refineries during the early stages of exploitation, as exemplified by those of Kuybyshev, Perm and Ufa, situated on the Volga–Urals field. However, after lagging behind supply, larger new refineries are now being established in all the main areas where the oil products are consumed, with products pipelines radiating outwards. To accommodate the huge oil flows, the Soviet pipeline manufacturing industry at Chelyabinsk in the Urals and other centres has been required to produce very large diameter pipes of 120 cm. (48 inches) or more.

Natural gas (Table 8.2)

There are two contrasting situations in which gas may occur in the earth as 'natural gas' (i.e. not manufactured in gasworks from coal). Natural gas is very often found in association with crude oil within the containing sedimentary rock formations, and is extracted during drilling for the oil. Many of the Soviet oilfields yield large quantities of this oil-well gas. Natural gas may also occur alone as 'dry' or lean gas and not associated with oil. It is this gas that has, together with oil, contributed to the vastly increased use of hydrocarbon fuels in the USSR in recent years.

The oil-well gas or 'wet gas' is commonly encountered first during drilling as it often rests on top of the oil in the containing rocks. The gas can be used in unprocessed form, for instance as fuel in the generation of electricity in power stations; or it may be 'flared' or burnt. Both alternatives are wasteful, because the heavier constituents can be utilised in gas-processing plants to produce ethane, the raw material for ethylene manufacture,

butane, the bottled liquefied petroleum gas, and natural gasoline.

During the rapid exploitation of the west Siberian oilfields, the recovery of this useful associated gas failed to keep up with the pace of oil extraction, and it was wastefully flared. Thus in the development of the giant Samotlor oilfield more than 8 billion m^3 of oil-well gas was wasted by flaring in 1975, because of the absence of gas-processing plants and of gas pipelines of sufficient length to reach such plants. This tremendous waste of gas is now being reduced by the establishment of additional processing plant, as set out in the tenth Five Year Plan (1976–80). Part of the gas is however to be transmitted by pipeline to the Kuzbas industrial area of west Siberia, where it is to be used instead of coal in electric power stations, thus reducing urban pollution, and also to serve as a basis for the petrochemicals industry of Kemerovo.

The pattern of natural gas exploitation in the Soviet Union has to some extent followed that of oil. As the two forms of fuel are commonly found together in sedimentary rocks, the exploitation of natural gas first occured in the north Caucasus region. Large-scale production did not occur until the later 1950s, as with crude oil. In 1950 it was less than 6000 million m^3, rising to 28 000 million in

Table 8.2 Geographical Distribution of Soviet Gas Production (billions of m^3)

	1965	1970	1975	1979	1980	1981
USSR	128	198	289	406	435	465
RSFSR	64	83	115	220	(245)	
Europe	62.5	70	53	(45)	(45)	
Komi ASSR	0.83	6.9	18.5			
Urals	1.2	2.3	22	(50)	(50)	
Orenburg field	—	—	18			
Siberia	0.6	11.0	40	(125)	(145)	
Tyumen Oblast	—	9.3	37.6			
Medvezhye field	—	—	30			
Vyngpur field	—	—	—			
Urengoy field	—	—	—			
Oilfield gas	—	—	3			
Ukraine	39.4	60.9	68.7	(65)	(55)	
Azerbaydzhan	6.2	5.5	9.9			
Kazakhstan	0.03	2.1	5.2			
Uzbekistan	16.5	32.1	37.2			
Turkmenia	1.2	13.1	51.8			

Figures in brackets are estimates.
Source: Narodnoye khozyaystvo SSSR, RSFSR, various volumes, Shabad (1978), *Soviet Geography*, **19**, pp. 273–293 and others.

1958. The gas came from the North Stavropol field, one of the first large deposits to go into full production; this, together with gas from other 'dry' gas fields in the Krasnodar area, was supplied by pipeline to Moscow and other cities of the Central Industrial region and also in a southward direction to Transcaucasia. Other dry-gas fields utilised at this period were the Dashava field, acquired from Poland after World War II and the Shebelinka field in the Ukraine.

Larger gasfields were brought into production during the 1960s and 1970s. Immense reserves were discovered in Central Asia in both the Uzbek and Turkmen republics; but, as in the case of oil, very long pipelines were necessary to convey the fuel to consuming centres. By 1965 a new gasfield in the Uzbek republic, Gazli, was supplying fuel to industrial centres in the Urals such as Chelyabinsk by means of pipelines more than 2000 kilometres in length; in 1966 the Gazli fields were yielding over 22 billion m^3 of gas, of which more than 80 % was piped to Urals industry. The remainder was piped eastwards to the cities of Central Asia. A new city, Navoi, was founded in the vicinity of the Gazli field, using the gas for the production of thermal electricity, nitrogen fertilisers and synthetic fibres. Gas from the Turkmen fields of Darvaza and Achak was also piped northwards for consumption in Moscow, Leningrad and the Baltic republics. Newer fields now being brought into the Soviet gas supply system from Central Asia are the Uchkyr field near Gazli and the Shatlyk field west of Mary.

The Volga–Urals oilfield began producing natural gas with the discovery of the giant Orenburg gasfield in 1966. The location of this field was favourable for transmission to the western industrial areas of the USSR and for export by pipeline to eastern Europe.

In the later 1960s the huge potential of gasfields in northern Europe and northern Siberia began to be realized. Development of this gas was extremely difficult and costly as the deposits were located within some of the remotest parts of the Soviet Union where extensive swamps, bogs, forests and permafrost hindered operations and where no transport facilities, apart from rivers, were in existence. As an example, equipment for working the Medvezhye gasfield was brought down the Ob River to the Gulf of Ob and then upstream along the Nadym River to Nadyms which became the base town; this was possible only during the short 3-month ice-free season and, during winter trucks and lorries used temporary cross-country roads. Even greater difficulties of access were encountered during the work on the Urengoy gasfield where drilling rigs carried by truck convoys had to be transported for many miles across tundra.

The giant Vuktyl gas field in the Komi ASSR became incorporated into the Soviet gas pipeline network in 1968 by a major transmission link called the Northern Lights, designed also to bring west Siberian gas southwards and westwards towards European USSR along large diameter pipes. Part of this flow is planned to reach Leningrad. Siberian natural gas, however, has the greatest future potential. The explored gas reserves of fields in west Siberia, such as the Medvezhye field and the Urengoy field, both situated in the Tyumen oblast, increased from 400 billion m^3 in 1965 to about 16 000 billion in 1975. Urengoy, the largest, began production in 1978 and is to reach its full capacity of 100 billion m^3 a year in the early 1980s.

Other important gas deposits are those of Yakutia, in eastern Siberia, and those which supply the town of Norilsk, in the far north of Siberia. The latter are rapidly replacing coal as the main source of power for the mining and metal industries of Norilsk; one of the fields yields a gas condensate which at Dudinka is converted to petrol or gasoline and used as fuel for trucks and other motor vehicles in the area. This reduces the need for importing this fuel from distant sources.

The gas pipeline network
From the above outline of the natural gas resources of the Soviet Union, it will be apparent that the country is now criss-crossed by an elaborate network of gas pipelines, to some extent separate from that which carries oil, yet with similar general directions. This network expanded in the 1970s at an average rate of 5000 km a year and consisted of large-diameter pipes with a marked concentration of pipeline systems towards Moscow and the industrialised Centre, leading from the southern gasfields of the north Caucasus region and Central Asia (Fig. 8.3). Linked systems carry the gas farther west to cities in the Baltic area and onwards to eastern Europe. The Donbas is also linked to this main flow, which is reinforced by gas from the Orenburg field. A sub-system embraces cities of Central Asia such as Tashkent, Frunze and Alma-Ata.

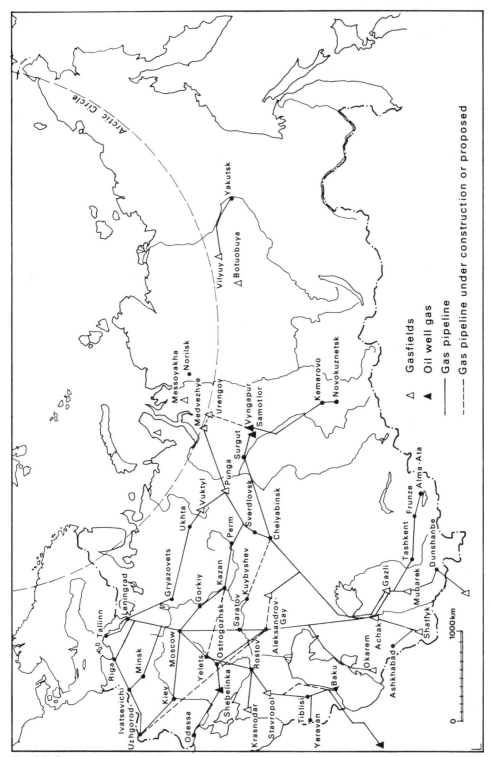

Fig. 8.3 Gas resources and pipelines

The European USSR is also the main focus of the increasing output of gas from the huge northern fields, particularly those of western Siberia. From the Medvezhye and Urengoy fields gas is carried along two basic pipeline routes, westwards and southwards. The westward route runs over the Urals to join the pipeline from the Ukhta field of the Komi ASSR, feeding gas to Vologda, Cherepovets and onwards through Torzhok to the Czechoslovak border for export to western Europe. The southward route runs through Surgut to Chelyabinsk. The flow of dry gas from these northern fields is supplemented by the wet gas associated with oil production of the more southerly oilfields which is piped to industrial centres of southern Siberia.

Coal

The output of solid fuels has increased during each period of the successive Five Year Plans since the end of World War II. Although their relative importance in the national fuel balance was decreased by the rapid growth in the output of oil and gas in the 1960s and early 1970s, the tenth Five Year Plan (1975–80) provided for a large increase in coal output (Table 8.3). This maintains the Soviet Union in first place in the world in terms of actual tonnages, although her output is lower than that of the USA in terms of heating value as it contains larger tonnages of soft brown coal (lignite), inferior to hard coal.

Table 8.3 Geographical Distribution of Soviet Coal Production (millions of tonnes)

	1965	1970	1975	1979	1980	1981
USSR	578	624	701	719	716	704
Anthracite	76.5	75.8	77			
Coking Coal	139	165	181	554		
Other bituminous	212	235	280			
Lignite	150	148	164	165		
shaft-mined	437	457	475			
strip-mined	141	167	226			
RSFSR	325	345	381	395		
coking coal	49	65	76.6			
Europe	99	99	103			
Moscow Basin	41	36	34			
Pechora Basin	17.6	21.5	24.2			
coking coal	4.7	12.7	14.4			
Urals	55	47	36			
Siberia	172	199	242			
Kuznetsk Basin	97	110	139	(150)		
coking coal	37.5	46.9	56.2			
Kansk–Achinsk	14	19	28			
Ukraine	194	207	216	(220)		
coking coal	77.0	80.7	84.7			
Donets Basin	206	216	222			
coking coal	80.6	84.3	88.5			
Kazakhstan	45.8	61.6	92.2	(106)		
Karaganda Basin	30	38.6	46.3			
coking coal	11.0	16.9	18.1			
Ekibastuz Basin	14.3	22.8	45.8			
Uzbekistan	4.5	3.7	5.3			
Kirgizia	3.7	3.7	4.3			
Tadzhikistan	0.90	0.89	0.87			
Georgia	2.6	2.3	2.05			
coking coal	2.05	1.8	1.7			

Figures in brackets are estimates.
Source: Narodnoye khozyaystvo SSSR, RSFSR, various volumes, and others.

The most northerly gas pipelines in the world are in the USSR: the Mesoyakha-Norilsk line in June, with pipes for doubling the line being brought by truck and trailer

Soviet coal reserves

According to recent published figures, the Soviet Union has vast reserves of coal, estimated at nearly 7000 billion tonnes. However, this quantity includes two areas in eastern Siberia, the Tunguska basin and the Lena basin, where the existence of coal is not proven or measured but only inferred; together these two basins are thought to contain about 3500 billion tonnes of hard coal and lignite. They are both inaccessible and remotely situated and do not figure in published details of coal production.

Much more realistic are the quantities of solid fuel that have been measured or proved and which form the actual basis of the Soviet coal industry in the future. As shown in Table 8.3 these reserves are 255 billion tonnes—still a very substantial amount and among the world's largest. The hard coals include the coking coal essential for steel production, of which the reserve is 65.5 billion tonnes. The remainder would be used for fuelling electric power stations. Both types of coal are deep-mined to depths of 1800 m and are of high calorific value. Lignite, because of its lower heat/bulk ratio is mined from surface or shallow workings and is used for thermal electricity production in power stations adjacent to the mines as its inferior qualities do not justify transport costs.

Table 8.3 and Fig. 8.1 emphasise the wide dispersal of Soviet coal deposits. As the reserves in the western coalfields become exhausted, more and more of the output is originating in the Asian coalfields such as the Kuznetsk basin and this gives rise to long rail hauls of fuel to the consuming centres. This trend is to increase in the 1980s with the projected development of the large measured coal reserves of the Kansk-Achinsk lignite basin.

The coalfields

The most productive coalfield in the Soviet Union is still the Donets basin, or Donbas, and it is by far the most favourably located, being conveniently close to its chief markets, the Ukraine and the Central Industrial region. Since the middle of the 19th century, hard-coal production has been dominated by this one field except during the German invasion of the USSR, during the Second World War. In 1913, during Tsarist times, it provided no less than 87 per cent of the total output and in 1940 it still yielded one-half of the total tonnage. Its share of the total output was, however, declining, as newer coalfields in western Siberia and Kazakhstan were rapidly increasing production. The importance of the latter two areas became critical during World War II when both the Donbas and also part of the Moscow field were in enemy hands. The coals produced in the Donbas are of high quality, having a high calorific and carbon content and, although sulphur is present, they are of great importance for the production of coke for use in blast furnaces, hence the location of large steel-manufacturing enterprises near the coalfield. Several kinds of coal are mined; in addition to coking fuels there are also steam coals, gas coals and anthracite; but many seams are discontinuous and rather thin, less than about one metre, and lie at considerable depth, so that extraction costs are higher as the deeper seams are worked. This places Donets coals at a disadvantage in competing with those of the Kuznetsk basin where mining conditions are more favourable.

The coalfield extends across two administrative divisions, the eastern Ukraine and the Rostov oblast of the Russian republic; but of the production of the entire field 85% is from the Ukrainian portion. Reserves of coal in the Donets basin are still sufficient to warrant the active development of recent years including the new large deep mines in the main producing areas and also numerous shallower mines in the western part of the basin, particularly in the Pavlograd area of Dnepropetrovsk oblast. Here new coal towns have appeared, Pershotravensk and Ternovka, with populations of about 25 000 in the later 1970s. Yet production targets have not been reached, for the 1980 plan of 231–233 million tonnes for the Donbas had to be reduced to 229 million tonnes and even this figure was not attained.

The western Ukraine contains also a relatively small, yet locally important bituminous coal deposit, the Lvov–Volhynian basin which feeds steam coals to adjacent power stations which form part of the grid supplying electricity to eastern Europe. Lignite obtained from the Dnepr lignite basin in the Ukraine is converted to briquets for local use.

Lignite is also produced in the Moscow basin, an extensive area extending in a continuous arc to the south and west of the capital through the urban areas of Tula and Novomoskovsk, which are among the chief mining centres. The output comes from opencast or surface mines and is moved to large thermal-electric power stations which transmit power to the industries of the region. The heavy demand for electricity in the area has necessitated a high output, which in former years formed over 10 % of the total Soviet production, but this is now slowly declining as the small reserves become used up and mines close down but are not replaced.

In the Urals, there is a lack of a sufficient supply of good quality coking coal for smelting the rich ore deposits, hence the import of coal over long distances continues to be a feature of the industry. Locally produced coal of suitable quality is thus of great importance and occurs in separate basins, whose aggregate production exceeded 10 % of the USSR total in former years reaching a maximum of over 60 million tonnes in the 1960s, but declining in the next decade to less than 45 million tonnes. The Kizel basin, situated in the Perm oblast, has a diminishing output of good bituminous coal, but elsewhere the Urals are limited to dispersed lignite deposits such as that of the Sverdlovsk field.

The drastic reduction in coal supplies from the Moscow basin during the last war, and the total loss of production from the Donets basin during the German invasion of 1942–3, impelled the Soviets to develop a third coalfield in Europe, in the remote far north of the Komi ASSR. From

here, the Arctic district of Vorkuta in the Pechora basin rails its coking coal more than 1600 km south-west to the steel-manufacturing centre of Cherepovets. Part of the 1975 output of 24 million tonnes was also railed to Lipetsk, in central Russia, and to Murmansk in the Kola peninsula. Reserves appear to be very small.

The Asian coalfields
The principal Asian coalfield is the Kuznetsk basin or Kuzbas, situated in south-western Siberia. It occupies a large depression in the valley of the upper Tom river, 300 km long and 160 km wide, flanked by spurs of the southern mountain ranges, the Kuznets Alatau in the east and the Salair ridge in the west. Although the output of coal from the Kuzbas (137 million tonnes in 1975) is below that of the Donbas (222 million tonnes in 1975), the rate of incremental increase of Kuzbas coal is much greater than that of the Donbas. Kuzbas is a much newer field, has greater reserves and contains high quality bituminous coal in thick undisturbed seams which lie much closer to the surface. A considerable part of the output, in fact, comes from surface mines. In such circumstances, Kuzbas coal is so much cheaper to raise than that of Donbas that it competes successfully with the latter even after the costs of a long railway haul to parts of the European USSR, 3000 km or more distant, are taken into account. Plans for Kuzbas envisage an output of 275–315 million tonnes by 1990, including both coking coal and steam coals and much of this will be mined from the undeveloped part of the coalfield, the Yerunakovo district, 40 km north of Novokuznetsk, which contains large reserves suitable for strip-mining operations.

The importance of the role of the coalfield in the national industrial economy is indicated by the huge tonnages that move from Kuzbas to coal-deficient areas in several directions. It is railed westwards to the Urals and much farther to Cherepovets and Lipetsk; another flow goes southwards into Central Asia, and another eastwards to the Pacific coast for export to Japan. Kuzbas coal is even exported to western Europe, to, for instance, Belgium and West Germany.

Between the Kuzbas and Lake Baykal are several separate coal basins; this eastern Siberian group consists of the Minusinsk basin situated in the upper Yenisey valley, and further north, adjacent to the Kuzbas is the Kansk–Achinsk

The Kharanor open-cast coal mine in East Siberia is planned to increase output from 6.5 to 9 million tonnes by 1985. The mine is situated in remote mountainous country about 30 km from the Chinese frontier

basin; eastwards of the latter and north-west of Irkutsk, the Cheremkhovo deposit is found; this formed an important local fuel supply late in the last century for locomotives of the Trans-Siberian Railway and its steam coals are still worked at Tulun. The largest output from this group of coalfields, however, comes from the first-named, the Kansk–Achinsk deposit, now the basis of an important lignite working combined with thermal power stations close to the strip mines; this is a vast project, planned to produce up to 300 million tonnes of lignite each year for electricity generation. The power would be utilised partly by local power-intensive industry but would also be transmitted thousands of miles westwards to the European USSR.

In the Soviet Far East, coal occurs in a number of scattered localities, often yielding lignite which is used for nearby thermal power stations, but also better quality coals. They include the Buryat basin and the Suchan area (now Partizansk) near Vladivostok; Sakhalin also has several coalfields, locally important. Larger scale developments are in progress in the South Yakutian basin in the upper Aldan river. The deposit consists of both coking and steam coals accessible from surface workings, with consequent low production costs. The coal provides fuel for the power station at Chulman, and the developments have given rise to

the new mining centre of Neryungri, founded in 1975. The reserves of coking coal in the basin are the basis of arrangements for the export of this fuel to Japan replacing the present more distant supply from the Kuzbas. Transport to the Pacific port of Nakhodka is provided by a branch of the Baykal–Amur Mainline, but part of the output is used locally within the BAM zone.

In addition to the Siberian coalfields of Soviet Asia, the USSR also obtains a significant output from deposits in northern Kazakhstan together with much smaller production from the Central Asian republics. The coalfields of Kazakhstan consist of the Karaganda basin and the Ekibastuz basin, neither of which has large reserves. The Ekibastuz deposit is bituminous coal of lower quality than that of other hard-coal fields such as the Kuzbas, having high ash content and inferior calorific value. It is, however, cheaply mined in extensive surface workings where the thick seams are easily accessible so that production can be maintained at a high level from sites such as the Bogatyr (Hero) pit, the Soviet Union's largest strip mine, where 35 million tonnes were extracted in 1977 (Shabad 1978). In the following year a total output of 35 million tonnes were attained by the entire field accounting for 22% of all Soviet surface-mined coal. This fuel was supplied to thermal-electric power stations in north

Kazakhstan and adjacent parts of west Siberia in cities such as Omsk, but the largest proportion was used in the Urals. An accelerated rate of production of Ekibastuz coal is planned for the future, in view of the Soviet fuel policy, and an output of 74 million tonnes is expected in 1980, rising to 115 million in 1985. With the objective of reducing rail hauls of coal, emphasis is being placed upon building huge power stations close to the workings around the city of Ekibastuz itself, creating a generating complex to transmit current to the unified power grid supplying destinations in the locality but also extending to the Urals and to central Russia.

The other major coal basin of Kazakhstan, the Karaganda basin, resembles to some extent the Donbas, in having hard coals, shaft-mined with a diminishing incremental growth. Coking coals and steam coals are produced, the total in 1977 being 48 million tonnes, part of which is exported to the Urals, although the bulk of the production is used in Kazakhstan and in Central Asia.

The four Central Asian republics import coal from the Kuzbas and Karaganda, as only small tonnages are produced in their scattered basins. Several of the best deposits occur in the Fergana valley or in the hilly country around it. The deposit at Angren, where lignite is mined, has been important in local industrial development in Uzbekistan. Kirgizia also has important lignite deposits at Kok Yangak, Kyzyl Kiya and Sulyukta.

Oil shale

A small but significant part of the fuel balance of the USSR is derived from oil shale; oil products and petrochemicals can be obtained from the shale after heating, refining and distilling or it may be burnt as solid fuel for boilers in electric power stations. It has a large ash content and a calorific value similar to the poorer-quality lignites.

Proved reserves of oil shale amount to 6.6 billion tonnes, the bulk of which is found in European USSR in Leningrad oblast and Estonia and smaller deposits in Kuybyshev oblast along the Volga River. In all these areas, the shale is mined both in deep mines and strip mines. In Estonia the shale-mining industry has undergone rapid expansion, providing fuel for large electric power stations, either directly or as shale-oil and gas, obtained from the shale after a retorting process. Estonia has a surplus of electricity from

this source after fulfilling her own requirements, and is able to transmit current to neighbouring Lativia and the Leningrad area. Narva in Estonia and Slantsy in the Leningrad oblast are the two main centres associated with the industry.

Peat

The USSR has vast quantities of peat, estimated at 60% of the world's total resources. Most of this occurs in the coniferous and southern tundra areas, where the cool, humid summer and cold winter, combined with deficient drainage, provide the conditions for the accumulation of plant residues as peat. Extensive areas of peat are also found in the centre and west of European Russia, in the Baltic republics and Belorussia, where peat occupies basins and hollows which were formerly lakes. This latter area is the main producing and consuming region where peat is used either as fuel or as a soil-conditioning fertiliser for agriculture. About 10% of the total reserves are found here, but much larger reserves occur in west Siberia (25%) and in the Urals (35%).

Peat has the lowest heating value of all the fossil fuels, and provides less than one-third that of bituminous coal; as it contains a high proportion of water, it requires to be dried in the open air, a process dependent upon the summer weather. However, within the centre and west of the European USSR where demand for energy is so high and regional fuel resources so meagre, the use of peat as a power station fuel has long been of some importance, and output has remained fairly constant since the end of the last war, averaging about 46 million tonnes annually, but with production levels low in years when drying was affected by bad weather. An increasing amount has been required for agriculture, particularly in the northern parts of the centre and west where the widespread podzolised soils of low fertility are capable of improvement by the addition of peaty organic material.

At the present time there is renewed emphasis on the use of peat as a source of power because of the shortage of other boiler fuels in central Russia. Expansion of the Shatura station and the construction of other stations in oblasts such as Smolensk and Pskov, based on local peat deposits, are evidence of the continued importance of this fuel in the USSR. West Siberia has one peat-fired plant at Tobolsk.

TABLE 8.4 INSTALLED ELECTRICAL
GENERATING CAPACITY AND OUTPUT

	1965	1970	1975	1980	1981
Total Capacity					
USSR (million kw)	115	166	218	266	
Thermal	81	123	162	186	
Hydro	22.2	31.4	40.8	52	
Diesel and misc.	11	9	9	9	
Nuclear	0.9	1.6	6	19	
Total output (thousand million kilowatt hours)	506	741	1039	1295	1325

Sources: Narodnoye khozyaystvo SSSR, various years
and others.

Nuclear power

Nuclear power in the USSR is undergoing very
rapid development (Table 8.4). During the course
of the tenth Five Year Plan (1976–80), it was
expected that about 14 000 MW would be added to
the 5500 MW in 1975 making a total of roughly
19 400 MW in 1980. This implies that the contribution of nuclear-generated electricity to the total
electricity from all Soviet sources will have grown
from its 1975 total of $2\frac{1}{2}\%$ to the anticipated
total in 1980 of almost 7%. Nuclear generating
capacity should reach 50 000 MW by the mid-
1990s or earlier (Dieres, 1981).

A feature of the development is the almost total
concentration of this industry in the western third
of the USSR, the European area. Only one of the
atomic power stations is in Siberia, namely the
Bilibino station, situated in the remote north-east.
This contrast in distribution is explained by the
abundance of fuel and energy sources, natural gas,
oil and hydro-electricity, in Siberia, and the relative deficiency of such sources in the European
area, where the needs arise from the greater
concentration of population and industry. Central
Asia, like Siberia, also has substantial reserves of
natural gas, together with rapidly increasing
hydro-electricity facilities, although not so well
endowed with coal and oil.

The USSR built its first reactor at Obninsk, near
Moscow, in 1954; this was a research project of
small capacity, but Obninsk has remained a centre
of research and in the future is also to be concerned
with the training of atomic scientists. Later in the
1950s a new 600 MW unit was established, known

as the 'Siberian', believed to be engaged in the
development of atomic weaponry; its location is
not known but is believed to be not in Siberia but
at Troitsk, in the southern Urals. By 1972, the
USSR had only two large commercial atomic
power stations excluding the 'Siberian' unit; these
were located at Beloyarskiy in the Urals and
Novovoronezhskiy in central Russia, on the
River Don, south of Voronezh (Fig 8.4). By 1975
new reactor units had been installed at Kola and at
Bilibino in the far north, at Shevchenko, on the
Caspian Sea in Kazakhstan, and Sosnovy Bor
near Leningrad. The Shevchenko unit was the first
full-sized commercial breeder reactor to be installed in the Soviet Union; such reactors are able
to produce more fissionable material than they
consume. A larger breeder reactor of a new and
advanced design is now under construction at
Beloyarskiy.

The tenth Five Year Plan gave rise to considerable expansion of nuclear power capacity, as
previously observed, including both new units at
existing sites and the installation of reactors at
additional sites. New units were started up in
1977–8 at Kursk and in Armenia and at
Chernobyl in the Ukraine, with additional capacity added to that of Novovoronezhskiy; new
sites were also planned for Smolensk, Nikolayev
and Kalinin.

In addition to the planned expansion of nuclear
power, the USSR has also begun a project for the
installation of a plant for the production of reactor
vessels and other equipment for use in atomic
power stations. This is known as 'Atommash'
(atomic machinery) and is being built at the town
of Volgodonsk, a riverside location on the Don
river, allowing large, heavy units to be taken by
water to other sites in European USSR. The
building of nuclear power plants for export is also
a feature of the Soviet programme; such stations
have been installed in East Germany and in other
satellite countries of eastern Europe and one in
Finland.

Applications of nuclear energy, apart from
power station installation work, have also included the Soviet Union's use of sub-surface
explosions for canal and reservoir excavations and
the development of atomic-powered ice-breakers.
The latter, such as the *Lenin, Arktika* and *Sibir*,
are required to keep open channels for navigation in ice-bound waters such as the Arctic
Ocean.

Fig. 8.4 Nuclear power stations in the USSR, including major stations under construction or approved for construction

The Soviet authorities argue that nuclear power stations constitute no hazard to public safety in view of the high quality of their design and the skill and efficiency of their operation. Hence the possibility of environmental hazards from the discharge of radioactive material is not given high priority in the choice of site. Site factors that are taken into account include the following: proximity to cooling water supply, to fuel manufacturing sources, to road or rail transport, and access to an independent electrical power supply. The site should also be on impermeable rock to prevent the accidental diffusion of radioactive liquids; it should also be downwind from populated areas, and near to sites where waste radioactive substances could be discharged safely into the ground. Nuclear waste materials are usually solidified and then placed within concrete and stainless steel containers; the Soviet practice is then to bury them near the surface where they can be readily examined, or utilised when, in the future, technological advance makes that purpose possible. As regards distance from urban centres, no Soviet atomic power station has so far been built closer than about 40 km from a major city, and each has had a protective zone from which all residential buildings for the power station personnel are excluded. However, Soviet interest in the possibility of using waste heat from atomic power stations for heating settlements or for producing greenhouse crops may in future be a factor in reducing this distance.

The geography of uranium resources
Data are not published relating to the geographical distribution of the Soviet Union's basic nuclear fuel supply, uranium. Shabad (1978) estimated that the production tonnage was the equal of that of Canada, at 4700 tonnes in the late 1970s. This figure is just above half that of the United States with about 9000 tonnes. Other producers are South Africa (2600 tonnes); France (1700 tonnes); and Niger, with 1200 tonnes.

In the absence of information upon the actual distribution of the resource, tentative data have been inferred by Shabad from Soviet publications referring to the development of urban settlements in the USSR. Settlements with high administrative status but relatively small populations, which would normally not allow them to qualify for such status, may be assumed to be associated with uranium mining and processing. Another

indication of industries connected with uranium mining is provided by a reference in Soviet publications to a mining site but omitting a discussion of the material produced. The sites of uranium mining on the basis of Shabad's (1978) information may be divided into two groups. Some are definitely known to exist, having been publicly recognised and long established, in some cases before the Second World War. A second group can be only tentatively named as urban centres probably associated with uranium mining; in some cases they have relatively small populations not compatible with their elevated urban status, and they may not be marked on Soviet maps.

A recognised location of uranium mining in the USSR is the city of Zheltyye Vody (Yellow Waters), situated in the Ukrainian SSR. Here the uranium minerals occur in very ancient (Pre-Cambrian) crystalline rocks associated with the iron deposits of the Krivoy Rog deposit. It is a large city of 52 000 inhabitants, having grown rapidly since the start of the uranium activities in 1948. Another well-established uranium centre is Sillamae, situated in Estonia on the Baltic coast near Narva, where uranium minerals occur in the form of phosphatic ores in sedimentary clay formations. This is a small city of 15 400 inhabitants but has a very large municipal area and has the status of republic-level city, indicating its economic significance. In Central Asia there are several known uranium-mining sites: Min-Kush is an urban settlement in the Tyan-Shan mountains which is involved in the manufacture of nuclear fuel. Mill concentrates from Min-Kush are transported for processing 208 km northward to a plant at Kara-Balta, in the Chu valley. Kara-Balta, a republic-level city with a population of about 45 000, is also a centre for agricultural industries. Other sources of uranium concentrates associated with the processing plant in Kara-Balta are Kadzhi-Say, one of the earliest Soviet uranium mining sites, situated on the south shore of Lake Issyk-Kul in north Kirgizia; and also several mining settlements at the eastern end of the Chu river valley, including Orlovka, which was granted urban status in 1969.

Additionally, a number of recognised uranium sources occur in the west-east ranges of the Tyan-Shan mountains bordering the Fergana valley. Taboshar, near the western end of the valley, originally associated with radioactive minerals became an official urban settlement in 1937. With the increasing need for advanced processing of nuclear fuel, it grew in importance after the Second World War. Renamed Chkalovsk, it had a population of over 24 000 in 1970. To the north-east is a more recent development, the uranium-fluorspar mine of Naugarzan, a mountain site, with its own urban status granted in 1964, although administered as part of Chkalovsk.

Siberia contains two places which appear to be concerned with uranium mining; Vikhorevka is a settlement in the Irkutsk oblast of significantly rapid development. It is sited where the meta-morphic Pre-Cambrian rocks of the Angara shield, likely to contain titanium-uranium ores, are accessible to mining. It is close to Bratsk and is linked by rail to the Trans-Siberian main line. The second Siberian settlement, Krasnokamensk, is in the Chita oblast; it was promoted in 1969 to oblast rank although not previously recorded as an urban place, and in 1977 was made the ad-ministrative centre of the rayon of that name. It has a location where the igneous geology may give rise to ores containing uranium. Similarly there are several locations in Kazakhstan likely to be involved in uranium extraction.

Hydro-electricity

Hydro-electricity clearly offers important advan-tages when compared with other power sources: by utilising precipitation and runoff it exploits a naturally renewed resource which can be re-used by locating several units along the same river. It avoids air pollution; may provide flood control and benefit navigation; the reservoirs may provide water for cities, industries and irrigation; they often form a recreational resource and may develop useful fisheries. But there are also adverse features such as losses of water by evaporation from large water surfaces, and flooding of agricultural land.

A significant contribution to the total power output from hydro-electricity has occurred during the past half-century in the USSR, which today is one of the world's leading countries in terms of developed water power; yet only a part of the potential has been realised. About 82 % of the potential lies in the Asian USSR and only 18 % in the European part. More than half the total potential is located within Siberia and about one-fifth is found in Kazakhstan and the Central Asian republics where there are increasingly heavy de-mands for water for irrigation as well as for power (Fig. 8.4).

In the early years of the development of the Soviet Union's resources, water power con-tributed about 11 to 14 % of the electricity supply. With the construction of both large-capacity thermal-power stations and large hydro-electric stations the contribution of the latter to the supply is about 13 to $14\frac{1}{2}$ %, falling to about 12 % in dry years. The actual generating capacity is, however, about 19 % of the total for the USSR, higher than the power production, as the hydro plants operate part-time and generate electricity when peak load demands occur, whereas the thermal stations are adapted to work continuously to fulfil the base-load demand.

The development of hydro-electric power in the Soviet Union began a few years after the 1917 Revolution, in the European part of the USSR under the direction of GOELRO (The State Commission for the Electrification of Russia). The Volkhov station near Leningrad was completed in 1926 and this was followed by the construction at Dneproges, near Zaporozhe, of the great Dnepr dam in 1932. The power station had a capacity of well over half-a-million kilowatts and for many years it was the largest water-power project in Europe. Rebuilt and improved after its destruc-tion in the Second World War this scheme together with more recent projects continues to provide power for Ukrainian industry, particu-larly power-intensive industries such as the manu-facture of aluminium and electric steels. Like other schemes it is a multi-purpose unit as the reservoir provides water for the irrigation of the semi-arid steppe and the increased depth of water eliminated the series of rapids which had obstructed navi-gation.

The exploitation of the potential of the Dnepr river has continued since the 1950s with the addition of five other stations and the expansion of the original station for peak-load requirements. They are relatively small-capacity stations though their combined capacity is in excess of 2000 MW; they consist of Kakhovka (1956), Kremenchug (1960), Kiev (1964) Dneprodzerzhinsk (1964) and Kanev (1972). The very large Kakhovka reservoir provides irrigation to the dry steppe of the southern Ukraine in partial compensation for the extensive farmland of the Dnepr valley lost by flooding when the reservoirs were formed.

Contemporary developments have also taken place within the Kama–Volga basin; the seasonal flooding of the river has been regulated by massive

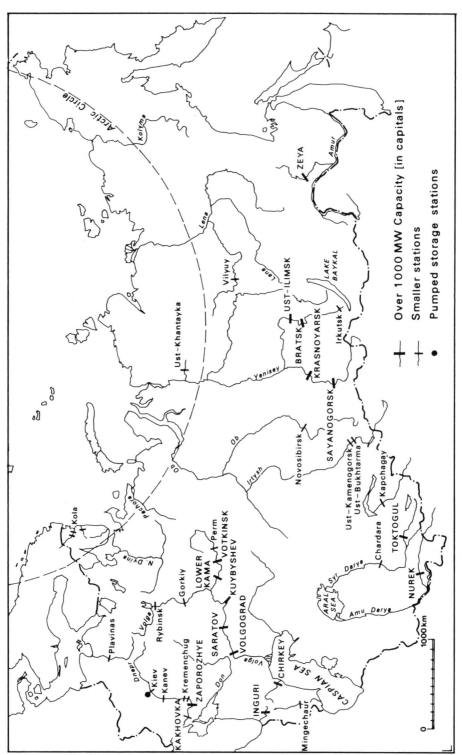

Fig. 8.5 Principal hydro-electric power stations in operation

dams which impound very large multi-purpose reservoirs, linked by canals forming a continuous navigable waterway. The canals traverse low watersheds between river basins by a series of locks allowing inter-basin navigation and water transfer. Thus, a dam on the Volga with a hydro-electric power plant near Ivankovo (built 1937) provided water for the Moscow Canal, the navigational link between the Volga and the Moscow River. In 1940 a second dam and hydro-electric unit was added at Uglich, followed the next year by further dams on the upper Volga, creating the Rybinsk reservoir which at the time was the world's largest man-made lake. The power produced at the Rybinsk dam supplies Moscow and other cities in the area, and the lake provides a fresh-water supply and a recreational amenity. In the post-war years, Volga projects became larger. These units, all based on vast reservoirs on the Volga and the Kama, are at Perm (1954–8), Kuybyshev (1955–7), Volgograd (1958–61), Votkinsk (1963) and Balakovo, near Saratov (1970). The Lower Kama project, the third on the Kama, began generating in 1979. All have capacities of over 1000 MW with the exception of that at Perm with 504 000 kW, and the largest is that of Volgograd with 2500 MW; this takes water from a gigantic lake extending about 640 km upstream. Very high-voltage power lines carry electricity from the Volga stations to Moscow and to the Urals; these have become an integral part of a nation-wide electricity transmission grid linking up the many hydro or thermal stations with their consumers.

Hydro-electricity in the European north was developed early in the Soviet period, with the harnessing of swift streams flowing from numerous lakes. It is generated mainly in the Kola peninsula, in Murmansk oblast and in the Karelian ASSR, by small stations with a combined capacity of about 1600 MW.

The development of the huge hydro-electric potential of the Siberian rivers began in the 1950s with a small unit on the Ob above the city of Novosibirsk. This was soon to be dwarfed by the exploitation of the huge potential of the Yenisey river and its tributary, the Angara. The latter is particularly suitable for power development as it rises in Lake Baykal which, with its enormous volume, provides an almost constant flow of water; in addition, its constricted, steep-sided valley slopes sharply downstream and is cut into

resistant rocks. Hence the ideal conditions of a large head of water combined with solid foundations for dam construction are fulfilled.

The first dam, built near the city of Irkutsk, provided water for the Irkutsk power station, opened in 1958 with a capacity of 660 000 kW, supplying power for large aluminium reduction plants. Downstream was the newer Bratsk scheme, based on the great Bratsk dam across the Angara gorge; this began generating in 1961 and was upgraded in the 1970s to 4500 MW. In the meantime, work on other power projects further downstream was in progress. Ust-Ilimsk designed to be a twin of the Bratsk scheme and to have a capacity of about 4300 MW; the power being used by a large wood-pulp mill with surplus power fed into the central Siberian grid. Bratsk and Ust-Ilimsk together represent significant examples of large industrial enterprises established in remote areas of the boreal forest, far to the north of the main line of communications, the Trans-Siberian Railway. Huge areas of forest have been cleared; houses, shops, roads and other infrastructure have been provided for workers and their families. By 1978 the population of Bratsk had grown to 209 000 from 43 000 in 1959. Further developments on the Angara are taking place several hundred miles downstream at Boguchany where work began in 1977, utilising power for operations supplied by Bratsk, with supplies of material brought by truck convoys along cross-country winter roads from Bratsk.

On the Yenisey river there are even larger projects, designed to operate in conjunction with thermal power stations whose fuel supply is furnished by the Kuznetsk basin and the Kansk-Achinsk basin, so that reserve hydro-electric power can be used at peak load periods. These are the Krasnoyarsk station which approached its 6000 MW design output in 1978, supplying current to the aluminium works; and also the Sayan-Shushenskaya project upstream from Krasnoyarsk where generation began in 1978. Aluminium production is planned for the new city of Sayanogorsk, near the hydro station. Other stations on the Yenisey are planned for the middle section of the river, consisting of one of 6400 MW at Yeniseysk, near the confluence of the Angara and the Yenisey, and also one of 6100 MW at Osinovo near the confluence of the Stony Tunguska river and the Yenisey. Farther downstream, the lower Yenisey is to have a hydro station of 5000 MW at Igarka; and finally Norilsk, the non-ferrous metals complex near the mouth of the Yenisey, derives part of its power supply from hydro-electricity. Other hydro-electric sites in Siberia are the Vilyuy station in Yakutia, and, in the Far East, the Zeya and the Bureya stations situated on the rivers of those names, supply power for the economic development associated with the Baykal–Amur Mainline project. The Zeya station began generating in 1975.

In Central Asia, the earliest large hydro-electric schemes were sited on the Syr Darya river and combined power production with the requirements of irrigation; the projects included the Farkhad and Kayrak-kum dams together with the Chardara station. Much more important were the several major schemes of the 1960s and 1970s designed to produce power for a high-voltage electricity grid for the whole region, combined with output from large gas-fired power stations. Two of these projects are on the swift-flowing Vakhsh river, the Nurek station, having a capacity of 2700 MW, and completed in 1972–3, and the Rogun station with a capacity of 3200 MW. Nurek was to furnish power for aluminium and other industry in Tadzhikistan. The Naryn river in Kirgizia has been similarly harnessed by the Toktogul project of 4400 MW, and completed in 1975, having a function for peak-load output. Two other sites on the Naryn river are being utilised for power development, namely the Kirpsay and the Kembarrata.

In Kazakhstan, the Irtysh river system is exploited for power supplies for the important non-ferrous mineral industry in the northern part of the republic. The Ust-Kamenogorsk hydro station of 331 000 kW, completed in the 1950s and the more powerful Bukhtarma project, further upstream, completed in 1966, were both designed primarily for power production with detriment to irrigation and navigation. The need to regularise river flow has given rise to plans for an additional project downstream, the Shulba Dam.

Although the Caucasus region with its heavy precipitation and steep gradients has favourable conditions for water power, the developments until recently have been of modest capacity, for peak load operation only. However, much larger stations have now been built, or planned, in Dagestan, Azerbaydzhan, and western Georgia.

In Dagestan a series of hydro stations is being built to harness the Sulak, the largest being the Chirkey station which reached its 1000 MW ca-

pacity in 1975 (Shabad, 1976), for peak operation to supplement thermal power. This is to be exceeded in the future only by the planned Inguri station in Georgia with 1600 MW designed for a more constant output for base-loads, a prolonged and expensive project requiring the construction of the world's highest concrete arched dam. In Azerbaydzhan, the only major project is the Mingechaur station on the Kura river with a capacity of 359 000 kW, but smaller projects are planned for the same river. In Armenia, a series of hydro stations sited along the Razdan river, the outlet of Lake Sevan, provided much of the republic's power supply; but increasing erosion and falling lake and water table levels have caused so much concern for the environment that the stations have been closed until conditions may be rectified. Meanwhile, the future of Armenia's power supply is to be based on gas-fired steam electricity together with nuclear power.

The Soviet Union is experimenting with pumped-storage hydro-electric developments similar to those developed in western countries. These are two-way systems, equipped with reversible turbines which pump water from a lower to an upper reservoir during off-peak periods and then are switched to their normal function during peak times when water from the higher reservoir is brought into use. Such installations would be particularly advantageous in European Russia where further conventional sites for power development are limited, and where the demand for electricity is so great.

FERROUS METALS

The Soviet Union is the world's foremost producer of iron ore with abundant reserve supplies, estimated at 111 billion tonnes. The bulk of the ore is relatively low in iron content as the higher grade ores have been approaching exhaustion and this low-grade ore requires concentration or beneficiation before use in blast furnaces.

As Table 8.5 indicates, the European part of the USSR dominates iron ore production, yielding over 80 % of the total mined in 1978, the remainder originating in Kazakhstan and Siberia. The most important European deposit at the present time is in the Krivoy Rog basin of the Ukraine, where the ore consists of highly metamorphosed Pre-Cambrian rocks containing magnetite, mined by both shaft and surface excavations. There are several separate mining and concentrating com-

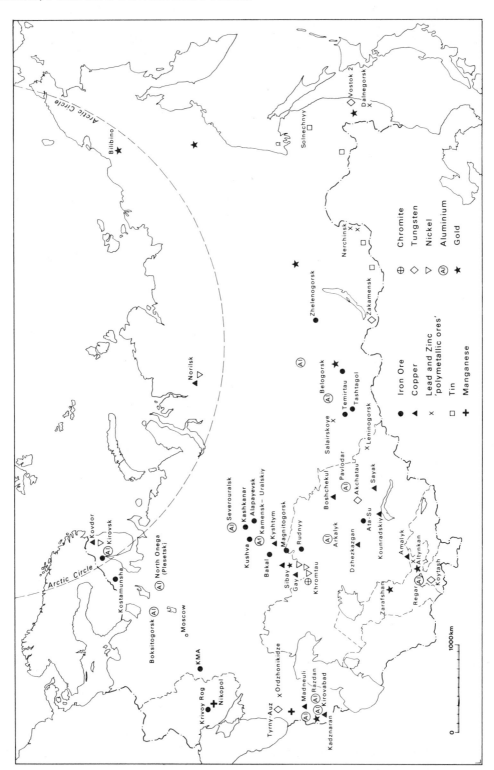

Fig. 8.6 Principal ferrous and non-ferrous metal deposits

Table 8.5 *Geographical distribution of Soviet Iron-ore Production (million tonnes; usable ore)*

	1970	1975	1977	1980	1981
USSR	196	233	240	245	242
RSFSR	64.7	86.8	88.6	89.4	
European Russia	24.4	45.3	47		
Kola peninsula	7.6	9.5	9		
Kursk district	17.8	35.8	37.9		
Urals	26.5	26.1	27		
Siberia	12.9	15.5	15		
Kazakhstan	18.2	21.4	23.4		
Ukraine	111.2	123.3	126.4		

Sources: Narodnoye khozyaystvo SSSR, RSFSR, various volumes; Shabad (1978) *Soviet Geography,* **19,** pp. 273–293 and others.

plexes within the basin, converting the low-grade iron quartzite into concentrated material, commonly in the form of pellets. Current plans call for expansion of production but the highest rate of production increase has been in the second great iron deposit west of the Urals, the Kursk Magnetic Anomaly (KMA) in central Russia, north-east of Krivoy Rog. The ancient shield rocks, consisting of magnetites and iron-bearing quartzites are mined from the surface or from pits and concentrated before transport to the nearby Lipetsk iron and steel works or to the three major steel centres in the Urals, Magnitogorsk, Chelyabinsk and Novotroitsk. Two main mining centres, Gubkin and Zheleznogorsk, produced jointly in 1978 40 million tonnes. The USSR exports a considerable part (about 20 %) of the production; the bulk of this is from the KMA and is railed to many of the countries of Europe, including not only the Soviet satellites but also Britain and Italy.

The Kola peninsula in the north of European Russia is the third main iron-producing area west of the Urals; low-grade ores are mined at Kovdor and Olenegorsk in Murmansk oblast and about 10 million tonnes of the concentrate are railed to the iron and steel centre of Cherepovets on the Rybinsk reservoir in northern Russia.

An additional source of iron became available in north European Russia in 1973. An agreement with Finland was made to develop the Kostamuksha iron-quartzite deposit in the Karelian ASSR, near the Finnish border, and production began in 1978. Concentrates from the mines are sent to Cherepovets and supplement the supplies from the Kola peninsula.

In the Urals, the complex of igneous, metamorphic and sedimentary rocks contains a great variety of mineral deposits, of which iron ores were originally among the most abundant, and provided the basis of the traditional iron and steel industry of the region. There are several iron-mining centres, although production in them all is declining as the deposits become exhausted. The most important is Magnitogorsk where a large deposit of high-grade ore, the Magnitnaya Gora (Magnet mountain) formed the basis of the Soviet steel industry during the Second World War and in the early post-war years, supplying both Ural and Siberian steel works. Today, as the Ural iron production is insufficient for local needs, additional supplies from the KMA and Kazakhstan are brought in. Other deposits are the Kashkanar, a low-grade vanadiferous magnetite, and those of the Nizhniy· Tagil area at Kushva, Vysokaya, Blagodat and Alapayevsk. The Bakal deposit supplies the iron and steel mills at Chelyabinsk.

East of the Urals, very large reserves of low-grade iron ore are found in Kustanay oblast in north-west Kazakhstan. Here, a very extensive magnetite deposit is mined at Rudnyy, and the concentrated ore is railed to the Urals and east to the Kuznetsk basin. Open-pit methods are used as the ores lie close to the surface; production is rising and about 12 million tonnes were sent to the Urals in 1979. Another ironfield in Kazakhstan is at Atasu from which the ore is railed to the steel plant at Temirtau.

In Siberia, the Kuznetsk basin contains iron-ore deposits, mined in the southern rim of the basin at Temirtau and Tashtagol, known as the Gornaya Shoriya district. Production is insufficient for the needs of the Kuzbas steel industry and is supplemented from the Rudnyy mines in Kazakhstan and from Zheleznogorsk-Ilimskiy, east of Bratsk.

Ores of non-ferrous metals (Fig. 8.6)
The ores of all the non-ferrous metals are distinctive in their relatively low percentage of pure metal, commonly less than 5 %; hence the need for a preliminary process of concentration prior to smelting. Many are associated with igneous activity during which metallic minerals were formed by the agency of heated gases and vapours, representing a late stage in the intrusion and cooling of a magma.

COPPER

Copper is among the most important of such deposits, because of its value in the electrical industry as a conductor and for electrical machinery. Many other industries need copper, exemplified by the motor-car and truck industries, and the metal is extensively used in the manufacture of alloys such as bronze and brass.

The USSR has large deposits of this valuable metal and has been among the chief producing countries for a long period, mining having begun in the Urals in the seventeenth century. In addition to the older Ural centres of Krasnouralsk and Kyshtym, new sources have been exploited at centres such as Sibay, Gay and Uchaly.

As the older deposits in the Urals become exhausted, the greater reserves of Kazakhstan are being increasingly used by the Ural smelters; in central Kazakhstan the great copper complex at Dzhezkazgan has become the principal copper centre of the Soviet Union, with steady expansion since the beginning of production in the 1960s. It rails concentrates to the Urals and to the Balkhash complex farther south (Chapter 9) where the industry is supported also by the Kounradskiy mine and by the newer Sayak mine. Other centres in Kazakhstan are at Orlovka, a new complex in the east, and at Bozshakol, where a copper-molybdenum deposit is being developed during the course of the current Five Year plan.

An important contribution to the USSR copper industry is supplied by Georgia, Uzbekistan and Armenia. Madneuli, in south Georgia, near the town of Kazretiy, is a new non-ferrous metals complex yielding copper, barites, zinc and lead; the first ores were mined here in 1973. The Armenian SSR has a copper-molybdenum site at Kadzharan, near the border with Iran. The Uzbek republic's output of copper is centred upon the Almalyk copper and zinc concentrator. This receives copper-molybdenum ore from the Sarycheku deposit, situated in the Kurama mountains east of Almalyk, exploitation of which began in late 1973.

Norilsk, in the far north of the RSFSR, is being continuously developed as a non-ferrous metals complex, with copper its most important product. The scale of the operation is indicated by the 'October' mine, one of the largest sites, where there are numerous vertical shafts more than 1000 metres in depth and an extensive system of tunnels. Hydro-electricity and natural gas provide power to the area which is linked by rail to the Yenisey river terminal of Dudinka.

A new source of copper, the Udokan deposit in east Siberia, is planned to begin production in the 1980s. This will be associated with the new settlement of Naminga and with the BAM railway system.

LEAD AND ZINC

Minerals containing these metals are commonly found together, often in rocks affected by thermal metamorphism or where heated solutions have deposited veins of the metal in limestones. They are complex deposits and the lead/zinc ores may also yield gold, bismuth, selenium and other metals. The industrial uses of lead and its compounds are manifold; for accumulators, for piping, foil, ammunition and for various alloys.

The USSR appears to rank very high in the scale of world producers, probably second after the USA. An early centre of production was Ordzhonikidze, in the Caucasus, where the Terek River supplied hydro power for the plant, which acquired new mines and a concentrator recently. The Kazakh SSR appears to contain half the lead and zinc deposits of the USSR at Leninogorsk in the Altay region, and also at Chimkent, Achisay, Karagayly, and Tekeli. A major expansion of the lead/zinc industry took place after the Second World War in eastern Kazakhstan, with zinc refineries at Ust Kamenogorsk and Leninogorsk. (Chapter 9) Almalyk in Uzbekistan is another important centre. Other deposits are in western Siberia (the Salairskoye group), eastern Siberia (Nerchinsk group) and the Far East, where the lead mining centre of Tetyukhe has been renamed Dalnegorsk ('far mountain'). The latter mine yields both bismuth and silver.

TIN

Cassiterite, or tin oxide, is found in veins in certain types of granite, often associated with copper pyrites and wolfram. However, most tinstone is recovered as grains from placer washings in weathered soil, or in alluvial silts and gravels of river beds. The metal is important in the engineering and chemical industries and the manufacture of alloys and tinplate.

Tin is one of the non-ferrous metals not abundant in the USSR, and supplies are imported from Malaysia and Indonesia. The principal sources in the USSR are the Solnechnyy complex near

Komsomolsk and Dalnegorsk, both in the Far East, and in Chita oblast in eastern Siberia. Tin is also mined with tungsten in the far north-east of Siberia in the Chukotsk peninsula.

MANGANESE
This is abundant in the USSR; it is obtained on the Chiatura plateau in the southern foothills of the Caucasus, between Poti and Tbilisi, and also in the Ukraine, at Nikopol. At the latter site the ore-bed occurs near the Dnepr river within hollows on deeply weathered Pre-Cambrian gneiss.

CHROMITE
Like manganese, this is an important mineral used in the production of alloys, in this case its use is for making chrome steel, stainless steel, and for refractory materials. The USSR is the world's principal producer of chromite, and it comes from the Khrom-Tau (chrome mountain) area in north-west Kazakhstan, where it occurs in ultra-basic intrusive rocks.

TUNGSTEN
The ores of tungsten are wolfram and scheelite, the former often associated with tinstone in acid igneous rocks. Tungsten's chief use is for machine-tool steels and for electric filaments. The main source is the open-pit mine and concentrating plant in Zakamensk mining area of the Buryat ASSR in eastern Siberia. Other tungsten producing sites are at Tyrnyauz in the north Caucasus region, Akchatau, in central Kazakhstan, Koytash in Central Asia, Iultin in the Chukchi A O and several sites, notably Vostok 2, in Primorskiy kray.

NICKEL
This ore is found in certain types of intrusive igneous rock. The main deposits of nickel ores are located in Murmansk, the Urals, the Kazakh SSR and in north Siberia, at Norilsk. The mines at Norilsk, together with the smelters there, account for a major part of the USSR production, and this complex also yields copper, iron, gold, silver and platinum.

MERCURY
This is a rather rare metal, though it is found in several sites in the Soviet Union and is required in the chemical, electrical and instrument industries. The principal producing centres are Nikitovka,

a suburb of Gorlovka in the Ukraine and Khaydarken, on the southern margins of the Fergana valley in the Kirgiz SSR. Other centres are the Anzob complex of the Tadzhik SSR, the Shorbulag mine of Azerbaydzhan, the Plamennyy mine in north-east Siberia, and the Aktash deposit in the Altay mountains.

ALUMINIUM
The aluminium industry has undergone rapid development since the end of the Second World War. In the 1930s it was a relatively small operation located in European Russia where bauxite, the principal source of aluminium, was mined near Tikhvin–Boksitogorsk, in the Leningrad region. Hydro-electricity, generated at Volkhov, was used for the process of reduction into aluminium metal. Later, alumina was railed southwards to the new Dnepr hydro-electric plant at Zaporozhye for conversion into aluminium.

Apart from bauxite, aluminium ores include nephelines, alunites, cyanites and sillimanites. The Soviet Union supplements her own resources of bauxite with imported supplies, but also obtains the alumina from nepheline and alunites which are mined at various sites. The industry is therefore widely dispersed, an important locational factor being abundance of electricity for the final process of conversion of the alumina into aluminium metal. The Kola peninsula, Transcaucasia, the Dnepr region, the Urals, Kazakhstan, Siberia and the Leningrad region all contribute to the present increasing production of aluminium in the USSR.

Post-war developments have included the use of nephelite in the production of aluminium; the centre of nepheline and apatite mining is the town of Kirovsk, east of Lake Imandra, in the Kola peninsula, where hydro-electric power is used in the aluminium refineries of Kandalaksha and Nadvoitsy. Nepheline from the Korovsk area is also converted to aluminium at Volkhov, the intermediate process of alumina production being carried out in the Boksitogorsk area. A newly discovered deposit of bauxite ore has become available in the European north-west, named the north Onega deposit. It is a high-grade ore body but is in a remote area of waterlogged terrain at the confluence of the Onega and Iksa rivers.

In Transcaucasia, alunite deposits at Zaglik, near Kirovabad in the Kura river valley, are the basis of the alumina plant at Kirovabad; the final process of aluminium production takes place at

Yerevan and Sumgait. Yerevan also receives supplies of alumina from Razdan in Georgia.

The aluminium industry in Central Asia utilises the clay material, kaolin, as a source of alumina; the deposit is obtained in the Uzbek and the Tadzhik republics and was planned to support the aluminium reduction plant at Regar, in the Gissar valley west of Dushanbe, where the hydro-electricity of the Nurek project is available; alumina from the Urals or from Pavlodar in Kazakhstan is also used at the Regar plant.

The German occupation of much of European Russia during the war years, 1941–1944, resulted in a significant movement of the Soviet aluminium industry to the east. In the Urals, bauxite and alunite had been worked for several years and production increased at centres such as Kamensk–Uralskiy and Severouralsk, with part of the raw material being railed to Siberia. The post-war years have seen vast expansion of the industry into the Asian part of the USSR based upon the exploitation of newer sources of the different aluminium-yielding ores, together with the availability of abundant hydro-electricity in the reduction plants at Bratsk and Krasnoyarsk. Thus, bauxite is now mined at Arkalyk and at Krasnooktyabrskiy, both in Kazakhstan; and Pavlodar has become important, sending alumina to the Novokuznetsk and Shelekhov aluminium plants. More recently, new plant has been added at Achinsk, producing alumina from nephelite from Belogorsk, using thermal-electricity derived from the lignites of the Kansk–Achinsk coalfield.

GOLD

Gold is abundant in the USSR, and the country is second only to South Africa in world production. Gold mining was one of the earliest industries of the upper Lena region in Tsarist times, where placer deposits were obtained from washings of alluvial gravels. This method is still used in the middle Yenisey region, operated on a very large scale by huge dredges. Commercial gold mining began in the Urals in 1814 and was followed by the discoveries in Siberia, notably in the Vitim and Aldan plateau areas, where mining still continues. Other Siberian gold mining sites are in the Magadan oblast, and at Bilibino, in the Chukchi autonomous okrug where atomic power is used for the mining operations.

The traditional domination of the Urals and Siberia in Soviet gold production is, however, being changed by newer developments in the south of the country. In Armenia, the Zod deposit is an important lode, mined east of Lake Sevan, and the metal is concentrated at Ararat. Important developments in Uzbekistan, based on lodes, are at Altynkan on the slopes of the Kurama mountains in the Fergana valley; the Kochbulak mine in the same area and the Zarafshan complex in the central part of the Kyzylkum desert. It seems clear that with these developments Uzbekistan will become one of the principal gold producing areas of the USSR.

BIBLIOGRAPHY

Campbell, R. W. (1968), *The economics of Soviet oil and gas*, John Hopkins Press, Baltimore.

Danielson, A. L. and Delorme, C. D. (1979), 'An alternative analysis of the effects of energy prices on energy consumption in the Soviet Union,' *Soviet Studies*, **31**, pp. 581–4.

Dewdney, J. C. (1976), *The USSR, Studies in industrial geography*, Dawson, Folkstone.

Dienes, L. (1977), 'Basic industries and regional economic growth: the Soviet South,' *Tijdschrift voor Economische en Sociale Geografie*, 1977 No. 1, pp. 2–15.

Dienes, L. and Shabad, T. (1979), *The Soviet energy system*, Wiley, New York.

Dienes, L. (1981), in Jt. Economic Committee US, *Energy in Soviet Policy*, Washington, 101–19.

Godman, M. I. (1980), *The enigma of Soviet petroleum: half full or half empty*, Allen and Unwin, London.

Kelly, W. J. (1978), Effects of the Soviet price reform of 1967 on energy consumption, *Soviet Studies*, **30**, pp. 394–402.

Lydolph, P. E. (1979), *Geography of the USSR, topical analysis*, Misty Valley, Elkhart Lake, Wisconsin.

Pryde, P. R. (1978), 'Nuclear energy development in the Soviet Union,' *Soviet Geography*, **19**, pp. 75–83.

Shabad, T. (1978), News Notes. *Soviet Geography*, **19**, pp. 273–293.

Shabad, T. (1969), *Basic industrial resources of the USSR*, Columbia University Press, New York.

9 Industry

Industrial development in the Soviet Union has had to overcome difficulties which have been no less formidable than those which faced agriculture. It is true that the climate does not pose nearly so many problems for industrialists, though it does impede some industrial activities, such as mineral extraction and movement of goods and labour, and the water resources are very unevenly distributed. Industrial development also is not hindered, generally, by soil variations. On the other hand, the great extent of the country, which has conferred reserves of land on Soviet agriculture, has meant great transport problems for industry, both in the assembly of raw materials and labour at suitable locations, and in the distribution of finished or semi-finished goods. Strategic issues have also posed problems for Soviet planners, with a constant need to balance development in the European parts which have the greatest population and, therefore, demand, against the wish to locate as much industry as possible in the less accessible regions where they are safer from invasion and aerial bombardment. Economic issues have likewise presented problems in whether to locate industries near the raw materials, many of which are in the eastern regions, or in the areas of main demand, where raw materials are fewer. In either case, specialised regions of industry mean long transport hauls, whereas a more even distribution of industry throughout all populated regions means less dependence on centralised or specialised industrial areas and more regional security.

The problem of ensuring a sufficient supply of labour and of, in particular, skilled labour, has also always been paramount in Soviet industry. Although after the emancipation of the serfs there was considerable migration from the farms to the towns, the workforce was not particularly well adapted or sufficiently well educated for skilled work. Later generations have benefited from being brought up in an urban and industrial environment, but the newcomers reinforcing the industrial ranks have almost always been from rural sources and in need of training. In later years the flow of migrants from the rural areas has slackened as the reserves of manpower have become less, and industrial planning has had increasingly to think in terms of coping with actual labour shortages, particularly in the less attractive regions. It has been increasingly necessary for labour reasons, as well as being politically desirable, for industrial development to be speeded up in Central Asia rather than in Siberia, the increase among the traditionally Moslem peoples of the Central Asian republics being the most rapid in the Soviet Union, whereas population has increased only slowly in Siberia, with much outward migration to areas of better climate.

Against the advantages of location in either Siberia or Central Asia have been the attractions of greater economies of operating manufacturing industries in the western or European areas, where skills and training facilities are best developed and contacts most readily established with the Soviet Union's partners in COMECON, as well as with the capitalist countries in western Europe and North America, on whom the USSR has depended for much of the expertise required to develop modern industries.

In 1917 the new government inherited a considerable range of industries from Tsarist times but industrial development had depended very much on foreign engineers and foreign capital. For example, British capital developed textile mills (which employed managers and overseers from Lancashire), east of Moscow and at Narva in Estonia. German capital was invested in engineering and in the chemicals industry and was particularly important in the Baltic region, where there was a large German minority. Ukrainian heavy industry was financed by British, French and Belgian money, and the city of Donetsk was founded by a Welsh ironmaster, Hughes, being originally named after him (Yuzovka). French money was also liberally invested in railway development and Swedish money in telephones, while the Nobel millions were made in the Baku oilfields, to name but a few examples. The Tsarist authorities gave the greatest encouragement to industries which might help Russia strategically and St. Petersburg, then the capital, grew as an industrial centre supplying the Imperial armed forces. As noted in Chapter 1, manufacturing industry was relatively well developed around Moscow, the traditional commercial capital of the country, while the coal and iron ore of the Ukraine attracted heavy industry. Added to the industries of the Tsarist empire were also the textile manufacturing of Lodz and the coal and iron-making of Dabrowa, for much of Poland was then under Russian control.

Nevertheless, in 1914, two-thirds of the manufactured goods required by Russia had to be imported and over three-quarters of manufacturing industry was controlled by foreign capital. Many simple everyday needs were still supplied to the market by peasant industry and much commerce continued to pass through the traditional great fairs, like that of Nizhniy Novgorod (now Gorkiy).

SOVIET INDUSTRIAL DEVELOPMENT

When the Bolsheviks seized power in 1917 they proclaimed workers' control of industry but in the confused conditions of the Civil War (1918–21) this was curtailed, central planning was developed and by mid-1918 all major industries had been nationalised. After this period of 'War Communism' Lenin permitted more freedom in what

became known as the New Economic Policy. After his death in 1924 no clear programme emerged until Stalin took control and initiated an ambitious industrialisation drive in the first of the Five Year Plans (1928–33). His aim to create 'socialism in one country' resulted in almost total centralisation of economic planning with the emphasis on basic industries such as coal, steel and heavy engineering.

Since the Soviet leaders were not prepared to permit industrial development by private entrepreneurs there was no possibility of letting individuals make the decisions on capital investment and location of industry and then suffering if the decisions turned out to be bad ones. With the State as the only entrepreneur there was need for an immense and complex bureaucracy to make the decisions and guide development. The principal organ for industrial development was GOSPLAN, the State organisation for industrial planning, itself guided by the leaders in the Communist Party.

Gosplan laid down directives proposing the spread of industry more evenly over the country by development of the eastern regions; the development of regional specialisation at the same time as maximum overall development in the major planning regions; and encouragement for any development which reduced the burden on transport. In the early years, planning suffered from a gigantomania, illustrated by the concept of the Ural–Kuzbas Kombinat. This was a vast inter-regional link-up between industries in the Ural region and in western Siberia. Kuzbas, in west Siberia, was to ship its coking coal by rail to the Ural region, where suitable fuel was lacking, with return loads of iron ore. The idea was not entirely new, a similar project using water transport having been suggested by a Commission in 1916, but it was inadequacy of the railways to handle the bulk freights demanded that weakened the scheme. From the early 1930s also, supplies of Karaganda coal began to reduce the Ural's dependence on Kuzbas output while discovery of iron ore in western Siberia reduced the Kuzbas need for ore from the Urals. By the mid-1930s, the Ural region emerged as the second great metallurgical producer after the Donbas as its large new iron and steel works went into operation.

Much publicity was given to the development of the eastern regions but some of the greatest but least advertised achievements were in industrial construction in European Russia, notably in the Moscow and Gorkiy districts, while new industries began to appear in Baykalia and in the Far East in response to the strategic threat created by Japanese control of Manchuria. Some regional economic development in the 1930s had, however, strong political undertones. For example, the Moslem lands of Central Asia, of uncertain allegiance, were tied more tightly to the rest of the Soviet Union by increasing economic interdependence. Land in Central Asia was turned over increasingly from food to industrial crops (e.g. cotton), urgently needed for industries in other parts of the country, while Central Asian food deficiencies were made good by Siberian wheat sent along the Turksib railway, completed in 1931. Central Asian manufacturing industry was also made heavily dependent on raw metal and chemical supplies sent from the Ural region and Siberia, or even from European Russia. It was not until the wartime emergency that iron and steel making was established in Central Asia (Begovat/Bekabad) to use locally available scrap, and the region was kept continually dependent on pig iron and alloy metals from Siberia and the Ural region.

As the world situation deteriorated in the late 1930s, developments with obvious strategic implications were planned, such as the opening of the Pechora coalfield, the working of metallic minerals on the lower Yenisey and exploitation of the Ural–Volga oilfields, while further progress was made in industrialisation in the Ural region and Siberia. Of these developments, few were anywhere near completion by the time of the German invasion. As much equipment as possible was removed from the path of the advancing German armies and re-erected east of the Volga, notably in the Ural region and in Siberia. Central Asia acquired food and textile plants among others. Many of the evacuated plants left the machinery in their 'temporary' sites when they returned to European Russia where they were re-equipped after the German defeat. This accounted in part for the surprising growth of machine tools and transport equipment in the Ural region and western Siberia after the Second World War. The 'eastern regions' also benefited from new plants erected there after having been dismantled as reparations in Germany: this was marked, for example, in the chemicals industry of western Siberia.

Postwar planning

After the war, reconstruction was achieved under the strict centralised control favoured by Stalin, with first priority being continued for the producer goods industries. Khrushchev introduced the first major reforms in the late 1950s. His decentralisation of management to regional economic councils (*sovnarkhozy*) (Chapter 12) did not lead to the greater production he had hoped for and after his removal from power the central ministries were again given full control over the most important branches of the economy. Nevertheless, under Khrushchev the economy became somewhat better balanced in terms of production of consumer goods, the reconstruction of the chemicals industry was seriously begun, the motor vehicle industry was expanded and the production of petroleum products substantially increased.

With planning more centralised again under Brezhnev's leadership reforms have been modest. There has been a trend towards grouping enterprises and in 1973 it was decreed that associations (*ob'edineniya*) would become standard in basic industry in order to achieve economies of scale and enhance technical progress. Production associations (*proizvodstvenninye ob'edineniya*) link enterprises horizontally or vertically, while industrial associations (*promyshlennye ob'edineniya*) execute ministerial requirements at all-Union or republic level in selected industries such as fuel and power. As with individual enterprises, it appears that associations have to accept economic accountability (*khozraschet*), which has been increasingly demanded as a means of avoiding waste of resources.

Integration is stressed also in the creation of territorial production complexes. Much stress was placed during the 1970s on these areal forms of organisation which are intended to facilitate both specialisation of individual enterprises and integration of overall regional production. The planning for such complexes embraces both long-established industrial regions such as the Donbas and pioneer areas like those being built in association with the Baykal–Amur railway.

Official literature stresses the part played by the planning bodies of each republic, oblast and rayon in the construction of plans by the Gosplan organisation. The Gosplan of each republic is supposed to take account of all territorial requirements and it is presumably through these processes that individual enterprise managers bid for their own places in the national plans, in terms of both production and supplies. It is clear, however, that national interests are supreme in the formulation of each five year plan and the longer-term plans that are accepted as essential for full development of the economy.

Postwar planning has generally favoured industrial development in the better placed areas and the relatively weak regions have hardly improved their position. Thus, approximately half the total national investment has remained in European Russia, while the rate of industrial growth in Transcaucasia and Central Asia has generally been below the national average. In Kazakhstan and in Belorussia, however, it has been above the national level, and investment per head of population has been greatest in Siberia, Kazakhstan and north-west European Russia. Major mining, metallurgical and railway developments in southern Siberia, and giant new hydro-electric barrages providing cheap power for large new electro-metallurgical and electro-chemicals industries provide the basis for widespread developments.

Despite the lack of satisfactory statistics, there is every indication that European Russia (including the Ural region) remains the main location of industrial output, contributing well over half the total output. As much as one-fifth of total output may come from the Ukraine; another fifth from the Central Industrial region; over one-tenth from the Ural region and a little less may now be contributed by the Volga lands. Siberia and the Far East together contribute probably between 10 and 15%. The geographical pattern of industry represents a product of the struggle between the centripetal tendencies to locate plants in the most economic sites and the centrifugal tendencies to spread industry as widely as possible throughout the country for strategic reasons.

INDUSTRIAL DEVELOPMENT IN THE FUTURE

The Soviet Union is now among the most developed nations industrially, but the average standard of living of its inhabitants is substantially below that common in western Europe and North America, and the Communist Party and government of the USSR will undoubtedly continue to plan for continued advancement of the economy in an effort to 'catch up with the West', an aim

which has dominated their history ever since the revolution. In order to continue development the Soviet Union must achieve further utilisation of its primary resources, especially agricultural and mineral, to provide raw materials. It must also improve supply of fuel and power and the harnessing of its labour resources.

During the 1970s the energy crisis in the world as a whole focused attention on the position of the Soviet Union. Largely because of its great size the USSR has far greater fossil fuel and water power resources than has any other country. However, it is not easy to satisfy all the demands, especially for oil, within the country, for export to the other countries of COMECON, which are heavily dependent on Soviet oil, and for export to the west to earn foreign currency. A great deal was achieved during the 1950s and, especially, the 1960s, in increasing the efficiency of utilisation of energy resources but little more can be expected in this direction.

The development of energy and mineral resources requires increased investment, in spite of the fact that since the Five Year Plans which commenced in 1928, some three-tenths of all productive capital invested in industry has gone to the energy industries. Much of this investment will have to be made in the eastern regions since that is where the resources lie. The European USSR provides only about 60% of its energy requirements from its own territories and this figure will steadily diminish. While oil, natural gas and electricity can be transported over great distances by pipelines and high voltage transmission lines, the losses entailed in these forms of transport are quite considerable, between 5 and 15% being reported in varying forms of transmission.

The attractions of locating the maximum industry practicable in the eastern regions is apparent, for then there is minimum transport of energy and minerals to the point of manufacture or processing. As the markets are mainly in the west there is then, however, the necessity to transport finished products. Furthermore, labour supply is limited in Siberia and the Far East, though plentiful in Central Asia, which is the only major region in which the total labour supply can be expected to increase significantly in the coming decades. Hence the advantages of each location for each industrial development must be carefully balanced by Gosplan before a decision is taken. There are clear advantages in locating in the east the industries catering for local consumer needs, as in the cases noted above. Less obvious in transport terms are some of the others developed in the east but these are commonly located there in response to some specific overwhelming advantage, such as cheap power for the aluminium and electrochemical industries in Siberia and Central Asia.

Thus, there can be no general rule about the economic desirability of an eastward spread of industry as a whole and many branches will continue to be developed predominantly in the west irrespective of the riches of the east. Strategically also there is clash of interests between emphasis on development in the east and in the west. There is powerful motivation to encourage Soviet people to move into the regions bordering China, with its 1000 million population posing a threat, at least in Soviet eyes, to the Siberian and Far East lands, the legal possession of some of the border territories being, in any case, in dispute. On the other hand the integration of the Eastern European economies with that of the USSR and the need for trade with 'the West' make the European regions more attractive for investment. In all probability the Soviet rulers will continue to apportion investment to both east and west, with the bulk going to the west, where the population is densest, but with every opportunity for selective investment in the east being taken to the accompaniment of much publicity of Soviet achievements in these rich but harsh territories.

THE MAJOR INDUSTRIAL GROUPS

Each of the main groups of manufacturing industry will now be reviewed, followed by a résumé of the principal industrial regions.

The metal production industries

The comparatively rich endowment of the Soviet Union with minerals, detailed in Chapter 8, has been a considerable aid to industrial growth. Exploitation of deposits in the harsh physical environments of northern Siberia and Central Asia has posed many problems and a dilemma. The choice is whether to save on transport by installing expensive refining and purifying equipment at the mines, or to save such investment but pay heavier transport costs by evacuating raw ore for refining and treating elsewhere, carrying away considerable quantities of what is ultimately 'waste'. Solution of the equation is difficult since factors such as nature, size and location of the deposits, the relative priority of development of different minerals and ease of provision of transport, as well as labour supply, are all involved.

Fuel minerals are well represented. Coal has ceased to be the principal source of energy, having been displaced by petroleum and being now rivalled by natural gas (Table 9.1). Coal deposits of varying quality are widely scattered. Most significant are those suitable for metallurgical coking coal, the continuing supply of which does give rise, however, to some anxiety. An important influence on industrial development has been the great improvement in availability of oil and natural gas as detailed in Chapter 8, while a wider spread territorially of deposits has eased the supply problem.

Iron ore, generally in quality better than deposits currently used in the Western world, has also been shown to be available in generous proportions and there is a rich endowment with most of the more important alloy metals, especially manganese. The wide spread of deposits is again an important locational influence. The

TABLE 9.1 PRODUCTION OF FUELS BY TYPE (CALCULATED IN STANDARD UNITS)

Year	All	Petroleum	Natural Gas	Coal	Peat	Shales	Wood
1913	100	30.5	—	48.0	1.4	—	20.1
1940	100	18.7	1.9	59.1	5.2	0.3	17.3
1950	100	17.4	2.3	66.1	4.8	0.4	9.0
1960	100	30.5	7.9	53.9	2.9	0.7	4.1
1970	100	41.1	19.1	35.4	1.5	0.7	2.2
1980	100	45.3	27.1	25.4	0.4	0.6	1.2

Source: Narodnoye khozyaystvo SSSR, various years.

situation for non-ferrous metals is a little less happy, notably because of the adverse physical environment in which several important 'deficiency' metals (e.g. tin) are found, but also because some metals are poorly represented. A special office of COMECON deals with intra-communist bloc use of these metals and recovery of non-ferrous scrap.

It should also be borne in mind that the Soviet Union is the major supplier of raw materials to the COMECON countries of eastern Europe, and has encouraged these countries' dependence on Soviet supplies for political reasons. Soviet regional economic policy, with its emphasis on a high degree of regional self-sufficiency and reduction of the burden on transport, has encouraged development of deposits, even where these have been unpromising in quantity and quality and are consequently expensive to exploit.

A special note should also be made of electricity, which occupies a notable place in Marxist–Leninist dogma: Lenin said 'Communism is Soviet power plus electrification of the whole country'. The greater part of the electricity generated is by thermal power stations. A little over an eighth of the current is generated by hydro-electric stations. Because of the remoteness and great physical difficulties, it is unlikely that more than a small proportion of the immense water power potential of Siberia will be harnessed in the foreseeable future. The creation of a national grid for electricity distribution presents problems because of the great distances involved, but this may be overcome by Soviet advances in high tension transmission technology, allowing greater economical distances for electricity 'transport'. Meanwhile, several regional grids have been constructed. It has been argued that availability of conventional fuels and water power make the necessity to develop atomic powered generating stations less urgent in the Soviet Union than in western Europe, though the Soviet Union has a number of nuclear power plants in operation and is believed to have adequate nuclear fuel mineral deposits.

IRON AND STEEL MAKING

The major iron and steel producer is the Dnepr–Donbas district. Although of lower relative importance than formerly, it still produces about one-third of all Soviet steel. Heavy metallurgy consumes about 40 % of the Donbas coal output.

A particularly important group of works lies on the western flank of the Donbas coalfield, obtaining iron ore from Krivoy Rog and Kursk, and comprising plants at Donetsk and Makeyevka, which together smelt half the output of pig iron in the Donbas, and also Yenakiyevo, while Gorlovka is a large coking centre. At Kramatorsk there is electric steel production. The plants of the eastern Donbas concentrate on specialised work such as pipe rolling at Lugansk, complicated sections at Kommunarsk and special pig iron at Almaznaya, while Taganrog is important for tubes, pipes and boilers. Gorlovka coke, Yelenovka limestone and a mixture of Kerch and Krivoy Rog ores are used at Zhdanov, where there are some of the largest rolling mills in Europe. The highly phosphoric Kerch ore is suitable for tube and welding steels. Although an ore producer, Krivoy Rog imports Donbas coal and coke to smelt its own fragile ores that do not stand transporting elsewhere. An

The Berezniki (Urals) titanium-magnesium plant

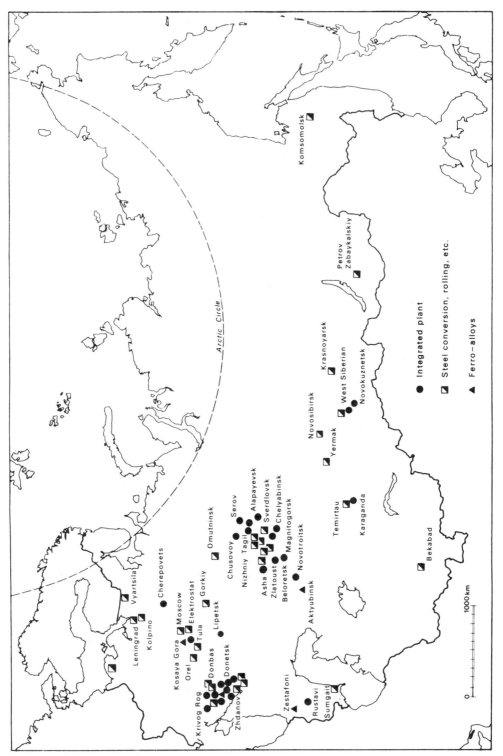

Fig. 9.1 Distribution of major iron and steel plants

intermediate location in the bend of the Dnepr marks large plants at Dneprodzerzhinsk and Dnepropetrovsk, while Zaporozhye, using cheap Dneproges electricity, makes electric steels and cold rolls, and has a ferro-alloy plant. Nikopol, with manganese mines, is also a rolling mill centre. The Dnepr area has a big advantage in its water supply, which contrasts with the water-deficient Donbas.

The second main centre, producing about 30 % of the total, is the Ural region. The low cost of Ural ore offsets the high costs of coke and coal imported from western Siberia and Kazakhstan, but it is now insufficient and ore is imported from as far afield as Kursk. Unlike the Donbas, there is not such a difficulty in the Ural region in obtaining the large quantities of water needed for processing, except in the southern areas. Manganese is often used generously in place of flux. The main plants lie mostly on the eastern slope of the Ural ranges along a belt of intense mineralisation which supplies their raw material. Nizhniy Tagil, one of the largest works, is supplied from nearby mines such as Vysokaya Gora and Blagodat or most recently from Kachkanar, with coal and coke mostly from the Kuzbas. There are also some old charcoal smelting plants in the area. The Sverdlovsk district depends mostly on converting engineering scrap into steel for electrical engineering, while Polevskoy has one of the largest Soviet tinplate works. Since 1943, quality and alloy steel has been made at Chelyabinsk, using Bakal ores and Karaganda and Kuzbas coal and coke. Zlatoust makes instrument steels. One of the largest of all Soviet plants is Magnitogorsk, which uses local ores from the Magnetic Mountain (Magnitnaya Gora) and recently from Kazakh deposits, with coal and coke brought from the Kuzbas and Karaganda. A serious problem has been the supply of water for processing in the dry steppe, largely overcome by a barrage across the Ural river near the town. In the southern Ural, Novo–Troitsk has a large modern works, using the chrome-nickel-iron ore from Khalilovo and imported coal and coke. The small works on the western flanks of the Ural mostly concentrate on rolling, plating or drawing.

Western Siberia was developed first as a steel producer in association with the Ural region as part of the Ural–Kuzbas *Kombinat* of the early Five Year Plans. One of the largest integrated iron and steel works in the USSR is sited at Novokuznetsk, where a second large plant is being developed, and where there is also a big ferro-alloy plant. Novokuznetsk has one of the world's largest continuous sheet mills. Coal and coke are available locally and ore comes from Tashtagol, Shalym and Abakan, and from the more distant Angara, Ilim and Pit basins, with coal from a new field at Chulman in southern Yakutia. Plans have been put forward for a steelworks at Tayshet and modernisation of the old Petrovsk–Zabaykalskiy works.

The Central Industrial region around Moscow has traditionally had high production costs offset by low transport charges to local consumers, but its future has been transformed by the KMA development. Coal and coke come from the Donbas, while ore is drawn from Krivoy Rog and other areas, but some ore is also mined locally. Tula and Lipetsk are the main smelters, while the latter has large rolling mills and a continuous strip mill, as well as a large diameter tube plant and a cold rolling mill. Both Kosaya Gora and Lipetsk produce very high quality steels for special purposes. Some steel conversion from scrap is carried on in Moscow at large engineering works. The upper Volga has some small rolling mills (e.g. Gorkiy). The Moscow and Leningrad regions are also now supplied from Cherepovets (near the Rybinsk reservoir) which uses Vorkuta coal and Karelian ore. Leningrad converts steels for local engineering plants and Vyartsilya in Karelia makes electric steel.

Using Donbas and Caucasian coal and Dashkesan iron ore, the Transcaucasian Rustavi iron and steel works near Tbilisi, opened in 1955,

A blast furnance of the Karaganda iron and steel works at Temirtau

supplies the Sumgait tube works near Baku. At Zestafoni, using local ores and cheap hydro-electric current, is one of the main Soviet ferro-alloy plants. In Kazakhstan, based on Atasu ores and Karaganda coals, there are new iron and steel works at Temirtau and Karaganda and a large ferro-alloy plant is being built at Yermak (Pavlodar), while the Aktyubinsk ferro-alloy works uses ore from Khrom-Tau. To use available scrap and convert imported Siberian pig iron, a steelworks was opened in 1943 at Bekabad (Begovat) near the Farkhad dam in Uzbekistan. In the Far East, Amurstal at Komsomolsk serves a similar purpose, and it also has important tinplate works.

Non-ferrous metallurgy
Some of the important locations of the non-ferrous metals industry have already been mentioned in connection with the steel industry, and others in describing the occurrence of important ore bodies in Chapter 8. It is necessary, however, to stress that this is a vast and vital branch of industry, of no less importance than the steel industry, to the functioning of the modern complex economy, and to note the main plant locations.

COPPER
The Ural region has supported copper smelting since the early part of the eighteenth century. Relocation has occured as local deposits have become exhausted, with the southern area becoming dominant as new metal deposits have been discovered. Verkhnyaya Pyshma, near Sverdlovsk, is the largest refining centre. Concentrates are shipped in from other ore-rich regions including Kazakhstan. Within the Kazakh SSR, the Balkhash plant, near Lake Balkhash, refines concentrates from the several ore bodies of the area. A major new East Kazakhstan copper refinery is being developed to use the Nikolayevsk deposit and concentrates from other ore bodies. Armenia has one of the oldest copper smelters at Alaverdi. This plant has been rebuilt in Soviet times and is now a major works. Copper smelting has also been developed in Uzbekistan, using Uzbek and Tadzhik ores.

NICKEL
Nickel is worked along with copper in several plants, notably at Monchegorsk and Nickel in the Kola Peninsula and the Norilsk area in northern Siberia. In copper and nickel working the emphasis is increasingly on very large smelters, which achieve marked economies of scale and enable valuable by-products to be recovered. This is, in turn, facilitated by modern concentration methods which reduce the amount of waste material transported from the mining areas.

ALUMINIUM
Production involves even more transport than does the movement of concentrated copper and nickel ores to smelters, because the reduction of alumina to aluminium metal requires immense inputs of electric power for electrolysis, about 18 000 kilowatt-hours per tonne of metal produced, and hence the most favoured locations are in areas of major hydro-electric stations. On the other hand, ore is not usually available conveniently nearby and in any case has first to be smelted. Fortunately, the alumina is suitable for long distance transport to the reduction works.

The first Soviet aluminium reduction plants were built at Volkhov (1932), near Leningrad, and Zaporozhye on the Dnepr (1933), the former location being influenced by the availability of bauxite in the Leningrad area. Bauxite deposits also influenced the location in the Ural region of the third and fourth plants. All post-World War II plants, however, have been located in the regions of cheaper power—Novokuznetsk, Volgograd, Sumgait (Azerbaydzhan), Yerevan (Armenia) and, in eastern Siberia, at Shelekhov near Irkutsk, Krasnoyarsk and Bratsk, all three in the 1960s. Over one-half of the Soviet output of aluminium is now produced in Siberia. Aluminium plants have, however, also been constructed in Karelia and Kazakhstan, and Central Asia has also been selected for development of this industry because of its hydro-electric resources. All the locations in the east have become more attractive with the use of nephelines and other ores as alternatives to bauxite (Chapter 8).

MAGNESIUM AND TITANIUM
Like aluminium these are of great strategic importance through their application in the aerospace, nuclear and other advanced technologies. For the early applications of magnesium, the need was met from the plants at Zaporozhye (1935), on the Dnepr, and the two plants in the Urals, Solikamsk (1936) and Berezniki (1943). Pro-

duction of titanium began only in 1954 and the two metals are now produced together at Podolsk, south of Moscow, Zaporozhye, Berezniki and Ust–Kamenogorsk, a large new plant in Kazakhstan dating from 1965, and at a similar large plant at Kalush in the western Ukraine. Titanium production requires a very high consumption of electricity, greater than that for aluminium, so availability of power is crucial in location. In the ores, however, titanium is found in association with vanadium, tantalum and other minerals and integrated processing plants make for the greatest economy of extraction of all these light metals and associated elements.

LEAD AND ZINC

Smelters for these metals were formerly located in coalfield areas as the retorts used large quantities of coal and coke. Old smelters of this kind are still found in the Urals, Ukraine and Kuzbas. More modern methods of handling the polymetallic ores, however, have now been adopted. Mining areas now have concentrating plants, the concentrates being treated in integrated plants typically using natural gas for smelting lead, which results in production of sulphuric acid as a by-product, which is then used in the electrolytic refining of the zinc concentrates. For the latter processes, large quantities of electricity are needed, which, together with the location of ore bodies, has resulted in an emphasis on these industries in the eastern regions. The largest centre is Ust–Kamenogorsk in Kazakhstan, dating from 1947 but since much expanded. It is fairly close to large hydro-electric stations on the Irtysh as well as the Zyryanovsk metal deposit. It produces lead, zinc, cadmium, copper and other metals together with sulphuric acid and zinc sulphate. The titanium-magnesium plant already mentioned is located nearby. Other major refineries have been developed at Leninogorsk, not far away, and at Almalyk in Uzbekistan. Also in Uzbekistan, Chimkent smelts lead while zinc concentrates from the area are railed to electrolytic refineries. In the Urals, only Chelyabinsk produces zinc. Belovo in the Kuzbas is similarly the only zinc producer in Siberia, while lead is smelted at Tetyukhe in the Far East. Otherwise, ores from the areas east of Lake Baykal are shipped as concentrates to other regions. In the North Caucasus, the Ordzhonikidze zinc plant, dating from Tsarist times, has been developed into a major integrated plant for lead and zinc, while another old plant at Konstantinovka in the Donbas, has been modernised and operates wholly on concentrates from distant areas.

TIN

As tin deposits are relatively small and scattered (Chapter 8), no major centre for smelting has yet emerged near the ore bodies. Concentrates are shipped to the existing smelters at Podolsk, south of Moscow, and at Novosibirsk. Hence, there is a large transport input. Promising new fields are being developed in the Far East and processing is beginning there.

It will be seen that when the basic metal processing industries, whether iron and steel, base metals, polymetallic or light metals, are examined, certain regions recur repeatedly in the analysis. Although these clusters were indicated in the brief regional introduction to this chapter, such a cursory survey could not stress the importance of the modern complex plants that have developed. Nor does the traditional emphasis on the iron and steel industry adequately indicate the breadth and variety of the plants that produce the metals for the engineering, constructional and other industries that in turn produce and transport the goods required for further processing, (and, indeed, the processing of the minerals and metals themselves), for transport services and for all other forms of consumption. It will now, however, be clear that in addition to the older industrial regions (the Centre, the Donbas–Dnepr area and the Urals) that of western Siberia and Kazakhstan, in particular, has received an immense amount of investment in basic production facilities in recent decades. Though water supply remains a major problem it has become a formidable addition to Soviet industrial regions. Central Asia and Transcaucasia are also emerging as considerable industrial regions in their own right through the availability of mineral resources and hydro-electric power. These trends will be confirmed in examination of other industries, including those producing chemicals, but first, the main users of metal, the engineering industries, will be reviewed.

Engineering

The use of metals in all branches of the economy depends on metal-cutting and shaping equipment and the machine-tool industry is thus of fundamental importance. Over a hundred enterprises

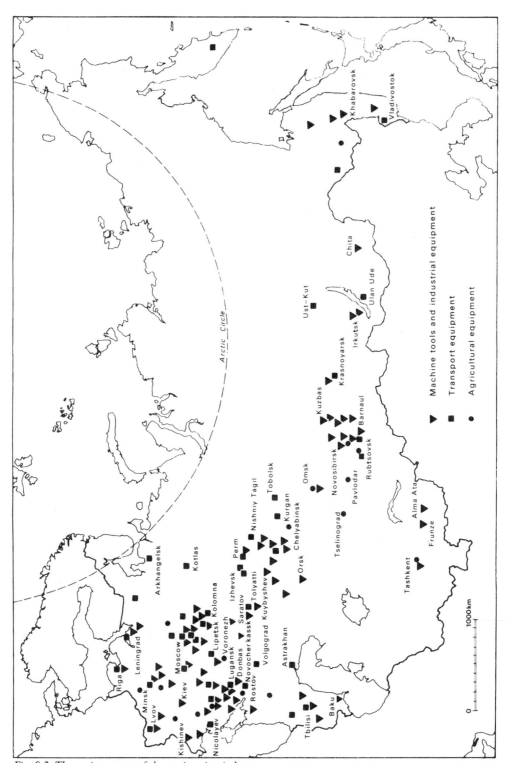

Fig. 9.2 The main centres of the engineering industry

manufacture major metal-working machines, forges and presses, lathes and tools of all kinds. More than half of the total are classed as automatic or semi-automatic, many having digital programme control. The Soviet Union claims to be the birthplace of the most advanced machines for electrophysical and electrochemical working of metals.

The Moscow area and Leningrad, traditional centres of the machine-tool industry, remain dominant in this form of engineering, but many plants have been built in the Urals, especially in Orenburg and Chelyabinsk, the Volga area centred on Saratov, the Lower Don and the North Caucasus, the Ukraine, Belorussia, especially Vitebsk and Minsk, Lithuania and Transcaucasia (Fig 9.2). Novosibirsk is the main centre in Siberia, while in Central Asia as yet only Kirgizia has developed a machine-tool industry. Design and labour skills, markets and the availability of steel are important in location of these plants. Instrument-making factories have expanded particularly rapidly with the accelerating demand for all forms of control units, calculators and computers, electronic equipment and photographic apparatus. High labour input and demand for special skills cause these factories to be located mainly in Moscow, Leningrad, Kiev, Lvov and other large urban centres. Availability of female labour is a particular advantage, both in terms of numbers and the traditional dexterity of feminine fingers.

The construction of heavy machines, providing plant for ferrous and non-ferrous metallurgy, mining, power stations, cement and chemical plants, however, is more often located in metal-producing regions because of the large and heavy content of metals in the products. The Donbas, Dnepr and Ural areas are leaders in these branches. Other major works are sited in the Kuzbas, Novosibirsk, Petropavlovsk in North Kazakhstan, Irkutsk, Krasnoyarsk and Alma Ata, the last three being especially concerned with mining equipment for their areas. Turbines, generators and steam turbines are produced mainly in Leningrad, Kharkov and Sverdlovsk.

Machinery for the textile, food and other light industries is produced in great quantities and varieties in Leningrad, with the Moscow area also important. The old textile centres of Ivanovo and Kostroma are prominent in textile machinery. Like the food industry itself, the manufacture of equipment for processing food is extremely widespread. The greatest number of plants is located in the Ukraine, with the Central, Volga and Transcaucasian areas also important, but the industry spreads all the way across to the Far East where there is specialisation in equipment for the fishing industry. Other regional specialisations include the manufacture of special dredges and mining equipment in eastern Siberia where gold and diamonds are mined, and oil drilling equipment in Transcaucasia, near the first Russian oil-producing area.

Prior to the revolution some railway vehicles were built in Russia but most were imported. Among the now numerous railway works are the old but reconstructed plants at Voroshilovgrad (formerly Lugansk), Kharkov and Kolomna, which build a range of vehicles. Electric locomotives are constructed at Novocherkassk, Riga and Tbilisi and diesel locomotives at Gorkiy and Ulan Ude in Siberia. Moscow's underground and suburban lines are equipped largely from the Mytishchi works. The heavy demand for railway wagons in the industrial districts of the Donbas and Ural regions is covered largely from Dneprodzerzhinsk and Nizhniy Tagil respectively, those of northern and central Russia from Kalinin and Kolomna. There is a considerable amount of specialisation, for example, tank wagons at Zhdanov and refrigerator vehicles at Bryansk. The only constructional plant in the eastern regions is at Novoaltaysk. There is now considerable interchange with the other members of COMECON.

The Soviet Union has greatly increased production of motor vehicles in recent years. Whereas in 1950 lorries accounted for 80 per cent of production, which totalled 363 000 vehicles, in 1980 2 199 000 units were produced, of which 787 000 were goods vehicles, with 85 300 buses and 1 327 000 motor cars and similar light vehicles. The largest plant for cars is that at Tolyatti on the Volga, named after the Italian Communist because the plant was built under contract by the Fiat Company. Other plants producing small cars are at Moscow and Zaporozhye while larger cars are made at Gorkiy. Cars are also produced at Ulyanovsk and Miass in the Volga and Ural areas respectively.

The most important lorry producing plants are at Minsk and Zhodino, both in Belorussia. A major plant is being built at Naberezhniye Chelny on the Kama River in the Tatar ASSR and there are numerous smaller plants, some of them associated with car factories. Some of the buses are also produced in these factories, notably in Moscow and Gorkiy, but there are also specialised enterprises in Lvov, Likino (near Moscow), Pavlov (near Gorkiy), Riga and Kurgan.

There are now also specialised works for motor vehicle engines, the first being at Yaroslavl and others at Ulyanovsk, Kharkov and Barnaul in Siberia. It will thus be seen that altogether the Soviet motor industry is now of major importance with plants widely distributed, although with the majority still in the European regions.

In contrast to the publicity given to new motor plants, the Soviet Union maintains as much secrecy as possible on the location of its aircraft constructing plants, and reveals no information at all on the number of aircraft produced or in service with either military or civil air fleets. The industry is organised by design bureaux which tend to specialise in particular types of aircraft, for example Tupolev, involved mainly with large transport aircraft, bombers and long-range reconnaissance types, often based on the same fundamental designs. There is no hard and fast rule, however, and the Yakovlev designs range from light aircraft through fighters to transports. Most of the design bureaux and research facilities are in Moscow but there are newer establishments at Kuybyshev, Kazan, Perm, Novosibirsk, Omsk, Sverdlovsk and Ufa, i.e. mainly in the east for strategic reasons. Production factories are not directly linked with particular design bureaux but more often with the production of particular classes of aircraft—transports, strike aircraft, helicopters, etc. Most were rebuilt in the eastern regions during the war and these have been further developed though there are new plants also in European Russia.

Building of river vessels occurs on the main rivers; for example, on the Volga at Rybinsk, Gorkiy, Krasnoarmeysk and Astrakhan, with Perm and Votkinsk on the Kama; while the Dnepr is supplied from Kiev and Nikopol. Kotlas is the main yard for the Northern Dvina and Tobolsk supplies the Ob–Irtysh basin, while the Yenisey receives its ships from Krasnoyarsk and the Lena from Ust–Kut. Sea-going vessels (mostly naval) are built at Nikolayev and Leningrad, but major repair facilities are available on other seas—Arkhangelsk and Murmansk in the north and Vladivostok for the Pacific waters. Astrakhan and

Kaspiysk build Caspian vessels. Many ships are bought from foreign yards.

Widespread agricultural engineering usually reflects local needs, with works both in engineering centres and in the countryside. Numerous large tractor works are scattered across the country: Kharkov, Volgograd and Chelyabinsk are most important, but Lipetsk is also a significant plant and Rubtsovsk supplies Siberia. Grain combines, first built in 1930, are made mostly in grain growing regions—Zaporozhye, Omsk, and Barnaul have important works and the Rostselmash plant at Rostov-na-Donu builds one-fifth of all Soviet farm machinery output. Tula makes potato harvesters and sorters; Bezhetsk, flax processing machinery; in Transcaucasia (Batumi, Tbilisi, Poti) production is mainly of machinery for citrus fruit cultivation and tea growing; machinery for Central Asian oasis cultivation comes from Tashkent, Chirchik and Frunze. Tselinograd and Pavlodar supply machinery, notably to the 'virgin lands' area of Kazakhstan and southern Siberia, while Perm makes silage cutters and threshers and Kurgan, dairy machinery. There are many other large works.

The chemicals industry (Fig. 9.3)
A large and diverse chemicals industry is essential for a modern industrial state, and its importance is likely to increase further with the development of new processes and materials, both in the heavy ('industrial') and light (pharmaceuticals, cosmetics) sectors. The Soviet chemicals industry has been developed intensively since the late 1950s. Raw material supply tends to be a most significant locational factor for heavy chemicals production, so that plants are tied closely to mineral deposits or to other industries whose waste or by-products form raw materials. Light chemicals tend to be sited near to consumers and in centres of skill and research.

The emphasis put on agriculture since the mid-1950s has brought corresponding development of artificial fertiliser manufacture, for which abundant raw materials are available, though often in inconvenient locations. There is a marked agglomeration of nitrogen plants in the Central Industrial and Black Earth regions of European Russia, while the Donbas produces sulphate of ammonia from coal by-products, which is also made at cokeries in the Ural region and western Siberia. Several large phosphate plants lie in

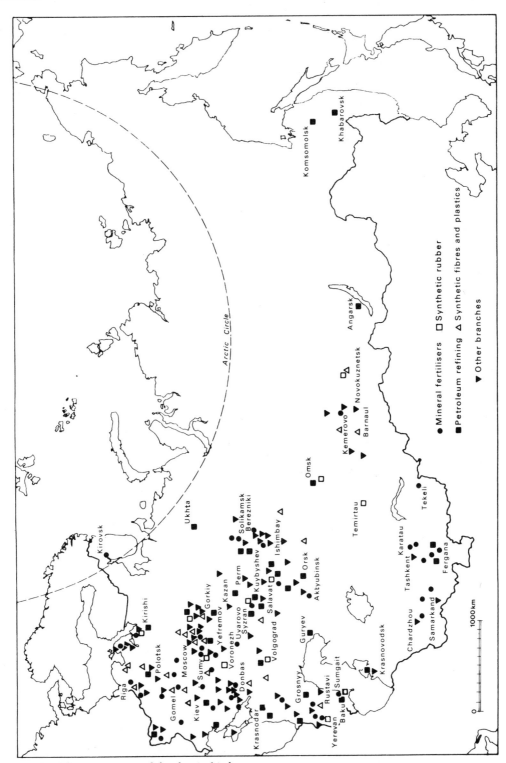

Fig. 9.3 The main centres of the chemical industry

European Russia (e.g. Voskresensk, Sumy, Zhdanov, Leningrad), in the Ural region, southern Kazakhstan and in Central Asia, where there are also nitrogen plants. Transcaucasia covers its own needs for artificial fertilisers. Large potash deposits are used at Solikamsk in the Kama basin as well as in Belorussia and Transcaucasia. Location of plants is usually near raw materials.

Sulphuric acid, a basic raw material in chemicals production, is made in many widely scattered centres from 'secondary' sources of sulphur (by-products, waste) but near to consumers since it is not easy to transport. Among the largest plants are Voskresensk and Novomoskovsk in the centre of European Russia, Leningrad, Solikamsk and Berezniki in the Kama basin and Aktyubinsk in Kazakhstan, as well as others in the Donbas coalfield and at Tekeli in Central Asia. Crude oil is an increasingly important source, especially in the Volga–Ural area. Soda production is chiefly from the Donbas, the Urals (Berezniki and Sterlitamak), Siberia and the Kara Bogaz Gol.

To reduce its dependence on imported rubber, the Soviet Union has developed artificial rubbers, though some natural latex comes from the *Sagyz* plants native to Central Asia. Synthetic rubber manufacture expanded rapidly after 1945, using German reparations equipment and processes. Plants at Yaroslavl, Voronezh, Yefremov and Kazan use ethylene derived from potatoes; calcium carbide is used at Yerevan and Temirtau (Kazakhstan); but production increasingly uses by-products of petroleum refining with the Volga area most important.

Petrochemicals and chemicals derived from coal have been developed into a major industry with a wide variety of products including plastics. The main groups of plants are at Moscow and elsewhere in the centre of European Russia, in the Donbas and on the Volga, but several major plants have been built elsewhere—notably in Belorussia, the Ukraine, Transcaucasia, Central Asia, Siberia and the Far East. Synthetic fibres are widely produced—the Central Industrial region, the Volga region, the Ukraine and the Baltic region all have plants. Cosmetics, pharmaceuticals and films are dominated by Moscow and its environs, though towns such as Kiev and Kharkov are also significant. Growth of this industrial branch is being helped by the purchase of foreign technology and plant, with British ICI and the German Krupp concern notably important.

As noted in connection with the metal industries there has been a marked spread of chemical plants away from the old centres of industry. Thus, Moscow and the Central region, Leningrad and Kiev areas have notable and long-established concentrations of chemical plants, relying mainly on imported raw materials. The Donbas–Dnepr area is another important chemical-industry region, better endowed with natural resources, except for water, which is in rather short supply. The western Ukraine has also developed chemical plants on the basis of local minerals (sulphur, rock salt and petroleum) but the expansion further north in Belorussia and the Baltic republics is based on imported materials. The Caucasus–Transcaucasus regions have notable developments based on oil and other local resources, as have the Volga–Ural areas. Natural resources are also the basis of most of the current developments in Central Asia and the Far East.

Timber, wood chemical and building industries

A marked overlap in these branches of industry occurs because of the role of timber in the production of building materials, but timber is also important in the chemical industry and pulp and paper production. Also, although much reduced by more advanced methods of harnessing energy, timber is still widely used as a fuel in forested and mountainous areas. Siberia and the Far East contain almost 80% of the Soviet Union's timber resources so in European areas there is now urgent need for conservation of timber stands.

The first stage of exploitation, that of logging, is carried out by *lespromkhoz* units which are also responsible for storing and some processing of timber, and for replanting. Large plants with powerful machinery and drying kilns have largely replaced small sawmills in the most productive areas. Factories, producing packaging materials, furniture and prefabricated building items, plywood and chipboard are commonly integrated with the timber milling plants. Several such complexes, extending to the manufacture of pulp and paper, are being developed in Siberia, at Bratsk and in the Ob, Yenisey and Amur river basins of Siberia and at Arkhangelsk and Kotlas in the European North. Most of the plywood enterprises are, however, located in the European northwest, especially Belorussia, the Centre and the western parts of the Urals, 95% of the plywood output

Paper factory timber yards in Siberia—one of the industrial plants using power from the Bratsk hydro-electric scheme

being from the European forest areas, with the eastward shift a relatively new feature. A number of sawmills are found at the mouths of northern rivers, catering for the export trade which is mainly in sawn timber.

The pulp and paper branch of industry is dominated now by large plants, notably those at Solikamsk on the Kama river, where there are many smaller plants, while Balakhna on the northern reaches of the Volga is another important location. Most of the older plants are in the European areas, but, as already noted, major new complexes are being built in the eastern areas. Associated with these new integrated developments, in particular, are wood-hydrolysis plants which produce a variety of chemical products such as the familiar resins, turpentine and acetic acid and the newer technical oils, formalin, acetate phenols, special glues and pharmaceutical and other products in ever-increasing diversity.

The manufacture of furniture has also been developing in the eastern regions but traditionally it has been a market-oriented industry, with most factories in Moscow and Leningrad, with other cities, notably the capitals of the Union Republics in the European areas, also important. Valuable

beech, oak, hornbeam and other hardwood resources have ensured the North Caucasus region an especially important role in this industry.

Timber is one of the Soviet Union's most valuable resources and even more valuable because it is renewable. As yet only the European areas, a relatively narrow strip of forest along the Trans-Siberian Railway and areas around mining and other settlements in Siberia have been exploited. Future development must be increasingly in the east, but even more important in the long term is the improvement of utilisation practices. Timber is a renewable resource, but only if conservation is constantly kept to the fore alongside exploitation will these resources be available for future generations. The USSR, like most countries, has in the past allowed extravagant use of timber, careless extraction, unnecessary burning and waste through bad transport and processing methods. It has yet to be seen how efficient the timber enterprises have become in an age which recognises the need for, but all too rarely implements, conservation and restoration of natural resources.

One aspect of the economy in which the use of timber has declined, at least relatively, with the development of alternative materials and methods, is the building industry. While timber still provides the preferred material for many purposes, such as window and door frames and some kinds of flooring, and almost everything deep in the forest zones, cement and concrete have become the basis of most large-scale construction, including the ubiquitous Soviet blocks of residential flats. The USSR claims to be the leading world producer of cement, asbestos-cement and pre-cast concrete. Formerly, large-scale cement production was based on the few deposits of good quality marls near Novorossiysk on the Black Sea coast and in the Volga area near Volsk. Now, however, there is a widespread industry based on limestones, blast-furnace slags and other waste materials. Many other materials as well as the familiar bricks enter into the building industry's requirements and, as far as possible, factories are distributed to minimise transport and hence are near large centres of population, subject to availability of raw materials. Glass is a case in point, with most works in the Donbas, the Centre and Belorussia, where materials are available reasonably close to demand. The largest plant is, however, at Saratov, with emphasis on economies of scale.

Light industries

Although the classification of industries into heavy and light is not entirely satisfactory, partly because there is overlap from the timber, chemicals and other branches into the consumer goods industries, such as furniture, domestic plasticware and toiletries and cosmetics, the industries traditionally classed as light still tend to have a freedom in location not found in heavy industry. This is because light industry is mainly concerned with the utilisation of raw materials which can be readily transported so that they can be processed near to markets, or use more ubiquitous materials such as some agricultural products. The finished products represent high value-added items, as in the case of textiles and clothing, which can withstand distribution costs of fairly high level, but which in any case present no particular problems in transport, or which, like processed foodstuffs, present no problems if distribution is kept within moderate bounds, as in the case of bread and milk. Excessive distances in these cases do impose problems so plants are generally distributed in some degree comparable with the pattern of population. Hard and fast rules cannot,

however, be laid down. The pattern of location varies according to the particular product, the sophistication of the transport and distribution network, etc. but, as there are not normally very heavy loads, noxious processes or severely limited origins of raw materials, at least a substantial degree of flexibility is possible.

TEXTILES
The cotton industry is the most important of the textile group of industries. Spinning mills are mainly in the Central region, which accounts for about 75 % of output. This is mainly explained by historical circumstances, the raw cotton being transported from Central Asia or, originally, the importing ports. The advantages of the Central region lay in the availability of an adaptable workforce, accessibility for the foreign interests that provided much of the capital, and availability of markets, as well as of suitable skills for maintenance of machinery, and ease of providing the required degree of humidity. These conditions no longer restrict location and large cotton mills have been developed in Central Asia, especially Tashkent, near the source of the raw material, in the Ukraine, Estonia and western Siberia, with lesser developments in other regions, showing the flexibility that is possible although most of the cotton will continue to come from Central Asia.

Wool manufacturing has also spread widely. Early centres, using imported wool, were developed in the Baltic cities and in the Central region. As internal supplies of wool became more important the industry was expanded in the Ukraine, Belorussia and the North Caucasus. The large number of sheep in the Caucasus, Kazakhstan and Central Asia led to increased emphasis on processing in these regions, and a number of mills have been built in Siberia. Again, flexibility is possible and a very large number of centres are now engaged in processing local and transported wools and in making garments. The traditional carpet-making craft industry remains in Central Asia but large mechanised enterprises using both wool and artificial fibres have been developed in Transcaucasia and other regions.

The linen industry, with a more restricted demand for its products, has remained in its traditional location in the Central and north-west areas, with expansion also in Belorussia and the Baltic republics, close to the flax-growing areas and also to the main markets.

Designing clothes in the Salut garment factory, Moscow

Of the silk mills, most are close to the supply of raw material in Central Asia and Transcaucasia, but with weaving and finishing in the Central and other European areas. The true silks remain important commodities in the USSR but, as in other countries, rayon and synthetic fibres have become increasingly important. They are manufactured mainly in the Centre and other European areas and, in the case of fibres derived from the petrochemical industries, western Siberia, and other areas with major oil resources, appear likely to become increasingly important.

The clothing and knitwear industries are eminently suited to locations with no special advantages except an appropriate labour force so are often used to initiate industrial development in small and relatively isolated towns. There are, however, numerous such establishments in Moscow, Leningrad and other major cities so it can be said that this is an industry of which the distribution accords closely with that of the population, though with some specialisation.

The leather and footwear industries, though of a handicraft nature originally and correspondingly widely distributed, have become more concentrated in response to mechanisation of production and are located mainly in the European areas, but with some expansion in other areas to make for a more even distribution. The fur industry, associated with one of the oldest sources of wealth in Russia, is based predominantly on the forests of the European and Ural areas with a major centre at Slobodskoy, where an ancient trade route from Siberia crossed from the Ural mountains to the Vyatka river. Other historic trading centres such as Kazan and Chita are among the other locations of the fur industry.

St. Petersburg was the original home of the Russian china industry, where the market of the court and wealthy citizens of the former capital provided ample stimulus. Leningrad today is an important centre of the china and pottery industry which has also been long developed in the Novgorod–Volhynsky area, the Moscow area and the Ukraine. The output includes porcelain and ceramic goods for industrial and building uses, glazed and wall tiles and domestic goods. Factories have more recently been built in the Central Asian and other areas to provide local supplies of such goods as well as employment.

The manufacture of consumer goods generally is widespread but with the main centres in the European regions, especially the Moscow and Leningrad areas, where technological expertise and labour are both available. A substantial portion of the output of factories producing photographic equipment, watches, radios, sporting guns, etc. is earmarked for export but all such light and valuable items can be distributed also to all parts of the Soviet Union at costs low in relation to their value.

FOOD INDUSTRIES

Food manufacturing plants are scattered widely over the country in relatively small units. The aim has been to use local produce to keep transport to a minimum and there is a relatively low level of development of such modern processes as freezing, dehydration and even of canning. Factories that do carry out such processes are, however, situated in areas producing the vegetables, fruits, etc. involved, for ease of supply of fresh products. Similarly, sugar-beet processing, and the production of wines, butter, cheese and other products

from perishable commodities are located in the primary producing areas. In the case of town milk supply the producers are taken, so to speak, to the consumers, the farms being established near the cities. This is true also of horticulture for table vegetables to be fresh. Meat processing plants are being increasingly concentrated in areas of specialisation on beef cattle and pig production east of the Volga and there are large fish processing factories in the Far East where the major fishing fleets are based. Poultry processing is another branch that has become characterised by large units, particularly in the European areas. Whereas cattle can be transported to processing plants (although costly), this is not practicable on a large scale with poultry.

A certain amount of relocation has been attempted on a planned basis in some of the major food industries. On the principle that flour is more expensive than grain to transport and more susceptible to deterioration, flour mills have been built widely outside the main grain growing areas and within about 50 km of consuming cities. This was done on a modest scale in the 1930s in

Quality inspectors checking tomatoes in a cannery in the Kirgiz SSR

Transcaucasia, Belorussia and the eastern regions, and in the 1960s larger plants were built in Central Asia, Siberia and the Far East. Bread and confectionery are essentially localised enterprises located near consumers. Similarly, while wineries must be located in the grape growing areas because ripe fruit cannot be transported, bulk wines can be transported and it is more economic to bottle the wines in the areas of consumption. Production of spirits is also traditionally linked with the wine areas and the potato growing areas of the central European USSR but new distilleries and bottling plants were built in the 1960s in large cities of the Urals, Siberia and the Far East to reduce the transport of bottled vodka and other spirits. In virtually all branches of the food industries the aim is to replace small, inefficient and sometimes unhygienic units with modern factories located in accordance with principles of transporting the commodity which is easiest or least costly to transport in the stages from farm to consumer.

Although not a part of industry in the ordinary sense, the retail establishments provide an essential part of the distribution network. The Soviet organisation of retailing has lagged far behind the development of the production side of the economy and most shops are small and very traditional in their methods of handling and selling goods. Combined with unsophisticated and often crude forms of packaging this results in shops looking very unattractive to western eyes, while purchasing is a slow and complex procedure. There is, however, one advantage resulting from this situation, the Soviet Union has little of the rubbish problem that affects both town and countryside in the west, most packaging is scanty and easily degradable and there is relatively little of it, while disposal is facilitated by education of children from an early age not to scatter litter and by an army of otherwise perhaps unemployable persons to sweep and clean public places.

THE MAJOR INDUSTRIAL REGIONS

To draw together the diverse patterns of the various industries which have been described, the principal regions within which Soviet industry is concentrated will now be considered briefly (see Fig. 9.4). The regions of spatial concentrations here described overlap administrative divisions of

all levels, as do the agricultural regions described in Chapter 7. The distribution of industry and of agriculture in each of the formally designated Major Economic Regions, used for large-scale planning purposes in the USSR, will be dealt with in Chapter 12. The more detailed treatment of industrial aspects of the regions has been reserved for Chapter 12 because it is for the official Major Economic Regions that comparable statistics are made available from year to year from Soviet sources.

The Industrial South

The European Industrial South is formed by the sub-regions of the Donbas, the Dnepr Bend and Krivoy Rog and is closely linked to the great industrial towns of Kharkov and Kiev. The resource base is the coal (much of coking quality) of the Donbas, the iron ore of Krivoy Rog, Kursk and Kerch, Yelenovka limestone, Nikopol manganese, salt, imported petroleum and natural gas. Hydro-electric current from the Volga and Dnepr barrages is augmented by local thermal generators. A locational problem of the dry south is finding adequate water supplies for industry. It is the most important region for iron and steel making, notably on the coalfield at centres such as Donetsk and Makeyevka, on the orefield at Krivoy Rog and in the Dnepr Bend (notably ferro-alloys). Coking by-products and local salts plus imported raw materials are the basis of a heavy chemicals industry, notably on the coalfield. Raw metal and a large local market attracted heavy engineering both to the coalfield and to nearby centres. Well served by railways, its products are distributed widely throughout the country.

The Central Industrial Region

The Central industrial region includes Moscow and its environs, the textile towns of the Klyazma basin, and the Tula lignite field. Lignite and peat are used for electricity generation, but many thermal stations formerly using imported coal have turned to oil or natural gas supplied by pipelines. Some electric current is obtained from the Volga region. Nearly all raw materials have to be imported and the area is a major focus of the Soviet railway system, with 11 main lines converging on Moscow. A large local market and soft water were important factors in attracting textile manufacture, despite having to import raw cotton and wool, and this remains the principal Soviet

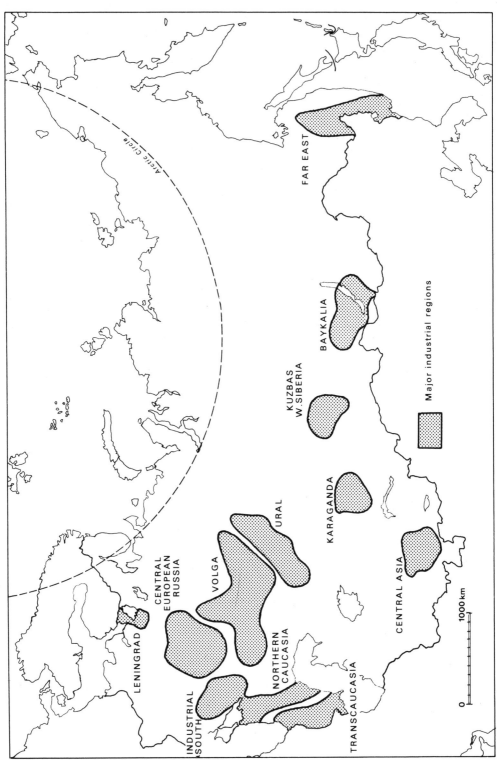

Fig. 9.4 Major industrial regions of the USSR

centre of the industry. The chemicals industry depends on imported raw materials plus local lignite and phosphates, but there is also a large pharmaceuticals sector based on the Moscow market and research facilities. Engineering includes a wide range of branches, particularly the more sophisticated ones such as aircraft and vehicles, and those requiring a large market, as well as good design and development facilities and a pool of highly skilled labour, so that some of the principal Soviet plants are found in or around Moscow.

The resource base of the Centre was transformed by the discovery of the vast iron ore deposits of the Kursk Magnetic Anomaly (KMA) in the 1950s. These are now claimed to be the largest known deposits in the world, with reserves of at least 30 000 million tonnes of rich ores, more than the total of all other Soviet deposits. New works at Novo-Lipetsk have been added to the basic production facilities at the old centres, such as Tula and Gorkiy, and the northerly Cherepovets integrated steelworks built in the 1950s. Other developments are projected, as a result of which this area is now being looked on as the third metallurgical base, a term previously applied to western Siberia. The development of the KMA will facilitate increases in production in the Ural and in the South, with which the Centre will virtually merge.

The Ural Region
The Ural region comprises a number of industrial clusters separated by forest and mountain country. The main metallurgical plants which form the basis of Ural industry lie on the eastern slope of the mountains where iron ore and other metallic ores are found. Chemicals associated with local salts or petroleum are typical of the western flanks where there is some coal around Kizel. The Ural region is, however, generally deficient in fuel, and coal and coke are imported from western Siberia and Kazakhstan, though local fuels—coal, peat and wood—are also used to generate electricity. The physical nature of the Ural mountains makes them unsuitable for hydro-electric development. Petroleum and natural gas are imported from the Ural–Volga oilfields, Central Asia and from western Siberia. The production of iron and steel, non-ferrous metals and heavy chemicals from the Ural region is widely distributed by railway to other regions, while, since the Second

World War, the production of heavy engineering and transport goods has begun on a considerable scale. This region, however, is still regarded primarily as an iron and steel producer, the 'second metallurgical base'.

Western Siberia and North Kazakhstan
The Kuzbas coalfield is the focus of industrial western Siberia, which includes several large towns lying at some distance from the coalfield, such as the engineering centres of Novosibirsk and Rubtsovsk and the textile town of Barnaul. Kuzbas coal and local iron ore are used by the iron and steel industry (notably at Novokuznetsk), while there is also smelting and refining of non-ferrous ores. By-products of these industries, plus wood from the tayga, form the basis of chemicals production. Development of vast resources of water power will provide cheap electric current and lead to an emphasis on electrochemicals and electro-metallurgy in the future. This would be the core for possible development of a larger 'metallurgical base' of southern Siberia. For transport, the region depends on the Trans-Siberian Railway and supporting rail routes and the airways. North Kazakhstan is virtually an extension of this region. It has a new integrated iron and steel works and a new ferro-alloys plant but industrial development is hindered by a shortage of water only partly overcome by the Irtysh-Karaganda canal.

The Middle Volga Region
A newly emergent industrial region is the middle Volga, using its own natural gas, petroleum and salts, while timber is easily obtained from the northern forests and coal from the Donbas, which along with the Ural and Centre regions can also supply raw metal. It has developed electrochemicals and electro-metallurgy, consuming current from its own large hydro-electric barrages, while petro-chemicals have developed in new refineries. Engineering developed during the Second World War and a vast car assembly plant has been built at Tolyatti, between Ulyanovsk and Kuybyshev. It is a major cement-producing region. Crossed by several railways and served by the Volga–Kama and associated waterways, it enjoys a nodal position in the Soviet transport system.

Other industrial regions
Other regions are of much less importance. Leningrad shows a notable dependence on manu-

facturing from materials imported from home or abroad. Textiles, engineering and chemicals are all represented and ship-building is important. Transcaucasia has local resources of ferrous and non-ferrous metals, petroleum and coal. It is a major producer of ferro-alloys and synthetic rubber and has a new integrated steelworks at Rustavi. Novorossiysk in northern Caucasia is one of the largest cement producers in the USSR. There is a specialised engineering industry for the Caucasian oilfields. Central Asia has a rich assortment of minerals and fuels augmented by supplies of raw materials from Siberia. There is engineering (textile machinery) in Tashkent, chemicals—notably fertilisers—at several centres, and Tashkent and Frunze have textile mills using local cotton. New hydro-electric stations offer great scope for industries with high power needs. Industry in the Far East has a strong strategic character and primarily serves local needs.

In conclusion, the achievements of the USSR in its rapid industrialisation may be indicated by figures for output of major products (Table 9.2).

These are spectacular achievements by any standards yet in spite of such successes it still remains true that many consumer goods are in short supply in the Soviet Union and many bottlenecks are reported in the production process. The complexity of modern society is such that it appears to defeat centralised planning, at least when it is carried to the extent of supplanting virtually all individual enterprise.

TABLE 9.2 PRODUCTION OF INDUSTRIAL GOODS IN THE USSR—1928, 1950, 1965, 1978, 1980, 1981

	1928	1950	1965	1978	1980	1981
Electrical energy—milliard kWh	5.0	91.2	507	1,202	1,295	1,325
Petroleum—million tonnes	11.6	37.9	243	572	603	609
Natural gas—milliard m³	—	5.8	128	347	406	465
Coal—million tonnes	35.5	261	578	724	716	704
Pig iron—million tonnes	3.3	19.2	66	111	107	—
Steel—million tonnes	4.3	12.3	102.2	151	148	149
Sulphuric acid—million tonnes	0.2	2.1	9.7	22.4	23	24
Mineral fertiliser—million tonnes	0.03	1.2	7.4	23.7	25	26
Synthetic resins and active constituent plastics—million tonnes	—	0.06	1.1	3.5	3.6	4.1
Synthetic fibre—million tonnes	—	0.02	0.5	1.1	1.2	1.2
Motor tyres—million units	0.09	7.4	29.6	59.0	60.1	60.5
Mainline diesel locomotives—units	—	125	1,497	1,392	1,378	—
Mainline electric locomotives—units	—	102	388	438	429	—
Railway freight wagons—thousand units	7.9	50.8	43.8	68.3	63.0	61.0
Motor vehicles: all types—thousand units	0.84	362.9	728.8	2,151	2,199	2,197
Tractors—thousand units	1.3	116.7	405.1	576	555	—
Grain combines—thousand units	—	46.3	101.2	113	117	106
Excavators—thousand units	—	3.5	21.6	41.1	42	42
Paper—million tonnes	0.3	1.2	3.8	5.5	5.3	5.4
Cement—million tonnes	1.8	10.2	84.8	127	125	127
Cloth—all types—milliard m²	2.2	3.4	8.2	10.6	10.7	11.0
Leather footwear—million pairs	58.0	203	561	740	744	739
Radio sets and radiograms—million units	—	1.1	6.4	8.7	8.5	8.7
Television sets—million units	—	0.01	4.9	7.2	7.5	8.2
Granulated sugar—million tonnes	1.3	2.5	11.0	12.2	10.1	9.5
Meat—million tonnes	0.7	1.5	6.5	15.2	15.0	15.2
Processed meat—million tonnes	—	0.5	2.0	9.5	9.2	9.2
Butter—million tonnes	0.08	0.3	1.1	1.4	1.4	1.2
Vegetable fats—million tonnes	0.4	0.8	2.8	3.0	2.7	2.6
Tinned food—milliard standard tins	0.1	1.5	8.9	15.0	15.3	15.9

Source: Narodnoye khozyaystvo SSSR, various years.

BIBLIOGRAPHY

Abouchar, A. (1979), 'Regional industrial policies in the USSR, the 1970s,' *Regional development in the USSR*, NATO colloquium, Oriental Research Partners, Newtonville, pp. 93–103.

Bater, J. H. (1976), *St. Petersburg: industrialisation and change*, Edward Arnold, London.

Cole, J. and German, F. (1970), *A geography of the USSR*, Butterworth, London.

Conolly, V. (1967), *Beyond the Urals*, Oxford University Press, Oxford.

Conolly, V. (1975), *Siberia today and tomorrow*, Collins, London.

Current Digest of the Soviet Press (1949–), Joint Committee on Slavic Studies, Washington, DC.

Dewdney, J. C. (1976), *The USSR, Studies in Industrial Geography*, Westview Press, Boulder, Colorado.

Dienes, L. and Shabad, T. (1979), *The Soviet energy system*, Wiley, New York.

Dobb, M. (1966), *Soviet economic development since 1917*, Routledge and Kegan Paul, London.

Dyker, D. A. (1976), *The Soviet economy*, Crosby Lockwood Staples, London.

Hamilton, F. E. I. and Linge, G. J. R. (1979), *Spatial analysis, industry and the industrial environment, I– Industrial systems*, Wiley, Chichester.

Hutchings, R. (1971), *Seasonal influences in Soviet industry*, Royal Institute of International Affairs, London.

Kalesnik, S. V. and Pavlenko, V. F. (eds.) (1976), *Soviet Union; a geographical survey*, Progress Publishers, Moscow.

Kistanov, V. A. and Epshteyn, A. S. (1972), 'Problems of optimal location of an industrial complex,' *Soviet Geography*, **13**, pp. 141–52.

Lavrishchev, A. (1968), *Economic geography of the USSR*, Progress Publishers, Moscow.

Linge, G. J. R., Karaska, G. J. and Hamilton, F. E. I. (1978), 'Appraisal of Soviet TPC concept', *Soviet Geography*, **19**, pp. 681–97.

Lonsdale, R. E. (1977), 'Regional inequity and Soviet concern for rural and small-town industrialisation,' *Soviet Geography*, **18**, pp. 590–602.

Lydolph, P. E. (1979), *Geography of the USSR, topical analysis*, Misty Valley, Elkhart Lake, Wisconsin.

Mathieson, R. S. (1975), *The Soviet Union; an economic geography*, Heinemann, London.

Matrusov, N. D. (1970), 'Geographical problems in the development of machine-building in the Ob-Irtysh complex,' *Soviet Geography*, **11**, pp. 464–71.

Mellor, R. E. H. (1964), *Geography of the USSR*, Macmillan, London.

Narodnoye khozyaystvo SSSR v . . . (various years), *Statisticheskiy ezhegodnik*, Tsentralnoye Statisticheskoye Upravleniye SSSR, Moscow.

NATO Economic Directorate (1979), *Regional development in the USSR*, NATO colloquium, Oriental Research Partners, Newtonville, Mass.

Nove, A. (1977), *The Soviet economic system*, Allen and Unwin, London.

Pallot, J. and Shaw, D. J. B. (1981), *Planning in the Soviet Union*, Croom Helm, London.

Pryde, P. R. (1968), 'The areal deconcentration of the Soviet cotton-textile industry,' *Geographical Review*, **58**, pp. 575–92.

Shabad, T. (1969), *Basic industrial resources of the USSR*, Columbia University Press, New York.

Woroniak, A. (1973), 'Regional aspects of Soviet planning and industrial organization,' in V. N. Bandera and Z. L. Melnyk (eds.), *The Soviet economy in regional perspective*, Praeger, New York.

10 Urban and Rural Settlement

In response to the creation of a powerful industrial structure in the Soviet Union since the late 1930s, there has been a vast movement of people from country districts both into established towns (which have grown substantially) and into new towns founded in the process of economic development. Although the population of the USSR rose from 147 million in 1926 to 263.4 million in 1979, growth in town population was even more impressive since the number of country dwellers fell from 120.7 million in 1926 to 98.8 million in 1979. Marxist–Leninist views on social, economic and ideological organisation have made the town the focus of attention. Although great changes have been made in towns, many long-standing features of the Russian town remain. Great changes have also been brought to the village—the outcome of Communist reorganisation of agriculture and the need to raise the standard of living of country dwellers to the level of the townspeople, while many experiments have been made to develop new forms of rural settlement adjusted to the contemporary economic and social conditions.

TABLE 10.1 POPULATION GROWTH IN TOWN AND COUNTRY

	Urban	Rural	Total
		Millions	
1897 census	20.0	108.1	128.2
1926 census	26.3	120.7	147.0
1979 census	163.6	98.8	263.4
Change 1926–1979	+137.3	−21.9	+111.4

Source: Soviet statistical handbooks.

At the Tsarist census of 1897, within the boundaries of the Russian Empire of the time, only 16 % of the people were living in towns, but the most strongly urbanised parts of the empire—Russian Poland and the Baltic countries—were lost as a result of the First World War. During the Revolution and subsequent civil war, several million people left the starving and disrupted towns to find shelter and sustenance in the countryside, from which many had come a decade or two earlier. In 1926, the Soviet authorities, believing some measure of stability to have been reached, made an exceptionally detailed census that showed that some 82 % of the people were still resident in rural districts. But this proportion was to begin to change rapidly two years later when the first of the new economic plans was put into operation and the transformation of the economy started.

The 1939 census showed that urban population had risen to 33 %, but shortly afterwards the destruction and disruption of the German invasion again drove people out of the towns of the occupied areas and large numbers fled into the Volga region and further east, to work in factories which had been evacuated from the path of the German armies. An official post-war estimate of 197.9 million was issued in 1956 and showed that 45 % of the people were living in towns—a higher proportion than many people had expected. The first post-war census of 1959 showed that of the 208.8 million people, 48 % were now urban dwellers and by 1961 it was estimated that 50 % of the population of 216.2 million were in urban areas. In 1979, of the 263.4 million people, 62 % were living in towns. According to a recent Soviet view, the urban population will have risen to 68 % by the mid-1980s and it will comprise 75 % of a population of 333 million by the year 2000.

TOWN POPULATION AND REGIONAL VARIATIONS

Migration to towns

An important aspect of the increase in town population and its relationship to changes in the rural population is the process of population growth. One of the main mechanisms has been migration, usually into comparatively nearby towns from rural communities. This occurs most commonly within European Russia, but also often from both towns and country districts in European Russia to towns in the eastern regions. Towns in European Russia, notably in the westernmost parts, have been important suppliers of settlers to the towns of Siberia. Movement has commonly been a voluntary choice, in response to encouragement given by the authorities in the form of better housing, pay incentives and 'fringe benefits', and has been marked by a high proportion of young single people or young married couples, though in some remote and inhospitable environments (such as Magadan in the Far East) there has been difficulty in recruiting sufficient women to build a balanced sex-ratio. Forced migration cannot be omitted, since it played a part in Tsarist times (when the dreaded prison settlement, the *katorga*, was the destination of many exiles) and even after the Revolution, notably in the Stalinist period. Many towns in the Soviet Arctic were peopled at their inception mostly by politically unreliable elements and even by criminals, as, for example, Norilsk in the late 1930s when it was a wooden shanty town. Tsarist and Soviet governments have often forced migration of whole communities to carry out their population policy. Some Ural towns, for example, were founded by enforced migration of serfs in the eighteenth century.

Town population has also grown by natural increase, which accounted for a fifth of the growth in town dwellers between 1939 and 1959, whereas migration into towns comprised over half the total increase in numbers. The balance is accounted for mainly by boundary changes or by changes in status. The difference between the urban birth and death rate (both lower than in the countryside) has

been less than in the country, with a consequently lower rate of natural increase. Families are generally larger in the countryside, despite the proportion of women of child-bearing age being higher in towns. Although the rate of natural increase in the countryside has been markedly higher than in the towns, the drift from the country to town has been so strong that it has caused an actual fall in numbers of rural population. The number of people classed as urban has also increased by administrative measures; first, by giving town status to settlements as soon as they have reached the legal threshold for such designation, and, second, by expanding the boundaries of towns to encompass adjacent suburbs or rural districts.

Regional variations in urbanisation

The considerable regional variation in the proportion of town dwellers in the total population is shown in Fig. 10.1. It can be seen that this ranges from around 20 % in the oasis areas of Central Asia such as Kashka–Darya, Surkhan–Darya and Khorezm to about 80 % in Magadan oblast of the Far East and to 90 % in Murmansk oblast in northern European Russia. The proportion of urban dwellers is generally below the national average (62 %) in the farming districts of western and central European Russia, northern Caucasia and the Ukraine, all areas comparatively densely settled by Soviet standards. The proportion of urban dwellers is well above average in much of Siberia, the Ural region and the Karaganda district of Kazakhstan: these are all areas where industrial development has been pushed ahead since the early 1930s. It suggests that such lands have, in Soviet times, been settled primarily for industrial or transport development and that migration has been focused into towns and workers' settlements—the rural settlement of the eastern regions has been much less important, though some change came with the inception of the virgin lands scheme in the mid-1950s. Evidence shows that many towns in Siberia and the Far East, for example, lie in virtually uninhabited and undeveloped country. In Magadan oblast, 1 199 100 km^2 in area, 365 000 people (78 %) out of a total population of 466 000 are classified as urban dwellers—122 000 'urbanites' are found in Magadan city alone—so that the density for the whole oblast is 0.4 persons per km^2, while for rural districts it is under 0.05 persons per km^2.

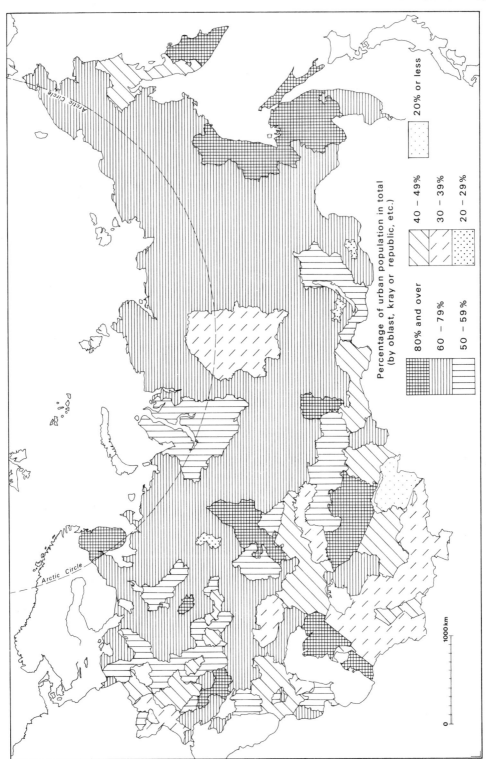

Fig. 10.1 Percentage of urban dwellers in the total population. With some 61 % of the national population living in towns, the average is substantially exceeded over most of Siberia, whereas the richer agricultural areas of European Russia and the native societies of Central Asia and Transcaucasia show below-average levels of urbanisation

Numbers of towns

In January 1979, there were in the Soviet Union some 2061 towns and 3845 'settlements of town type', falling into the size categories shown in Table 10.2 Between 1926 and 1979, the number of towns had risen by 1352 and the 'settlements of town type' by 2629.

Definition of a town

What criteria are used in the Soviet Union to define a town and a 'settlement of town type'? Fundamentally, the definition is strictly an economic concept, based on a minimum adult population and a minimum level of employment outside agriculture. The requirements vary somewhat among the 15 Union Republics in response to local conditions, and are generally least exacting in the less developed republics, and some similar concessions are made even in the less developed parts of the RSFSR. Conditions for selected republics are shown in Table 10.3. Once a settlement has the status of a town, its progression up the urban administrative ladder is related to the level of local government to which it is subordinated—whether to the rayon, the oblast (or kray) or to only the republic (as in the case of, say, a capital of a republic). If fortune is adverse, however, a settlement may be downgraded—several small market towns in the western territories, incorporated into

the Soviet Union in 1945, suffered the fate of being reduced to village status. A 'workers' settlement', the first stage on the road to urban development, may even be dissolved and disappear should the reason for its existence, such as a large construction project or a mine, fail or be abandoned. Nevertheless, many villages may be designated as

A boulevard in Tbilisi. People are gathered around a kvass cart, kvass being fermented fruit juice.

TABLE 10.2 SIZE DISTRIBUTION OF URBAN SETTLEMENTS IN THE USSR

Number of inhabitants	Number				Population (millions)			
	1926	1959	1975	1979	1926	1959	1975	1979
TOWNS								
Less than 5 000	141	205	175	⎫	0.5	0.7	0.4	n.a.
5–20 000	350	726	825	⎬ 1744	3.8	8.6	10.2	n.a.
20–100 000	187	600	803	⎭	7.9	25.1	33.5	n.a.
100–500 000	28	123	201	272	4.1	24.2	43.1	47.0
More than 500 000	3	25	39	45	4.1	24.2	44.6	51.8
	(2)	(3)	(13)	(18)	(3.6)	(9.49)	(26.2)	(31.9)
TOTAL	709	1679	2043	2061	21.7	83.0	131.8	
SETTLEMENTS OF URBAN TYPE								
Less than 5 000	927	1542	2015	n.a.	2.0	4.5	5.7	n.a.
5–20 000	281	1368	1673	n.a.	2.4	11.8	14.2	n.a.
20–50 000	8	30	⎫ 51	n.a.	0.2	0.7	⎫ 1.4	n.a.
More than 50 000	—	—	⎭	—	—	—	⎭	n.a.
TOTAL	1216	2940	3739	3845	4.6	17.0	21.3	n.a.

Figures in brackets refer to cities of one million or more inhabitants.
Source: Narodnoye khozyaystvo SSSR, various years.
n.a.: not available.

TABLE 10.3 SETTLEMENTS OF TOWN TYPE: CRITERIA FOR DEFINITION IN SELECTED REPUBLICS

Republic	EMPLOYMENT STRUCTURE (% WORKERS IN INDUSTRIAL SECTORS AND MEMBERS OF THEIR FAMILIES)			MINIMUM TOTAL POPULATION IN THOUSANDS		
	Workers' settlements	Settlements of town type	Towns	Workers' settlements	Settlements of town type	Towns
RSFSR	not less than 85%	non-existent	not less than 85%	3	non-existent	12
Ukraine	preferably majority	over 60% (50% for rayon centres)	preferably majority	0.5	2	10
Georgia	non-existent	not less than 75%	not less than 75%	non-existent	2	5
Moldavia	preferably majority	not less than 70% (not less than 60% for rayon centres)	preferably majority	0.5	2	10

Source: Khorev, B. Gorodskiy poseleniya SSSR, Moscow, 1968.

a workers' settlement or even as a 'health resort' earning them the classification of 'settlements of town type' and may ultimately be given the status of town (*gorod*). Such elevation in status takes place also as the result of industrial development or where an important transport function emerges (as on a new railway or at a road-rail junction), or even through development of a significant resort.

The town plays an influential part in the political geography of the Soviet Union, since Marxist–Leninist theory has regarded it as an excellent milieu for the evolution of a Communist society and the 'victory of the proletariat'. It has, therefore, been seen as a vital focal point from which to disseminate Marxism-Leninism to the countryside, for so long markedly resistant to Communist views. The towns form a series of nodes on which the territorial-administrative framework is hung, since each unit in the system—rayon, oblast or kray, or republic—must have a suitable town as its centre. The concept of the basic territorial-administrative unit—the oblast (or kray in less developed areas)—is seen as the hinterland of its major 'proletarian' centre, and such a view is found to pervade the whole spectrum of Soviet regional planning. It is thus perhaps easier to understand why urban status itself is conceived in economic terms rather than in functional, morphological or demographic measures.

Historical aspects

Towns within the Soviet Union date from most ancient times to the most recent. Not all owe their origin and character to Slav peoples—in the Baltic region and the western frontier districts, German, Polish and Rumanian influences have been strong; in Transcaucasia and Central Asia, Iranian, Indian and even Chinese influences have been found. Some towns in Central Asia, Transcaucasia and the Black Sea littoral may be traced back to pre-Classical and Classical times, though they have not always been on exactly the same site. Mary, in the Turkmen SSR for example, is believed to be one of the oldest town foundations in the world, while Samarkand (as Maracanda and Afrosiab) dates from the third millenium BC (Fig. 10.2). In the Baltic littoral, German influence—first introduced in early medieval times by missionaries, traders and knightly orders—remained influential until the latter part of the nineteenth century, as may still be seen in Riga and Tartu (Dorpat). There are also other towns which lay for long periods outside the Russian state but which have been absorbed since 1945—for example, Polish Lwów (Austrian Lemberg—now Lvov), Uzhgorod, Mukachevo and Chernovtsy (Rumanian Cernauti), while Königsberg, a typical German Baltic town until 1945, when it was badly damaged, has been rebuilt

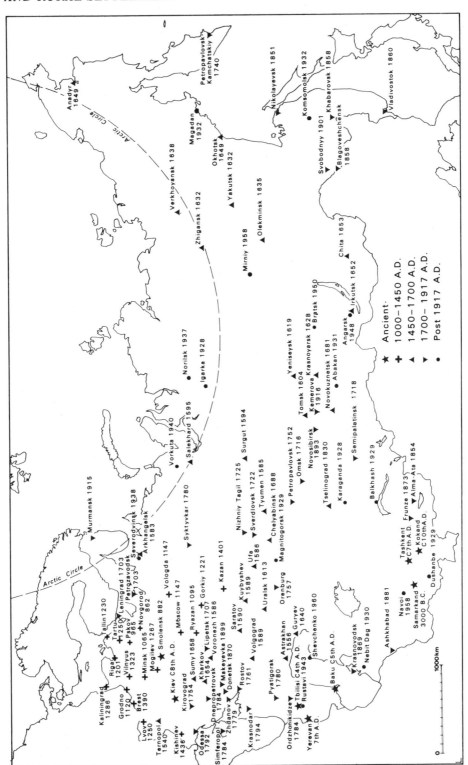

Fig. 10.2 Dates of foundation of towns. The early dates of town foundation in Central Asian oasis lands and parts of European Russia contrast with the much later spread into the Trans-Volga lands and Siberia, though in all regions major foundations of the Soviet period are to be found

as a characteristic Soviet town and renamed Kaliningrad.

The early town in the Russian lands was a close association of defensive, administrative and trading functions. The administrative functions were usually exercised from within a walled enclosure (*gorod*) within which lay a castle or *kreml* (in northern Russia, *detinets*). There was also frequently a cathedral or monastery, though in some parts of northern Russia, the ecclesiastical functions completely replaced the administrative and defensive roles. Outside but also walled was the *posad*—the traders' and artisans' quarters. Beyond this there was in some cases a peasant settlement, the *sloboda* outside the walls or forming part of the *posad*. The kreml (still seen in Moscow, Gorkiy, Tula and many other towns) usually lay on high ground or on a bluff above a river, while the merchants' and traders' quarters stood on lower ground, not uncommonly some distance away. The early Russian towns date from the three or four centuries before the catastrophic Tatar invasion (1240) which laid the majority of them in ruins. These towns lay in areas where reasonable farming land and good fishing were available, especially at break-of-bulk points on river portages (of which Smolensk is the 'classical' example), and were thus scattered through the wooded steppe, the better parts of the mixed forest or the fringe of the boreal coniferous forests. A few venturesome towns lay towards the steppe fringe, though here they suffered most from interference by raiding steppe nomads. Everywhere wood was the common building material, though from the thirteenth century stone began to be used for churches and fortifications—Vladimir was already renowned far and wide by the mid-twelfth century for its stone buildings.

EXAMPLES OF SOVIET TOWNS

Moscow

Moscow, capital of Russia, except in the period 1708–1918, is one of the world's largest towns, with a population of 8.2 million in 1980. It commands the 'mesopotamia' between the main river routes and portages of the centre of the plain of European Russia. On the east, it was protected by the marshes of the Klyazma and Oka basins, though to the south it lay open to the wooded steppe and was defended by a number of fortified monasteries. The first record of Moscow is in

A view of Moscow from the river showing some of the most desirable residential flats and a new high-rise administrative block

1147 AD when there was a wooden kreml on a bluff above the Moscow river, protected on either flank by small streams. Around this nucleus, the town grew. In the fourteenth century, a solid wall was built round the fortress and, separated from it across the Red Square, arose a traders' quarter, the *Kitaygorod* (from the Tatar meaning 'fortified town'), which in 1534 also received a substantial wall. In 1520, Moscow reputedly had 45 000 houses and was claimed to be larger than London. As the town grew, there developed the 'White Town', the home of courtiers and rich citizens, around the kreml: in 1586, it also received a wall. Beyond it newer suburbs began to emerge, the 'Earthen Town', named from the clay wall around it, and settlement spread across the Moscow river. Beyond the Earthen Town, a number of suburbs for foreigners grew up, like the German suburb— *Nemetskaya Sloboda*—in the north-east.

The kreml ceased to be mainly a defensive point in the seventeenth century and was then much ornamented and elaborated (mostly to foreign designs). In the early eighteenth century, the outermost suburbs were surrounded by a wall with 14 customs barriers (*zastavy*). Despite the ornate churches, the brick kreml and stuccoed wooden palaces, most streets remained unpaved and low timber houses, set in large gardens with high wooden fences and many outhouses, gave the town the appearance of a vast village. Even though the houses and palaces of the aristocracy and the rich began to be finished in central European style, basically they remained of wooden construction. The Napoleonic attack on Russia was marked by the firing of Moscow (1812) and three-quarters of its buildings were destroyed. But even though the capital had been moved to St. Petersburg, the town quickly recovered and began to increase its commercial and manufacturing functions.

The industrialisation of late nineteenth century Russia was essentially focused upon Moscow. New and squalid industrial slums appeared, and the old walls were pulled down and boulevards made in their place—the wall of the Earthen Town, for example, was replaced by a park-like ring, the *Sadovaya*. The line of the old walls can still be seen as broad green circles in the contemporary plan of Moscow, and some of the old barrier names remain (e.g. the Kaluzhskaya Zastava). Industry had gathered particularly in the south near the river harbour or in the east. The growth of railways created a ring of terminal stations roughly along the line of the old *zastavy*. Brick, stone and concrete have been increasingly used, but even now many wooden buildings remain, though in the early 1960s a determined effort was begun to remove them.

The return of the capital to Moscow after the Revolution brought a new significance and a change in the town's function, with the meteoric rise in the bureaucratic superstructure of the Soviet state. The population of 600 000 in 1897 had risen to 1.6 million by 1912 and to 2.03 million in 1926, while the 1939 census enumerated 4.14 million people. Industry was expanding, using the pool of skilled labour available, and workers for the new bureaucratic machine flowed in. In the early 1930s an elaborate development plan was drawn up, with the widening of streets and removal of the last remains of the old walls, as well as

The tourist industry is one of the main sources of foreign currency as well as employing many people – here Soviet and foreign tourists stream into Petrodvorets, the summer palace of Peter the Great near Leningrad.

the laying out of new parks. In the central districts extensive changes were made in the street pattern and many new official buildings erected, though some of the more grandiose architectural concepts were never realised. Great improvements were made in public transport: construction of an underground railway began and suburban railways were electrified, besides expansion of the bus, trolley bus and tram networks. To increase rail mobility, a ring railway was built (to be augmented by an outer ring line after the Second World War) and in 1937 the Moscow–Volga Canal provided a shorter route to the Volga than the winding course of the Moscow and Oka rivers. The southern river port at Nogatino was now augmented by installations in the northern part of the town at Khimki.

During the inter-war period, building of homes received a relatively low priority, but from the early 1950s expansion of residential accommodation has produced vast new housing quarters (mostly large blocks of flats with supporting services) around the city. The growth of motor traffic, even though still below Western levels, has led to the provision of widened streets and appropriate junctions, while during the mid-1960s a ring motorway was built. Many new buildings have been added, including the erection of skyscrapers. Nevertheless, the side streets remain poorly paved and wooden houses are still common. Moscow is a mixture of architectural styles: beautiful old structures such as the Kremlin or the former palaces; dismal, late-nineteenth century buildings; a few buildings in a clean functional style of the early 1930s and a vast assortment in the heavy, ornate, almost bizarre style of the Stalinist period. A return to a more functional style has been made since the death of Stalin, with much use of concrete and glass, reflected in the striking headquarters of COMECON, several hotels in the central area and a variety of other buildings.

Leningrad

Leningrad (St. Petersburg or Petrograd) in its elegance and farsighted central layout is in great contrast to Moscow. It owes its origin to Peter the Great, an admirer of western Europe, who built it in Russia's then most-westerly territory with access to ice-free waters through which he hoped European ideas would find a way into the backward and inward-looking Russia of the early eighteenth century. The town was founded in 1703 on the flat, marshy delta of the Neva, subject to autumn and spring floods, especially when onshore winds ponded back the waters of the river. The town lies at the base of a narrow isthmus between the Gulf of Finland and Lake Ladoga, and was protected by its outer fortresses, like Petrokrepost on Lake Ladoga and Kronstadt on Kotlin Island in the Gulf of Finland. St. Petersburg was built by some 40 000 peasants recruited in the countryside around, steadily replaced by new recruits as their numbers were depleted by accidents and illness, and directed by Italian and other foreign artisans. In the soft sub-stratum, all the larger buildings had to be supported on piles and the problem of their weight tended to restrict their height—the low, even skyline, broken by fine, tall and spindly spires is characteristic of the older part of Leningrad. The generous and roomy appearance of the central districts is given by wide radiating streets, broad arms of the delta and drainage canals and a fortunate balance between open space and buildings.

The focus of the town was the low-walled fortress of Peter–Paul, but around the eighteenth century core, there is a broad belt of less attractive buildings of the nineteenth and twentieth centuries, mostly flats and factories, in style similar to other Russian towns. Along the coast lie, however, a number of small and pleasant holiday resorts, while the southern side of the delta is the site of Leninport which, although closed by ice in winter, remains one of the largest and busiest Soviet harbours.

Kiev

Kiev, capital of the Ukraine, lies in the marchlands between the northern forests and the southern steppe alongside a major north—south routeway, the Dnepr river. A settlement appears to have existed on the high right bank of the Dnepr before the ninth century, from which the later nucleus developed. It was an easily defensible position on bluffs overlooking the river, and isolated by deeply incised valleys to either flank. To the south lay the later royal village of Berestovo, site of the Pechersk Monastery, one of the main centres for the dissemination of Christianity to the Russian lands, especially under Vladimir in the tenth century. Internal dissension and attacks from steppe nomads brought the decline of Kiev in 1230, and its fortunes were seldom good until it passed back into the Russian state in the seventeenth century. With the expansion of the Russian hold throughout the Black Sea littoral and the Ukraine, Kiev began to revive. Houses spread along the high river bank and in the deeply incised valleys that dissected it. A broad open site by the confluence of the Dnepr and Pochayna river, known as Podol, became a centre of artisans and the site of the river port, changing in the nineteenth century into Kiev's industrial district. During the late 1930s and in the post-war period, development on the eastern (the low meadow) bank included the large industrial suburb of Darnitsa, while in the 1960s an underground railway was built to link the two sides of the river.

Novgorod

Novgorod is an example of the oldest Russian towns and has been restored as an historical 'monument' since extensive damage in the Second World War. Lying in poor agricultural country, but enjoying a commanding position on the Volkhov river, part of the important early medieval trade route from the Baltic to the Black Sea, at a point to which portages across the Valday Hills from the Volga basin led, Novgorod was one of the earliest great trading centres in the Russian lands. On a low but steep bluff on the western side of the river lay the kreml whose walls also enclosed the cathedral, and around this but separated from it by a broad square was the administrative and ecclesiastical quarter, the *Sofiyskaya Storona*, itself surrounded by a wall and a moat. Across the river but joined to the western bank at an early date by a bridge, lay the traders' and artisans' quarter—the *Torgovaya Storona*—behind its own wall, where a large square served as the main trading point. To Novgorod came merchants from the Hansa and from Visby as well as Russian and Asiatic traders. The town was largely built of wood and was renowned for the beauty of its buildings, but it was razed by Ivan the Terrible, who reputedly slew 60 000 citizens, and never fully recovered its former glory. Much of the present town is composed of the dreary early post-war style of Soviet architecture.

Siberian towns

Town foundations in the Volga lands and the steppe in the sixteenth and seventeenth centuries and in Central Asia in the eighteenth and early nineteenth centuries were a process of consolidat-

ing hard-won territory, and most began life as fortified posts. The Siberian towns were fortified wooden trading posts commonly situated to take advantage of relief for defence and to use better patches of ground where some cultivation might be undertaken. As the rivers and portages were main routeways, most towns were situated along rivers, particularly at points where portages began or where there were ferries. Wooden stockades surrounded low wooden houses set behind high fences, brightly painted wooden churches and administrative buildings, with white-washed stucco (but wooden-frames), that lined wood-paved streets. Deep open drains were often framed over with wood to make a pavement or sidewalk; these still exist in the older parts of Siberian towns. In the nineteenth century, some of the more important towns like Irkutsk became rich and could afford better buildings, parks, museums and other signs of municipal affluence. With a fund of exiled intellectuals to draw on, Siberian towns were distinguished by their museums and literary and philosophical societies.

The wooden town is still being built in Siberia: Divnogorsk, near Krasnoyarsk, on the banks of the Yenisey, is a new town of large wooden blocks of dwellings set amid the tayga, with roughly graded roads and simple facilities.

The coming of the railway in the late nineteenth century brought a new wealth and purpose to towns that lay at points where railway and river crossed and many of these came to outshine towns on the old *trakt*, the former main highway across Siberia. In this way, Novonikolayevsk, a mere insignificant village in the early 1890s, grew into the city of Novosibirsk, with its large theatre, administrative buildings, industrial plants, and the now world-famous 'Academic City' (Akademgorodok) nearby: it now greatly outshines the formerly more important town of Tomsk, with its university which was established in 1880—Novosibirsk has 1.3 million people and Tomsk a mere 421 000 (1979).

There are in Siberia many boom towns: apart from the foundations of the interwar years like Komsomolsk, postwar foundations have included Angarsk in 1948, now a town of 245 000 people, while in the west Siberian oilfields, Surgut has risen from 6 000 people in 1959 to 137 000 in 1981, while Nizhnevartovsk has rocketed from 16 000 in 1970 to 134 000 in 1981.

Soviet Central Asia and Transcaucasia

Distinctive native towns are found in Soviet Central Asia and in Transcaucasia. These lands, which passed to the Tsarist empire in the nineteenth century, already had their own strongly developed native society with a moderate scatter of towns much influenced by Indian or Persian culture. The native towns of Central Asia, for example, were composed of a mass of small alleyways along which lay low clay courtyard houses with flat roofs and few, if any, windows facing on to the streets. They were dominated by mosques and minarets, often beautifully decorated with coloured tiles, if somewhat dilapidated. A central market place (*registan*) was surrounded by bazaars composed of small shops and one-roomed workshops. These towns usually lay within a towered wall, also made of sun-dried mud bricks, and some were commanded by an old fortress. Adjacent to many of these ancient towns lies the Russian foundation—originally a garrison town—with regular tree-lined streets, small Russian-style houses and public buildings also in the style of European Russia. The Russian barracks usually took up a generous part of the town and, where the railway existed, a large area was occupied by copious sidings and a station

Flats in Ordzhonikidze in the north Caucasus region, the design being similar to those found all over the Soviet Union. The mural painting draws attention to Soviet military strength.

enclosure. In the Soviet period, these towns have been changing—the old and less salubrious parts of the native towns have been slowly cleared and replaced by multi-storied blocks of flats or by more open spaces. Nevertheless, in places, the older native buildings of interest have been retained as historical monuments. The contemporary architectural style, while distinctively 'Soviet', has sought to incorporate a local motif as well as designs on the basis of the slogan 'national in style, socialist in content'. Reports from Central Asia suggest, however, that the native people have commonly been reluctant to move away from traditional homes into Russian-style houses or blocks of flats.

Towns 'of socialist realism'

Latest among the Soviet towns are the towns of 'socialist realism', mostly foundations of the late 1940s and thereafter. These are often associated with major industrial developments, though to this group may also be added many of the towns built in the early prewar Five Year Plans (e.g. Magnitogorsk, Karaganda, Komsomolsk) whose growth has allowed the incorporation of the current concepts. The towns focus on their main plant, though they are often separated from it by a green belt, lake (reservoir for industrial water) or a recreational area. Within the built-up area is a careful evaluation of a balance between population, employment, services and amenities. The design is usually one of distinct 'neighbourhood units', with all supporting services. The striking feature, as in so many Soviet towns, is the fewness of shops, but it should be recalled that each shop has a very carefully estimated population to serve. Some of these towns, for example, Karaganda, comprise within one administrative area, a series of industrial enterprises or mines, each with its own settlement linked to a central administrative and service core, so that the whole pattern of territorial occupancy by buildings is loose and diffuse. These new towns have been criticised for failings in their planning concepts: for example, too many were conceived with too great a compactness in building intended to give the 'big city effect', so that there is monotony and overcrowding of buildings that are too high and line overwide streets. Many plans have been criticised for being too geometric, especially in focusing too forcefully on the main industrial plant.

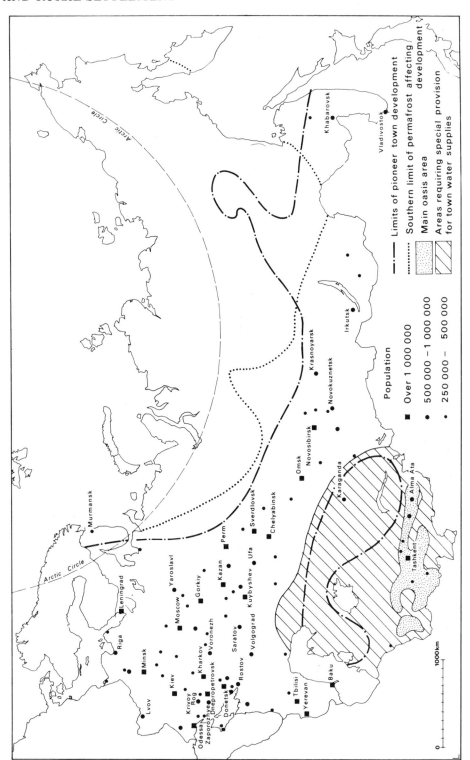

Fig. 10.3 The largest contemporary towns. The distribution of the largest towns within the main populated triangle with its base between the Baltic and Black Seas and its apex in western Siberia is impressive. Beyond this triangle, factors of the physical environment play a significant role in town foundation

In the growth and planning of towns, several problems face the Soviet authorities. Housing for too long received only a low priority, but the demands for improved standards of living, together with the hygienic and social problems arising from overcrowding, have forced attention to the large deficit in most towns. Large new housing and neighbourhood units of prefabricated blocks of flats have been erected, usually accompanied by all essential services. Some of these schemes have been markedly successful, as for example in Kharkov, where the new districts stand amid attractive wooded gullies. In some towns, these new buildings are erected in the gardens of old wooden houses whose residents are moved into the new homes on completion. An attempt has been made to enforce a vigorous policy of issuing 'residence permits' in the towns with the most serious housing deficits. The vigorous migration from country to town creates difficulties in educating rural people to town life and in catering for the countryman's need of such things as a small allotment garden to cultivate and to keep a few domestic animals such as rabbits. These allotment gardens are, nevertheless, a useful contribution to the problems of distributing food and nourishing urban populations, since the distributive industries appear to have been an intractable problem under central planning concepts.

The growth of towns in inhospitable environments—the arid lands of Central Asia or the intensely cold Arctic Siberia—has presented questions of design and form. One of the major problems in both areas has been water supply: in arid areas, reservoirs need to be built to collect water (e.g. at Magnitogorsk) or aqueducts built to carry water from other areas. An aqueduct is presently being built from the Irtysh to Karaganda and Temirtau in Kazakhstan. The oil-mining town of Shevchenko in the Mangyshlak peninsula, developed in the 1960s, has an elaborate atomic-powered water desalinisation plant, and Krasnovodsk receives fresh water by tanker across the Caspian Sea. Over much of Siberia, permafrost, a distinctive civil engineering hazard requiring special methods of construction, makes water supply and sewage disposal difficult (Fig. 10.3). Wooden frame buildings are preferred in many places because they adjust more readily with the movement of the sub-stratum permafrost caused by an upset of the thermal balance. The importance of shade and greenery in arid lands as an amelioration of the micro-climatic environment is also stressed: in western Turkmenistan, in the largest settlements there are 3–4 m² of greenery for each inhabitant, but the Soviet authorities maintain that this must be increased to 25 m².

The problems of assembling labour and building materials in remote and virgin country present many transport headaches: the building of Bratsk demanded a temporary workers' settlement and special electricity supply across 700 km of virgin and empty country. Little could be achieved until a railway branch line of several hundred kilometres had been built to the site. Once a settlement is established, it has to be fed and this adds a further burden on transport. It is common to develop glasshouses and special installations to provide fresh food—Norilsk and Igarka are supplied from a state farm on a sandy island in the middle of the Yenisey, whose massive volume of warm water creates a local positive temperature anomaly and consequently keeps the island free of permafrost. Reports suggest that the mining settlement of Deputatskiy in north-eastern Siberia has been built under a gigantic roof supported in the permafrost by adjustable supports and with the buildings, partly subterranean, suspended from this roof. It should not be forgotten that in the worst Siberian blizzards, it is almost impossible to move about outside, even in towns.

Optimum size of a town

A long discussion has taken place in the Soviet Union on the optimum size of the town so that the best amenities may be provided and the best return may be had on investment while running costs are kept to a minimum. Various proposals have been made—in the early 'thirties the concept of the vast multi-million town was accepted in the then-prevailing 'gigantomania', but since then views have changed several times. One view will not accept communities of less than 250 000 or more than 500 000 as within the optimum limits in relation to local circumstances. In the mid-1950s, Soviet planners appeared to reject the view that any city should exceed 400 000 people, but the continued growth and the difficulty in controlling growth of large cities has led to estimated populations being exceeded anything up to a decade earlier than forecast. Examples of rapid urban growth have already been quoted for Siberia, but others include the new motor vehicle manufacturing town of Naberezhnye Chelny on the Kama which has grown from 16 000 in 1959 to 346 000 in 1981, or the nearby Nizhnekamsk that has risen from 49 000 in 1970 to 143 000 ten years later. Another vehicle manufacturing centre, Tolyatti, has also risen from 72 000 in 1959 to 533 000 in 1981, perhaps the best example of the Volga basin's boom towns. In the commuting sphere around Moscow, Zelenograd has risen from 7000 in 1959 to some 130 000 in twenty years, while Staryy Oskol in the newly developing Kursk iron ore district has moved from 27 000 in 1959 to 130 000 in 1981 and will continue to grow substantially as the planned new metallurgical complex is further developed.

It is suggested that the type of industry basic to a new town is an important guide to the eventual likely size to which the town should be expanded. In some instances, however, estimates for ultimate size have had to be revised steeply upwards in the light of real growth—the chemical town of Volzhskiy on the Volga, with 220 000 people (1981), was planned originally as unlikely to exceed 50 000, but further projections suggest that 300 000 should be the upper limit. Soviet planners maintain that the tendency has been to design for too *few* rather than too *many* potential inhabitants. Plans for Navoi in the Uzbek SSR changed from 50–70 000 to 250–300 000, though it had not reached 100 000 inhabitants by 1981. Angarsk, founded in 1948, was planned on too small a scale, with the subsequent problems of adjustment to a much greater population of 245 000 by 1981.

The geographer Pokshishevskiy, speaking to the press in 1970, said, 'practical experience has shown that the further expansion of giant cities has become very undesirable. Vigorous efforts have already been made to limit their growth and their share in the total will presumably diminish considerably by the year 2000'. It has been calculated that the 45 major cities (all over 500 000), which account for 20 % of total population and 32 % of urban population, will drop to 13 % of total population and 17 % of urban population by 2000 AD, if growth of population for the group does not exceed 10–15 %. Pokshishevskiy then says, 'alternative types of communities—small towns and urban-type communities—are unable to provide their residents with a sufficiently high level of services . . . It is much less economical to provide amenities of various kinds in small urban communities. That is why Soviet town planning

theory recommends avoidance of unduly small urban communities while restricting the growth of giant cities. A part of the existing small communities will presumably have grown into medium-sized towns by the year 2000 and the setting up of new communities will depend on economic requirements. In 2000 the bulk of the urban population will probably be living in well-appointed, very healthy and exceedingly economical medium and large communities but not giant cities'. However, by no means all Soviet planners agree with these views and many argue the 'progressive' nature of urban agglomerations.

THE VILLAGE

The Russian lands were traditionally lands of villages, while the village was the common unit of settlement in the sedentarily settled areas of Central Asia and Transcaucasia as well as in the non-Russian parts of European Russia. Moreover, wherever Russian settlers went, they took the concept of the village with them. In form, size and house type, there were, however, regional variations (Fig. 10.4).

TABLE 10.4 NUMBER OF VILLAGE SOVIETS IN THE USSR

Year	Soviets
1928	72 997
1950	74 863
1964	39 623
1968	40 558
1977	41 249
1981	41 511

Source: Narodnoye khozyaystvo SSSR, various years, Moscow.

In European Russia, the village played a vital part in the emergence of Russian society—particularly through the village council, the *mir*—and was distinguished in Tsarist times according to whether it had a church (*selo*)—and was, therefore, a focal point of the countryside—or whether it was without (*derevnya*). Such a distinction no longer exists in the Soviet view and now villages are important if they are the seat of a collective or state farm or a village Soviet.

In northern European Russia, villages tend to be small—many are of a dozen or so houses only—in widely scattered positions on drier ground such as sandy mounds or river terraces. In the central

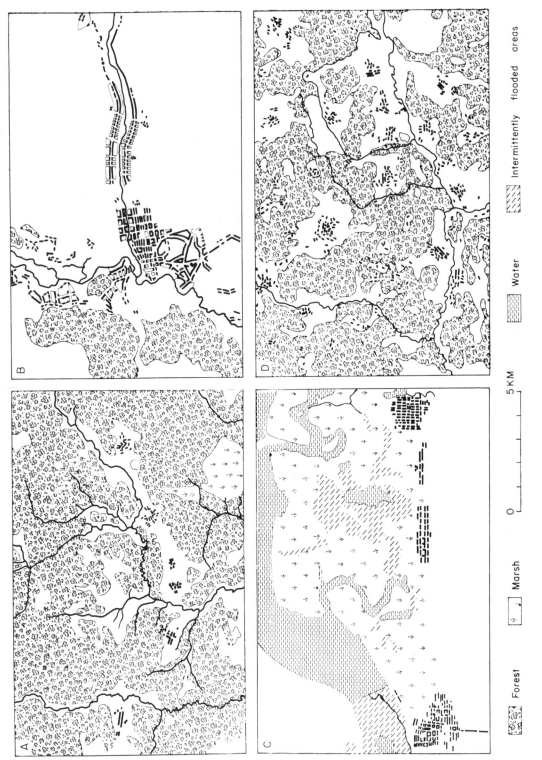

Fig. 10.4 Rural settlement types   A Southern Karelia   B Ukrainian steppe   C Northern Caucasia   D Valday Hills

Great Russian districts and in the north-west and Belorussia, villages are larger with several dozen houses, though the type of house varies considerably in size and richness of its appearance from district to district: especially poor and meagre are the villages of the wet lands such as Polesye. The most common Russian village type is the street village, a simple line of houses scattered along either side of a broad and unpaved street, but small nucleations do now more frequently occur as the result of growth around farm centres, where educational, cultural and technical facilities are concentrated. Several villages may belong to one collective or state farm and some have a little handicraft industry.

The steppe villages tend to seek shelter from the cold winter winds that sweep across the open steppe: thus villages are commonly sited in valleys or erosion gullies, particularly where water is available. The villages are usually large and several may be strung out along a gully or a valley, forming an uninterrupted line of buildings for several kilometres, though each community can usually be distinguished by its village pond. Particularly large chessboard villages of a rectangular street plan are common in the newer settled areas of the steppe in the Ukraine and notably in northern Caucasia, as, for example, in the Cossack village type (*stanitsa*) of the Kuban. The villages of southern Siberia on the steppe fringe are often large and prosperous looking and make a generous use of space.

Other settlement types

Non-Slav peoples show other settlement types. In the Baltic republics, villages still tend to be small, comprising 20 houses or so, and the land reform of the nineteenth and twentieth centuries led to the development of scattered individual farms. Houses were often long and low with a mansard roof. Since re-incorporation in the Soviet Union, collectivisation has tended to encourage nucleation. Small hamlets and villages or even scattered farms, distinguished by large houses with barns, are also found in Karelia. In the Volga lands, Tatar settlement areas have been identified by their irregularly shaped villages, usually close to a river or spring, though they are not found on the best lands from which they were displaced by early Great Russian colonisation. The Bashkirs, who only abandoned nomadism in the nineteenth century, live in villages of the street type, and until

recently, with simple housing of mud bricks and plaited wattle. Air-dried bricks or wattle frame houses clad by mud or plaster and colour-washed are common in the southern Ukraine and Moldavia. These houses often have long verandahs.

The Caucasian mountain villages are irregular in their plan but closely nucleated. Low stone houses, usually with flat roofs, stand on easily defended slopes amid guard towers. In the lower hill lands, villages are commonly large and houses have spacious verandahs or balconies. Some Caucasian houses show strong Turkish influence of stone basements with overhanging upper floors in wood. Central Asian oasis villages are large and commonly closely nucleated, surrounded by a low wall. The flat-roofed courtyard houses crowd along narrow alleys (with open sewers), but in many places the Russian-style house, and more recently, houses and flats of bricks or concrete, have begun to appear, especially where nomads have recently become sedentary. In nomadic lands, settlements are mobile and consist of tents and *yurts* of various kinds and shapes, but in the Arctic and sub-Arctic in Siberia, native winter houses are partly below ground, built of wood, sods and stone; in summer they are deserted for tents or wooden huts, in some cases raised above ground on stilts. Nevertheless, even in these regions, the Russian wooden house—the *izba*—has been widely adopted.

Modern ideas on rural settlement

Modern Soviet ideas on rural settlement have been centred on ways to bring rural life into line with life in towns. A major deficiency has been the amenities of village life: a large proportion of villages have until recently had no piped water and no electricity and complaints about the state of rural roads have been common. Encouragement has been given to nucleation—outlying settlements have been encouraged to move into central collective and state farm villages where better amenities can be provided. A concept reintroduced by Khrushchev was the *agrogorod*—the 'agricultural town'. The first was tried in the 1930s on a state farm in northern Caucasia and this form appeared again on the immense state farms of the virgin lands of northern Kazakhstan. It can offer all the amenities of the small town and provides the authorities with a better supervision of the community. Each day workers are taken to the fields in

A Tadzhik village with new houses and farm buildings among the old

lorries or buses, as commuters are taken to work in a town. Plans formulated in the 1960s earmarked about 16 % of the existing villages for development, while the remainder were to stagnate or even die away, but such radical changes are now regarded generally as unrealistic though grouping of villages for more efficient provision of services continues widely.

The Soviet town provides the urban geographer with a study of the problems of massive urbanisation in a rapidly industrialising economy set in a generally harsh physical environment, especially in arid Central Asia and Arctic Siberia. The application of Marxist–Leninist concepts in the framework of a rigorous central planning also introduces influences in the evolution and growth of towns not experienced in the western world. At the same time, the great historical traditions of the town in the Soviet lands should not be overlooked, while the nature of the village, in its varying forms, from which so many towns have evolved, has been an important factor in the emergence of the Soviet society.

BIBLIOGRAPHY

Adams, R. B. (1977), 'The Soviet metropolitan hierarchy: regionalisation and comparison with the United States,' *Soviet Geography*, **18**, pp. 313–328.

Bater, J. H. (1980), *The Soviet city*, Edward Arnold, London.

Bugromenko, U. N. (1979), 'Complex planning of a city and the study of its spatial structure,' *Soviet Geography*, **20**, pp. 160–169.

Burlachenko, G. F. (1979), 'Problems and prospects of development of rural nonfarm places in the USSR,' *Soviet Geography*, **20**, pp. 305–309.

French, R. A. and Hamilton, F. E. I. (1979), *The socialist city*, John Wiley, Chichester.

Hamilton, F. E. I. (1976), *The Moscow city region*, (*Problem Regions of Europe*), Oxford UP, Oxford.

Hamm, M. (ed.) (1976), *The city in Russian history*, UP of Kentucky, Lexington.

Harris, C. D. (1970), *Cities of the Soviet Union – Studies in their functions, size, density and growth*, Rand McNally, Chicago.

Hooson, D. J. M. (1969), *The growth of cities in pre-Soviet Russia*, University of California Slavic and East European Series, Berkeley.

Khorev, B. S. (1975), *Problemy gorodov*, Mysl', Moscow.

Kochetkov, A. V. and Listengurt, F. M. (1977), 'A strategy for the distribution of settlement in the USSR: aims, problems and solutions.' *Soviet Geography*, **18**, pp. 660–674.

Konstantinov, O. A. (1977), 'Types of urbanisation in the USSR.' *Soviet Geography*, **18**, pp. 715–728.

Kravchuk, Ya. T. (1973), *Formirovaniye novykh gorodov*. Izd. Literatury po Stroitelstvu, Moscow.

Kitovka, O. P. (1980), 'Urbanisation in the USSR: problems of spatial differentiation,' *Soviet Geography*, **21**, pp. 30–36.

Lappo, G., Chikishev, A. and Bekker, A. (1976), *Moscow, capital of the Soviet Union*, Progress, Moscow.

Mellor, R. E. H. (1963), 'The Soviet town.' *Town and Country Planning* **31**, pp. 90–94.

Mellor, R. E. H. (1976), 'Sowjetunion. IV' – *Bevölkerungsverteilung und ethnische Zusammensetzung*, Harms Erdkunde, Verlag Munich.

Pallot, J. and Shaw, D. J. B. (1981), *Planning in the Soviet Union*, Croom Helm, London.

Saushkin, Yu. G. (1964), *Moskva–geograficheskaya kharakteristika*, Mysl, Moscow.

Saushkin, Yu. G. (1966), *Moscow–geographical characteristics*, (Trans.: T. Kapustin), Progress, Moscow.

Shaw, D. J. B. (1978), Planning Leningrad, *Geographical Review*, **48**, pp. 183–200.

Smirnov, N. V. (1979), 'Stages in the development of the demographic structure of large cities,' *Soviet Geography*, **20**, pp. 219–224.

Tikhomirov, M. (1959), *Towns of ancient Russia*. Foreign Languages Publishing House, Moscow.

Underhill, J. A. (1976), *Soviet new towns – Housing and national urban growth policy*, US Government Printing Office, Washington.

11 Transport

A modern industrial state depends on an adequate transport system to assemble raw materials for its factories, to carry food from the country or ports to its townspeople, and to distribute the products of its industry, as well as to move people for recreational and employment reasons. The selection of the means of transport to do these tasks depends on the nature of the traffics generated in relation to distance and volume and in relation to the physical environment through which they will have to move.

In the immense and diverse continental environment of the Soviet Union, development of the transport system has been a key to the feverish creation of a strong economic structure based on large-scale industry since the Revolution. Policy has demanded an even spread of development among the regions, despite a clearly uneven distribution of natural resources and conditions, and has thus accentuated the significance of transport. National self-sufficiency has demanded provision of transport to remote mining areas far beyond the existing limits of sedentary settlement. Yet at the same time it has required the burden on transport to be kept as low as possible, in order to reduce to the minimum level investment of scarce national resources in transport rather than in more productive growth sectors of the economy. Transport has, therefore, been an almost decisive factor in such aspects as the evolution of high-cost arctic agriculture (rather than carry cheap food from southern producers) or the relation between plant location and raw material supply among inter-linked areas like the Ural, western Siberia and Karaganda.

TRANSPORT IN A SETTING OF THE PHYSICAL ENVIRONMENT

A basic Soviet transport problem is distance. The USSR, the world's largest compact political unit, is three times the area of the United States and 90 times the area of the United Kingdom, while its east to west extent is so broad as to give a ten-hour difference in time. Moscow is some 9200 km by rail from Vladivostok and there is a seven-hour time difference: the two towns are further apart than London and New York. Moscow is also 370 km *further* by rail from Tashkent than it is from Paris.

The influence of the climate

The strongly continental climate has an important influence on transport. The anomalous cold, with winter considerably exceeding summer in duration over most of the country, and the related phenomenon of permafrost (reputedly affecting 47% of the country's area) are a hindrance over wide areas to construction of roads and railways or even buildings. Intense cold also can cause brittleness in metals, affect ferro-concrete and the working tolerance of machinery or reduce the fluidity of oils and increase thermal loss from heat engines. Frost heaving breaks up roads and upsets the alignment of railway tracks, besides affecting the stability of bridges, but it does at least provide a hard surface over which to move, so that winter has been traditionally a period of movement, when even bogs, almost impassable barriers in spring and summer, and some rivers, can be used by temporary 'winter roads'.

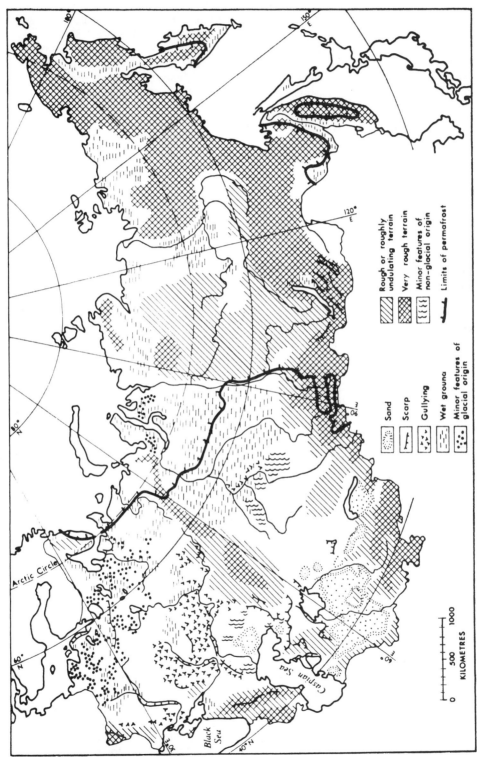

Fig. 11.1 Terrain problems for transport

Throughout the greater part of the country, rivers, lakes and even coastal waters suffer ice hazards for 100 days or more each year (Fig. 11.1). Ice makes access to Russia's coasts difficult, except for a few favoured ports seldom seriously troubled or which may be kept open easily by ice breaker, so it is not surprising that the Soviet Union has contributed much to the design of ice breakers and of merchant ships for navigation in ice. In some waters, notably on the Pacific coast and in the Arctic, mist and fog even in the open-water period are also a major hazard; dust storms in spring and summer in the Black Sea can seriously reduce visibility, while along the Caucasian Black Sea coast very strong föhn winds off the shore can make entry to some ports (e.g. Novorossiysk) awkward.

The spring thaw, traditionally the *rasputitsa* (the 'roadless' season), results in bad roads, because the lower layers of the soil remain frozen and the thawed surface layer produces large areas of standing water and floods, turning the ground to a quagmire. The water level in rivers rises and currents increase, while ice floes endanger shipping and bridge supports or pile up in bends and constrictions to form temporary dams whose collapse releases masses of water to sweep downstream as destructive floods. Low-lying areas of the 'meadow banks' (usually the left bank) are regularly flooded and avoided by settlement, and shipping is forced to lie in winter harbours until the period is past. In Siberia, the upper southern reaches of the rivers thaw first and water flows north on to still-frozen lower sections, turning areas like the west Siberian lowlands into huge shallow swampy lakes that are gradually reduced to vast swamps by summer. In late summer, many rivers suffer from low water, forcing navigation to a halt, while the heavily silt-laden streams of Central Asia are plagued by ever-shifting shoals and banks, making them of little navigational value. In the spring quagmire, it is often only railways, raised on low embankments, which can keep moving; while sudden vicious summer thunderstorms can bring traffic to a halt and disrupt urban trams by damage to overhead lines. Thunderstorms help to settle the dust, frequently a visibility hazard, and stop drifting dust or sand that can block roads and railways.

Physical obstacles to the development of the transport network

The relief map of the Soviet Union suggests few obstacles to easy transport: vast plains and moderately dissected plateaus form large areas of the heart of the country (Fig. 11.2). Even the parallel Ural ranges that lie across the main east-west transport arteries are low and marked by clearly defined through-ways, particularly in their central section. High mountain terrain lies mainly in the southern and eastern peripheries, areas of underdevelopment until recently, and border areas where international transport has not been encouraged for strategic reasons. It is perhaps paradoxical that minor features of relief commonly form more troublesome obstacles to the development of the transport network than do the major features.

In the northern part of the great plains, because of low temperatures (insufficient for evaporation to exceed even the meagre precipitation) and the exceptionally gentle gradients which impede drainage, the land suffers from too much water and is characteristically wet and marshy. Drainage of roads and railbeds is a critical problem since saturation causes bad running and frost heaving in winter. Railbeds are often laid on several feet of sand, and are usually raised on low embankments, which also prevent snow drift in winter and inundation in spring. The softness of the substratum and its poor bearing capacity are also a hindrance to railways, demanding additional or unusually long rail sleepers (ties) or imposing severe weight and axle-load restrictions. Despite the moistness of the northern forests there is a fire danger in summer, and wide avenues alongside railway tracks are cleared as spark arresters and to prevent trees blown down in winter blizzards from fouling the track.

Southwards and eastwards, the plains become drier, turning to steppe and even desert. Low precipitation is exceeded by high summer evaporation, and sudden thundery downpours fall on parched ground unable to absorb the moisture, causing much loss by run-off, so that gullying easily occurs, especially where the vegetation cover has been broken. In winter, when the thin snow cover is quickly blown away, or even in a dry spring or summer, the parched, friable ground can be easily eroded by high winds sweeping unimpeded across these open plains. Roads and railways need to be protected against drifting dust and

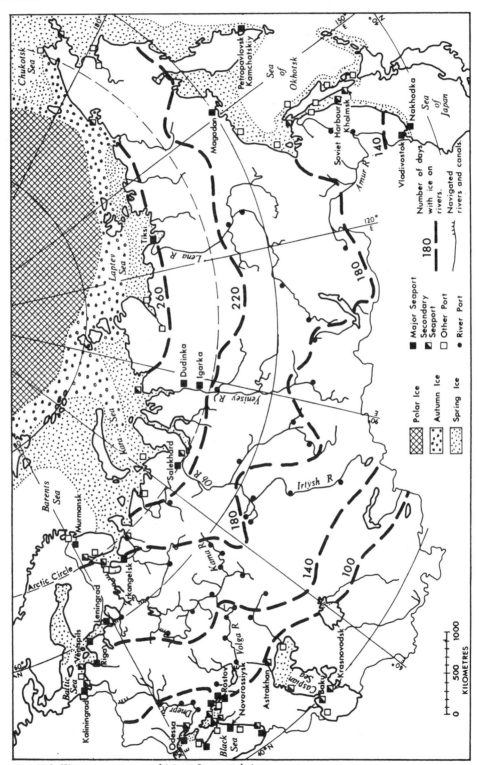

Fig. 11.2 Waterways, ports and icing of seas and rivers

sand by long shelter belts, a notable feature of the landscape in the steppe and even in parts of the farmed forest belt. The first were laid out along the Moscow–Gorkiy railway in 1861 against snow drift; by 1900 some 3982 km of track were protected by shelter belts and by 1950 the length exceeded 37 450 km. (23,371 miles). In the desert, protection against sand drift often requires belts extending up to 120 m from the track.

In the northern forest, there is a rough mantle of glacial debris where drier morainic ridges provide routes between the marshy hollows. The southern plains beyond the limits of glaciation have a cover of loessic materials, sands and clays into which gullying to varying degrees has taken place. Where this process has extensively developed, the steep-sided troughs are obstacles to the ready construction of roads and railways and require numerous bridges or culverts, while routes tend to become sinuous to avoid gullies or to follow them along their marshy floors. With a deep mantle of loosely consolidated material and few solid rock exposures, a problem is to find suitable aggregate for track ballast or road surfacing. Stone work is replaced by bricks (often air-dried in the south), but concrete is nowadays commonly used.

In the mountains and uplands, in addition to several of these problems there are other difficulties, and the choice of routes is generally more clearly defined by major relief features. The dissected plateau of central Siberia and mountainous north-eastern Siberia, immense undeveloped areas, are largely without roads or railways and rivers remain the main routeways linked together by convenient portages. The few roads are mainly for heavy lorries and there are primitive tracks and recognised 'winter roads'. Railway building can only be justified when traffic becomes large enough to warrant the high capital cost of construction. Numerous grandiose railway plans have been proposed for northern Siberia, but it is unlikely that many will warrant realisation. Essential communications are maintained by aircraft, and airfields are cheaper to build and to operate than land transport in these remote areas. Southern Siberia is a complex mass of old mountain structures and great tilted blocks of country, with particularly rough terrain east of Lake Baykal. The Trans-Siberian Railway circuitously traverses these Baykalian lands following river valleys and suitable low passes, while the new Baykal–Amur trunkline is being built through

similar rough terrain. Here are found some of the steepest gradients on Soviet railways, while the Trans-Siberian, the Kuzbas–Tayshet, and now the Baykal–Amur lines account for a substantial share of the total length of railway tunnels in the Soviet Union. There are also problems caused by patches of permafrost, especially in the wet lands of the Amur valley.

The north-south parallel ranges of the Ural, traditional divide between Europe and Asia, present no major obstacle, because their central section is low and open and there are a number of useful if restricted routes following well-defined valleys, such as that along the Chusovaya river, while the main north-south rail artery runs along the more open country on the piedmont edge of the eastern Trans-Uralian peneplain. In south-west European Russia, the Carpathian mountains have convenient passes of great historical and strategic significance allowing easy access to the Hungarian plains. Modern arterial roads and railways follow the central Veretskiy Pass, but the Uzhokskiy and Jablonka Passes also remain important.

The Caucasian isthmus is dominated by the alpine ranges of the Great Caucasus separated from the rugged Little Caucasus by a broad trough blocked at its western end by the granitic Suram range. Railways from the north follow the eastern and western coastal shelves into Transcaucasia, and the main east-west line from Batumi to Baku via Tbilisi takes a narrow and steeply graded route through the Suram range. Steep gradients are also found on the Tbilisi–Leninakan line, while on some branch lines reaching into the Great Caucasus, mainly to serve mountain health resorts, gradients are so steep that it is necessary to have rack working, adhesion being gained by gearing a cogwheel driven on an axle of the locomotive to a toothed rack set between the rails. The mountain tribes of the Great Caucasus were not finally subjugated by the Tsars until the latter part of the nineteenth century, and their military campaigns led to the building of some excitingly engineered roads across the mountains, notably the magnificent Georgian, Osetian and Sukhumi Military Highways.

In the mountains of Central Asia ancient routes linking China to Europe through the oases of the Silk Roads still exist, though some are little better than camel and mule tracks and in places follow gorge-like valleys along narrow ledges or even wooden catwalks, crossing torrents on simple but efficient wooden suspension bridges. The few railways found in these mountains usually follow well-defined valleys to reach large and fertile intramontane basins like the Fergana valley, but some modern roads have been engineered into the high and rugged Pamir territory of Gorno–Badakhshan. One ancient route whose strategic importance remains is through the Dzungarian Gate, leading from Kazakhstan into Chinese Turkestan, followed by a road and by a part-completed project for a railway from Aktogay in the USSR to Lanchow in China.

In Siberia, the great streams which rise in the southern mountains reach gigantic size in their lower courses along the shores of the Arctic Ocean. Large ocean-going vessels can sail 720 km up the Yenisey to Igarka, where the river is still over 5 km wide, but the Lena delta has many shallow and winding arms, and on the Pacific coast the Amur estuary is closed by a shallow bar. The rivers of the central Siberian uplands cannot be easily navigated since they have ungraded profiles, with strongly flowing rapids and narrow gorges in places. The great rivers present serious obstacles across the routes of roads and railways and long bridges are common, extending not only across the river but also across the flood plain regularly inundated by spring floods. Bridges over 60 m long form two per cent of the total number but 22% of the total length: for example, the Trans-Siberian Railway crosses the Yenisey on a bridge 854 m long, while the recently completed bridge across the Amur at Komsomolsk is over 1.5 km long.

Vehicle ferries for cars and lorries have long been common on most rivers where traffic has not warranted building a bridge and many settlements grew up round such a ferry. In winter, a crude roadway is laid across the ice. There has also been the use of ferries for railway traffic—the classic example was the short-lived ferry across Lake Baykal until completion of the Trans-Siberian Railway round the south shore. From the early 1950s a train ferry across the Strait of Kerch has provided a short cut from the Ukraine to north Caucasia, and from the late 1950s a train ferry has operated across the Caspian Sea from Baku to Krasnovodsk. Elsewhere reference is made to replacement of the train ferry across the Amur at Komsomolsk by a bridge and the introduction of a train ferry from Vanino to Sakhalin; a later addition has been the Ilyichevsk–Varna train ferry linking the Soviet Union to Bulgaria. Change-of-gauge wagons can also enter the Soviet Union using the train ferry from Travemünde in West Germany to Hangö in Finland.

TRAFFIC AND OPERATION OF TRANSPORT

It is evident from Tables 11.1 and 11.2 that in the percentage share of total national traffic—i.e. the *effort* of carrying goods or people—the railways predominate even though their overall share has tended to fall.* As a goods haulier, the railway fits Russian conditions well, because it is able to handle effectively and cheaply bulk freights (coal, ore, etc.) with reliability over the long distances necessary in the Soviet Union, reflected in an average haul of coal of 676 km in the Soviet Union compared to 80 km in the United Kingdom. The largest proportion of railway passengers is in commuting traffic, but this has been increasingly eroded by expanding bus services, while long distance passenger traffic has likewise fallen victim to air competition. There is reason to believe that the importance of railways has been artificially maintained by a strong railway lobby in Soviet government circles.

Compared to the Western world, road transport long made a poor showing in the Soviet Union, but growth in the 1970s was dramatic as big investment programmes in production facilities for vehicles and in roads began to pay off. Nevertheless, despite construction of such large plants as that for light vehicles at Tolyatti on the Volga and the Kama lorry plant at Naberezhnyye Chelny, the USSR still produces less than twenty per cent of the world's motor vehicles. Private car ownership, though growing vigorously, also lags well behind the industrial countries of the West, but the length of hard-surfaced road in the Soviet Union still remains at less than a tenth that in the United States which has a smaller area. Long distance road transport is little developed because of the poor, inadequate road network and because it cannot compete with railways over the distances required, besides being more likely to suffer

* Traffic is the effort of carrying a given volume of goods or passengers over a stated distance, e.g. one tonne-kilometre represents the effort of moving one tonne of goods over one kilometre distance. Originating tonnage or passengers represent the volume of goods or people to be moved irrespective of the distance they have to be carried.

TABLE 11.1 PERCENTAGE SHARE OF THE PRIME HAULIERS IN TOTAL NATIONAL TRANSPORT, 1913–1978

	Percentage share of total for the country				
	1913*	1940	1950	1960	1978
Goods Transport					
Railways					
Traffic	60.4	85.2	84.4	79.7	57.7
Tonnage originating	72.3	38.0	29.5	17.5	13.4
Roads					
Traffic	0.1	1.8	2.7	5.2	6.6
Tonnage originating	4.6	55.0	65.6	78.7	81.8
Shipping					
Traffic	16.3	4.9	5.5	6.9	13.9
Tonnage originating	6.8	1.9	1.1	0.7	0.8
Waterways					
Traffic	22.9	7.4	6.5	5.3	4.1
Tonnage originating	16.1	4.6	3.3	1.9	1.9
Airways					
Traffic	—	. . .†	0.02	0.02	0.05
Tonnage originating	—	. . .†	. . .†	. . .†	. . .†
Pipelines					
Traffic	0.1	0.7	0.7	2.7	17.6
Tonnage originating	0.2	0.5	0.5	1.2	2.1
Passenger Transport					
Railways					
Traffic	93.2	92.4	89.5	68.5	39.5
Passengers originating	94.4	66.5	51.1	14.5	5.9
Roads					
Traffic	. . .†	3.2	5.4	24.6	42.9
Passengers originating	. . .†	29.5	46.4	84.3	93.7
Shipping					
Traffic	3.0	0.8	1.2	0.5	0.3
Passengers originating	1.4	0.4	0.3	0.1	0.1
Waterways					
Traffic	4.0	3.5	2.7	1.7	0.7
Passengers originating	4.2	3.6	2.2	0.8	0.2
Airways					
Traffic	—	0.1	1.2	4.7	16.6
Passengers originating	—	. . .†	. . .†	0.1	0.2

* In contemporary boundaries   † Share too small to allocate.
Source: Narodnoye khozyaystvo SSSR v 1978.

seasonal disruption. Nevertheless, the transfer of all hauls of less than 50 km to roads from the railways is being undertaken. Table 11.1 reveals, however, that the greatest proportion of the total *originating* tonnage and passengers is handled by road transport (including trams and trolley buses), reflecting the predominantly short hauls involved, especially in towns or as feeder movements to railways in the countryside.

The most striking change has been in traffic handled by waterways, the traditional carrier, whose proportion of total freight traffic has fallen from nearly a quarter in 1913 to a little under 5 % currently, despite an increase in the originating tonnage and in traffic. An important factor has been the predominantly north-south alignment of the rivers while the present day major traffic flows are mostly on an east-west axis. The river is, of

A trolleybus line; Simferopol to Yalta, Crimea

TABLE 11.2 SOVIET FREIGHT TRANSPORT PERFORMANCE
(milliard tonne-kilometres)

	1928	1940	1955	1970	1978	1980
Rail	93.4	420.7	970.9	2494.7	3429.4	3439.9
Sea	9.3	24.9	68.9	656.1	827.7	848.3
Inland waterway	15.9	36.1	67.7	174.0	243.6	244.9
Pipeline	0.7	3.8	14.7	281.7	1099.1	1196.8
Road	0.2	8.9	42.5	220.8	395.2	432.3
Air	—	0.02	0.25	1.9	2.86	3.1
TOTAL	119.5	494.4	1165.0	3829.2	5947.9	6165.3

Source: Narodnoye khozyaystvo SSSR v 1978.

TABLE 11.3 TONNAGE OF MAIN COMMODITIES MOVED BY PRINCIPAL MEDIA *(million tonnes)*

	1970				1977			
	Rail	Sea	I.W.	Road	Rail	Sea	I.W.	Road
TOTAL	2,896.0	161.9	357.8	14,622.8*a* 3,810.0*b*	3,728.2	228.3	568	24,142 6,456
Coal	647.2	9.3	17.6	77.0	731.6	9.6	23.8	
Petroleum	302.8	75.1[1]	33.5	31.2	422.7	109.9[1]	41.3	
Metals	141.6	6.7	2.0	109.6	191.8	12.6	4.5	Not available
Timber	178.8	11.0[2]	91.2[4]	55.0	146.9	10.6[2]	71.2[4]	
Ores	245.6	13.6	—	13.0	315.7	18.8	—	
Building Materials (mineral)	691.0	15.3	180.9	1,322.9	956.5	18.6	378	
Fertilisers	70.9	5.5[3]	—	5.9[3]	115.8	8.1[3]	—	
Grain	106.1	6.5	6.8	116.3	135.2	8.0	6.5	

a All branches incl. farm transport   *b* Public Service transport
[1] incl. other liquid cargoes   [3] incl. other chemicals
[2] incl. 0.4 m. tonnes by raft   [4] incl. 20–25 per cent floating (raft etc.).
Sources: Narodnoye khozyaystvo SSSR v 1980: Transport i svyaz' SSSR (1972).

course, a cheap bulk carrier and should compete readily with railways, but unfortunately the long winter and spring period of disrupted river traffic and the summer low water period compare unfavourably with the reliability of the railway for 'moving belt' delivery and a much greater choice of route mobility. River systems are usually self-contained and canal construction to join systems together offers relatively limited possibilities and could be done only at great cost. Regionally, however, rivers do remain important, as, for example, the Volga, the Lena and the Yenisey, the latter two serving as the prime arteries of movement for large areas of Siberia.

Apart from some restricted waters which suffer little or no ice, sea transport is also markedly seasonal, with the interruption varying from a few days to many months. Because Soviet seas are separated from each other by long coastlines under foreign control, coasting traffic between them is negligible, but even within the individual seas it is poorly developed, except the Black Sea and the Sea of Azov. The growing trading relations with the world at large are increasing the importance of sea transport and account primarily for the rise in its share of total traffic. The Soviet merchant fleet has grown rapidly since 1945 and comprises mostly excellent modern vessels, many built in other countries. To conserve foreign currency, the Soviet Union has tried to carry as many of its cargoes as possible in its own vessels or those of East European socialist countries like Poland and the German Democratic Republic. Soviet *bloc* shipping has also taken an aggressive policy to get into Western markets for shipping services.

The growth of air transport has been particularly striking and the Soviet Union, with its great physical difficulties and vast distances, has become an unusually air-minded country. Not only is air travel over such great distances immensely quicker than land travel, especially in territories not served by railways, but it is also in many instances cheaper than first class rail travel. Aircraft are ideally suited to journeys across immense Siberian lands lacking roads and railways, so that air transport has been recognised as a key to the economic development of these remoter areas, where the helicopter has begun to play a major role. If the Soviet Union were to offer positive encouragement for foreign airlines to operate across its territory which lies astride many excel-

lent great circle routes from Europe to the Far East and Australasia, or from western North America to India and Africa, the role of air transport could increase very greatly. International connections are operated principally via Moscow by Aeroflot and foreign airlines, as for example, between Europe and Pakistan, India and the Far East across Central Asia or Siberia, while connections exist at Moscow between these services and North America and Africa.

Pipelines, a cheap means of moving gaseous and liquid freights, also reduce the burden on other forms of transport. It is estimated that the Friendship Pipeline from the Ural–Volga oilfields to the East European socialist countries has released some 10 000 20-tonne tank cars on the railways, while pipeline transport costs one third of railway traffic. The development of both the large Ural–Volga oilfields and the immense oil and gas deposits of western Siberia has resulted in the laying of long pipelines to refinery and consuming centres, just as long gas lines have been laid from Central Asia to the Ural industrial towns and from northern Caucasia to the Moscow region and to Leningrad, as described in Chapter 8. Even in 1913 there were 1100 km of pipeline in Russia; by 1946, the length reached 4400 km and by 1966, 29 400 km to which could also be added 47 000 km of gaslines. By 1980 there were 69 700 km of oil pipelines and 132 000 km of gaslines.

In the Soviet Union, the share of the different means of transport in the total traffic is conditioned not only by their economic and technological suitability to handle particular traffics but also by the allocation of tasks and of resources determined by central planning policy, with special attention given to the eradication of wasteful crossflows or duplicated movements of the same or interchangeable goods. The planners have also aimed to minimise the demand on the limited transport capacity available by reducing as far as possible the contrasts in levels of development between planning regions. Wide differences still remain, however, and will continue to do so because of the widely variant potential of the different regions. Density of the transport network in any region is, therefore, a crude index of the degree of current development. It is not surprising that the densest transport network is in European Russia, south of Leningrad and west of the Volga, where on one sixth of the country's area live two-thirds of the Soviet population, the core of the so-called 'settled triangle' whose base lies between the Baltic and the Black Sea and whose apex rests in western Siberia.

In recent years Soviet literature on transport has been concerned to emphasise that within the Soviet Union there is a 'unified system of transport', where the role of each mode of transport is fully co-ordinated to eliminate wasteful effort. The emphasis is placed on transport as an integral constituent of the economic infrastructure, a vital link in the chain of production though itself not regarded as 'productive'. It is claimed that the systematic and proportional development of the Soviet economy conditions the rational development of transport, both in terms of inter-media relations and in the regional provision of a transport system. This system is regarded as 'unified' because each mode of transport is combined into a structure where it performs the tasks it can best undertake and it is not in unnecessary competition with other media. As noted, the effort is directed at achieving the requirements for movement of goods and people by the most economical investment in the transport infrastructure: it is essentially a 'minimum input–maximum output' equation. Each movement is regarded as a specific flow from origin to destination for which the most economical 'media mix' is set up in relation to parameters such as distance, volume, frequency and orientation. All movement is classified on a scale ranging from 'local' to 'interregional', 'national or trunk' and 'international'.

We must consequently look at the overall transport map in this light. The basic framework is composed of railways, though in the remoter regions of Siberia and Central Asia, lorry roads and rivers form a continuation to these routes, and in places, they are also continued by shipping on the peripheral seas, as in the Black Sea, the Baltic, the Caspian, the Arctic basin and the Pacific coast. In the more thickly settled areas, particularly within the 'settled triangle' already described, this basic framework is augmented by an interstitial transport system of feeder services, mostly provided by road transport but including some branch railways and even rivers. Airways may be seen as superimposed on this framework of surface transport for special tasks, though in particularly remote regions (for example, in the Arctic and northern Siberia), air transport essentially provides a continuation of the main framework.

The railways

Though the first railway ran from Pushkin to Leningrad in 1837, it was not until completion of the Leningrad–Moscow mainline in 1851 and the Leningrad–Warsaw railway in 1861 (later extended to Vienna) that development began in earnest. These were quickly followed by lines built to replace old portages linking river systems and, during the latter 1860s, by lines from the grainlands of the Ukraine to carry grain to Baltic and Black Sea ports or to the Moscow region, where several short branches also served the central black-earth lands. By 1872 the Volga had been reached, after which railways began to appear in the Ural in the latter 1870s. In 1892, construction of the Trans-Siberian Railway from Chelyabinsk started: it had reached Krasnoyarsk five years later and Irkutsk in 1898. In 1905, the train ferry across Lake Baykal was replaced by a through railway route along the precipitous southern shore, but railway communication entirely across Russian territory to Vladivostok was not opened until 1916 with completion of the Kuenga–Khabarovsk section, following the loss of control over the Chinese Eastern Railway across Manchuria via Mukden.

The last 20 years of the nineteenth century saw a great burst of railway building: there was rapid growth of the railway system in the industrial south, focused on the Donbas where in 1884 a vital line from the Donbas coalmines to the iron ore mines of Krivoy Rog had been completed. Between 1881 and 1899, the Trans-Caspian Railway from Krasnovodsk to Tashkent had been built in Central Asia, primarily for military reasons in the conquest of this territory. A link from this area to the Volga was established in 1905 by the opening of the Trans–Aral Railway, able to carry Central Asian cotton to the growing textile industry of the Moscow region. This was also a period of railway building in Transcaucasia, but these railways were not linked to the rest of the system in Europe until 1900. In 1913, 80 % of the 70 000 km of route was in European Russia.

Unlike the rest of Europe and North America, where building trunk routes had virtually ended by 1914, trunk line construction continues in the Soviet Union and since the Revolution the Turksib (Turkestan–Siberian), Yuzhsib (South Siberian) and the long Sredsib (Central Siberian) railways have been completed and steady progress has been made on the greatest project of all, the

A mainline train passing through the Donetsk coalfield

new Baykal–Amur trunkline. In the 50 years of Soviet power, the length of railways has almost doubled, with the bulk of new building in the eastern regions, especially in western Siberia and Kazakhstan.

THE BAYKAL–AMUR TRUNKLINE
Indicative of the major part still played by railways in the Soviet transport scene is the fact that the central task begun in the tenth Five Year Plan has been to build a trunk railway some 3 200 km long between the Lena river and the Amur at Komsomolsk on a trajectory some 150–300 km north of the existing Trans-Siberian Railway by 1983. The concept of this line dates back to the years when Court Witte was planning the original Trans-Siberian Railway, because at this period American interests were trying to wrest a concession from the Tsar for a railway along roughly the same northern alignment as the present project. This so-called Siberian–Alaskan Railway would have, however, branched in the Bureya basin, one route going south to Khabarovsk and the other north to the Amur delta at Nikolayevsk and then along the coast to the Chukotsk Peninsula.

The idea was again revived in the 1920s and an actual survey made and work began on branch lines north from the Trans-Siberian Railway to give access to points along the proposed trajectory from which constructional work would begin. By the mid-1930s the Never-Tynda, Izvestkovaya–Urgal and Volochayevka–Komsomolsk lines were being built, but work halted in 1941 and the Never–Tynda line was dismantled and the rails

sent to build strategic railways near Stalingrad. The whole project had been revealed in the third Five Year Plan of 1938, where the details of the so-called Baykal-Amur Trunkline to duplicate the Trans-Siberian Railway were set out. Priority was given to the western section from Tayshet on the Trans-Siberian to the river Lena at Ust-Kut, for the railway was needed to carry constructional materials for the great hydro-electric barrage at Bratsk on which work was to begin, but the threat which the Japanese posed to the Amur section of the Trans-Siberian from their hold on Manchuria gave an added urgency to this new trunkline.

Little subsequent information about the project was released by the Russians and Western observers assumed work was continuing in a low key, using prisoner-of-war or forced labour. This was partly true: in 1945, news came of completion of a railway from Pivan opposite Komsomolsk across the Sikhote Alin to a new port, Sovetskaya Gavan, on the Tatar Strait. In 1947, it was announced that the line from Tayshet to Bratsk was complete and by 1950 the Lena river had been reached, while by the mid-1950s the line from Izvestkovaya to the Bureya coalfield near Urgal was ready.

The silence about work on the rest of the railway now seems to have been because of major revision of its trajectory, especially between the Lena and Lake Baykal and on the Vitim—Laba section, where increased knowledge of the topography, physical geography and resource wealth called for new surveys. The resurvey seems to have been completed about 1961 and resulted in a southward shift of the alignment compared to the pre-war original. Some of the change appears to arise from more advanced technology and better constructional methods now available that make tunnel-building more acceptable, so allowing distances to be shortened by avoiding circuitous valley routes and by cutting directly through mountains instead of finding trajectories with acceptable gradients across them. The basic plan remained, however, for a single track route, though this was now to be built for eventual double track electrification. Use of diesel instead of the original steam traction also allowed changes in the original plans for operating sections and for maximum gradients.

In 1973, the main project was reactivated with reconstruction of the line to Tynda on an improved trajectory from the Trans-Siberian Railway, while the train ferry across the Amur from Komsomolsk to Pivan was replaced by a 1.5

km-long bridge. As lines like that from Abakan to Tayshet and from Khrebtovaya to Ust–Ilimsk were completed, the work teams were transferred to the Baykal-Amur trunk route. Work on the easternmost sector from Urgal to Komsomolsk is already well advanced and the section from Ust-Kut to Tayura (site of a bridge across the Lena) and some way beyond is complete, though the route from the Lena to Nizhneangarsk is one of the most difficult sections requiring a bridge across the Lena and a trajectory through the Baykal mountains. Since 1971 work has been under way on several major civil engineering structures notably a 15 km-long tunnel under the North Muy range and a rather shorter one through the Baykal mountains, though it now appears that pre-liminary work on these had begun in the late 1950s. To cope with the rising traffic supplying the construction gangs at the western end, the Tayshet–Ust-Kut line has been double tracked and electrified.

The task of building this railway is immense, for it runs through virgin tayga and across large swamps, besides having to cross seven mountain ranges, with some exceeding 3000 m in elevation. About 40 % of the route is across ground affected by permafrost, while between Lake Baykal and the Olekma river seismic problems have to be over-come. Constructional and operational difficulties arise from the climate, with temperatures below −50°C in winter and over 35°C in summer. In such empty country, all constructional workers have to be brought in and housed in special camps, so that provision of the necessary infrastructure (e.g. living accommodation, medical, welfare and educational facilities as well as roads) has to be completed before major work on the railway itself can begin. Some survey and work teams in the remotest parts are entirely dependent on air support (mostly by helicopter). Work has been pressed into the tayga from the railheads at Ust-Kut, Tynda, Urgal and Komsomolsk, but the underdevelopment of the territory through which the line is to pass is such that a main settlement is planned approximately every 50 km, with stations and passing places at 20 km intervals. The double track passing places will be between 3 km and 12 km in length, to make passing and overtaking at speed possible. All traffic will be centrally controlled, with radio communication used on trains and at stations. Because of the extreme climatic conditions, special diesel and electric locomotives will be needed.

Even now the extension of this line westwards from Bratsk to the foot of the Ural mountains is being discussed, while the bridge across the Amur at Komsomolsk and a train ferry from Vanino near Sovetskaya Gavan to Kholmsk on Sakhalin Island (whose railway system has been expanded by completion of a north-south trunk route) suggest a new interest in the Far East.

RAILWAY OPERATIONS

Operating conditions on Soviet railways are eased by the generally low gradients prevailing, so that three-quarters of the route length has gradients gentler than 1 : 166 while less than one-fiftieth of the route length has gradients steeper than 1 : 60; some three-quarters of the route is straight track. Over large areas of the plains, the fact that Russian railways have been constructed as cheaply as possible has had little adverse effect on gradients or the radius of curves, but in rougher terrain such cheapness of original construction has made it impossible to avoid severe gradients and sharp sinuous curves. This makes long-term operating costs higher than if more had been spent initially on civil engineering works and keeps down per-missible speeds and axle loads and consequently the density of traffic.

Rapid growth in traffic in the 1950s and 1960s had demanded heavier, faster and more frequent trains without the expensive provision of alterna-tive routes or doubling of track, except in special cases, so that faster and more powerful motive power was seen as an important clue to the solution of the problem. The steam locomotive at this time reigned supreme (Table 11.4) except for a few routes where special circumstances prevailed,

TABLE 11.4 PROPORTION OF FREIGHT TRAFFIC HANDLED BY DIFFERENT TYPES OF RAILWAY TRACTION

Year	All forms of traction	Electric	Diesel	Steam
1940	100	2.0	0.2	97.8
1950	100	3.2	2.2	94.6
1960	100	21.8	21.4	56.8
1966	100	42.0	46.8	11.2
1975	100	51.2	48.2	0.6

Source: Nikolskiy, I. V. *Geografiya transporta*, Moscow 1979.

because its operating reliability, simple maintenance and its initial cheapness to build, besides the
ready availability of fuel, more than offset its low
thermal efficiency and water supply problems in
arid or permafrost areas or even its limited
operating radius. One solution was obviously
more powerful steam locomotives, but if these had
rigid frames it meant much heavier axle-loads and
greater radius curves (including points and station
trackwork) which demanded strengthening the
track and civil engineering works, using better
ballast and heavier rails. Time and cost and the
added demand for steel to carry out such work
eliminated such a solution, because even the need
to lengthen passing places and sidings for longer
trains and to provide additional passing places for
faster and more frequent services imposed sufficient strain on constructional work and rail
production. Existing track standards could have
been maintained by using articulated steam locomotives, but these were disproportionately more
costly to build and more complicated to maintain,
while their power/weight ratio was not com-
pensatingly better.

A strikingly better power/weight ratio could
only be obtained using electric or diesel traction. A
rapid improvement in the supply of petroleum, as
output in the Ural-Volga oilfields expanded, encouraged the use of diesel locomotives, either as an
interim measure on routes marked for electrification or as a replacement for steam on lightly
loaded routes where electrification was not considered economic. Diesel locomotives had been used
in the early 1930s in the oil-producing areas of
Trans–Caspia, but they found little favour until
after 1945 when Russian-built locomotives were
developed from imported American proto-

types. These locomotives have demonstrated a
better thermal efficiency in cold weather and make
possible a 90 % water saving (important in water
shortage areas) compared to steam locomotives.

Blessed by Lenin, electrification has always had
substantial support in the Soviet Union, so that
electric traction was planned for main trunk routes
where the high cost of installation could be quickly
recovered. It has, however, been dependent on
current generating capacity available along the
selected routes, and the several large power
stations under construction in southern Siberia
favoured the choice of the Trans-Siberian route as
the largest single project envisaged, with the
optimal conditions of very heavy traffic and
available current supply. Similar factors have
underlain electrification of arterial routes in
European Russia, and this has also been applied
on commuting lines around some of the largest
towns. The Soviet authorities have favoured electrification at 25 KV, because this system allows
industrial current to be used without costly sub-
stations and is also economical in copper for the
overhead wires (copper has been in relatively short
supply in the Soviet bloc). Electrified sections still
account, however, for only 30 % of the total route,
but they handle, nevertheless, 52 % of all freight
traffic.

Soviet railway operation is a mixture of
American and European practice, with a rising
frequency of heavier and faster trains, but as is
characteristic of most railway systems, traffic
density is very unevenly spread over the network.
Some 86 % of all freight traffic is carried by 46 % of
the total route length, while the 28 % of route
length which is double track handles no less than
67 % of all freight traffic. Loadings of some

TABLE 11.5 GOODS TRAFFIC ON RAILWAYS BY TYPES OF FREIGHT

	Total traffic (milliard tonne-km.)	Coal and coke %	Petro- leum goods %	Ferrous metals %	Wood %	Grain %	Ores %	Mineral building materials %	Mineral fertil- iser %
1913	65.7	19	5	—	8	15	—	—	—
1928	93.4	20	7	5	12	16	3	—	—
1940	415.0	26	9	6	11	8	5	7	1
1950	602.3	29	9	8	12	5	5	8	1
1960	1504.3	22	14	7	14	6	5	10	2
1970	2494.7	17	14	8	12	4	7	12	3
1980	3439.9	18	13	8	7	4	7	13	4

Source: Narodnoye khozyaystvo SSSR, various years.

sections are particularly heavy and the average freight traffic density on Soviet railways is among the world's highest.

Tables 11.3 and 11.5 reflect the predominance of heavy bulk goods on the railways, but, as might be expected, the share of coal in the traffic has fallen and its place has been taken by petroleum, while compared with pre-Soviet times, grain has also declined, though there has been an increase in mineral building materials and chemical fertilisers. Despite attempts to keep the length of haul down, there has been a slow upward trend, with some goods moving very great distances (e.g. cotton moving over 3000 km) but all hauls are exceptionally long by western European standards. Careful planning of freight movements on such hauls is important because of the great amount of empty running which may result if return freights are not available, though some wagons (e.g. tank cars) necessarily have to be allowed to run empty on return. Originating tonnages show some remarkable concentrations at a few goods yards or railway directorates on the system: reputedly half the coal loadings are by the railway directorates of the Donets and Western Siberia (Kuzbas), while 20 % of all ferrous metal semi-finished goods are shipped from three yards (Magnitogorsk, Sartan in the Donbas and Zaporozhye), and 55 % of all iron ore shipments come from the Dnepr Directorate.

Passenger traffic, (Tables 11.6 and 11.7) regarded as less important, has risen by little over ten times since 1913 compared to a 44-fold increase in freight traffic. A third of the passenger traffic is in commuting and over 90 % of the originating passengers are commuters, with an average journey of 29 km. The average non-commuting journey is 598 km. The Moscow commuting sphere, served by 1200 pairs of trains a day, extends up to

TABLE 11.7 NUMBER OF PASSENGER JOURNEYS (millions)

	Rail	Inland waterway	Bus, etc.	Sea
1940	1377	73.4	590.0	9.7
1965	2301	133.9	18 656.6	37.2
1970	2930	145.2	27 343.8	38.5
1980	3559	138.0	42 175.9	51.7

Source: Narodnoye khozyaystvo SSSR v 1980.

167 km (e.g. to Kalinin) and handles well over 750 000 travellers in each direction daily. Passenger service frequencies otherwise are generally poor. On secondary lines there is usually one train a day (often a mixed train) in each direction. On trunk routes there may be between seven and twenty trains in each direction daily, though only on selected sections do the best trains exceed 72 km/hr. Moscow, with nine terminal stations, dispatches 200 long distance trains daily with about 150 000 passengers in the summer season, a much busier season for travellers than winter. Short distance railway journeys are being eroded by buses, while very long distance trips are being taken over by air competition. A problem of long distance trains is that one train in each direction daily may need as many as 20 or more sets of carriages to operate the service. The through carriages from Adler in the Caucasus to Vladivostok take 204 hours for the journey!

A dominant T-shaped distribution is seen in the principal flows of both goods and passenger traffic (Figs. 11.3 and 11.4). There is a main north-south artery, with interchange between the industrial South (chiefly the Donbas) and the North-West (mostly from Leningrad and environs), passing through the Central Industrial region at the western end (chiefly around Moscow and its satellites) of the major east-west artery. The main east-west artery from the Moscow region joins the Volga lands to the Ural and Siberia. The bulk of the remainder of the system acts as a feeder to this T-shaped arterial core. Railway traffic between the Soviet Union and its neighbours, with the exception of Finland, has been hampered by a difference in gauge, with 1524 mm in Russia* and elsewhere 1435 mm, European standard gauge; but since

TABLE 11.6 SOVIET PASSENGER TRANSPORT PERFORMANCE (milliard passenger-kilometres)

	1928	1940	1955	1970	1980
Rail	24.5	100.4	141.4	265.4	332.1
Sea	0.3	0.9	1.5	1.6	2.5
Inland Waterway	2.1	3.8	3.6	5.4	6.1
Bus, etc.	0.2	3.4	20.9	202.5	389.8
Air	0.0	0.2	2.8	78.2	160.6
TOTAL	27.1	108.7	170.2	553.1	891.1

* Since January 1972, this 'traditional' gauge has been modified to 1520 mm, a simpler metric measure.

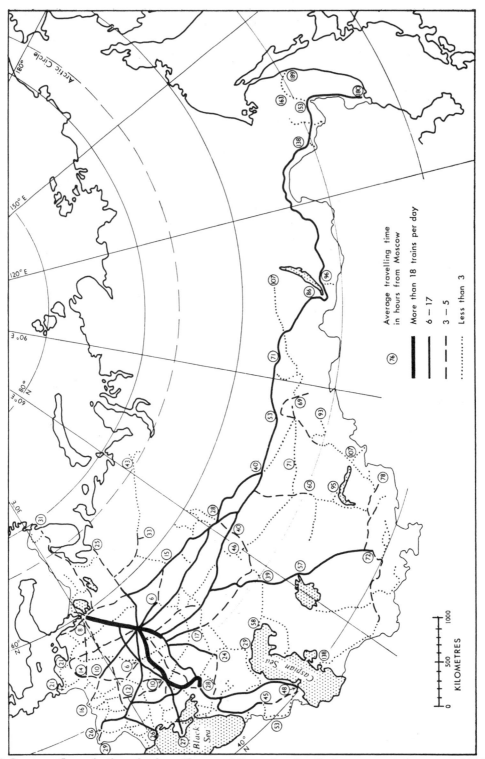

Fig. 11.3 Dominant flows of railway freight traffic, annual figures based on Soviet sources relating to period 1960–65

A railway station on the Trans-Siberian Railway

1945 efficient methods of changing the gauge on wagons and carriages have been developed. There are now through passenger workings from Moscow to several European capitals and these are also possible to Peking and Pyongyang. Increasing shipments of coal and ores to Poland, Hungary, Czechoslovakia and the German Democratic Republic have been handled by large Soviet hopper wagons run on to overhead gantries at frontier points (e.g. Chop, Przemysl and Terespol) to empty into European standard gauge wagons, but the large demand of the new East Slovakian Ironworks at Košice for ore and coal has been solved by building an 80-km long broad-gauge railway across the Czechoslovak border to the plant. Soviet railways have been active in promoting use of containers and a regular service of container trains across the Trans-Siberian Railway now handles traffic between Japan and Europe. Highly competitive in cost and delivery time with sea transport, the main constraint is the capacity of terminal facilities and trains to cope with rising demand.

The roads

The earliest 'roads' in Russia were vaguely defined tracks (*trakty*) that shifted across broad avenues of country as sections became impassable because of mud, dust or rutting. The first ballasted road did not appear until 1817 while no true road linked Moscow and Leningrad until 1834. Traditionally, roads served only as feeders to the rivers or across portages. Even today, motorable roads do not penetrate into every corner and do not even link the country right across from west to east. Road transport is most important in and around towns and in the less developed parts of the country like Siberia or Central Asia, where railways have not yet been built and where roads are frequently described as 'routes without rails'. There are still only 31 km of hard surfaced road per 1000 km^2. This varies between republics, however, from 14 km per 1000 km^2 in the Turkmen SSR to 534 km per 1000 km^2 in the Estonian SSR. Choice of surface is, however, difficult since intense winter frost and bad drainage over large parts of the country are peculiarly damaging: preference remains for grit rather than for tar or cement, though dust is a problem in summer. In the northern forest, 'corduroy' roads made of tree trunks covered by grit are laid and in the swamps 'winter roads' are roughly staked out across what in summer is impassable morass. Unembanked grit or earth roads turn into quagmires in the

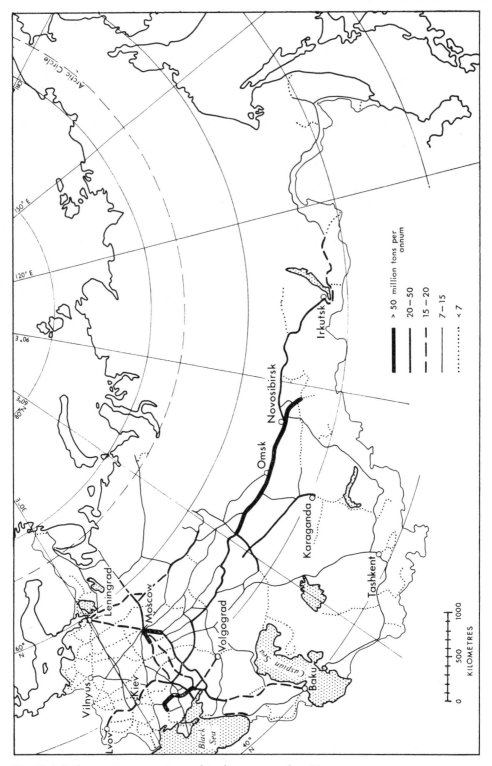

Fig. 11.4 Railway passenger services and isochrones centred on Moscow

A public service bus in the mountains, Tadzhikistan

rasputitsa, as the German motorised columns found to their cost in the campaigns of 1941–43. Snow and ice add to winter hazards, while in arid areas there are hazards from gullying, washouts and drifting sand, and roads are often lined for great distances by shelter belts.

The country west of the Volga contains a widely meshed but expanding system of roads designed for comparatively fast traffic over long distances and used by inter-city lorries and buses, but once away from these roads, most country roads are merely tracks. East of the Volga, the mesh of roads is much wider than west of the river and few high quality routes exist. In Siberia, a reasonable system exists in the south, notably along the railway zone, but even here some local systems are interlinked only by a single road while in eastern Transbaykalia and Amuria, the local systems are not even interlinked and movement between them depends on the railway. A better developed system exists in the Maritime Kray of the Far East, radiating from Vladivostok, and the Ussuri Highway runs north to Khabarovsk. In north-eastern Siberia, a road runs from Magadan to the mines of the upper Kolyma and to Yakutsk, from which a good road (the Aldan Highway) runs to the Trans-Siberian Railway at Never. Regular if infrequent bus services operate on these roads in Siberia. In Central Asia and in Caucasia are numerous interlinked local systems carrying bus and lorry traffic and reference has already been made to the well-engineered mountain highways in these areas.

In both town and country, traffic is dominated by buses and lorries, and light motor cars are mostly taxis, but trams and trolley buses operate in many towns. The local nature of road haulage is reflected in an average goods haul of 14 km and an average bus journey of under 7 km. Of the goods originating, building materials and the collection and distribution of goods to and from railway stations and river quays are the main items. Horse carts are still seen in provincial towns and the countryside, while camels are used in Central Asia, and in the tundra and forest lands of Siberia, reindeer and dog teams remain a common means of native transport.

The waterways
From the earliest times rivers were used in the Russian lands: Scandinavian contact with Byzantium was first established via the Volkhov, Lovat and Dnepr rivers—in Nestor's words, the 'route from the Varangians to the Greeks'—while the later conquest of Siberia similarly moved along one river system and across a convenient portage to the next. Several of the great historical towns of Russia (e.g. Smolensk) owe their importance to being astride portages. Until the coming of the railways, rivers like the Dnepr and the Volga carried grain from the lands in the south producing surpluses to the food-deficit areas of the north: the Volga boatmen's song records the harshness of getting the heavily laden boats upstream. To link the systems together, a few simple canals were built in the late eighteenth and early nineteenth centuries, but these fell into disuse in the railway age. Some have been replaced by modern canals, where traffic has justified the great cost, though these have also commonly been associated with electricity generation or irrigation as well as navigation. Examples are the Volga-Don Canal (1954), making possible voyages from the Volga and Caspian to the Sea of Azov and the Black Sea; and the Volga-Baltic canal (1964), which replaced the old Mari canal, opening up the possibility of a voyage from the Caspian via the Volga to the Baltic. In the interwar years, a series of short canals were built to join together the lakes of the Karelian isthmus and form a waterway from the Baltic to the White Sea, while a current plan among other schemes projects a major waterway link from the Dnepr via the Pripyat and Bug to the Vistula.

Improvements in navigation and large hydro-technical schemes sometimes create undesirable side-effects. Even modest dredging or straightening out meanders can affect the local water table, but large schemes usually include barrages that inundate extensive areas which have to be cleared of settlement or even forest. By slowing the flow of water, such schemes can mean longer periods with ice, or, by altering the thermal regime of the water, affect fauna and flora. It has been claimed that the vast new Volga barrages have held back so much water from the Caspian that they have helped to accelerate its naturally induced fall in water level, so that former anchorages like Prorva are now dry and a special channel has to be dredged to the Volga delta port of Astrakhan. The reduced inflow has meant less nutrients for fish, while some species spawning in the Volga have had their breeding habits upset by the change in the thermal gradient.

Two-thirds of all river-borne freight traffic is on the Volga–Kama waterways. The two principal freights are timber (including firewood) and mineral building materials (including cement), but on the Volga–Kama system, petroleum products are an important element: average length of haul is about 450 km. Despite the cheapness of river transport and its ability to handle very large quantities, official encouragement to use rivers and suitable tariff-rigging have not been strikingly successful and river transport has shown the lowest growth rate of all forms of transport. Unfortunately the long winter freeze and other delays interrupt traffic and users have to hold large stocks to tide them over or rely on available surplus railway capacity at such times, both difficult to achieve in the Soviet economy. River passenger traffic is also under competition from faster hauliers, unless these are absent (as in parts of Siberia), but average journey distance is surprisingly short at about 35 km.

Sea transport

Sea transport plays relatively little part in the internal transport system of the Soviet Union, but a substantial increase in goods and passengers moved reflects the growing contact with the outside world. Despite the great length of the Soviet coastline, some 42 000 km, giving a frontage on several seas, political and economic conditions, quite apart from the problems of physical background, have made sea transport relatively unattractive. Traffic from one Soviet sea to another (e.g. from the Baltic to the Black Sea) has been insignificant because of the long and circuitous distances between them. The Northern Sea Route along the Arctic coast, with serious inherent physical difficulties confronting navigation, has

The harbour at Yalta

not provided a really usable 'Soviet Canal' from western to eastern waters. Transport on both a local and an international scale has therefore been organised generally on the ports of each sea individually.

In the Black Sea—Sea of Azov, 55 % of the traffic is to non-Soviet ports and 45 % to Soviet ports on the same or other seas. Some 80 % of the traffic is petroleum, ores or coal: Tuapse, Batumi and Novorossiysk send petroleum to Odessa, Kherson and other Ukrainian ports, while coal moves from Zhdanov to Odessa and Poti, with manganese ore shipped from Poti to Ukrainian and Danubian ports; but there are also shipments of cement and grain from northern Caucasian ports, and Transcaucasian ports send semi-tropical fruits and tea in return for grain, salt and timber from Ukrainian ports and the Don estuary. Odessa is a major port for overseas passenger journeys.

The Baltic is particularly important for its traffic to North Sea and Atlantic ports. About 40 % of all coal, grain and metals exported from the Soviet Union pass through Baltic ports, as well as 30 % of all timber and manufactured goods, while the Baltic handles Ural–Volga petroleum brought by pipeline to a terminal at Ventspils. Leningrad is one of the largest Soviet ports. From the Barents and White Seas are shipped large amounts of northern timber and minerals such as apatite from the Kola peninsula, but 70 % of the traffic is coastwise.

The seas of the Pacific coast supply outposts of settlement in north-east Siberia and also maintain services with Sakhalin, so that 80 % of the turnover is local coastwise traffic. Timber, petroleum, fish products, salt and general goods are the main cargoes. Vladivostok, the main port, is nowadays closed to foreign vessels, which use Nakhodka, fortunately ice-free longer, and another new port has been built nearby at Vostochnyy. An oil terminal at Moskalvo on Sakhalin ships petroleum to Japan and south-east Asian buyers.

The Northern Sea Route, operated by scheduled services since 1935, is open for 70–120 days each year, though the shallow Vilkitskiy Strait may be closed throughout some summers by grounded icebergs and the Laptev Sea has very bad ice and fog conditions most summers. The route is used by about 100 ships each season, even though comparatively few pass through its whole length. Igarka and Dudinka on the Yenisey ship wood

and minerals, while the eastern parts also ship minerals but most services are for victualling Arctic settlements. Attempts to get more use of the costly investment in the Northern Sea Route by opening it to foreign vessels has not been successful, because the charges for pilotage, etc., and the conditions of passage have been unattractive to foreign shippers between the Atlantic and Pacific. With the Suez Canal back in use, and quick services for containers across the Trans-Siberian Railway, this arctic route will be even less of interest. Of the traffic on the inland Caspian Sea, 85 % is petroleum, but there are also movements of wood, minerals, fish and salt, and there is also some passenger traffic.

Air transport

In time and monetary saving, great distance favours air transport, so that an average haul of 1000 km for passengers and 1310 km for goods reflects this advantage, though the number of passengers and the tonnage originating are both small compared to the railways or roads. Physical conditions in the Soviet Union favour flying: large flat spaces are available for airfield construction; there is a lack of serious relief obstacles; and there are long periods of anticyclonic conditions with still air and good visibility in winter, though greater turbulence and poorer visibility characterise summer.

Since the first scheduled civil airline opened in 1923 from Moscow to Gorkiy, state policy has encouraged air-mindedness. The state airline, *Aeroflot*, one of the world's largest operators, has a virtual monopoly of both internal services and Soviet international traffic, but there are a few specialised operators, like the Chief Administration of the Northern Sea Route. In all, some 908 000 km of route are flown (700 000 km within Soviet borders), moving over 93 million passengers and 2.7 million tonnes of goods and mails. Besides the main trunk routes flown by jet airliners, there is an elaborate system of secondary routes served by more modest machines, and aircraft are widely used in maintaining contact with Arctic stations, winter ice observations at sea, forest fire surveillance, agricultural work (as noted in Chapter 7), helping reindeer herders to find pasture and muster their herds, while aircraft are reputedly even used in wolf-hunting! The principal international traffic centre is Moscow, which has four airports, but other important internal centres

Tupolev Tu 134 airliner of Aeroflot on display in the Exhibition of Economic Achievement in Moscow

are the Union Republic capitals and such cities as Novosibirsk, Sverdlovsk, Irkutsk, Khabarovsk, Kharkov, Kuybyshev and Volgograd. Equipment is supplied by a well established Soviet aircraft industry as discussed on page 172.

A study of transport is a useful way of appreciating the problems inherent in the vastness of the USSR, for distance remains one of the most difficult problems to surmount in welding the huge and differing major economic regions of the country into an effective economic and political unit spread across continental dimensions.

In making comparisons between the Soviet Union and other parts of the world, care must be taken to make allowance for these dimensional contrasts and the harshness of the physical environment. It would be false to think, for instance, that continued predominance of the railway indicates technical backwardness—it has been shown that for physical and technical reasons neither road nor river transport can serve the country's needs as effectively as the railway raised to a high technical level.

BIBLIOGRAPHY

Armstrong, T. (1952), *The northern sea route*, Cambridge UP, Cambridge.

Armstrong, T. (1975), 'The northern sea route,' in Symons and White (eds.), 1975, pp. 127–141.

Biryukov, V. (1980), 'The Baykal-Amur mainline – a major national construction project,' *Soviet Geography*, **21**, pp. 225–270.

Blackman, J. H. (1957), *Transport development and locomotive technology in the Soviet Union*, Columbia.

Briliant, L. A. (1975), *Geografiya morskogo sudokhodstva*, Transport, Moscow.

Crouch, M. (1979), Problems of Soviet urban transport, *Soviet Studies*, **31**, pp. 231–256.

Danilov, S. K. (1977), *Ekonomicheskaya geografiya transporta SSSR*, Transpechat, Moscow.

Dubrowsky, H. J. (1975), *Die Zusammenarbeit der RGW – Länder auf dem Gebiet des Transportwesens*, Berlin.

Dubrowsky, H. J. (1963), Ekonomicheskiye svyazi i transport, *Voprosy Geografii*, **61**, Moscow.

Galitskiy, M. I. *et al* (1965), *Ekonomicheskaya geografiya transporta*, Moscow.

Garbutt, R. (1950), *Russian railways*, Sampson Low, London.

Greenwood, R. H. (1975), 'The Soviet merchant marine,' in Symons and White (eds.), pp. 106–126.

Hunter, H. (1957), *Soviet transportation policy*, Harvard UP, Cambridge, Mass.

Hunter, H. (1968), *Soviet transport experience: its lessons for other countries*, Brookings Inst., Washington.

Kalinin, U. K. *et al* (1970), *Obshchiy kurs zheleznikh dorog*, Moscow.

Kazanskiy, N. N. *et al* (1969), *Geografiya putey soobshcheniya*, Moscow.

MacDonald, H. (1975), *Aeroflot, Soviet air transport since 1923*, Putnam, London.

Malashenko, V. (ed.) (1977), *The great Baykal–Amur railway*, Moscow.

Medvedkova, E. A. and Misevic, K. N. (1978), 'Die Erschliessung der BAM-Zone unter ökonomisch–geographischen Aspekten,' *Petermanns Geographische Mitteilungen*, **122**, pp. 37–43.

Mellor, R. E. H. (1959), 'Motive power and its problems on Soviet railways,' *Locomotive*, **65**.

Mellor, R. E. H. (1964), 'Some influences of physical environment on transport problems in the Soviet Union,' *Advancement of Science*, **20**.

Mellor, R. E. H. (1976), *Die Sowjetunion. VI–das Transportwesen*. Harms Erdkunde, List Verlag, Munich.

Mellor, R. E. H. (1975), 'The Soviet concept of a unified transport system and the contemporary role of the railways,' in Symons and White (eds.), 1975, pp. 75–105.

Miller, E. B. (1978), 'The Trans-Siberian landbridge—a new trade route between Japan and Europe,' *Soviet Geography*, **19**, pp. 222–243.

Nikolskiy, I. V. (1960, 1978), *Geografiya transporta SSSR*, Moscow, 1960, 2nd edition, 1978.

Parker, W. H. (1979), *Motor transport in the Soviet Union*, Research Paper 23, School of Geography, Oxford.

Sarantsev, P. L. (1957), *Geografiya putey soobshcheniya*, Moscow.

Shafirkin, B. I. *et al* (1971), *Ekonomicheskiy spravochnik zheleznodorozhnika*, Moscow.

Slezak, J. O. (1963), *Breite Spur – Weite Strecken*, Transpress, Berlin.

Spring, D. (1975), 'Railways and economic development in Turkestan before 1917,' in Symons and White, (eds.), 1975, pp. 46–74.

Stanislavyuk, V. L. (ed.) (1977), *Razvitiye yedinoy transportnoy seti SSSR v desyatoy pyatiletke*, Moscow.

Symons, L. (1975), Soviet air transport, in Symons and White, (eds.) 1975, pp. 142–163.

Symons, L. (1975), 'Soviet civil aviation—objectives and aircraft,' in Fallenbuchl, A. M., *Economic development in the Soviet Union and Eastern Europe*, I, *Reforms, technology and income distribution*, Praeger, New York, 1975, pp. 221–237.

Symons, L. and White, C. (eds.) (1975), *Russian transport: an historical and geographical survey*, Bell, London.

Tonyaev, V. I. (1977), *Geografiya vnutrennykh vodnykh putey*, Transport, Moscow.

Tupper, H. (1965), *To the Great Ocean*, Secker and Warburg, London.

Westwood, J. N. (1964), *History of Russian railways*, Allen and Unwin, London.

Westwood, J. N. (1963), *Soviet railways today*, Ian Allan, London.

White, C. (1975), 'The impact of Russian railway construction on the market for grain in the 1860s and the 1870s,' in Symons and White, (eds.), 1975, pp. 1–45.

12 The regions

The larger a country's territory, the more difficult it is to organise and develop that territory in a planned, integrated and comprehensive manner, a fact which applies whatever form of economic and political system may be adopted. In the case of the Soviet Union, which is the world's largest state and where a planned and highly centralised economy is one of the most noteworthy features, these difficulties are particularly significant. It is not surprising therefore that, throughout the period since the Revolution, special attention has been paid in the USSR to the matter of regionalisation and numerous systems have been devised for dividing the country into regions of various kinds as a framework for administration, planning and economic development.

ADMINISTRATIVE DIVISIONS

Administrative divisions of the USSR fall into two categories: those which, in addition to their administrative function, also have political status and are directly represented in the organs of central government, and those which are solely administrative and are thus not represented. In the first category we have the *Soviet Socialist Republic*, the *Autonomous Soviet Socialist Republic*, the *Autonomous Oblast* and the *Autonomous Okrug*, while the second category involves two units, the *Oblast* and the *Kray*. The two types together form a complex, multitiered hierarchy, which is shown diagramatically in Fig. B (p. 4). Within this hierarchy, each level is subordinate to the one above it and the degree of administrative autonomy which an area enjoys depends on its position in the hierarchy.

Political-administrative divisions

Table 12.1 gives a full list of the 53 political-administrative divisions within the Soviet Union, are mapped in Fig. A (p. 2). At the summit of the hierarchy, of course, stands the Soviet Union itself or, to give it its full title, the Union of Soviet Socialist Republics (USSR). The highest legislative and administrative body of the USSR is the Supreme Soviet, which comprises two chambers: the Soviet of the Union and the Soviet of Nationalities. The Soviet of the Union is elected by universal adult suffrage, and for this purpose the whole country is divided into electoral districts, each with a population of about 300 000. Membership of the Soviet of Nationalities, however, is based on the division of the country into the various political-administrative units discussed below, which are themselves based primarily on the nationality of the local population. Each Union Republic sends 32 deputies to the Soviet of Nationalities, each Autonomous Republic sends 11, Autonomous Oblasts five and Autonomous Okrugs one member each. The aim of this system is to ensure that, since all measures must be passed by both houses, the interests of the smaller nationalities are not overwhelmed by those of the larger groups. Thus, for example, both the Armenian republic, with a population of less than 3 million, and the Russian republic, with 135 million, are equally represented in the Soviet of Nationalities, to which they send 32 members each. In the Soviet of the Union, on the other hand, the Russian republic will have over 400 members and the Armenian republic nine or ten.

The USSR is a federation of 'Union Republics', at present numbering 15. The largest of these, the

TABLE 12.1: POLITICAL–ADMINISTRATIVE DIVISIONS OF THE USSR, 17 JANUARY 1979

Key No.*	Division	Area 000 km²	Population (000's)	Capital
USSR		22 402.2	262 442	Moscow
	Soviet Socialist Republics			
I	Russian SFSR	17 075.4	137 552	Moscow
II	Ukrainian SSR	603.7	49 757	Kiev
III	Belorussian SSR	207.6	9 559	Minsk
IV	Lithuanian SSR	65.2	3 399	Vilnius
V	Latvian SSR	63.7	2 521	Riga
VI	Estonian SSR	45.1	1 466	Tallin
VII	Moldavian SSR	33.7	3 948	Kishinev
VIII	Georgian SSR	69.7	5 016	Tbilisi
IX	Azerbaydzhanian SSR	86.6	6 028	Baku
X	Armenian SSR	29.8	3 031	Yerevan
XI	Kazakh SSR	2 717.3	14 685	Alma–Ata
XII	Kirgiz SSR	198.5	3 529	Frunze
XIII	Tadzhik SSR	143.1	3 801	Dushanbe
XIV	Uzbek SSR	447.4	15 391	Tashkent
XV	Turkmen SSR	488.1	2 759	Ashkhabad
	Autonomous Soviet Socialist Republics			
16.	Bashkir ASSR	143.6	3 848	Ufa
17.	Buryat ASSR	351.3	901	Ulan–Ude
18.	Dagestan ASSR	50.3	1 627	Makhachkala
19.	Kabardino–Balkar ASSR	12.5	675	Nalchik
20.	Kalmyk ASSR	75.9	293	Elista
21.	Karelian ASSR	172.4	736	Petrozavodsk
22.	Komi ASSR	415.9	1 118	Syktyvkar
23.	Mariy ASSR	23.2	703	Yoshkar–Ola
24.	Mordov ASSR	26.2	990	Saransk
25.	North Osetian ASSR	8.0	597	Ordzhonikidze
26.	Tatar ASSR	68.0	3 436	Kazan
27.	Tuvinian ASSR	170.5	266	Kyzyl
28.	Udmurt ASSR	42.1	1 494	Izhevsk
29.	Checheno–Ingush ASSR	19.3	1 154	Groznyy
30.	Chuvash ASSR	18.3	1 293	Cheboksary
31.	Yakut ASSR	3 103.2	839	Yakutsk
32.	Kara–Kalpak ASSR	165.6	904	Nukus
33.	Abkhaz ASSR	8.6	506	Sukhumi
34.	Adzhar ASSR	3.0	355	Batumi
35.	Nakhichevan ASSR	5.5	239	Nakhichevan
	Autonomous Oblasts			
36.	Adygey AOb	7.6	404	Maykop
37.	Gorno–Altay AOb	92.6	172	Gorno–Altaysk
38.	Yevreysk (Jewish) AOb	36.0	190	Birobidzhan
39.	Karachayevo–Cherkess AOb	14.1	369	Cherkessk
40.	Khakass AOb	61.9	500	Abakan
41.	South Osetian AOb	3.9	98	Tshinvali
42.	Nagorno–Karabakh AOb	4.4	161	Stepanakert
43.	Gorno–Badakhshan AOb	63.7	127	Khorog

*As used in Fig. A, page 2.

Autonomous Okrugs*

44.	Aga–Buryat AOk	19.0	69	Aginskoye
45.	Komi–Permyak AOk	32.9	173	Kudymkar
46.	Koryak AOk	301.5	34	Palana
47.	Nenets AOk	176.7	47	Naryan–Mar
48.	Taymyr (Dolgano–Nenets) AOk	862.1	44	Dudinka
49.	Ust–Orda Buryat AOk	22.4	133	Ust–Ordinskiy
50.	Khanty–Mansiy AOk	523.1	569	Khanty–Mansiysk
51.	Chukot AOk	737.7	133	Anadyr
52.	Evenki AOk	767.6	16	Tura
53.	Yamalo–Nenets AOk	750.3	158	Salekhard

* National Okrugs Until 1977.
Source: Narodnoye Khozyaystvo SSSR v 1978 godu, Moscow 1979.

Russian republic, has been referred to as 'a Union within a Union' on account of the large number of subordinate units which it contains, a situation reflected in its cumbersome title of the Russian Soviet Federated Socialist Republic (RSFSR). This covers about three-quarters of the country, including the Russian homeland in the east European plain together with the whole of Siberia and the Far East, regions of Russian colonisation where people of Slav origin are in an overall majority. The RSFSR has large thinly populated areas and its inhabitants comprise some 52% of the total Soviet population. 82% of those living in the RSFSR are Russians; the remaining 18% include representatives of virtually every other Soviet nationality, some numbering several millions.

The remaining 14 Union Republics, officially Soviet Socialist Republics (SSRs), fall into a number of regional groupings, the arrangement of which reflects the distribution of the larger and more advanced non-Russian peoples of the USSR as discussed elsewhere in this volume (Chapter 6). The 15 Union Republics purport to be partners in a voluntary political association and, in theory at least, each has the right to secede from the Union. This theoretical right has a significant effect on the political-administrative structure of the USSR for it means that no SSR can be established which does not have a boundary with the outside world. Political divisions in the interior of the country can never be raised to SSR status since they would then have the right to secede, thus creating the possibility of the 'political anomaly' of an independent state completely surrounded by the remaining territory of the USSR, a situation unacceptable to Soviet theorists.

Subordinates to the Union Republics within which they lie are the Autonomous Soviet Socialist Republics (ASSRs). At present these number 20, of which 16 are in the RSFSR, two in Georgia and one each in Azerbaydzhan and Uzbekistan. These units, too, tend to occur in clusters, indicating the distribution of important minority groups. There are six ASSRs in the zone between the middle Volga and the Urals, a region inhabited by various Finno-Ugrian and Turkic peoples, another eight in the Caucasus and Transcaucasia, two in the north European section of the RSFSR and three in Siberia. Finally there are eight Autonomous Oblasts (AOb) and 10 Autonomous Okrugs (AOk.; until 1977 known as National Okrugs, NO), representing smaller and less advanced minority groups. The majority of these are in Siberia and there are several in the Caucasus. Autonomous Okrugs occur only in the RSFSR.

Although these political-administrative divisions are named after particular national groups, it should not be imagined that each is inhabited solely by one group or that it contains all the members of one group. Long-continued migration movements within the Soviet Union have ensured that every areal unit has an ethnically mixed population. In particular, since the dominant migration movements have been from the European to the Asiatic parts of the country, the Slavs, especially the Russians, are found in sizeable numbers in most areas. In the case of the SSRs, the titular group (i.e. the group after whom the republic is named) is in a majority in all but two cases, the exceptions being Kazakhstan, where Kazakhs are outnumbered by Russians, and the Kirgiz SSR where the Kirgiz, though still the largest group, form less than half that republic's population. In the great majority of the lower-grade units, the titular group is very much in a minority. An extreme example is provided by the Yevreysk (Jewish) AOb, which had a 1970 population of 172 449 of whom only 11 452 were in fact Jews (0.5 % of all Soviet Jews) and 144 286 were Russians. A further point is that the system of political-administrative divisions is flexible and an area may be raised to a higher status as its population grows and its economy develops. Demotion is also possible, and a number of ASSRs were abolished in the late 1940s on the grounds that their populations had collaborated with the enemy. However, the present pattern of political-administrative divisions has remained unchanged since the early 1960s.

Administrative divisions

In addition to the four types of political-administrative division discussed so far, there are two other units which are purely administrative and economic in function and are not represented in the Soviet of Nationalities, though they often form electoral districts sending deputies to the Soviet of the Union. These are the Oblast and the Kray, of which there were 121 and six respectively in 1979. Those parts of the RSFSR which do not enjoy ASSR status, together with the majority of SSRs (the exceptions are the smaller republics—Lithuania, Latvia, Estonia, Moldavia, Georgia, Azerbaydzhan and Armenia) are divided into oblasts, which are the basic units of local government. The boundaries of these units are shown in Fig. A. The organising centre of an oblast is usually an industrial centre of some importance from which the oblast takes its name (Moscow oblast, Kiev oblast, Karaganda oblast, etc.). The half dozen krays, which occur only in the RSFSR, now have functions similar to those of the oblast. The lowliest political units, the AOb and the AOk, are in fact subordinate, as far as local government is concerned, to the ASSR, oblast or kray in which they are situated.

Below the level of the ASSR, oblast and kray are a variety of smaller units. The country is divided into 3196 rayons which contain 41 511 village soviets, 2089 towns (the larger of which are further subdivided into urban rayons) and 3 863 'settlements of urban type'.

ECONOMIC DIVISIONS

In addition to the system of political and administrative regionalisation outlined above, there is a second, parallel system by which political and administrative divisions are grouped to form various kinds of economic regions. The details of this second type of regionalisation have undergone several major changes during the Soviet period, reflecting changes in the attitudes of Soviet planners towards the principles on which economic regions are based. Throughout most of the period since the Revolution there have been at least two levels of economic regions, of which the more stable has been the division of the country into a relatively small number of large units known as Major Economic Regions. Their actual number has varied between 13 (Fig. 12.1) and 23; the present division is into the 19 units shown in Fig. 12.5, which have remained unchanged since the mid-1960s. These are essentially economic planning regions and are also the basis for the tabulation of economic and other data in various official statistical publications. In addition, Soviet geographers frequently use the Major Economic Regions as the main regional divisions in their textbooks.

Economic–administrative areas

The lower tier of economic regions, because they have usually consisted of small groups of administrative units, are often referred to as economic-administrative areas, and it is these which have been subject to the most frequent changes, particularly in the 1950s and 1960s.

Until 1957, the economic-administrative areas were simply the smaller political and administrative units already described, namely the oblasts, krays, ASSRs and small SSRs. In practice, under the highly centralised forms of political and economic organisation characteristic of the Stalin period, these units had very little economic autonomy. They were responsible only for the organisation of agriculture and of 'industries of local importance', the greater part of their economic activities being under the direct control of the various government ministries in Moscow.

In 1957, however, as a result of Khrushchev's desire to decentralise control of the economy, the economic powers of economic-administrative areas were much enhanced by the establishment of the *Sovnarkhoz* system, under which the country was divided into 105 Sovnarkhoz regions (Fig.

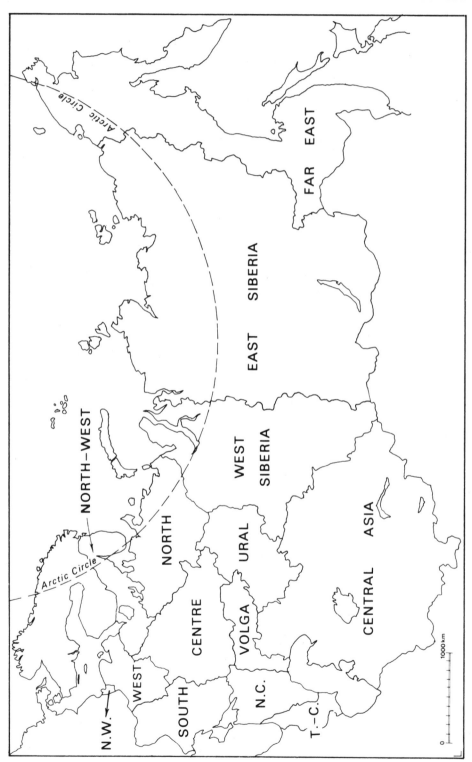

Fig. 12.1 Major Economic Regions, 1940–1960

12.2). The majority of these comprised a single oblast, kray, ASSR or SSR, but in a few cases several oblasts were amalgamated to form one of these units. Each Sovnarkhoz region was given planning, managerial and budgetary responsibility for practically all forms of economic activity within its boundaries, and only a few items, such as the construction of major hydro-electric plant and the defence industries, remained under centralised control. At the same time, the various production ministries, each responsible for a particular industry throughout the country, were abolished.

In the early 1960s, it was decided that the decentralisation of economic control had gone too far, and that the Sovnarkhoz regions were too small for efficient management of the economy. Consequently they were re-grouped into 47 larger units known as Industrial Management Regions (Fig. 12.3) and for a while it appeared likely that these would provide a long-term solution to the regionalisation problem and would perform both planning and managerial functions. In 1965, however, there were further moves back towards centralisation. The regional economic councils which had been in charge of the 47 regions were abolished and the central industrial ministries re-established. Since the mid-1960s, the economic powers and functions of the administrative divisions have again been very restricted and the control of industry has remained in the hands of some two dozen ministries, each responsible for a particular industry over the USSR as a whole. To avoid the excessive centralisation of the Stalin period, however, some of the powers of these All-Union Ministries have been devolved to Union-Republican Ministries responsible for a particular industry within a single republic, and much greater responsibility has been given to the managements of individual farms, factories and other economic enterprises.

Major Economic Regions
Throughout these changes, the Major Economic Regions have remained in being, though their boundaries have been altered on several occasions (Figs. 12.1, 12.4 and 12.5), and are still used for economic planning (as distinct from management) purposes and as 'standard regions' for data tabulation. Before proceeding to a discussion of each of these regions, a brief consideration of the general pattern (Fig. 12.4) is necessary. It will be seen that, in many cases, the boundaries of the Major

Economic Regions coincide with those of the Union Republics, and it is in fact a general rule that political-administrative boundaries must be preserved intact in any system of economic regionalisation. Thus, while an economic region may be a sub-division of an SSR, or may unite several SSRs, no economic region may be established which takes part of one republic and joins it to another republic.*

These regions vary greatly in size and there is a marked contrast between the relatively small, compact units of the more densely settled European part of the country and the small number of very large units in the Asiatic sector. As Table 12.2 indicates, the variation in population size is less marked. While regions (excluding the special case of Moldavia, which is 'a republic outside the system of Major Economic Regions') range in area from 6.2 million km² (Far East) to 110 700 km² (South), their populations vary between 6.8 million (Far East) and 28.9 million (Centre).

The attitude of Soviet economic planners towards the form and functions of the Major Economic Regions has varied. At different times they have extolled the virtues of both regional self-sufficiency, whereby each region attempts to produce the widest possible range of agricultural and industrial commodities thus lessening its dependence on other regions and reducing the volume of inter-regional freight traffic, and of regional specialisation with each region concentrating its efforts on producing, for the country as a whole, those commodities which it can most easily supply. In reality, neither complete regional self-sufficiency nor complete regional specialisation is possible, or even desirable. The resource base of each region is unique, and there are inevitable shortages of particular commodities in each region which can only be made good by 'imports' from other regions. At the same time it would be most illogical, in a country the size of the USSR, to concentrate production of a particular commodity in a single region if that commodity is required throughout the country. In practice, the 'choice' between regional self-sufficiency and regional specialisation has never been a true choice but a matter of emphasis on one or other of the two

* A single exception to this rule has been allowed in the case of the Kaliningrad oblast, a detached portion of the RSFSR annexed from Germany in 1945, which has been placed in the Baltic economic region.

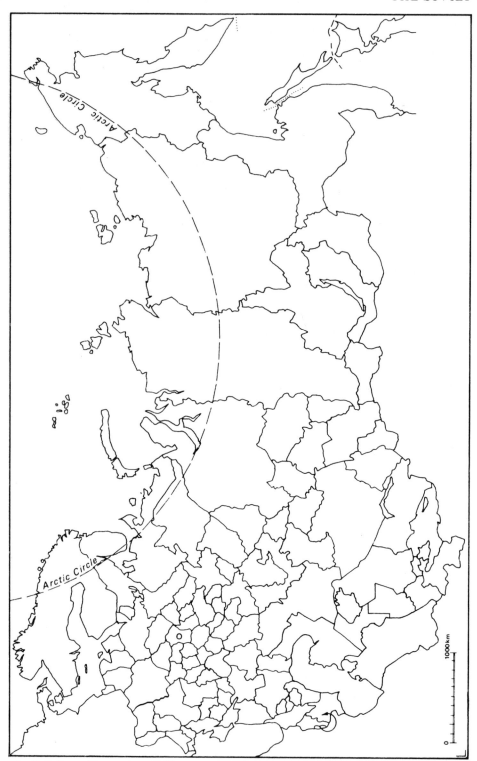

Fig. 12.2 Sovnarkhoz regions, 1957

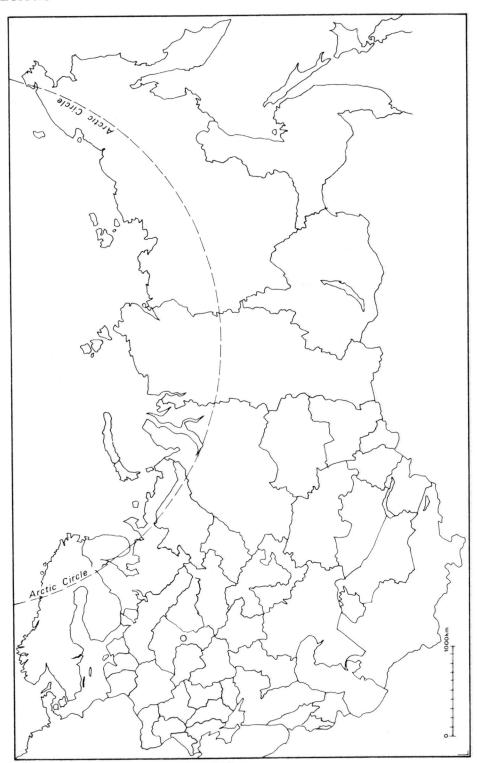

Fig. 12.3 Industrial management regions, 1963

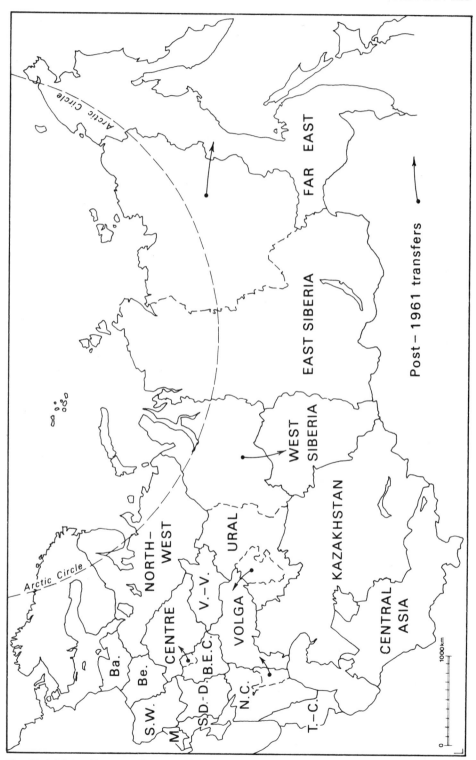

Fig. 12.4 Major Economic Regions, 1961

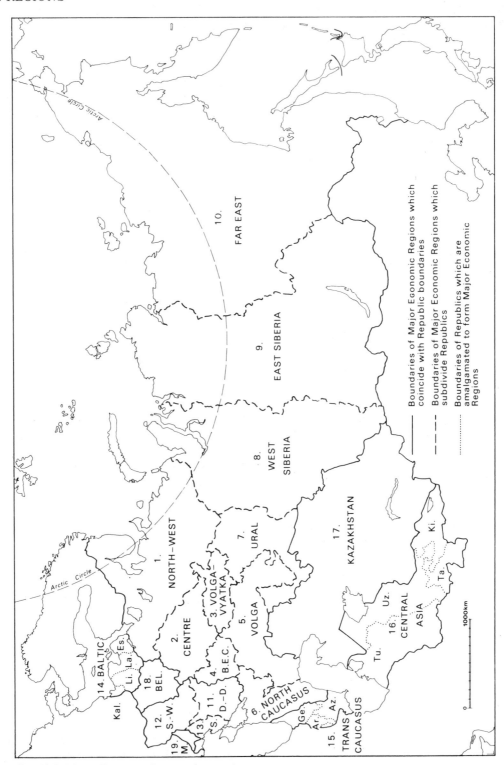

Fig. 12.5 Major Economic Regions (current)

TABLE 12.2: MAJOR ECONOMIC REGIONS, 17 JANUARY 1979

Region	Area 000 km^2	%	Population 000	%	per km^2	urban %	Sown %
1. North-west	1 661.8	7.4	13 275	5.1	8.0	79.5	1.9
2. Centre	485.2	2.2	28 947	11.0	59.7	78.4	30.1
3. Volga–Vyatka	263.2	1.2	8 343	3.2	31.7	62.3	27.0
4. Black Earth Centre	167.7	0.8	7 797	3.0	46.5	52.1	65.9
5. Volga	680.0	3.0	19 393	7.4	28.5	65.6	41.9
6. North Caucasus	355.1	1.6	15 487	5.9	43.6	54.9	43.9
7. Ural	680.4	3.0	15 568	5.9	22.9	74.4	24.1
8. West Siberia	2 472.2	10.8	12 959	4.9	5.2	67.7	7.7
9. East Siberia	4 122.8	18.4	8 158	3.1	2.0	68.7	2.0
10. Far East	6 215.9	27.8	6 819	2.6	1.1	74.5	0.5
11. Donets–Dnepr	220.5	1.0	21 045	8.0	95.4	75.4	63.6
12. South-west	269.8	1.2	21 578	8.2	80.0	47.1	48.1
13. South	110.7	0.5	7 134	2.7	64.4	62.8	59.4
14. Baltic	189.1	0.8	8 192	3.1	43.3	66.2	28.0
15. Transcaucasia	186.1	0.8	14 075	5.4	75.6	55.4	13.4
16. Central Asia	1 279.3	5.7	25 480	9.7	19.9	40.7	5.1
17. Kazakhstan	2 715.1	12.1	14 685	5.6	5.4	53.9	13.1
18. Belorussia	207.7	0.9	9 559	3.6	46.0	55.0	30.0
19. Moldavia	33.7	0.2	3 948	1.5	117.2	39.3	52.9
USSR	22 402.2	100.0	262 440	100.0	11.7	62.3	9.8

Source: *Narodnoye khozyaystvo SSSR v 1978 godu*, Moscow, 1979.

extremes. As a broad generalisation we can say that, in the inter-war years, the emphasis favoured regional self-sufficiency and this was reflected, for example, in the establishment of small steel industries in the Far East and Central Asia. Since the mid-1950s, much more attention has been paid to relative costs of production (including transport costs) at different locations, resulting in a greater emphasis on regional specialisation. As evidence of this, we may note the division of the Centre region of the inter-war years into a smaller, predominantly industrial Central Region and a mainly agricultural Black Earth Centre, or the separation of the industrial Donets–Dnepr region of the Ukraine from the predominantly agricultural South-west and South.

Recent statements by Soviet authors bear witness to the fact that, while regional specialisation remains the dominant theme, each region aims at a diversified economy. Implicit in their arguments is the idea that no system of regions can be permanent, and that boundaries must change as the economy develops and new patterns of economic activity emerge. It remains to discuss the present regions individually, to indicate their relative importance to the Soviet economy and to assess

the extent to which they fulfil the requirements of the theorists.

THE MAJOR ECONOMIC REGIONS

(1) The North-West

This is the largest of the European regions and also the one with the lowest population density and the smallest proportion of cultivated land. It contains a number of diverse elements. The greater part, including Karelia, the Kola peninsula and the basins of the Northern Dvina and Pechora rivers, is remote and inhospitable, with a coastal tundra belt and large areas of coniferous forest and swamp. Consequently agriculture is of little significance and the traditional activities are reindeer herding, fishing, hunting and lumbering. However, this part of the region also contains valuable mineral resources which have been vigorously exploited over the past 40 years, including coal, oil and natural gas in the Pechora basin (Komi ASSR), bauxite in the valley of the Onega river (Arkhangelsk oblast) and nickel, iron ore and apatite in the Kola peninsula. There are valuable hydro-electric sites in Karelia.

The south-western part of the region, including the Leningrad and neighbouring oblasts, is very different. Although wholly within the tayga belt, this zone is more densely settled and contains the bulk of the region's farmland. However, agricultural potential is limited by the harsh climate and the large stretches of poorly drained land so that much food has to be brought in. Leningrad, with 4.6 million inhabitants, is the second city of the Soviet Union, contains a third of the entire population of the north-western region and is a major industrial complex concerned with a wide variety of engineering activities, particularly those of the more highly skilled kind, and produces ships, machinery, electrical equipment, chemicals, textiles and consumer goods.

The north-western region thus contributes to the Soviet economy in a variety of ways. First and foremost it is a source of primary products, notably timber, fish, furs, coal, oil, natural gas and metallic minerals. Secondly it plays a major role in the country's foreign trade through its ports of Leningrad, Murmansk and Arkhangelsk. Thirdly it contains an important centre of manufacturing industry, supplying goods which are used throughout the country. The main internal transport links help to connect the diverse parts of the region. The railways to Arkhangelsk and Murmansk carry imports and exports and tap the minerals of the Kola peninsula; the Vorkuta-Kotlas line, built during the Second World War and now paralleled by oil and gas pipelines, carries fuel and timber from the remote north-east to the Leningrad industrial complex, to the Baltic republics and to the Centre.

(2) The Centre

The Centre, which appears quite small on a map of the Soviet Union but is in fact nearly as large as France, is among the most densely populated and highly urbanised regions. Its pre-eminence in so many branches of the Soviet economy has been achieved despite a lack of natural resources. The Centre has no coal, oil or natural gas, though there are large deposits of lignite and peat, and its hydro-electric potential is small. There are only modest iron ore deposits and no other minerals apart from mineral salts. Lying for the most part in the mixed forest belt, the Centre has a greater agricultural potential than areas further north but climate and soil conditions are inferior to those of more southerly regions.

The Centre is a region which benefits more from its location than from its natural wealth. It owes its importance, as its name suggests, to its centrality with respect, not to the territory of the Soviet Union as a whole, but to the more densely settled and highly developed European section, and to its historical function as the organising centre of the Russian Empire and the USSR. It was this region which became the political focus of the Empire from the sixteenth century onwards, and its centrality was confirmed, after the Revolution, by the choice of Moscow as the capital and by the establishment there of the most important organs of the highly centralised Soviet state.

The centrality of the region is most clearly expressed in the pattern of communication, both old and new, all of which tends to focus on Moscow. At the time when movement across the European plain was largely by water, the region had easy access to the main arteries, particularly the Volga, and it contains some of the earliest canals built to link the various rivers. When, in the late nineteenth century, rivers and canals were largely (but never entirely) replaced by railways, the network took a radial form centred on Moscow, which thus gained direct links with all parts of the Empire. Similar developments have occurred in recent decades with respect to the modern road system—it was the roads radiating from Moscow which were the first to be improved. Again, the highly developed network of internal airlines focuses on Moscow and provides a means of rapid contact with all parts of the Union. Other forms of modern 'transport'—electric power lines, oil and gas pipelines—though they cannot perhaps be said to centre on Moscow, feed into the region the power supplies necessary to maintain its varied and growing industries. Thus Moscow sits at the centre of a spider's web of communications and the Centre as a region benefits enormously.

Until the opening up of the steppelands in the nineteenth century, the Centre was the most densely populated part of the Empire, and its large population provided the necessary labour for the development first of handicrafts and then of mechanised factory industry. This has given the region a tradition of skilled craftsmanship and technological innovation which has enabled it to take the lead in many of the most sophisticated branches of modern industry.

The growth of urban populations as a result of industrialisation stimulated agricultural development. Some 30 % of the land area is under crops, a proportion exceeded only in the steppelands, and the land is devoted to what are, by Soviet standards, highly productive systems of mixed farming, producing large quantities of meat, milk and vegetables. There is scope for further expansion of agriculture, particularly by means of swamp reclamation, but it is highly unlikely that the Centre could ever approach agricultural self-sufficiency and large quantities of foodstuffs, particularly grain, must be brought into the region.

The heavy industrial base is relatively small and the region produces less than 10 % of the country's steel. Although the iron ores of the Tula district support the production of some pig iron, there are large 'imports' of ore, pig iron, steel and coal, mainly from the Ukraine, though metal comes increasingly from the Black Earth Centre (see below). The Ukraine is also the main source of grain, so that the Centre's main inter-regional linkages are with its southern neighbours.

The Centre contributes about a quarter of all Soviet engineering products, among which the most important are machine tools, scientific instruments, transport equipment, machinery for the textile and other light industries, electrical equipment and consumer goods of all kinds. The region is also responsible for about 70 % of Soviet production of textiles. Particularly noteworthy is its dominant position in the cotton industry, which persists despite the need to import all the raw material from Central Asia. Over the past two decades, with the building of oil and gas pipelines, the Centre has also become of major importance in the rapidly-expanding chemical industry.

The Centre thus has links with practically every other region of the USSR, drawing food, fuel and raw materials from a very wide area and supplying its manufactures to all parts of the country.

(3) The Volga–Vyatka Region

There would appear to be little logic in the separation of this region from its neighbours. Its western part (the Gorkiy oblast) straddles the Volga and is in many ways an eastward continuation of the Central industrial region. Gorkiy, with a population of 1.3 million, is the fifth largest city in the Soviet Union and is a major engineering centre and a large-scale producer of motor vehicles. Power is derived from large hydro-electric stations on the Volga and from thermal stations

based on local peat and on oil from the Volga–Ural field.

The more easterly parts of the Volga–Vyatka region are relatively thinly settled and less developed economically. This applies particularly to the large Kirov oblast, which is, however, an important source of timber. Agriculture is fairly intensive along and to the south of the Volga, supplying meat, vegetables and dairy products to the towns of the region, but is much less productive to the north and east. Like the Centre, the Volga-Vyatka region as a whole relies heavily on outside sources of food and raw materials, supplying manufactured goods in return.

(4) The Black Earth Centre

One of the smallest of the 19 regions, the Black Earth Centre is among the more densely populated. At the same time it is one of the least urbanised—although the urban proportion has much increased in recent years—and has a higher proportion of its land under crops than any other region. As its name suggests, the Black Earth Centre lies mainly in the zone of chernozem soils and the wooded steppe and steppe vegetation belts. Thus conditions for agriculture are, by Soviet standards, particularly favourable and the region is characterised by highly productive mixed farming which supplies large quantities of wheat, sugar beet, sunflower, meat and dairy products and supports a dense rural population.

Although agriculture is still the dominant economic activity in this region, the situation is changing. Small-scale iron mining has long been carried on in the vicinity of Lipetsk and during the past decade this activity has expanded rapidly in several localities on the basis of the vast reserves of ferruginous quartzite contained in the 'Kursk Magnetic Anomaly'. Situated midway between the Donbas and the Centre, the Kursk Magnetic Anomaly already supplies iron ore to both these and is also supporting increased steel production in the Black Earth Centre itself. A major integrated plant has been built at Lipetsk and others are planned. There remain the problems of power supplies, which are a major weakness, but there is easy access to Donbas coal and oil and gas pipelines from the Volga and North Caucasus pass through the region. One of the earliest atomic power stations in the USSR has been built near Voronezh.

The towns of the Black Earth Centre are

growing rapidly and the large rural population has provided a labour force for industrialisation, leading to a high rate of rural depopulation. At present, engineering, chemicals and food processing are the main branches of manufacturing industry.

(5) The Volga Region

This large region comprises a collection of administrative divisions ranged along the Volga river from Kazan to the Caspian Sea. It also includes the Bashkir ASSR, formerly part of the Ural region, which in 1963 was transferred to the Volga economic region in order to unite the main producing districts of the Volga–Ural oilfield within a single economic unit. This transfer is of considerable significance as an indication of the greater attention now being paid to regional specialisation.

The Volga river has long been a major transport artery linking the industrial regions of the Urals (via the Kama and Belaya tributaries) and Centre with the grainlands of the steppe and, via the Caspian sea routes, with the Caucasus and Central Asia. This link function was enhanced in the 1950s by the construction of the Volga-Don canal connecting the Volga region to the Donbas and the Black Sea. Traffic along the river thus included industrial raw materials, oil, foodstuffs and manufactured goods from many different regions. In addition, major rail routes cross the Volga, connecting the European regions with Siberia, Kazakhstan and Central Asia. Important urban centres, such as Kazan, Kuybyshev, Saratov and Volgograd, developed at these crossing points, where trans-shipment between rail and water took place.

Over the past 40 years, however, both the nature of the regional economy and its significance to the economy of the USSR as a whole have changed dramatically, mainly as a result of its emergence as a major source of power, producing great quantities of oil, natural gas and electricity. The development of the oil resources of the Volga

A village on river terraces in a Caucasus mountain valley

region was greatly accelerated during the Second World War when the Caucasian fields appeared likely to fall to the enemy. During the 1950s and 1960s, as oil made up an increasing proportion of Soviet energy supplies and as the Caucasian fields proved unable to maintain their share of the rapidly-rising total output, the Volga–Ural field was developed at an even greater rate. By the early 1970s it accounted for at least 70 % of Soviet oil production. Thus the Volga region has been the country's leading oil producer for a period of 30 years, a role which seems likely soon to be passed to West Siberia (see region 8). In addition to the development of oil and natural gas, there has been a massive development of the region's hydro-electric potential. Half a dozen major stations are now in operation, with others planned. Each involves a large barrage across the Volga, which now resembles a string of narrow lakes, and this, incidentally, has improved navigation and permitted the irrigation of large areas of the dry steppe.

From a region once deficient in power, the Volga region has been transformed into a major power base, supplying oil, gas and electricity to the Urals, Centre, Ukraine and more distant regions by river, rail, pipeline and cable. The development of power resources has led to other forms of industrialisation, and the region has become important in a variety of industries, which fall into three main groups. The first of these is concerned with supplying equipment used in power production, such as hydro-electric turbines and oil drilling and pumping machinery, items which the region now produces not only for its own needs but also for those of other regions. Secondly there are industries which have been attracted by the availability of electric power, including various forms of non-ferrous metallurgy and engineering. Noteworthy among the latter is the large motor vehicle plant, the biggest in the Soviet Union, at Tolyatti near Kuybyshev. Finally, and most rapidly growing of all, there are the chemical industries based on oil and natural gas.

The Volga region's industrial activities are found mainly in a series of clusters strung out along the river, of which by far the most important is that in and around Kuybyshev and its satellite towns.

(6) The North Caucasus Region

This is a region with several diverse elements and little internal unity. In the north, the Rostov oblast includes an extension of the Donbas coalfield industrial zone and the port cities of Rostov and Taganrog. This part of the region is highly urbanised and industrialised; its separation from the neighbouring Donets–Dnepr region of the Ukraine appears illogical and is imposed by the presence of the political boundary between the Ukraine and the RSFSR.

The remainder of the North Caucasus region is predominantly agricultural. Farming is most intensive in the west, particularly in the Kuban valley and along the foot of the main Caucasian range, producing wheat, maize, vines, rice, tobacco and fruit. The intensity diminishes eastwards towards the Caspian as conditions become drier. This part of the region is by no means devoid of industrial resources. Along the hillfoot zone is a string of small oilfields, which are still significant producers although their relative importance is much diminished, and the gasfields of the Krasnodar and Stavropol krays produce about 10 % of Soviet natural gas. The mountains themselves supply non-ferrous metals, notably lead and zinc, together with hydro-electricity. No major industrial complex has developed (except in the Rostov oblast) but the several medium-sized towns of the region have oil refining, food processing, chemical and light engineering activities. There are several health and holiday resorts in the foothills and on the Black Sea coast.

(7) The Ural Region

Boundary changes already referred to have reduced this region to the five oblasts of Kurgan, Orenburg, Perm, Sverdlovsk and Chelyabinsk, together with the Udmurt ASSR, territories which cover the central and southern parts of the Ural ranges and extensive foothill and lowland zones on either side. As the figures in Table 12.2 indicate, the overall population density is low when compared with the European regions to the west, but there is a high level of urbanisation. The greater part of the region lies in the tayga zone, but there are extensive areas of steppe in the south, and it is here that most of the agricultural land is to be found. Although a major producer of grain and livestock products, the region is by no means self-sufficient in foodstuffs.

The Ural region plays a fundamental role in the industrial economy as the Soviet Union's 'second metallurgical base' (i.e. second after the Donets–Dnepr region) and produces nearly a third of the country's pig-iron and steel. Prior to the Revolution, despite a long tradition of iron production, the Urals were of minor importance and the development there of the second metallurgical base is the product of a planning decision made in the 1930s. Among the many ore bodies developed since then, the most outstanding have been the high grade magnetites of Magnitogorsk and Nizhniy Tagil which, until recently, supported the bulk of the region's iron and steel industry. In addition, there are numerous valuable sources of other metals, notably copper, aluminium, nickel, chrome and platinum.

In contrast to its richness in metallic minerals, the Ural region is notably deficient in sources of energy. Although there are several sources of coal and lignite, these are quite inadequate to support the heavy industries of the region. There is a marked shortage of coking coal, which is brought in large quantities from the Kuzbas, some 1800 km away in West Siberia, and from Karaganda, 1100 km away in northern Kazakhstan. These linkages were established in the 1930s, and the movement of iron ore in the opposite direction permitted the establishment of iron and steel industries on the two coalfields. Although the Urals no longer send iron ore to the Kuzbas or Karaganda, the railway lines involved in the movement of coking coal to the Urals continue to be among the most heavily used in the USSR and indeed in the world.

By the 1960s it had become apparent that the Ural region, already deficient in coking coal, could no longer depend for its iron solely on its own ore deposits, some of which were nearing exhaustion. Alternative, though lower-grade sources have been found within the region, notably at Kachkanar, but there is a growing reliance on ore from the neighbouring Kazakh republic.

As might be expected, the manufacturing industries of the region are mainly in the heavy engineering group, machinery and equipment being supplied to many parts of the country. The lighter branches are less well represented, but timber-processing and chemicals are important, the latter based on local mineral salts and the oil and gas of the Volga–Ural field. With the removal of the Bashkir republic, the Ural region is no longer a major oil producer; sources in the Perm and Orenburg oblasts account for only eight per cent of Soviet output. Large quantities of oil and gas are brought into the region by pipelines from the Volga–Ural, Uzbek and West Siberian fields; a major new source of natural gas was discovered a few years ago in the Orenburg oblast.

The Ural region provides a particularly good example of a region with a changing resource base. The presence of high grade iron ores, together with the strategic advantages of a location in the interior of the USSR, led to the decision to develop the region as a metallurgical base. Once this decision had been made, the fuel deficit was overcome by the establishment of links with neighbouring energy-rich regions. Today, the mineral resources on which industrialisation was based are no longer sufficient and new inter-regional links have been made to overcome this problem.

(8) The West Siberian Region

Siberia and the Far East, which together extend from the Urals to the Pacific, constitute well over half the territory of the USSR but contain little more than 10 % of the population. About a fifth of this area and nearly half its inhabitants are in West Siberia. The latter falls clearly into two sections. The southern part, extending from the Trans-Siberian Railway to the Kazakh border and the Altay ranges, contains the bulk of the population, agricultural land and industrial capacity of West Siberia. Northwards to the Arctic Ocean, a distance of 1800 km, lies the vast, thinly settled west Siberian lowland. Here, the Tyumen oblast, one of the largest administrative divisions in the country, covers an area of 1.4 million km^2 and has a population of only 1.9 million; the large Khanty-Mansiy AOk and Yamalo–Nenets AOk within this oblast cover 1.2 million km^2 and have only 727 000 inhabitants. Until recently, the contribution of this area to the national economy was very small. Agriculture is virtually absent, lumbering is confined to the more accessible southern districts and the area's mineral resources were largely undeveloped. The significance of this zone has, however, been greatly increased over the past decade by the exploitation of its huge resources of oil and natural gas, now believed to exceed those of the Volga–Ural field. In 1980, the Tyumen oblast produced some 50 per cent of all Soviet oil and 36 per cent of the country's natural gas. Development of these resources in this remote area, with its extremely difficult physical environment, presented major technical problems, particularly in the case of natural gas, which is found mainly in the extreme north, and involved large-scale investment in pipelines to carry the gas and oil to other regions. Industrial development is not likely to proceed beyond the extractive stage and manufacturing industry is unlikely to be established on the West Siberian oil and gas fields.

The southern section of the West Siberian region is by no means uniform, but is given a certain unity by the Trans-Siberian Railway which runs across it and links its various parts. As far east as the Ob, the predominant activity is agriculture, which expanded rapidly in the 1950s and 1960s as a result of the 'virgin lands' scheme. This zone is devoted to extensive grain growing and livestock rearing and sends grain and meat to the European regions and to eastern Siberia. The most important element here is the Kuzbas coalfield, already mentioned in respect of its links with the Urals. The Kuzbas is a particularly rich source of coking coal, which it supplies not only to the Urals but also to Central Asia, and has the largest iron

and steel industry in the eastern regions. Major regional centres such as Novosibirsk, Omsk and Barnaul have varied manufacturing industries, based on Kuzbas coal and hydro-electric power from the Ob. In addition, the Altay ranges are a source of non-ferrous metals.

(9) The East Siberian Region
This region comprises the lowlands along the Yenisey, the western part of the central Siberian plateau and the mountains and basins of pre- and trans-Baykalia. As in western Siberia, there is a large thinly-settled northern zone and a smaller, more developed southern section along the Trans-Siberian Railway. The north, particularly the plateau section, is believed to contain valuable reserves of a variety of minerals and there are vast reserves of coal in the Tunguska and Taymyr basins, but all these remain virtually untouched. An exception is provided by the Norilsk district, near the mouth of the Yenisey, where a non-

A Siberian valley with limited cultivation and livestock rearing. Valleys such as this are highly dependent on the Trans-Siberian Railway

ferrous metal mining and smelting complex produces copper and nickel. This is linked to the rest of the country only by the Arctic sea route and by air.

The more developed areas of the south occur in a series of pockets along the Trans-Siberian Railway. This zone is most noteworthy for its large energy resources, which include the bituminous coal of the Cheremkhovo district (Irkutsk oblast), the lignites of the Kansk–Achinsk field (Krasnoyarsk kray) and the hydro-electric power of the Yenisey and Angara rivers. Prior to the 1950s, the most important industrial zone was along the upper Angara in the Irkutsk oblast, which had some significance in the engineering, chemical and timber industries. Over the past 25 years, a number of major developments have occurred in East Siberia, mainly in the field of energy production. The largest hydro-electric stations in the country have been built at Bratsk on the Angara and Krasnoyarsk on the Yenisey and others are under construction. The Kansk–Achinsk lignites are used on a large scale in thermal-electricity generating stations. The net result has been to make East Siberia a major power base—its per capita electricity production is the highest in the country—and this has attracted power-hungry industries such as aluminium smelting and timber-based chemicals. Important sources of iron ore and non-ferrous metals have been discovered, but their development has been less rapid than was at one time predicted, considerable difficulty being experienced in maintaining the necessary labour supply.

The agricultural potential of the region is considerable, but development has been hindered by the small size of the rural population, which totals only 2.5 million, and by physical difficulties. Consequently there is a large import of basic foodstuffs, mainly from West Siberia and Kazakhstan.

(10) The Far Eastern Region

In comparison with eastern Siberia, the Far East is yet more remote and thinly settled; covering more than a quarter of the Soviet Union, it contains less than 3 % of the country's population—seven million people in an area two-thirds the size of the United States. In parts the Far East has a rather more favourable physical environment than the rest of Siberia and it has a rich but generally undeveloped resource base. Coal is present in large

quantities in the Lena basin but only in relatively small amounts in the south. There is a large hydro-electric potential, little of which has so far been developed, on the Amur and its tributaries. Varied mineral deposits exist in the north, but exploitation has so far been confined to the more valuable items such as the diamonds of Mirny in the Vilyuy valley and the gold of the Lena valley. Oil is produced in Sakhalin, but reserves are small, while the extent of the oil and gas resources of the Lena basin has not yet been assessed.

As in the rest of Siberia, most of the settlement and economic activity occur in the southernmost districts; the Yakut ASSR together with the Magadan and Kamchatka oblasts cover 4.8 million km² but have a combined population of only 1.7 million.

A small steel plant was built at Komsomolsk in the 1930s, but this remains a very minor producer. Most manufactures, including basic items of industrial equipment as well as consumer goods, have to be brought in from the west and, despite the availability of large areas of fairly good agricultural land, the Far East is not self-sufficient in basic foodstuffs.

The low stage of development in this region is due in part to the small size of its population but also to a certain lack of attention to its problems by Soviet planners. The wave of intensive industrial development which has swept across the Urals into Siberia has barely touched the Far East. In view of current tensions between the Soviet Union and China, the underdeveloped nature of this region must be viewed with disquiet from Moscow and we may expect to see a more determined effort directed towards the development of the Far East in the coming decade. There is some evidence of this in the recent decision to begin work on the Baykal–Amur Mainline (BAM) railway. Running from Bratsk on the Angara to Komsomolsk on the Amur, some 300 km north of the Trans-Siberian, the BAM project was first mooted in the 1930s but is only now being built. This 3000 km-long railway is intended to lessen dependence on the Trans-Siberian, which runs uncomfortably close to the Chinese border, to strengthen the links between the Pacific coastlands and the rest of the country and to assist in the development of the industrial resources which lie along its route. Once this project is completed, we may expect the Far East to play a more important role in the Soviet economy than hitherto.

(11) The Donets–Dnepr Region

This is the most densely populated Major Economic Region and has one of the highest levels of urbanisation, yet at the same time is second only to the Black Earth Centre in the proportion of land under crops. The Donets-Dnepr region plays a leading role in the industrial economy as the Soviet Union's 'first metallurgical base', a function which it has now performed for more than 100 years, and produces more than a third of the country's coal, iron ore, pig iron and steel. The iron and steel industry became important in the second half of the nineteenth century on the basis of Donbas coal and carboniferous iron ores, but the Donbas was soon linked by rail to the Krivoy Rog iron ore field, thus permitting the establishment of a second iron and steel district in the Dnepr bend. A similar though smaller scale interchange, between Donbas coal and iron ore from Kerch in the Crimea, resulted in the building of steel plants at the coastal site of Zhdanov on the Sea of Azov. The Donbas and Dnepr bend areas still form two geographically separate industrial complexes, with a zone of mainly rural territory between them, but are completely interdependent economically, linked as they are by the vital interchange of fuel and ore. Each of the districts has additional advantages. The Dnepr bend, now a major source of hydro-electric power, with some oil nearby, has attracted a wide range of chemical and engineering activities. Chemicals are also important in the Donbas on the basis of local salts, coke-oven by-products and oil and gas piped in from the Caucasus and the Volga region.

The Donets–Dnepr region not only supplies steel, heavy engineering products and chemicals to a wide area of the European USSR, but also has large surpluses of raw materials and semi-finished products, including coal, coke, iron ore and pig iron, which it sends to regions deficient in those commodities, notably the Centre. In return it receives light industrial and consumer goods.

While industrial activity is most intensive in the Donbas-Dnepr bend zone, the region's largest city is Kharkov (1.4 million) which lies outside this zone but stands at the junction of routes between the Donbas, Dnepr bend and Centre. The city is now the centre of a rapidly growing engineering and chemical complex based on Shebelinka

natural gas and its contacts with the older industrial districts to the south.

Although the region is the scene of quite intensive and productive agriculture, this does not produce enough to support the large urban population and foodstuffs are brought in from the North Caucasus and western Ukraine.

(12) The South-west

In contrast to the Donets–Dnepr region, the South-west, which is considerably larger, is predominantly rural with only 47 % of its population living in towns. Until the re-organisation of Major Economic Regions in the 1960s, the South-west along with Moldavia and the present Southern region, were part of a single region, balancing the predominantly industrial eastern part of the Ukraine. Despite its low level of urbanisation, the South-west is among the most densely populated parts of the European plain, a fact which reflects the particularly favourable conditions for agriculture provided by its rich chernozem soils and relatively mild, humid climate.

The South-west is not without its industrial resources. Oil, coal and natural gas are all produced in the Carpathian hill-foot zone, which is also a source of sulphur and potash, and there are major hydro-electric plants on the Dnestr and Dnepr rivers. The major cities have a variety of engineering, food-processing, chemical and other industries. All these are expanding and the large rural population provides an adequate labour supply.

Despite these developments, industry still takes second place to agriculture which supplies grain, sugar beet, potatoes and livestock products to the eastern Ukraine and the regions of the forest zone to the north. This is a function which the region has performed since the nineteenth century, aided by a relatively dense network of communications linking it to its neighbours and to the Black Sea ports.

(13) The South

This is the smallest of the Ukrainian regions and is a good deal less densely populated than the other two. It comprises the drier steppelands of the southern Ukraine and Crimea, where agriculture has been intensified in recent years with aid of irrigation, and the high-value crop zone of the Crimean coast. Its main products are thus agricultural, including grain, livestock products, vines,

Summer day at a Simferopol suburban market, Crimea

fruit, vegetables and tobacco. The main industrial resource is the Kerch iron ore, which contributes to the Donets–Dnepr steel complex. The region gains added importance from its ports, particularly Odessa, which handles a large share of Soviet foreign trade, and from the health and holiday resorts of the Crimea.

(14) The Baltic Region

The three small Baltic republics of Estonia, Latvia and Lithuania, together with the Kaliningrad oblast of the RSFSR (formerly part of East Prussia) constitute the Baltic economic region. This is a region with a particularly poor resource base. Lying entirely within the forest zone and the podzol soil belt, with extensive tracts of poorly drained lowland, the Baltic region presents limited opportunities for agriculture. Although more than a quarter of the land is under crops, foodstuffs, particularly grain, have to be brought in from the Ukraine. In recent years, agriculture has become increasingly specialised on the livestock side, which would appear to be the most suitable agricultural activity for this region.

Industrial resources are extremely limited. Apart from timber and flax, which are the main items, the only materials available in quantity are

peat and oil shale (the latter in Estonia), both used for the generation of electricity. The three republics were detached from the USSR between 1917 and 1940 and thus were not affected by Soviet programmes of economic development, so that in the early post-war years, the region lagged behind the rest of the country. Since the mid-1950s, the significance of the Baltic region to the Soviet economy has increased. Power supplies have been augmented by the extension of pipelines into the region and by the development of hydro-electricity on the Western Dvina, and the Baltic ports have benefited from the growth of foreign trade. The problem of poverty in industrial raw materials remains, but the larger towns have their ship-building, engineering, chemical, food-processing and timber industries. Despite these developments, the Baltic region seems destined to remain of minor importance to the Soviet economy, not only because of its poor resource base but also as a result of its peripheral location with respect to the more highly developed parts of the country.

(15) The Transcaucasian Region

As its name suggests, this region, which unites the three republics of Georgia, Armenia and Azerbaydzhan, lies to the south of the main

Caucasian range. This location is largely responsible for the highly distinctive character of Transcaucasia, seen in its physical environment, history, culture and economy.

Although the cultivated area is small, the agriculture of the region is of special importance, since the local climates permit the growth of crops which can be produced in only a few parts of the Soviet Union. These include tea, citrus fruits, vines and tobacco, grown mainly in the humid lowlands of western Georgia, and cotton, grown under irrigation in the drier lowlands of Azerbaydzhan. These high-value crops, together with livestock products from the mountains, are sent to other parts of the USSR, but agricultural specialisation has led to a deficiency in basic foodstuffs, particularly grain, which has to be brought into the region.

Transcaucasia has a variety of mineral resources. The most important of these is oil, which, together with natural gas, occurs mainly in the Baku district of Azerbaydzhan. Baku oil was the region's main contribution to the national economy from the nineteenth century until the Second World War and, until the development of the Volga–Ural field, Baku and the North Caucasus together produced three-quarters of all Soviet oil. The decline in production which set in in the 1940s continues, despite the development of reserves beneath the Caspian, and Baku must now be considered only a minor producer. Much of the oil and most of the natural gas are now consumed within the region. Transcaucasia has a large hydro-electric potential. Until the 1950s this was developed on a limited scale, but over the past 20 years a number of important stations have been built, notably in Armenia. Coal and iron are both present, though in relatively small quantities, and there is an iron and steel plant at Rustavi. There are a variety of other metallic ores, including copper, lead, zinc, molybdenum and tungsten, but the only item of major importance is the Chiatura manganese deposit, one of the largest in the world.

The industrial resource base of Transcaucasia is varied but modest in size and the region is unlikely to become a major industrial zone. At present, its main contributions to the Soviet economy are in the form of foodstuffs and raw materials. Large-scale industry is confined to a few major cities, notably Baku, Tbilisi and Yerevan, which have engineering, chemical and food-processing plant. In this densely populated region, labour-intensive

light industries have developed quite rapidly, but remoteness from major markets is a disadvantage.

This is a region in which the varied resource base and an isolated location would suggest all-round development aimed at regional self-sufficiency. This has not so far taken place and attention has been concentrated on the production of items for which the region has special advantages, namely oil and high-value crops, and Transcaucasia is heavily dependent on other regions for both foodstuffs and manufactures. The industrial economy is being diversified, but the importance of this region to the USSR is appreciably less great than in the inter-war period.

(16) The Central Asian Republics

The four Central Asian republics (Kirgiz, Tadzhik, Uzbek and Turkmen) show certain similarities to the Transcaucasian region, particularly

The Registan square in Samarkand, one of the oldest cities in Central Asia

as regards their cultural distinctiveness and the level and nature of their economic development. The physical environment is extremely diverse, the major contrasts being between the desert, the mountains and the intervening hill-foot zone. As a result, Central Asia contains some of the most densely settled as well as some of the most thinly inhabited parts of the Soviet Union; the average density figure of 20 per km^2 given in Table 12.2 is very misleading—most areas are either well above or well below average.

The bulk of the population is associated with the intensive irrigated agriculture of the hill-foot zone and the river valleys. Agriculture is the region's main economic activity and Central Asia's leading contribution to the USSR's economy is its cotton, which constitutes more than 80% of the Soviet crop. Fruit, vegetables and livestock products are also important. Concentration on these high-value crops has, as in Transcaucasia, led to a grain deficit, which is made up by 'imports' from Kazakhstan.

Central Asia has a broad industrial resource base, with coal, iron, oil, natural gas, non-ferrous metals and a large hydro-electric potential, but has experienced only a modest degree of industrialisation. Industrial development has been selective and mainly post-Second World War. A small steel plant was built in the 1930s, but pig-iron and steel are still brought in from other regions. The oil, most of which occurs in western Turkmenia, is mainly shipped out via the Caspian, and ores and non-ferrous metals are also 'exported'. Over the past two decades, there has been more rapid industrial expansion, supported by natural gas and hydro-electricity, and the engineering, chemical, textile and food-processing branches have all expanded. Despite these developments, Central Asia's main function continues to be that of a supplier of primary products to the more developed parts of the country. The continuation of this traditional role is exemplified by the development of the large natural gas deposits in the Uzbek and Turkmen republics which now produce a quarter of all Soviet gas. Although these have certainly been used to strengthen the energy base of the Central Asian region, a large part of the output is piped to the energy-deficient Urals and Centre. Also as in Transcaucasia, a rapidly growing population supports industrial expansion, indeed Central Asia has a labour surplus, but there is a continuing

reliance on other regions for manufactured goods. This is another region in which the possibility of self-sufficiency appears to have been sacrificed to the requirements of the more developed regions.

(17) Kazakhstan

Second in size only to the RSFSR and much bigger than the whole of western Europe, the Kazakh republic is also one of the largest economic regions and contains several contrasting elements. Agricultural patterns reflect the varied physical conditions. In the north is a belt of steppe-land which runs across the republic from the southern Urals to the Altay. Along with the adjacent part of the West Siberian region, this zone was affected by the virgin lands scheme of the 1950s and now takes second place only to the Ukraine in the production of wheat which, together with livestock products, is 'exported' to the European regions, to Central Asia and to eastern Siberia. The steppe gives way southwards to the desert zone, where extensive stock-rearing is the dominant activity, supplying both meat and wool. Beyond the desert is a hill-foot zone, similar to that of the Central Asian region, where intensive irrigated farming is carried on. Thus Kazakhstan is a major source of both basic foodstuffs and high-value crops.

The republic has also been the scene of major industrial developments in the Soviet period. Among the earliest was the exploitation of the Karaganda coalfield as a source of coking coal for the Urals, which led to the establishment of an iron and steel industry at Karaganda itself. This no longer depends on the Urals for its iron ore, which now comes partly from the Atasu deposit, 150 km to the south-west. The significance of northern Kazakhstan to the Soviet iron and steel industry has been greatly enhanced by the discovery of large deposits of iron ore, mainly in the Kustanay oblast, which have been developed to supply the steelworks of the Urals and to support expansion at Karaganda. Another major development in this zone has been the opening up of the Ekibastuz coalfield, 250 km north-east of Karaganda, which now produces more coal than Karaganda itself, though of a lower quality. Ekibastuz coal is mined open-cast and is fed into large thermal generating stations nearby. These will eventually be linked to a high voltage grid connecting the Kuzbas, the Urals and the European regions. Thus northern Kazakhstan is becoming ever more closely linked to the West Siberian and Ural regions.

Kazakhstan also plays a major role in the production of ferro-alloy and non-ferrous metals. Major items include the lead and zinc of the upper Irtysh valley, the copper of Dzhezkazgan and Balkhash and several sources of chrome, manganese and bauxite. The development of these resources has placed Kazakhstan on an equal footing with the Urals as a producer of non-ferrous metals. In addition, the western part of the republic lies in the oil-rich zone around the Caspian. The Guryev (Emba) field has been in operation since the nineteenth century and the 1960s saw the development of oil and gas further south, in the Mangyshlak peninsula. The latter has, however, proved less rich than anticipated, and Kazakhstan produces less than five per cent of Soviet oil and gas.

Thus Kazakhstan has a rich and varied resource base and is increasing in importance to the Soviet economy. As an economic region it clearly lacks unity and linkages between the various industrial zones are weak. A more rational approach would be to link northern Kazakhstan to the Urals and West Siberia and the south to the Central Asian region. The policy of maintaining intact the constituent republics of the Union, rather than any real economic unity, would seem to be the main reason for the continued existence of Kazakhstan as a Major Economic Region.

(18) Belorussia
Belorussia shows many similarities to the Baltic republics. Like the latter, it has a poor resource base and, because much of present-day Belorussia lay within Poland until 1939, experienced little development before the Second World War. Agriculture is hindered by poor soils and bad drainage and is concerned mainly with potatoes, flax and livestock. The energy base is particularly weak, having been confined to peat, which is used in the generation of electricity. Oil and natural gas were discovered in the 1960s, but reserves appear to be very small. There are few minerals. Over the past two decades there has been some industrial development in the main towns, particularly Minsk (1.2 million), the capital, which have expanded their light engineering and chemical industries on the basis of electric power, oil and gas piped into the region, and local potash salts. Belorussia has long suffered from a degree of overpopulation and attempts have been made to offset this by the expansion of labour-intensive manufacturing industries. However, the republic continues to lie outside the mainstream of the Soviet economy, though clearly benefiting to some extent from the development of COMECON links.

(19) Moldavia
Under the present system, this small republic is not attached to any major economic unit, though in the past it was included in the Ukrainian economic region. Moldavia is characterised by a very low level of urbanisation accompanied by very high rural population densities, a situation reflecting favourable conditions for agriculture. Thus the republic specialises in high-value crops, notably vines, fruit and tobacco. Its main industries are concerned with processing agricultural products. In recent years there has been a marked expansion of light engineering activities, but Moldavia remains predominantly agricultural.

Conclusion
In the preceding section, an attempt has been made to indicate the characteristic features of the 19 regions rather than to give a complete systematic description of each. The various regions can be grouped, according to the nature of their contribution to the Soviet economy, into a number of types. One such group includes regions whose main function is as heavy metallurgical bases, providing steel and heavy engineering products—the Donets-Dnepr and Ural regions are clearly in this category whilst West Siberia performed the same function on a smaller scale but is now most significant as an energy source. One region, the Centre, stands in a class of its own, making a major contribution to the Soviet industrial economy owing to its advantages of location, despite its poverty in resources. Another, the Volga region, is primarily a source of energy and the same can be said of West and East Siberia, though all three are important in other respects as well. A further set of regions are important mainly for their agricultural production: the Black Earth Centre, the South-west, Moldavia and the South fall into this category. In contrast, Belorussia and the Baltic republics have very poor resource bases and are of limited importance in either agriculture or industry. Other regions are much less easy to allocate to a particular group. Kazakhstan, for example, is of major significance in both agriculture and industry. The North-west, East Siberia and the Far East contain zones of rapid develop-

ment and large stretches of undeveloped territory, while Transcaucasia and Central Asia have a varied resource base and are now developing quite rapidly, but remain somewhat peripheral to the Soviet economy as a whole.

The matters of the location of each region, the degree of development each has achieved and its contribution to the economy of the USSR are neatly summarised by Hooson's identification (Hooson, 1966, p. 121) of three types of region: the 'established core', embracing the Centre, the Ukraine and certain adjacent districts, the 'recent expansion funnel' covering a zone from the Volga to Lake Baykal, and the 'relatively marginal' or 'peripheral' areas of the Far East, the Arctic and Sub-Arctic zones, the Caucasus, Central Asia, Belorussia and the Baltic republics.

The difficulty of allocating the existing Major Economic Regions to groups with common characteristics draws our attention to the questionable nature of some of the present boundaries. The illogicalities which result from the insistence

that republican boundaries should remain inviolate have already been commented upon with respect to the splitting of the Donbas between the Donets–Dnepr and North Caucasus regions. In addition, there are several cases, of which Kazakhstan is the best example, but which also include the North Caucasus, Volga–Vyatka and others, of a combination of diverse and unconnected elements within a single region and the ignoring of clearly established inter-regional linkages. Many of these problems can still be attributed to the conflicting ideas of regional self-sufficiency and regional specialisation, neither of which can be wholly achieved. As the Soviet economy develops and new inter- and intra-regional linkages are established, the present set of economic regions, now in existence for nearly twenty years, seems likely to become even less satisfactory as a basis on which to plan the economy. There is increasing need for a radical reorganisation of the economic regionalisation of the whole country.

BIBLIOGRAPHY

Alampiyev, P. M. (1960), 'Problems of general economic regionalization at the present stage,' *Soviet Geography*, **1**, pp. 3–15.

Alampiyev, P. M. (1963), 'Economic regionalization and its place in economic geography,' *Soviet Geography*, **4**, pp. 60–67.

Alampiyev, P. (1964), *Economic areas in the USSR*, Progress Publishers, Moscow.

Altman, L. P. (1965), 'Economic regionalization of the USSR and new methods in economic-geographic research,' *Soviet Geography*, **6**, pp. 48–55.

Bone, R. M. (1967), 'Regional planning and economic regionalization in the Soviet Union,' *Land Economics*, pp. 347–354.

Chambre, H. (1959), *L'aménagement du territoire en URSS*, Mouton, Paris.

Dewdney, J. C. (1967), *Patterns and problems of regionalisation in the USSR*. Research Paper No. 8, Dept. of Geog., University of Durham.

Hooson, D. (1966), *The Soviet Union*, ULP (now Hodder and Stoughton), London.

Kalashnikova, T. M. (1969), *Ekonomicheskoye rayonirovaniye*, Moscow University.

Kazanskiy, N. N. and Khorev, B. S. (1976), 'Problems of economic regionalisation at the present stage,' *Soviet Geography*, **17**, pp. 637–645.

Kistanov, V. V. (1960), 'Aspects of the formation of economic regions in the eastern USSR,' *Soviet Geography*, **1**, pp. 52–59.

Kolosovskiy, N. N. (1961), 'The territorial-production combination (complex) in Soviet economic geography,' *Journal of Regional Science*, **3**, pp. 1–25.

Kurakin, A. F. (1962), 'Economic–administrative regions: their specialization and their integrated development,' *Soviet Geography*, **3**, pp. 29–39.

Linge, G. J. R., Karaska, G. J. and Hamilton, F. E. I. (1978), 'An appraisal of the Soviet concept of the territorial production complex,' *Soviet Geography*, **19**, pp. 681–697.

Melezin, A. (1968), 'Soviet regionalization: an attempt at the delineation of socio-economic integrated regions,' *Geographical Review*, **58**, pp. 593–621.

Mellor, R. E. H. (1959), 'Trouble with the regions: planning problems in Russia,' *Scottish Geographical Magazine*, **75**, pp. 44–48.

Mieczkowski, Z. (1965), 'The major economic regions of the USSR in the Khrushchev era,' *Canadian Geographer*, **9**.

Mieczkowski, Z. (1967), 'The economic–administrative regions in the USSR,' *Tijdschrift voor Econ. en Soc. Geografie*, **58**, pp. 209–19.

Moshkin, A. M. (1962), 'What is a territorial-production complex?,' *Soviet Geography*, **3**, pp. 49–55.

Moshkin, A. M. (1977), 'A typology of regional territorial-production complexes,' *Soviet Geography*, **18**, pp. 60–67.

Nikolskiy, I. V. (1975), 'Economic regions, administrative regions and territorial production complexes,' *Soviet Geography*, **16**, pp. 374–381.

Parkhomenko, I. I. (1966), 'Detailed (intra-oblast and lower level) economic regionalization in the USSR,' *Soviet Geography*, **7**, pp. 33–47.

Pokshishevskiy, V. V. (ed) (1964), *Geograficheskiye problemy krupnykh rayonov SSSR*, Mysl, Moscow.

Pokshishevskiy, V. V. (1966), 'Economic regionalization of the USSR: a review of research during 1962–64,' *Soviet Geography*, **7**, pp. 4–32.

Pokshishevskiy, V. V. (1975), 'On the Soviet concept of economic regionalisation,' *Progress in Geography*, **7**, pp. 1–52.

Probst, A. Ye. (1966), 'Territorial production complexes in the USSR,' *Soviet Geography*, **7**, pp. 47–55.

Probst, A. Ye. (1977), 'Territorial production complexes,' *Soviet Geography*, **18**, p. 195.

Rodoman, B. B. (1972), 'Principal types of geographical regions,' *Soviet Geography*, **13**, pp. 448–454.

Rodoman, B. B. (1973), 'Territorial systems,' *Soviet Geography*, **14**, pp. 100–105.

Saushkin, Yu. G. (1976), 'Economic regionalisation,' *Soviet Geographical Studies*, Academy of Sciences of the USSR, Moscow, pp. 57–73.

Saushkin, Yu. G. and Kalashnikova, T. M. (1960), 'Current problems in the economic regionalisation of the USSR,' *Soviet Geography*, **1**, 6, pp. 50–60.

Sdasiuk, G. (1962), 'The history of regionalisation of the USSR,' *Nat. Geog. Journ. India* (Varanasi), **8**, pp. 145–156.

Shabad, T. (1946), 'Political administrative divisions of the USSR in 1945,' *Geographical Review*, **36**, pp. 303–312.

Shabad, T. (1953), 'The Soviet concept of economic regionalization,' *Geographical Review*, **43**, pp. 214–222.

Shimkin, D. (1952), Economic regionalization in the USSR, *Geographical Review*, **42**.

Soviet Geography (1966), 'Bibliography on economic regionalization,' *Soviet Geography*, **7**, pp. 65–96.

Zawadskiy, S. (1973), *Osnovy regionalnogo planirovaniya*, Progress Publishers, Moscow.

Index

Abakan, 167, 213
Academic City, 193
Achak gas field, 141
Achinsk, 159
Achisay, 157
Adler, 215
administrative structure, 3, 188, 224–32
Aeroflot, 210, 221, 222
Afghanistan, 16, 21
Africa, 210
Afrosiab, 188
agricultural regions, 119–28
agriculture, 31, 35, 36, 41, 43, 68, 112–32
    historical, 6 ff, 16
    machinery construction, 172
    reclamation, 65; *see also* land improvement,
        virgin lands
agrogorod, 199
Agro-Industrial Associations, 131
Ainu people, 92
aircraft, agricultural, 130–1
aircraft industry, 172, 221
air transport, 208, 209, 210, 211, 221–2
    length of haul, 221
Akademgorodok, 193
Akatogay, 207
Akchatau, 158
Aktash, 158
Aktyubinsk, 168, 174
Alapayevsk, 156
Alaska, 12, 39
Alaverdi, 168
Alay mountains, 33
Alazeya plateau, 36
Aldan Highway, 219

Aldan plateau, 159
Aldan river, 30, 146
Aldan shield, 34–5
Aleut people, 92
Alexander I, 14
Alexander II, 15, 113
allotments, 196; *see also* personal plots
alluvial lands, 31, 74, 157, 159
Alma-Ata, 16, 76, 127, 141, 171
Almalyk, 157, 169
Almaznaya, 165
Alpine rocks and structures, 31–3, 35, 63
Altay kray and region, 21, 23, 97
Altay mountains, 34, 63, 92, 158, 240
Altay region, 125, 157
Altay-Sayan district, 31, 34
Altay steppe, 48
Altynkan, 159
aluminium industry, 151, 153, 154, 158–9, 168
Amu Dar'ya river and valley, 31, 33, 73–4, 78, 80,
        84, 97, 127
Amur-Maritime region, 23, 35, 207, 212
Amur river and valley, 15, 31, 35, 41, 59, 74, 92,
        117, 127, 206–7, 212–13, 219, 241
Amurstal, 168
Anabar shield, 30
Anadyr' peninsula, 36, 92
Angara basin, 167
Angara river and valley, 30, 73, 133, 153, 241
Angara shield, 151
Angarsk, 193, 197
Angren, 147
Angren river, 73
animal husbandry, *see* livestock
Antarctica, 38

Anzob, 158
Apatite, 158
Apsheron peninsula, 32, 137
Aragats, Mount, 33
Araks river and valley, 33
Aral' sea (Aral'skoye More), 30–1, 73, 80–1, 124
Ararat, 159
Ararat, Mount, 33
Archaean rocks and structures, 30
Archangel (Arkhangel'sk), 9, 13, 172, 174, 234, 235
Arctic Ocean and coasts, 21, 27, 31, 35, 39, 71–2, 85, 91, 119, 148, 204, 207, 220–1
Arctic regions, 34, 35, 43, 145, 196, 199–200, 211
Arctic sea route, 220–1, 241
Arctic tundra, see tundra
aridity, 39, 41, 50–1, 68, 73–86 passim
arid zones, 68, 73 ff, 119, 151, 167, 196, 219; see also desert
Arkalyk, 159
Arkhangel'sk (Archangel), 9, 13, 172, 174, 234, 235
Armenia (Armenian SSR), 33, 90, 91, 95, 106, 109, 148, 154, 157, 159, 168, 224, 243–4; see also Caucasus, Transcaucasus region
Armenians, 91–2
artesian water, 79
Ashkhabad, 33
Astrakhan', 9, 80, 137, 172, 220
Astrakhan' oblast', 124
Atasu, 156, 168, 245
Atlantic Ocean and ports, 85, 221
atomic power, see nuclear power
Australia, 39, 41, 49
Avars, 6
Azerbaydzhan, 12, 62, 106, 109, 134, 137, 154, 158, 168, 243–4
Azerbaydzhanis, 91–2
Azov–Caspian depression, 27
Azov, Sea of, 210, 219–21, 242

Bakal deposit, 156, 167
Baku, 12, 82, 91, 134, 137, 139, 161, 167, 206–7, 244
Balakhna, 175
Balakovo, 153
Balkhash, Lake, and basin, 16, 31, 34, 76, 81, 124, 168
Balkhash mineral complex, 157, 168, 246
Baltic economic region, 243
Baltic languages, 90
Baltic region, 16, 64, 141, 161, 176, 184, 188, 243

Baltic republics, 97, 104, 116, 119, 121, 131, 141, 147, 174, 176, 199, 243; see also Estonia, Latvia, Lithuania
Baltic Sea, coast and ports, 10, 12, 13, 14, 23, 25, 31, 116, 139, 150, 193, 211, 220–1, 243
Baltic shield, 23, 25
Barents Sea, 221
barites, 157
barley, 117, 121, 129
Barnaul, 48, 172, 181, 240
barshchina, 113
Bashkir ASSR, 68, 123, 136, 237
Bashkirs, 92, 199
Batumi, 49–50, 137, 172, 206, 221
bauxite, 158, 159, 168
Baykal–Amur Mainline (BAM), 139, 146, 154, 157, 162, 206, 211–13, 241
Baykalia, 21, 23, 30–1, 34–5, 162, 206, 240
Baykal, Lake, 30, 34–5, 38, 41, 73, 81–2, 92, 145, 153, 169, 206–7, 211–13
Baykal mountains, 19, 213, 240
Begovat (Bekabad), 76, 162, 168
Belaya river, 81, 237
Belgium, 145
Belogorsk, 159
Belogorye, 84
Belorussia (Belorussian SSR), 25, 64, 90, 104, 109, 116, 117, 119, 121, 131, 147, 163, 171, 174, 176, 179, 199, 246
Belorussians, 90
Belovo, 169
Beloyarskiy, 148
Beloye, Lake, 25
Berestovo, 192
Berezniki, 165, 168–9, 174
Berg, L.S., 54
Bering Strait, 12, 21
Bering, V., 12
Bessarabia, 91, 97
Betpak–Dala desert, 62
Bezhetsk, 172
Bilibino, 148, 159
bismuth, 157
black-earth (chernozem), 46, 48, 51, 117
Black Earth Centre region, 104, 109, 172, 236–7, 242
Black Land steppes, 75
Black Sea and ports, 10, 23, 25, 27, 32–3, 39, 62, 72, 116, 123, 137, 139, 176, 193, 202, 204, 210–11, 219–21
Black Sea coastlands, 6, 39, 49, 91, 188, 193, 238
Black Sea steppes, 13

Blagodat, 156, 167
Bogatyr', 146
bogs, 64–5, 72, 84, 136, 141, 202; *see also* marshlands, peat, swamps
Boguchany, 153
Boksitogorsk, 158
Bol'shevik Party, 18, 19, 113, 161
Bol'shoy Balkhan mountains, 33
Boshchekul, *see* Bozshakol'
Bosphorus, 13
boundaries, of USSR, 19–20, 97–8
Bozshakol', 157
Bratislava, 139
Bratsk, 65, 151, 153, 156, 159, 168, 174, 175, 196, 212–13, 241
Brezhnev, L. I., 162
brigades, farm, 116
Bronze Age, 6, 112
Bryansk, 139, 171
Buddhists, 92
Bug river, 219
building industry, 176
Bukhtarma HEP project, 154
Bulgaria, 20, 207
Bulgars, 6
Bureya coalfield, 212
Bureya mountains, 35
Bureya river, 35, 154
Buryat ASSR, 127, 158
Buryat basin, 146
Buryat people, 92
buses, *see* road transport
butter, 125, 182; *see also* dairy farming
Byrranga mountains, 30
Byzantium, 219

Caledonian structures, 21–4, 30–1, 33–4
California, 15
camels, 219
Canada, 38–9, 150
canals, 15, 82, 84, 153, 192, 219
   irrigation, 74 ff
Carboniferous strata, 30
Carpathian mountains, 19, 31–2, 60, 206
   minerals, 242
Carpathian region, 19, 23
Caspian Sea, 12, 16, 23, 30–1, 33, 61, 72–3, 78–9, 80–1, 84, 92, 123, 134, 137, 148, 172, 196, 207, 211, 219–20, 245
Caspian Sea oilfields, 139, 246
Caspian–Turanian lowlands, 21, 23, 30–1, 36
Caspian–Volga waterway, 139

Catherine II ('the Great'), 13
cattle, 115–28 *passim* herd size, 115–16 total numbers, 130
Caucasus area, agriculture, 124–6
   climate, 45–6
   historical, 6, 10, 14
   industry, 167, 174, 182
   minerals, 154, 157
   physical, 31–2, 68
   population, 45–6, 91, 95
   regional summary, 243–4
   transport, 204, 206, 215, 219
   villages, 199, 237
   water, 74
Caucasus mountains, 23, 31–3, 46, 62, 63–4, 75, 95, 116, 124, 126, 136, 157–8, 199
Caucasus, north, 74–5, 244, 247; *see also* North Caucasus
Central Asia (Soviet), 18
   agriculture, 112, 116, 119, 125–7, 131
   climate, 38–9, 45–6, 51, 85
   industry, 160, 162–4, 168–9, 171–2, 174, 176–7, 179, 181–2
   irrigation, 73–4, 76–9
   minerals, 137, 139, 141, 145, 146–8, 150–1, 154, 158–9
   physical, 21, 23, 31–3, 36
   population, 90–2, 95, 97, 101, 103, 105–6, 108, 109
   regional summary, 244–5
   settlement, 185, 188, 193–4, 196–7, 199–200
   soils, 61, 66
   transport, 204, 206, 210–11, 217, 219
Central Asian desert, 15, 41; *see also* desert lands
Central Asian economic region, 244–5
Central Blackearth (chernozem) region, 104, 109, 122, 172, 236–7, 242
Central Industrial region, 104, 109, 119, 141, 144, 146, 156, 163, 167, 169, 171–2, 174, 176–7, 179, 181, 215, 234–6, 246
Central Russian uplands, 27
Centre, *see* Central Industrial region
Cernauti, 188
Chancellor, Richard, 9
Chardara HEP scheme, 154
Chechens, 91
Cheleken peninsula, 137
Chelyabinsk, 29, 139, 140, 141, 143, 156, 167, 169, 171–2
Chelyabinsk oblast', 95, 117, 211, 238
chemical industry, 137, 172–4, 179, 181; *see also* fertilisers

Cheremkhovo coal deposit, 146, 241
Cherepovets, 139, 143, 145, 156, 167, 181
Cherkassy oblast', 95
Chernobyl', 148
Chernovtsy, 158
chernozem (black-earth), 46, 48, 51, 117
Cherskiy mountains, 36
chestnut and brown soils, 123
Chiatura, 158, 244
Chimkent, 139, 157, 169
China, 15, 16, 31, 34, 49, 74, 92–3, 127, 164, 188, 206, 241
china industry, 177
Chinese Eastern Railway, 211
Chinese Turkestan, 207
Chirchik, 172
Chirkey HEP scheme, 154
Chita, 177
Chita oblast', 127, 151, 158
Chkalovsk, 151
Chop, 217
Christianity, 9, 90, 192
chromite, 158
Chukchi AO, 158–9
Chukchi people, 92
Chukotka mountains, 36
Chukotsk peninsula, 158, 212
Chul'man, 146, 167
Chulym, 84
Chu river and valley, 31, 34, 76, 150
Chusovaya river, 206
Chuvash, 92
cities, 184–97 passim; foundation of, 12
citrus fruits, 49
Civil War, 18, 98
climate, 38–51, 66–8, 136
    and agriculture, 6, 43–4, 116 ff
    and industry, 160
    and transport, 44, 202–4
    see also winter conditions, permafrost
climatic changes, 84, 86
clothing industry, 177
clover, 117
CMEA, 20; see also COMECON
coal, 30, 34, 143–7, 161, 164–8, 179–82, 224–47 passim
    transport, 209, 214, 215
Colchis, see Kolkhid lowlands (Kolkhida)
collective farms, development, 18, 114–16, 119, 130–1
    production, 128–30
collectivisation, 76, 99, 114–15

COMECON, 20, 160, 163, 165, 171, 192, 246
commune, 7; see also mir
Communism, 113, 188
Communism, Mount, 33
Communist Party, 114–15, 161, 163
coniferous forest, 58 ff, 72; see also tayga
conservation, 63–9, 71, 79 ff, 175
Constantinople, 7, 9
consumer goods industry, 178
continentality, 38–9, 48, 116, 121, 202
co-operative farm enterprises, 131
copper, ores, 157, 158
    processing, 168
corduroy roads, 217
corn, see maize
Cossacks, 10, 13, 113–14
    village type, 199
costs, climatic, 50
    production, 119
    transport, 210, 221
cotton growing, 49, 76, 131, 162
    areas, 126–9
    historical, 15, 16
    output, 129
    temperatures required, 117
cotton manufacturing, 176
cows, numbers, 130
    yields, 129
    see also dairy farming
Crimea, 9, 13, 23, 27, 31–2, 45, 49–50, 62, 75, 76, 104, 126, 131, 209, 242–3
Crimean mountains, 32
Crimean peninsula, 32, 49, 62
Crimean War, 15
Cuba, 20
cultivation, 6 ff, 112
    oasis, 92
    see also field systems, grain, individual crops
Cumans, 7
Cyrillic script, viii, 90–1
Czechoslovakia, 20, 32, 98, 116, 143, 217

Dabrowa, 161
Dagestan ASSR, 32, 126, 139, 154
dairy farming, 46, 116–31 passim
Dalnegorsk, 158
Danube river and ports, 31, 84, 221
Dardanelles, 13
Darnitsa, 193
Darvaza gas field, 141
Dashava oilfield, 141
Dashkesan, 167

Dauria basin, 35
Deputatskiy, 196
desert and semi-desert lands, 15, 31, 33–4, 36, 38, 41, 49, 54, 61–2, 73 ff, 95, 97, 127–8, 204, 206
Desna river, 6
distilleries, 179
Divnogorsk, 193
Dmitry Donskoy, 9
Dnepr Bend area, 179, 242
Dnepr–Don area, 119, 165, 169, 247
Dnepr lignite basin, 145
Dneprodzerzhinsk HEP scheme, 151, 167, 171
Dneproges HEP scheme, 27, 151, 167
Dnepropetrovsk, 23, 167
Dnepropetrovsk oblast', 145
Dnepr railway directorate, 215
Dnepr, river and valley, 6 ff, 23, 25, 27, 64, 72, 74–5, 80, 123, 139, 151, 158, 167–8, 171–2, 179, 192–3, 219, 242
Dnestr river, 6, 242
Dokuchayev, V. V., 54
Don, river and valley, 8, 9, 25, 75, 80, 123, 148, 171, 221
Donbas, 15, 16, 17, 23, 82, 90, 95, 141, 144–5, 147, 161–2, 165, 167, 169, 171–2, 174, 176, 179, 181, 211, 212, 215, 238, 242, 247
Donets–Dnepr area, 27, 104, 109, 122, 139, 144, 145, 174, 215, 234, 238, 242–3
Donetsk, 161, 165, 179
Donetsk oblast', 95
Dorpat, 188
drainage, 49, 64, 74, 117, 204
    areas and development, 119
drought, 39, 41, 50, 74, 76, 117, 121–8 *passim*
dry farming, 49
dry steppe, 30
Dudinka, 141, 157, 221
Dushanbe, 159
Dzhagdy mountains, 35
Dzhezkazgan, 157, 246
Dzhugdzhur mountains, 35
Dzungarian gate, 34, 207

earnings, in agriculture, 129, 131
East European plain, 23–9, 36
East Germany, 148, 210, 217
East Kazakhstan, 168
East Siberia, 72–3, 97, 108, 145, 240–1
economic regions, 227–47
Edmonton, 38
Ekibastuz basin, 146–7, 245
Elbrus, Mount, 32, 63, 75

electricity, 133–4, 140, 165, 168–9, 179–82
    grid, 145, 146, 147, 153, 165
    in rural areas, 115, 130, 199
    location and fuelling of power stations, 144–50 *passim*
    nuclear stations, 148–50
    railways, 214
emancipation of serfs, 15, 113, 160
Emba oilfield, 137, 139, 246
energy, *see* fuel and power, oil, coal, nuclear power, etc.
engineering, 16, 169–83
England, 48
environmental problems, 63–9, 71, 79 ff, 150, 154, 220; *see also* pollution, soil erosion
Eskimo, 92
Estonia (Estonian SSR), 6, 13, 19, 90, 121, 147, 150, 161, 176, 217, 243
Estonians, 91
ethnic groups, 88–92, 225–7
European plain, 59
European platform, 31
European Russia: agriculture, 116–26, 131; historical, 6–20 *passim*; industry, 160–83 *passim*; minerals, 133–59 *passim*; physical, 23–9, 31–3, 36; population, 88–110 *passim*; regional summaries, 224–47; settlement, 185, 190, 194, 197; soils and vegetation, 54, 60, 64, 66; transport, 206, 210–11, 214; water, 72
Evenki AOk, 97
Evenki people, 92
exile system, 14
exports: coal, 145, 217; historical, 7; nuclear stations, 148; ores, 156, 217; petroleum, 139, 143

FAO/UNESCO soil units, 54–5
Far East, (Russian), 13, 15, 210; *see also* Far East (Soviet)
Far East (Soviet), 31, 35, 39, 54, 58–9, 74, 91–2, 95, 97, 99, 101, 103, 105–6, 108, 110, 116–17, 119, 127, 131, 139, 146, 154, 158, 162–4, 168–9, 171, 174, 178–9, 182, 185, 219, 234, 241–2; *see also* Pacific Ocean
Farkhad dam, 76, 154, 168
farming, 112–32; *see also* agriculture
Farm Machinery Association (*Sel'khoztekhnika*), 115, 130
Fedorovsk oilfield, 136
Fennoscandian shield, 23–5,
Fergana, 126, 139

Fergana canals and valley, 33–4, 76, 97, 147, 150, 158–9, 207
ferries, 207
fertilisers, 82, 117, 119–30 *passim*, 141, 147; manufacture, 172–4, 182; shortage of, 130; transport, 209
Fiat Company, 171
field systems, 7, 113
Finland, 14, 19, 25, 97, 148, 156, 207, 215
Finland, Gulf of, 25, 192
Finno–Ugrian language and people, 91–2
Finns, 91
fishing, 6, 151, 171, 220; Caspian and Aral' Seas, 80, 81, 119
Five Year Plans, 76, 79, 115, 130, 140, 143, 148, 157, 161, 163, 167, 193, 212
flax, 121, 128
flooding, in development, 65
   reservoirs, 74, 75, 80, 151
   spring, 72, 75, 204
fodder crops, 117, 119–28; *see also* hay
food processing, 178–9, 182
forest–fallow cultivation, 6, 7, 112, 122
forestry, 65, 68, 174–6
forest zone, 55, 57–60, depletion, 65–6
   development, 130 ff, 153, 224–47 *passim*
   settlement and population, 6 ff, 46, 90, 95, 104
   soils, 59–60
France, 150
'Friendship' pipeline, 139, 210
frontiers of USSR, 19–20, 97–8
frost, 39, 43, 48, 49, 116, 204
frost-free periods, 125, 126
fruit, 49, 119–27 *passim*
Frunze, 76, 141, 172, 182
fuel and power resources, 133–54, 163–4
fur industry, 7, 10, 12, 46, 119, 177
furniture industry, 175

gardens, 196; *see also* personal plots
gas, natural, 134, 135, 140–3, 144, 157, 164, 179–82, 210
Gay, 157
Gazli gas field, 141
geological structure, 21–36, 72, 79
Georgia (Georgian SSR), 10, 54, 90, 95, 109, 137, 154, 157–9, 188, 243–4
Georgian Military Highway, 10, 206
Georgians, 44, 91–2
German Democratic Republic, 20
Germans, 7, 18–19, 90, 91, 92, 161, 188, 191

invasion by, 144–5, 159, 162, 184, 219
Germany, 20, 98
Gissar mountains and valley, 33, 159
glaciation, 7, 25
glaciers, 32, 33
   in water supply, 73–4, 78, 79
goats, numbers, 130
GOELRO, 151
gold, 12, 157, 158, 159
Golden Horde, 7, 9
Golodnaya (Hungry) steppe, 76, 126
Gor'kiy, 121, 137, 139, 161–2, 171–2, 181, 190, 221, 236
Gorlovka, 158, 165
Gornaya Shoriya, 156
Gorno–Badakhshan AO, 207
gorod, 188, 190
GOSPLAN, 161–3
Goths, 6
grain combine harvesters, 182
grain crops, 17, 112, 116, 119–29 *passim*
   output, 44, 129
   transport, 15, 209–21 *passim*
   yields, 76, 117
   see also individual grains
grapes, 117; *see also* vineyards
grass, 117, 119 ff; *see also* hay, pasture, steppe
Great Britain, comparison with, 12, 16
Great Russia, 199
Greeks, 6, 91
green crops, 117
Gregorian Christianity, 91
Groznyy, 139
Gubkin, 156
Gur'yev, 139, 246
Gydan mountains, 35–6

Hangö, 207
Hansa, 193
hay, 119–28 *passim*
heat balance, 41
helicopters, 210, 213
   in agriculture, 130
   in oil development, 136
Hercynian structures, 21–4, 27, 29, 30–1, 33–5
high pressure system, 39
Himalaya mountains, 33
Hindu Kush, 33, 73–4
Hitler, A., 18
horses, 130
horticulture, *see* market gardening
housing, 185, 187, 190–6, 199

Hungary, 20, 116, 206, 217
Hungry (Golodnaya) steppe, 76, 126
Huns, 6
hunting, 6, 119
Huntington, E., 45
hydro-electric power, 65, 74, 80, 151–4, 157, 158, 159, 168

ice, 13, 39, 44, 48, 72–3, 141, 192, 204, 205, 217, 221
icebreaker vessels, 49, 148, 204
Igarka, 154, 196, 207, 221
Iksa river, 158
Il'ichevsk (Ilyichevsk) – Varna ferry, 207
Ilim basin, 167
Il'men, Lake, 25
Imandra, Lake, 158
India, 92–3, 188, 194, 210
Indigirka lowlands, 36
Indonesia, 157
industrialisation, 13, 16, 17, 133, 160–83, 191
industry location policies, 46, 161, 162–4, 176, 179, 202
    pollution by, 69, 81–2
    regions, 179–82
inland waterways, *see* canals, waterways
Intercollective Farm Co-operative Enterprises, 131
Iran, 33, 157; influence of, 188
Irkutsk, 65, 139, 146, 153, 168, 171, 211, 222
Irkutsk oblast', 13, 151, 241
Iron Age, 6, 112
iron and steel industry, 165–8, 179–82
    historical, 6, 13, 15, 16
    ores, 154–6
iron ore, 13, 15, 16, 154–6, 158, 161, 179–82
irrigation, 31, 41, 48, 49, 50, 64, 73 ff, 97, 116, 117
    development and extent, 119, 151, 154
Irtysh–Karaganda canal, 181
Irtysh river and valley, 10, 29, 34, 73, 84, 154, 169, 196, 246
Islam, 91
Issyk-Kul', Lake, 150
Italy, 156, 192
Iul'tin, 158
Ivan III (the Great), 9
Ivan IV (the Terrible), 9, 12, 193
Ivan'kovo, 81, 153
Ivanovo, 171
Ivdel'–Ob' railway, 65
Izvestkovaya–Urgal railway, 212

Jablonka Pass, 206
Japan, 145–6, 217, 221
Japanese, 15, 18, 19, 212
Jewish AO, 91
Jews, 91–2

Kabardins, 91
Kachkanar, 167, 239
Kadzharan, 157
Kadzhi–Say, 150
Kakhovka 75, 151
Kalinin, 148, 171, 215
Kaliningrad oblast', 19, 108, 121, 190, 243
Kalmyk ASSR, 124
Kalmyk people, 92
Kalush, 169
Kaluzhskaya Zastava, 191
Kama basin, 174
Kama lorry plant, 207
Kama river and valley, 81–2, 84, 151, 153, 171–2, 175, 196, 237
Kamchatka, 12, 15, 23, 36, 92, 119, 241
Kamchatka river, 36
Kamensk–Ural'skiy, 159
Kandalaksha, 158
Kanev HEP scheme, 151
Kansk–Achinsk basin, 144–6, 153, 159, 241
Kara–Balta, 150
Kara–Bogaz–Gol, 174
Karaganda, 106, 161, 167–8, 194, 196, 202
Karaganda basin, 97, 146–7, 185, 239, 245
Karaganda oblast', 97
Karagayly, 157
Karakum canal, 78–9, 84
Karakum desert, 31, 62, 73
Karatau mountains, 34
Karelia (Karelian ASSR), 13, 23, 25, 133, 153, 156, 167, 199, 219, 234
Karelians, 91
Karshi steppe, 78
Kasha–Dar'ya, 185
Kashkadar'ya river, 78
Kashkanar, 156
Kaspiysk, 172
katorga, 185
Kayrak–kum, 154
Kazakhs, 90, 92
Kazakhstan (Kazakh SSR)
    agriculture, 116–17, 119, 124, 127–8, 131
    climate, 41, 44–5
    industry, 163, 167–9, 171–2, 174, 176, 181
    irrigation, 73, 76–9

Kazakhstan (*contd.*)
  minerals, 134, 137, 139, 144, 146–8, 151, 154,
    155–9
  physical, 21, 23, 29–30, 34
  population, 90, 95, 97, 99, 101, 103, 105–6, 109
  regional summary, 245–7
  settlement, 185, 196, 199
  soils, 61–2, 66, 68
  transport, 207, 212
Kazakh steppe, 72
Kazan', 9, 10, 172, 174, 177, 237
Kazretiy, 157
Kembarrata HEP scheme, 154
Kemerovo, 140
Kerch', 165, 179, 242, 243
Kerch' straits, 207
Kerki, 78
Khabarovsk, 74, 211, 212, 219, 222
Khakass people, 92
Khalilovo, 167
Khanka–Ussuri lowlands, 35
Khanty–Mansiy AOk, 239
Khanty people, 91
Khar'kov, 171–2, 174, 179, 196, 222, 242
Khatanga depression, 29
Khaydarken, 158
Khazars, 6
Kherson, 22
Khibin mountains, 25
Khimki, 192
Kholmogory, 136
Kholmsk, 213
Khorezm, 185
khozraschet, 162
Khrebtovaya, 213
Khrom–Tau, 158, 168
Khrushchev, N.S., 162, 199, 227
Kiev, 7, 41, 46, 48, 95, 117, 151, 171–2, 174, 179,
    192–3
Kievan Rus, 7, 112
Kirgizia (Kirgiz SSR), 125, 127, 137, 147, 150, 154,
    158, 171, 244–5
Kirgiz people, 92
Kirovabad, 158
Kirovsk, 158
Kirpsay HEP scheme, 154
Kizel, 181
Kizel basin, 145
Klaypeda, 139
Klyaz'ma basin, 179, 190
Klyuchevskiy Peak, 36
Kochbulak mine, 159

Kok–Yangak, 147
Kola peninsula, 23, 25, 69, 119, 145, 148, 153, 156,
    158, 168, 221, 234, 235
Kolkhid lowlands (Kolkhida), 32, 39, 49, 63, 126
kolkhoz, 114, 115; *see also* collective farms
Kolmogory, 136
Kolomna, 171
Kolyma region, 35, 36, 63, 219
Komandorskiye Islands, 92
Komi ASSR, 137, 139, 141, 143, 145, 234
Komi people, 91
Kommunarsk, 165
Komsomol'sk (Komsomol'sk-na-Amure), 139,
    158, 168, 193–4, 207, 212–13, 241
Königsberg, 188
Konstantinovka, 169
Kopet–Dag mountains, 33, 79
Korean people, 92
Korovsk, 158
Koryak mountains, 36
Koryak people, 92
Kosaya Gora, 167
Košice, 217
Kostamuksha deposit, 156
Kostroma, 171
Kostychev, 54
Kotlas, 172, 174
Kotlin Island, 192
Kotur–Tepeh, 137
Kounradskiy, 157
Kovdor, 156
Koytash, 158
Kramatorsk, 165
Krasnoarmeysk, 172
Krasnodar, 141
Krasnodar kray, 238
Krasnokamensk, 151
Krasnooktyabrskiy, 159
Krasnoural'sk, 157
Krasnovodsk, 80, 139, 196, 207, 211
Krasnoyarsk, 139, 153, 159, 168, 171–2, 193, 211
Krasnoyarsk kray, 241
Kremenchug, 139, 151
Krivoy Rog, 150, 154, 165, 179, 211, 242
Kronstadt, 192
Kropotkin, Peter, 45
Kuban', 68, 199
Kuban' river and valley, 32, 75, 123, 238
Kuenga, 211
kulak, 113
Kulikovo, 9
Kulunda steppe canal, 78

Kuma–Manych canal, 75
Kuma river, 75
Kunda, 6
Kundag, 137
Kura river and basin, 33, 62, 127, 154, 158
Kurama mountains, 157, 159
Kurgan, 76, 84, 139, 172; oblast', 238
Kurile (Kuril') islands, 19, 36, 92
Kursk, 23, 148, 165, 167, 179, 197
Kursk Magnetic Anomaly, 156, 181, 236
Kushva, 156
Kustanay oblast', 156, 245
Kuybyshev, 41, 80, 82, 117, 137, 139, 153, 172,
    181, 222, 237, 238
Kuybyshev oblast', 76, 136, 147
Kuzbas, 34, 97, 140, 145–7, 156, 161, 167, 169,
    171, 181, 215, 239, 240, 245
Kuzbas–Tayshet railway, 206
Kuznetsk–Alatau mountains, 34, 145
Kuznetsk basin, 34, 144–5, 153, 156; *see also*
    Kuzbas
Kyshtym, 156
Kyzyl Kiya, 147
Kyzylkum desert, 31, 33, 62, 73, 159

labour, 46, 109, 116, 131, 160, 163, 171, 196, 212
Ladoga, Lake, 25, 192
lakes, 25, 34, 35, 64, 80 ff
    hydro-electric developments, 150–4
    pollution, 81–2
Lanchow, 207
land improvement, 76, 79, 84, 119; *see also* virgin
    lands
landlords (pre-revolutionary), 113
land ownership and tenure, 113–15
land reform, 17, 113–14, 199
languages, 90 ff
Latvia (Latvian SSR), 14, 19, 90, 121, 139, 147,
    243
Latvians, 90
lead ores, 157; processing, 169
leather industry, 177, 182
Lemberg, 188
Lena basin, 30, 35, 92, 144, 241
Lena river, 12, 21, 29, 31, 48, 73, 159, 172, 207, 210,
    212–13
Lenin, V. I., 15, 18, 19, 50, 114, 161, 165, 214
Leningrad, 13, 14, 18, 39, 43, 95, 116, 119, 121,
    139, 141, 147–8, 151, 158, 167–8, 171–2,
    174–5, 177–8, 181, 191–2, 210–11, 215, 217,
    221, 235; *see also* St. Petersburg, Petrograd
Leningrad oblast', 147

Leninogorsk, 157, 169
Lenin Peak, 33
Leninport, 192
Lesghians, 91
Liaotung peninsula, 15
light industries, 176
lignite, 145, 146, 159
Likino, 172
linen industry, 176
Lipetsk, 145, 156, 167, 172, 236
Lisichansk, 139
Lithuania (Lithuanian SSR), 10, 14, 19, 90, 104,
    109, 121, 131, 139, 171, 243
Lithuanians, 90
livestock, 5, 112, 114–15, 119–32 *passim*
Lodz, 161
loessic soils, 49, 112, 206
London, 191
Lovat' river, 219
Lugansk, 165, 171
L'vov, 171–2, 188
L'vov–Volhynian basin, 145
Lwow, 188

Machine–Tractor Stations (MTS), 114, 115, 130
Madneuli, 157
Magadan, 185, 219
Magadan oblast', 97, 159, 185, 241
magnesium, 168–9
Magnitnaya Gora, 156, 167
Magnitogorsk, 156, 167, 194, 196, 215, 239
maize, 117, 122–7 *passim*; areas, 128
Major Economic Regions, 179, 229–47
Makeyevka, 165, 179
Malaysia, 157
Manchuria, 15, 30, 162, 211, 212
Manchurian language and people, 91–2
manganese, 158, 167
Mangyshlak peninsula, 137, 139, 196, 246
Mansi tribe, 91
Maracanda, 188
Marco Polo, 16
Mari canal, 219
Mari people, 91
Maritime (Primorskiy) kray, 15, 23, 116, 158, 219
market-gardening, 46
markets, 119
Marshall Plan, 20
marshlands, 117, 119, 121; *see also* bogs, swamps
Marxism–Leninism, 15, 165, 184, 188, 200
Mary, 141, 188
Mazeikiai, 139

meat output, 129, 182
Mediterranean Sea, 6, 62
Medvezh'ye gas field, 141, 143
mercury, 158
Meshchera (Meshcherskiy) area, 64, 121
Mesolithic period, 6
Mesozoic rocks and structures, 21, 23, 30–6
metal ores, 133, 154–9, 165 ff; non-ferrous, 156–9
Miass, 171
mid-Russian heights, 123
migration, 45, 49, 51, 90, 97, 101, 103, 104, 105, 106, 108, 109, 160, 184, 196
milk output, 129; see also dairy farming
minerals, 133–59; see also coal, metal ores, oil, petroleum
Mingechaur, 154
Min-Kush, 150
Minsk, 25, 171, 246
Minusinsk basin, 34, 145
mir (commune), 112–13, 197
Mirny, 241
Moldavia (Moldavian SSR), 103–5, 126, 131, 188, 199, 229, 246
Moldavians, 91
molybdenum, 157
Monchegorsk, 69, 168
Mongolia, 127
Mongolian language and people, 91–2
Mongols, see Tatars
Mordov people, 91–2
Moscow (Moskva), 190–2, 197, 222
  historical, 8 ff
  transport, 202, 210–11, 217, 221
  see also Moscow region
Moscow canal, 82, 153
Moscow–Gor'kiy railway, 206
Moscow region, 235–6
  agriculture, 119, 121
  climate, 39, 41, 43, 46, 48, 50, 64
  energy supplies, 139, 141, 144, 145, 148, 153
  historical, 8 ff
  industry, 161–2, 169, 171–2, 174–5, 177–9, 181, 235–6
  physiography, 25, 27
  population, 88, 90, 95, 104
  transport, 211, 215, 217
  water supply, 76, 82
Moscow river, 82, 151, 192
Moskal'vo, 221
Moskva–Volga canal, 84, 192
Moslems, 12, 15, 91–2, 160, 162
motor vehicles, 192

construction, 171–2, 182, 197, 207
  see also road transport
mountain regions, 46, 63, 73, 75, 85, 112, 116, 117, 119, 145, 154, 204, 206, 213
  physiography, 21, 29–30
  villages, 199; see also individual ranges
Mugodzhar mountains, 124
Mukachevo, 188
Mukden, 211
Muraviev, N. N., 15
Murgab oasis, 79
Murgab river, 78
Murmansk, 95, 121, 145, 158, 172
Murmansk oblast', 95, 153, 156, 185
Muscovy, 9, 10
Muyunkum desert, 31
Mytishchi, 171

Naberezhnye Chelny, 171, 196, 207
Nadvoitsy, 158
Nadym, 141
Nadym river, 141
Nakhodka, 49, 146, 221
Namangan canal (Great), 76
Naminga, 157
Napoleon, 14, 191
Narodnaya, Mount, 29
Narva, 147, 150, 161
Naryn river, 76, 154
nationalities, 88 ff, 225, 227
'natural zones', 41, 43
Naugarzan, 151
Navoi, 141, 197
Near East, 6, 112
Nebit Dag, 137, 139
Neftezavodsk, 139
Nentsy people, 91
Neolithic period, 6, 112
nephelite, 158, 168
Nerchinsk, 157
Neryungri, 146
Neva river, 192
Never, 219
Never–Tynda railway, 212
New Economic Policy (1921), 18, 114, 161
New Zealand, 49
Nicholas I, 14
Nicholas II, 15, 16
nickel, 158, 168
Niger, 150
Nikitovka, 158
Nikolayev, 148, 172

Nikolayevsk, 168, 212
Nikopol, 158, 167, 172, 179
Nile river, 74
Nizhneangarsk, 213
Nizhnekamsk, 197
Nizhnevartovsk, 136, 139, 193
Nizhniy Novgorod, 161; *see also* Gor'kiy
Nizhniy Tagil, 156, 167, 171, 239
Nogatino, 192
Nogay steppe, 75
nomadism, 7, 16, 92, 112, 190, 199
Nordvik, 57
Noril'sk, 141, 144, 154, 157–8, 168, 185, 196, 240–1
North America, 38–9, 41, 43, 50, 57, 160, 163, 210–11
North Caucasus region, 95, 103, 105, 123, 136, 139, 140, 141, 169, 171, 175–6, 182, 185, 199, 207, 210, 221, 238, 247
Northern Donets river, 81
Northern Dvina river, 72, 172, 234
'Northern Lights' transmission link, 141
Northern Sea Route, 220–1, 241; *see also* Arctic Ocean
North Kazakhstan, 171, 181
North Muy mountains, 213
North Sea, 221
North-West region, 104, 215, 231–5
Novaya Zemlya, 29
Novgorod, 7, 9, 193
Novgorod–Volhynsky area, 177
Novoaltaysk, 171
Novocherkassk, 171
Novokuznetsk, 145, 159, 167–8, 181
Novo–Lipetsk, 181
Novomoskovsk, 145, 174
Novonikolayevsk, 193
Novopolotsk, 139
Novorossiysk, 32, 176, 182, 204, 221
Novosibirsk, 84, 117, 139, 153, 169, 171–2, 181, 193, 222, 240
Novosibirsk oblast', 97, 136
Novotroitsk, 156, 167
Novovoronezhskiy, 148
nuclear power, 148–50, 159
Nurek HEP scheme, 73, 154, 159

oases, 112, 116, 185, 199
oats, 117; areas, 128
Ob', Gulf of, 141
ob'edineniya, 162
Ob'-Irtysh basin, 172, 174, 239–40

Ob'lowland, 64, 174, 239–40
Obninsk, 148
Ob' river, 10, 29, 71–3, 84, 136, 141, 153, 174, 240
obrok, 113
ochagi (hearths of cultivation), 119
Odessa, 13, 41, 139, 221, 243
OEEC, 20
oil industry, 134–40, 179–82
  environmental effects, 65
  location of refineries, 139
  transport, 137, 210
oil shale, 147, 164
Oka river and valley, 8, 27, 46, 64, 81, 190, 192
Okhotsk, 13, 35
Okhotsk, Sea of, 12
Oleg, 7
Olekma river, 213
Olenegorsk, 156
Omsk, 65, 139, 147, 172, 240
Omsk oblast' 68, 97
Onega, Lake, 25, 81, 84
Onega river and valley, 84, 158, 234
Ordzhonikidze, 157, 169
Orenburg, 171
Orenburg oblast', 123, 141, 238, 239
Orlovka, 150, 151
Orsk, 139
Orthodox Christianity, 9, 91
Osetian Military Highway, 206
Osetins, 91
Osinovo, 153
Oymyakon, 36, 39

Pacific coast and ocean, 12, 21, 34, 35, 39, 48, 58, 90, 116–17, 139, 145–6, 172, 204, 207, 211, 241
Pakistan, 210
Paleo-Asiatic peoples, 92
Paleolithic period, 6
Paleozoic rocks and structures, 21 ff, 133, 136
Pamir–Alay mountains, 73
Pamir mountains, 15, 33, 44, 125, 207
Partizansk, 146
pasture, 119–28 *passim*
Pavlodar, 68, 139, 159, 168, 172
Pavlograd, 145
peasant farms, 114–15
peasants, 113–14, 192
peat, 64, 84, 147, 164; *see also* bogs
Pechenegs, 7
Pechora basin, 145, 234
Pechora coalfield, 162

Pechora–Kama diversion, 84
Pechora river, 72, 84, 234
Peking, 217
Perm', 95, 139, 153, 172, 239
permafrost, 39, 44, 48, 73, 118–19, 141, 196, 202, 213
Perm' oblast', 145, 238
Perm' plateau, 27
Pershotravensk, 145
Persia, influence of, 194
personal plots and livestock, 114, 115, 129
Peter I (the Great), 12, 13, 191, 192
petrochemicals industry, 140, 147, 174
Petrograd, 17, 18, 192; *see also* St. Petersburg
Petrokrepost, 192
petroleum, 164, 179–82, 209, 220; *see also* oil, gas (natural), pipelines
Petropavlovsk, 171
Petrovsk–Zabaykalskiy works, 167
pigs, 117–29 *passim*; farm size, 115–16; numbers, 130
pipelines, 137–9, 141–3, 144, 210; traffic, 208, 209
Pit basin, 167
Pivan', 212
Plamennyy, 158
planning, 224–47
   industrial, 162–4
   transport, 210–11
   urban and regional, 188, 194–200
   see also Five Year Plans
platinum, 158
Plock, 139
Pochayna river, 193
Podol, 193
Podolsk, 169
Podolsk–Volyn uplands, 27
Pokshishevskiy, V.V., 197
Poland, 10, 13, 19, 20, 90, 97, 116, 141, 161, 184, 210, 217, 246
Poles, 12, 90
   influence of, 188
Poles'ye, 27, 64, 199
Polevskoy, 167
political structure, 4, 225–7
pollution, 69, 81–2; control, 140
Polotsk, 139
Polovtsy, 7
population, 88–110
   age and sex, 99
   density, 92 ff, 185
   growth, 97 ff, 184 ff
   urban, 184–97

Port Arthur, 15
ports, 12, 13, 14, 15, 44, 48–9, 80, 192, 220–1
   oil, 139
potatoes, 117, 121, 123, 129
   areas, 128
   output, 129
Poti, 158, 172, 221
pre-Azov heights, 27
Pre-Cambrian rocks, 21, 23, 30–1, 133, 150–1, 154, 158
precipitation, 39 ff
pressure systems, 39, 48
pre-Volga heights, 27
Primorskiy (Maritime) kray, 15, 23, 116, 158, 219
Pripyat' river and marshes, 27, 64, 117, 219
private plots, *see* personal plots
processing of farm produce, 131
proizvodstvenniye ob'edineniya, 162
promyshlenniye ob'edineniya, 162
Prorva, 220
Protestant Christianity, 91
Przemysl, 215
Pskov oblast', 146
pulp and paper industry, 175, 182
Pushkin, 211
Putoran mountains, 30
Pyongyang, 217

Quaternary period, 27, 30, 32–6, 52

railways, 211–18, 222
   gauge, 215
   historical, 15, 16, 17–18, 44, 191–2, 193, 194, 202–9, 211
   length of haul, 144, 145, 161, 207, 215
   motive power, 213–14
   new developments, 153–4, 212–13
   vehicle building, 171, 182
rainfall, *see* precipitation
rayon (region), 227
   economic, 227–32
Razdan, 159
Razdan river, 154
rebellions, 113
recreation, 45, 46, 49–50, 65, 151, 153
Regar, 159
regionalisation, 224–32; *see also* planning, regions
regional specialisation, 229, 234, 247; *see also* planning, regions
regions, 224–47
   agricultural, 119–28
   economic, 229–47

industrial, 179–82
reindeer, herders, 91, 221
  pastures, 119
  rearing, 119
  transport, 119, 219
  vegetation depletion, 69
religious groups, 90, 91
reservoirs, 65, 74, 75, 76, 80, 84, 151, 196
  pollution, 81
retailing, 179
revolutions, 1, 14, 17, 18, 98, 113–14, 129, 151,
  184, 185, 191, 202, 211
rice, 117, 118, 126
Riga, 4, 139, 171–2, 188
Riga, Gulf of, 121
Rioni river and basin, 33
rivers, for electricity development, 153
  navigation improvements, 151, 153
  transport, 44, 141, 190, 193, 204–10, 219–20,
  222
river vessel building, 172
roads, 13, 44, 141, 153, 192, 202, 204, 217, 219
road transport, 44, 192, 207–10, 218–19, 222
  length of haul, 219
Rogun HEP scheme, 154
Roman Catholics, 90
Romance languages, 91
Romanov dynasty, 12–16
Romans, 6
Rostov oblast', 144, 238
Rostov-on-Don (Rostov-na-Donu), 27, 172, 238
RSFSR, 65, 116, 119, 121, 130–1, 156–7, 187–8,
  226; *see also* European Russia, Siberia
rubber manufacture, 174
Rubtsovsk, 172, 181
Rudnyy, 156
Rumania, 20, 116, 188
Rumanian language, 91
rural areas, population, 91–2, 97, 99, 103, 104–5,
  108, 109, 184
  settlement, 197–200
  see also agriculture, forestry
Rurik, 7
Rus, 6–7; *see also* Kievan Rus
Russian Empire, 6, 10–16, 60, 88, 90, 98, 192–4,
  197–9
Russian language, 92
Russian people, 44–5, 88, 90–2, 106, 226, 227
Russian republic, *see* RSFSR
Rustavi, 167, 182, 244
Ruthenia, 32
Ryazan', 139

Rybinsk, 172
Rybinsk reservoir, 80, 84, 151, 156, 167
rye, 117, 121; areas, 128

St. Petersburg, 12, 13, 15, 16, 17, 50, 161, 177,
  191–2
Sakhalin, 15, 19, 35, 92, 137, 139, 146, 207,
  213, 221
Salair mountains, 34, 145
Salairskoye, 157
salinity, soil, 79
Samarkand, 16, 33, 188, 244
Samotlor oilfield, 136, 140
sanatoria, 50
Saratov, 82, 137, 153, 171, 176, 237
Saratov oblast', 76
Saray, 7, 9
Sartan, 215
Sarycheku, 157
Sarysu river, 31
Sayak mine, 157
Sayan mountains, 34, 63, 92
Sayanogorsk, 153
Sayan region, 21, 23, 127
Sayan–Shushenskaya project, 153
Scandinavians, 6, 219
scheelite, 158
Schwedt, 139
sealing, 119
sea transport, 220–1; *see also* ports, shipping
selenium, 157
sel'khoztekhnika, 115, 130
serfdom, 7, 14–15, 17, 112–13, 185
settlements of town type, 187–8
Sevan, Lake, 33, 154, 159
Severoural'sk, 159
Shaim, 139
Shalym, 167
Shatlyk gas field, 141
Shatura, 146
Shebelinka gas field, 141, 242
sheep, 117–29 *passim*, 176
  flock size, 115–16
  total numbers, 130
Shelekhov, 159, 168
shelterbelts, 122, 206, 219
Sherabad steppe, 78
Shevchenko, 139, 148, 196
shipbuilding, 172
shipping, 220–1; oil, 139, 204, 208, 209, 210,
  211, 221
Shorbulag, 158

Shulba Dam, 154
Sibay, 157
Siberia, agriculture, 113, 116–17, 119, 121, 123–4, 127–9, 131
    climate, 39, 41, 43–6, 48–9
    energy, 133–54 *passim*
    historical, 6, 9, 10–11, 14, 15, 18
    industrial, 160–5, 167–9, 171–2, 174–7, 179, 181–2
    metal ores, 156–9
    physical, 21, 23, 29
    population, 90–2, 95, 97, 101, 103, 105, 109, 110
    soils and vegetation, 54–5, 57–60, 63–5, 69
    towns, 185, 193, 196
    transport, 204, 206–7, 210–11, 214–15, 217, 219–21
    villages, 199
    water, 71–2
Siberian plateau and platform, 21–4, 29, 30–1, 34
Sikhote Alin, 35, 212
silk, 126, 177
Silk Roads, Old, 206
Sillamae, 150
silver, 157, 158
Simferopol', 209, 243
Slantsy, 147
Slavs, 6 ff, 90–1, 106, 188
Slobodskoy, 177
Smolensk, 25, 148, 190, 219
Smolensk–Moscow ridge, 25
Smolensk oblast', 146
snow, 45, 48
    and agriculture, 116, 117, 127, 128, 130,
    and transport, 204–5, 219
    clearance, 82
    in water supply, 72, 73–5, 79
Sochi, 126
soil, 6, 52–70
    conservation, 119
    erosion, 27, 66–8, 82, 119, 125
Solikamsk, 168, 172, 174–5
Solnechnyy tin complex, 157
Sosna river and basin, 65
Sosnovy Bor, 148
South Africa, 150, 159
South Golodnaya steppe canal, 76
South region, 103–4, 181, 234, 242
South-west region, 109, 234, 242
South Yakutian Basin, 146
Sovetskaya Gavan', 48, 212–13
soviets (councils) 1, 18, 113–14, 197
sovkhoz, 115, 121; *see also* state farms
sovkhoz factories, 131

sovnarkhozy, 162, 227–9
spraying of crops, 130
Sredinyy mountains, 36
Sredsib railway, 211
Stalin, J. V., 18, 114, 161–2, 192
Stalingrad, 18; *see also* Volgograd
Stalinist Russia, 18, 185, 192
Stanovoy mountains, 35
Staryy Oskol, 197
state farms, 115, 119; size, 116
State Planning Committee of USSR (GOSPLAN), 161–3
Stavropol' kray, 123, 141, 238
Stavropol' plateau, 32
Stavropol' steppe, 75
steel industry, location, 144, 151, 165–8
    ores, 154–6, 158, 164–5, 167–8
steppe zone, 60 ff
    agriculture, 112, 122 ff
    development, 238–47 *passim*
    industry, 167
    irrigation, 74, 151
    population, 95, 97
    soils, 61
    villages, 199
Sterlitamak, 174
Stolypin reform, 113–14
Stony Tunguska river, 153
Strait of Tartary, 139
Strogonov family, 10
sub-tropical areas, 49–50, 62–3, 116, 126–7
Suchan, 146
Suez Canal, 78, 221
sugar beet, 117, 122–7 *passim*
    areas, 128
    output, 129
    temperature requirements, 117
Sukhona river, 84
sukhovey, 43, 68
Sukhumi Military Highway, 206
Sulak river, 154
sulphuric acid production, 174, 182
Sulyukta, 147
Sumgait, 159, 168
Sumy, 174
sunflower, 115, 117
Suram mountains, 33, 206
Suram Pass, 33
Surgut, 136, 139, 143, 193
Surkhan Dar'ya oasis, 185
Surkhandar'ya river, 78
Surkhob river, 33

Sverdlovsk, 145, 167–8, 171–2, 222
Sverdlovsk oblast', 95, 238
swamps, 64–5, 72, 84–6, 136, 141; *see also* bogs, marshlands
Sweden, 10, 12, 13
Swedes, 7
synthetic fibres, 176, 177, 182
Syr Dar'ya river and valley, 31, 34, 73, 76, 81, 84, 97, 127, 154
Szazhalombatta, 139

Taboshar, 150
Tadzhikistan (Tadzhik SSR), 33, 61, 66, 76, 103, 125, 137, 154, 159, 168, 200, 219, 244–5
Tadzhiks, 44, 91, 92
Taganrog, 165, 238
Tamara, Queen, 10
Tamerlane, 9
Tarbagatay mountains, 124
Tartu, 188
Tashkent, 16, 34, 49, 76, 79, 141, 172, 176, 182, 202, 211
Tashtagol', 156, 167
Tatar ASSR, 136, 171
Tatars, 7–10, 90, 92, 190, 199
Tatar Strait, 212
Taukum desert, 31
tayga zone, 10, 43, 57 ff, 86, 119, 121, 136, 213, 235, 238
  conservation, 69
  population, 95, 97
Taymyr AOk, 97, 240
Taymyr peninsula, 30, 240
Tayshet, 167, 212–13
Tayura, 213
Tbilisi, 33, 158, 167, 171–2, 187, 206, 244
Tbilisi–Leninakan railway, 206
tea, 49, 126
Tedzhen river, 78
Tekeli, 157, 174
Temirtau, 156, 167, 168, 174, 196
temperatures, 39ff, 116, 117
  accumulated, 41, 116
Terek–Kuma canal, 75
Terek river and valley, 10, 32, 75, 157
Terespol, 217
Ternovka, 145
territorial production complexes, 162
Tertiary rocks and structures, 21 ff
Tetyukhe, 157, 169
Teutonic languages, 91
textile industry, 176, 179, 182

Tikhvin–Boksitogorsk, 158
Timan range, 27
timber industry, 174–6
  effects, 65, 82
  transport of, 209, 220, 221
Timur the Lame, 9
tin, ores, 157–8
  processing, 169
titanium, 165, 168–9
tobacco, 126
Tobol river and valley, 10, 29, 84
Tobol'sk, 10, 147, 172
Tokhtamysh, 9
Toktogul HEP scheme, 154
Tolyatti, 171, 181, 197, 207, 238
Tom' river, 81, 84, 145
Tomsk, 65, 193
Tomsk oblast', 136
Torzhok, 143
tourist industry, 45, 46, 49–50, 191, 192
towns, 7, 14, 92, 184–97, 200
  definition of, 187
  numbers and size, 187
  oilfield, 136, 196
  uranium mining, 150–1
  see also cities, urban areas
tractors, 114, 115, 130, 182
trade routes, 8, 10, 12, 13, 16, 177, 193, 219
Transbaykalia, 219
Transcarpathia, 126
Trans-Caspian region, 137, 211, 214
Transcaucasian depression, 32
Transcaucasian peoples, 91
Transcaucasus region, agriculture, 116, 126, 131
  climate, 41, 49
  energy, 141, 158
  historical, 6, 7
  industry, 163, 167–8, 169, 171–2, 174, 176–7, 179
  physical, 32–3
  population, 91, 93, 95, 101, 103, 106, 108–9
  regional summary, 243–4
  soils and vegetation, 62–3
  towns, 188, 194
  transport, 206, 211, 221
  villages, 197
transport, 119, 131, 160, 161, 202–22
  pipeline, 134, 137–40, 141–3
  see also railways, etc.
Trans-Siberian Railway, 15, 29, 95, 97, 146, 151, 153, 175, 181, 206–7, 211–12, 214, 217, 219, 221, 239, 240, 241, 242

Trans-Uralian peneplain, 206
Travemünde, 207
Tsarist Russia, 9–18, 68, 159, 160, 169, 184–5, 194, 197, 206
Tselinograd, 172
Tselinograd oblast', 97
Tsimlyansk reservoir, 80
Tuapse, 137, 221
Tukuringra mountains, 35
Tula, 145, 167, 172, 179, 181, 190, 236
Tulun, 146
tundra, 43, 54–7, 65, 141, 219, 232, 235
    agriculture, 119–20
    conservation, 69
    population, 95, 97
tungsten, 158
Tunguska basin, 144, 240
Turanian desert, 97
Turanian lowlands, 30, 73, 79
Turgay Gate, 30
Turgay trough, 84
Turkestan, 34, 211
Turkey, 13, 199
Turkic peoples, 15, 91–2
Turkmeniya (Turkmen SSR), 33, 61, 78–9, 103, 134, 137, 139, 141, 188, 196, 217, 244–5
Turkmen people, 92
Turks, 9
Turksib railway, 162, 211
Tuva (Tuvinian ASSR), 19, 34, 127
Tuvinians, 92
Tver, 9
Tyan' Shan' mountains, 15, 33–4, 73–4, 124–5, 127, 150
Tynda, 212–13
Tyrnyauz, 158
Tyumen', 10
Tyumen' oblast', 97, 136, 141, 239
Tyumensk thermal power station, 65

Uchaly, 157
Uchkyr gas field, 141
Udmurt ASSR, 238
Udmurt people, 91–2
Udokan copper deposit, 157
Ufa, 172
Ufa oilfield, 139
Ufa plateau, 27
Ufa river, 81
Uglich, 153
Ukhta oilfield, 137, 143

Ukraine (Ukrainian SSR), agriculture, 112, 116–17, 119, 122, 128, 130–1
    climate, 39, 41, 45–6
    energy, 134, 137, 139, 141, 144–5, 148, 150, 151, 154, 238
    historical, 13, 15, 16, 18
    industry, 161, 163, 169, 171, 174, 176–7
    metal ores, 154, 158
    physical, 23, 27, 32
    population, 90, 95, 104
    regional summary, 234, 242–3
    soils and vegetation, 60–1, 64, 68
    towns, 185, 188, 192–3
    transport, 207, 211, 221
    villages, 199
    water, 74, 84
Ukrainians, 90
Ukrainian shield and massif, 23, 27
Ulan–Ude, 171
Ul'yanovsk, 171–2, 181
underground railways, 192, 193
UNESCO, 54
United Kingdom, 50, 92–3, 156, 202, 207
Ural–Altaic ethnic groups, 90–2
Ural river, 10, 81, 167
Ural–Kuzbas *Kombinat*, 161, 167
Ural mountains, agriculture, 117, 121, 123
    historical, 7, 10
    industry, 167, 171, 174, 176, 181
    minerals, 136, 139, 140–1, 143, 145–8, 153, 156–9
    physical, 21, 23, 27, 29–30
    population, 91–2, 95, 104
    soils and vegetation, 54, 58–60, 65
    transport, 202, 204, 206, 213
    see also Ural region
Ural region, agriculture, 121, 123
    climate, 45
    energy, 139, 141, 145, 147, 153, 156–9
    historical, 13, 16, 18
    industry, 16, 18, 141, 161–3, 167–9, 171, 174, 177, 179, 181
    population, 104, 109
    regional summary, 238–9
    soils and vegetation, 54, 65
    towns, 185
    transport, 202, 210, 211, 215
    see also Ural mountains
Ural'sk oblast', 76
Ural–Volga oilfields, 136, 139, 141, 162, 174, 181, 210, 214, 221, 236, 237–8
uranium resources, 150

urban areas, 184–97
  population, 94, 95, 97, 99, 103, 106, 108, 109
  stimulus to agriculture, 119
Urengoy gas field, 136, 141, 143
Urgal, 212–13
USA, 16, 38–9, 43, 50–1, 92–3, 143, 150, 157, 202, 207; *see also* North America
Usinsk oilfield, 137, 139
USSR, area and size, 1
  foundation, 16–18
  political structure, 1–5
Ussuri Highway, 219
Ussuri river and valley, 31, 35, 59, 117, 127
Ust'-Ilimsk, 153, 213
Ust'-Kamenogorsk, 154, 157, 169
Ust'-Kut, 30, 172, 212–13
Ustyurt plateau, 30
Uzbekistan (Uzbek SSR), 62, 76–8, 103, 137, 139, 141, 147, 157, 159, 168–9, 197
Uzbek people, 92, 105
Uzhgorod, 188
Uzhokskiy Pass, 206

Vakhsh river, 74, 78, 154
Valday glaciation, 25, 27
Valday Hills, 25, 193
Vanino, 207, 213
Varangians, 6
Vasyuganye swamp, 29, 64, 136
Vazuza river, 82
vegetables, 117, 119–29 *passim*
  areas, 128
vegetation, 36, 52–69
Ventspils, 139, 221
Veretskiy Pass, 206
Verkhnyaya Pyshma, 168
Verkhoyansk, 39
Verkhoyansk mountains, 35–6, 63
Vienna, 211
Vikhorevka, 151
Vikings, 6
Vil'kitskiy Strait, 221
villages, 184, 197–200, 237
Vilyuy river and valley, 30, 154, 241
vineyards, 32, 125, 126, 127, 242; *see also* grapes
virgin land schemes, 5, 41, 45, 119, 128, 130–1, 199
  erosion, 68
  harvest fluctuation, 44
  migration, 106
Visby, 193
Vistula river, 219

Vitebsk, 171
Vitim–Laba railway, 212
Vitim plateau, 159
Vladimir, 190
Vladimir–Suzdal, 7
Vladivostok, 15, 35, 48, 95, 146, 172, 202, 211, 215, 219, 221
Volga–Baltic canal, 219
Volga basin, 193, 197
Volga–Don canal, 219, 237
Volga–German Autonomous Republic, 91
Volga–Kama reservoirs, 80, 84
Volga–Kama waterways, 181, 220
Volga region, 9, 65, 72, 75, 82
  agriculture, 123–8
  energy, 136–7, 147, 151–3
  industry, 162, 163, 167, 171, 172, 174, 175, 176, 178–9
  population, 91–2, 104
  regional summary, 235, 237–8
  settlement, 191, 193, 197, 199
  transport, 207, 210–11, 215, 219–20
Volga river, 6, 25, 46, 72, 76, 80, 81, 82
Volga–Ural canal, 76
Volga–Ural oilfields, 136, 139, 141, 162, 174, 181, 210, 214, 221, 236, 237–8
Volga–Vyatka economic region, 74, 236, 247
Volgodonsk, 148
Volgograd, 18, 76, 153, 168, 172, 222, 236
Volgograd oblast', 76
Volkhov, 168
Volkhov HEP scheme, 151, 158
Volkhov river, 25, 193, 219
Volochayevka–Komsomol'sk railway, 212
Vologda, 143
Vol'sk, 176
Volzhskiy, 197
Vorkuta, 69, 145, 167
Voronezh, 23, 148, 174, 236
Voroshilovgrad, 171
Voskresensk, 174
Vostochnyy, 221
Vostok 2, 158
Votkinsk, 153, 172
Vozey oilfield, 137, 139
Vuktyl gas field, 141
Vyartsilya, 167
Vyatka, 9
Vyatka regions, 103–4
Vyatka river, 177
Vychegda river, 84
Vysokaya, 156

Vysokaya Gora, 167

War, Crimean, 15
War, First World, 97–8, 113–14, 129, 184
War, Second World, 98–9, 114, 129–30, 133,
    136, 141, 143–4, 150–1, 156–8, 162, 168,
    181, 192–3
Warsaw, 211
water, 71–87
  consumption, 82
  diversions, 84
  erosion by, 66–8
  hydro-electric developments, 151–4
  pollution, 81
  shortage, 49, 167, 174
  supply, 49, 82, 179, 196
  see also reservoirs
water balance, 41, 71–2
waterways, inland, 139, 153, 208, 209, 219–20; see
    also canals, river transport
Western Dvina river, 25, 243
Western Europe, 51, 143, 160, 163, 165
West Germany, 145, 207
West Siberia, agriculture, 112, 121, 123
  industry, 161–2, 167, 172, 176–7, 181
  oil and gas fields, 134–7, 139, 140–3, 239–40
  physical, 29–30, 36
  population, 91, 97, 105, 109
  regional summary, 239–40
  soils and vegetation, 60–1, 64–6, 68
  transport, 202, 204, 210–12, 215
  water, 84
wheat, 117–29
  expansion of area, 128
  yields, 129
  see also grains
White Sea, 9, 10, 25, 219, 221
wind, 43, 49, 116, 204–5
  erosion, 66–8
windbreaks, see shelterbelts
wineries, 179
winter conditions, 39 ff, 116, 117, 202–4, 217
Witte, Count S., 15
Wolfram, 158
wood chemical industry, 174
wooded steppe, 7, 10, 43, 46–8, 60, 117, 224–47
    passim
  population, 90, 95, 190

wood fuel, 164
wool manufacturing, 176

Yablonovyy mountains, 34–5
Yakutia (Yakut ASSR), 13, 30, 121, 154, 167, 241
Yakut people, 92
Yakutsk, 12, 13, 48, 219
Yalta, 49–50, 62, 209, 220
Yamalo-Nenetskiy AOk, 239
Yamyshevo reservoir, 84
Yano–Oymyakon plateau, 36
Yaroslavl', 139, 172, 174
Yefremov, 174
Yelenovka, 165, 179
Yenakiyevo, 165
Yenisey mountains, 30
Yenisey river and valley, 10, 21, 23, 29, 30, 34, 58,
    69, 73, 145, 154, 157, 159, 162, 172, 174, 193,
    196, 207, 210, 221, 240–1
Yeniseysk, 153
Yerevan, 159, 168, 174, 244
Yermak, 10, 168
Yerunakovo, 145
Yugorskiy peninsula, 29
Yukagir plateau, 36
Yuzhsib railway, 211

Zaglik, 158
Zakamensk, 158
Zaporozh'ye, 23, 27, 151, 158, 167–9, 171–2, 215
Zarafshan gold complex, 159
Zelenograd, 197
Zeravshan river and valley, 78, 126
Zestafoni, 167
Zeya–Bureya lowlands and plain, 35
Zeya HEP scheme, 154
Zeya river, 35
Zhdanov, 165, 171, 174, 221, 242
Zheleznogorsk, 156
Zheleznogorsk–Ilimskiy, 156
Zheltyye Vody, 150
Zhodino, 171
zinc, ores, 157
  processing, 169
Zlatoust, 167
Zod gold deposit, 159
zones, 'natural', 41, 43
Zyryanovsk, 169